Is It Still Good to Ya?

Is It Still Good to Ya?

Fifty Years of Rock Criticism, 1967–2017

ROBERT CHRISTGAU

DUKE UNIVERSITY PRESS *Durham and London* 2018

Designed by Matthew Tauch
Typeset in Minion Pro by Westchester

Library of Congress Cataloging-in-Publication Data
Names: Christgau, Robert, author.
Title: Is it still good to ya? : fifty years of rock criticism,
1967–2017 / Robert Christgau.
Description: Durham : Duke University Press, 2018. |
Includes bibliographical references and index.
Identifiers: LCCN 2018008218 (print) |
LCCN 2018009626 (ebook)
ISBN 9781478002079 (ebook)
ISBN 9781478000082 (hardcover : alk. paper)
ISBN 9781478000228 (pbk. : alk. paper)
Subjects: LCSH: Rock music—History and criticism. |
Popular music—History and criticism.
Classification: LCC ML3534 (ebook) | LCC ML3534 .C493
2018 (print) | DDC 781.6609—dc23
LC record available at https://lccn.loc.gov/2018008218

40+ materials © *Village Voice*. "Chuck Berry: 1926–2017"
and "Don't Worry about Nothing: Ornette Coleman"
© *Billboard* Magazine. "3. Spelled Backwards It's 'AIM,'"
"Shape Shifter: David Bowie: 1947–2016," "The Most
Gifted Artist of the Rock Era: Prince: 1958–2016," and
"Forever Old: Leonard Cohen: 1933–2016" © VICE Media.

Cover art: Christian Marclay, *untitled*, 2004. Photogram
on c-print paper, mounted on cintra board. © Christian
Marclay. Courtesy of Paula Cooper Gallery.

To Carola Dibbell

For Forty-Six Years and Counting

My Lover

My Life Coach

My Juiciest Editor

My Second Set of Ears

Contents

II   A Great Tradition

III   Millennium

IV   From Which All Blessings Flow

VI   Got to Be Driftin' Along

Robert Christgau's Greatest Hits: Volume III

Thank you for getting this far. Really—I mean it. Just by glancing at what the cover specifies is a collection, you have bucked the publishing truism that people don't buy collections—and concomitantly, don't read them. At the moment, you're reading one. So thank you.

The way I count, this is my third. Since I've also published three decade-spanning books based on my monthly Consumer Guide album reviews, others might say sixth, but let's call those alphabetical volumes, I don't know, compilations, because *I love collections.* I love them because they're read front to back, love them as successions of digestible units that reveal writers from angles that glance off each other to form a composite that resists closure. It was the many collections I read as the '60s shifted into high that turned my literary dreams toward journalism: pure essay collections by Norman Mailer, Dwight Macdonald, Pauline Kael, Susan Sontag, impure journalism collections by A. J. Liebling, Tom Wolfe, Gay Talese, Thomas B. Morgan (the forgotten profiling master class *Self-Creations: 13 Impersonalities*). Nor is the collection some golden-age artifact. I down four or five a year and treasure many, for instance Jonathan Lethem's *The Disappointment Artist*, Marshall Berman's *Modernism in the Streets*, and my very favorite, Dave Hickey's *Air Guitar*—all of which mess with a form that in the '60s group, Mailer's *Advertisements for Myself* excepted, straightforwardly sequences previously published essays, reviews, and reportage with no conceptual ado.

"Essays, reviews, and reportage," did I say? Instead let me enlist a bit of jargon that encompasses all three and whatever else you got: "piece," which is what magazine journalists tend to call their assignments, where in newspaper journalism it breaks down "story" or "column" or "review." *Is It Still Good to Ya?* is subtitled "Fifty Years of Rock Criticism, 1967–2017" because "Pieces on Music, 1967–2017" lacks gravitas, and collections need all the status they can get. But pieces is what it collects, almost every one condensed to make room for others and spruced up to mitigate stylistic shortfalls or correct factual errors but never to revise opinions or predictions gone awry, with a bunch substantially revised and marked as such, usually because they posed questions I originally lacked space or info to answer. Only a few qualify as pure exposition, including some repurposed lectures from the EMP Pop Conference, and the three longest are reportage even if one was reported mostly from my desk. But they're "cultural" reportage, meaning a critic's reportage, reportage that comes bearing opinions, which too much cultural reportage doesn't. Almost half are from *The Village Voice*, a weekly magazine masquerading as a weekly newspaper where I was employed from 1974 until 2006. Some three dozen of these were columns sporting the logo Rock & Roll &, which after I got fired in a hostile takeover followed me to *The Barnes & Noble Review*.

Ah yes, "column." High in status because it affords autonomy and valorizes judgment and analysis as well as reporting, resented because reporting remains journalism's pride, staple, and selling point, as it should—in hard news. Arts coverage oughta be different but often isn't, in part because hard-newsed dailies like to peg coverage to an event—if not a show, then at least an album release, about which you'd best nail down your precious opinion pronto and buttress it with reported context. For a rock critic, which is what I still call myself, one of several problems with reviewing on short deadline is that recorded music, unlike books or movies, is best enjoyed and understood via repeated exposure over lived time. Another is that the surrounding facts inflect the recording's meanings and pleasures less and less as it endures, and if it ain't gonna endure why bother with it? Because in its moment it's got the zap of news is the answer, and there are excellent collections—Simon Frith's *Music for Pleasure*, Chuck Eddy's *Terminated for Reasons of Taste*— that make a point of granting forgotten musical events and personages the symbolic permanence of book form. Without question such penny rockets brighten up the pop saga, and many relative obscurities come and go in the historical section that begins this book. But I had bigger stuff to stuff into *Is It Still Good to Ya?*

The staple is the kind of artist critiques that filled my 1998 collection *Grown Up All Wrong* and dominated Rock & Roll &, often tethered to an album plus show at the *Voice* or plus book at *B&N*, where Robin Kelley and Terry Teachout bios occasioned Monk and Armstrong lookbacks I'd mulled for years. Journalistically, the trick is to engage readers of widely varying knowledgeability by historicizing the event from a fresh perspective that educates newbies while keeping old heads on their toes. Of the seventy-five artists featured in *Grown Up All Wrong*, several were minor or eccentric by design, and by design all of these were better-known than designated penny rocket Pete Fowler. But there I also addressed every rock titan except Dylan, who had hogged four pieces in 1973's *Any Old Way You Choose It* (and gets four more here): Presley, Berry, Beatles, Stones, Brown, Franklin, Joplin, Wonder, Led Zeppelin, Young, Green, Clinton, Sex Pistols, Clash, Prince, Springsteen, Jackson, Public Enemy, Madonna, Nirvana. That's most of my pantheon as of 1998, although I apologized for omitting Louis Jordan, the Coasters, Monk, Dylan, Steely Dan, the Ramones, and Luamba Franco. Having folded Steely Dan into my 2015 memoir *Going Into the City*, I then got all but Jordan into *Is It Still Good to Ya?*, which repeats only eight artists from *Grown Up All Wrong*, three primarily because they died: Berry, Brown, Prince, Franklin, Youssou N'Dour, Sonic Youth, Nirvana, and my homeboys the New York Dolls.

Fifty-four artists get some variant of the Rock & Roll & treatment here, a total that includes zero penny rockets, two or three pans, and just four eccentricities: the Moldy Peaches complete with 9/11 hook, the Perceptionists giving alt-rap some, Boston-to-Nashville Lori McKenna, and best band in America Wussy. A few others are on the cusp, and no doubt some provincials will wonder why there aren't more Britons while looking askance at N'Dour, Franco, Fela, Ladysmith Black Mambazo, and Tom Zé, all titans by any civilized standard, and N'Dour the world's finest pop musician by me. From Louis Armstrong to Lady Gaga, however, most of these pieces essay straight-up major-artist analysis, sometimes informed by reporting that with a few takes over. And strikingly, eight including an Etta James tribute with a standard headline fall into a hitherto unnamed category. They're obits.

Of course I'd written criticism about dead people before—how could I bypass Janis or Jimi, Elvis Presley or John Lennon or Kurt Cobain? But as my work life worked out, the scattered obits I published at the *Voice* were marginal except for an absurdly "controversial" John Lennon all-nighter that I swear didn't call for Paul McCartney's assassination, as some charged. (See for yourself at robertchristgau.com, where also subsist many Consumer Guide takes on the artists dealt with here, although at the request of my publisher fifty-seven of these pieces will be embargoed online until two years after pub date.) I let it be because Lennon occasioned the longest piece in *Grown Up All Wrong*, a crucial one in *Any Old Way You Choose It*, an Xgau-penned *Encyclopedia Britannica* entry, a few pages of memoir, and enough already. But over the past two decades my work life has changed, and so has my regular life. In the wake of the born-again fundamentalism I spent my adolescence dissecting and rejecting, I've always taken death so seriously that I hit the high '60s with no use for hope-I-die-before-I-get-old bushwa. But now I *am* old, and how about that, so is rock and roll. Suddenly major artists are dying of relatively natural causes even if they could have been nicer to their livers. And given my seniority, editors often feel I should weigh in on the departed, as do I.

Having mentioned being old, I'd better acknowledge that the snappy, impressive, factually accurate subtitle "Fifty Years of Rock Criticism, 1967–2017" is a bit of a cheat. Because I used up so much material in my earlier collections, only four of these ninety-five pieces predate 1990 and only eight more predate 1998; some two thirds, in fact, were written after I turned sixty in 2002. So I got back to 1967 via my first serious piece of rock criticism as opposed to coverage: "Rock Lyrics Are Poetry (Maybe)," a soon-anthologized essay for the here-and-gone *Cheetah* that was so canonical by the time of *Any Old Way You Choose It* that I decided not to expend space on it there. Although still cited, it's no longer canonical, in part because its refusal to equate words on the page with words in the vocally inflected air quickly became a commonplace many excavated. But when I reread it I decided it was worth taking out of retirement, for ideas that haven't lost their bite and also for evoking the feverish musical ethos of the high '60s as discursive poetry (maybe).

Thus it filled a hole in the chronological overviews of the long introductory section "History in the Making," which go back to ancient Greece but bear down on the last twenty-five years. Sidestepping the artist focus of Rock & Roll & as well as the album focus of the Consumer Guide leaves me stretch room for the politics that imbue my aesthetic—an ear for democracy that responded from the dawn of "Maybellene" to the cocky class consciousness of wild-haired rockabilly and street-corner doowop, that believed from the git that the Americans I called Negroes were rock and roll's prime motorvators, and that loved the Shirelles sticking up for themselves and the Vandellas dancing in the street before the Beatles and the girls who loved them transformed popular music and world history.

My politics have always poked out of my criticism, enough to annoy people sometimes, and good. But they have come to feel far more urgent in the millennium that followed the apparent destruction of fascism than they were as the twentieth century staggered to an inequitable but uncatastrophic close. So of course they surface in the 9/11 and Africa sections that follow the run of artist essays designated "A Great Tradition." The way these self-contained units glance off each other to form a composite that resists closure is one way *Is It Still Good to Ya?* emulates the structural and thematic messing around of the three recent collections I cited. But not the main one. The main one reflects my desire to die the right way whenever it should transpire that I'm old enough to do so.

Rock and roll identified from the start as a youth music—at its very start, a rebellious teen music. And most of the panoply of styles, genres, subgenres, and hair-splitting subsubsomethings to arise in its wake have been claimed by tyros putting their stamp on them with varying force and acuity. But in the '60s, not to mention the '50s, it never occurred to us that each new generation and tendency would hang in there, nor that so many self-consciously maturing artists would keep such careful track of where they stood on life's through-line. Sure there are pop standards that address aging; my bed-ridden mother-in-law listened to Willie Nelson sing "September Song" over and over in the months before she passed at ninety-six. But due in part to the putative autobiography built into its songwriting model and the apparent self-expression built into its performance model—illusions, absolutely, but tricky, partial, and aptly seductive illusions—the former teen music with which I've cohabited for half a century keeps excavating fresh images of the youth and maturity that add up to mortality. I don't just mean the old guys, either. Among the '00s artists of the "Postmodern Times" section, I count Eminem, Kanye West, Jay-Z, Shakira, Brad Paisley, Miranda Lambert, Lori McKenna, Gogol Bordello, M.I.A., and Vampire Weekend, most of whom have crept past forty since I wrote about them and all of whom were on the theme well before they did.

Granted, forty would have seemed way old for rock and roll when twenty-five-year-old me crushed out "Rock Lyrics Are Poetry (Maybe)" in September 1967. But although the Mamas and Papas chart-topper as I wrote was the utopian "Twelve Thirty," subtitled "Young Girls Are Coming to the Canyon" after the laurel-wreathed opening line of its ecstatic chorus, in that very essay I single out the premonitory acid casualties thirty-two-year-old drug fiend John Phillips had already homed in on in a strange little number he called "Strange Young Girls." In both songs the youth counterculture of the Summer of Love was feeling its age as autumn leaves drifted by its window, and this generational unease proved permanent. The thirtysomethings of Fleetwood Mac wove Mamas-and-Papas beauty from romantic chaos as punk spat in their eye. The punks perfected a primitivist musical model whose durability and malleability recall blues while germinating an arty "postpunk" alt-rock whose stylistic range proved that some wankers were major innovators, some major artists, and some just major wankers. Soon Michael Jackson would launch his joyful, tortured transformation into history's most beatwise horror movie as project rejects synthesized the dozens, Jamaican sound systems, James Brown, and *Scarface* into a new music that conquered the world. A decade or so later, teenpop begat not just Britney but Beyoncé, who my dear friend Ann Powers will tell you evolved into a New Woman who's the pivotal pop hero of the current era.

Me, I've never enjoyed Beyoncé like I'm supposed to, although I certainly admire her, and expect I'd have devoted some column inches to figuring out why if I was still rolling out Rock & Roll &s. But one reason collections resist closure is that they're subject to the vagaries of journalism as a job. The longest artist essay here is Eminem's because some fool offered me big bucks to write five thousand words about him (and then found the result too "in" or something, leaving me with my kill fee and the kindness of *The Believer*); the Kanye West piece is barely nine hundred words because by that phase of the *Voice*'s ongoing clickbait trauma columns had shrunk to half the length of a decade before. Anyway, even a stylist as headstrong as I am comports himself differently in different places, because journalism generally targets a more specific audience than pop music (although not what I call semipopular music, but let's not get sidetracked). I flourished at *Barnes & Noble Review* not merely because I had two thousand words to play with, but because *B&NR*'s bookish older readership compelled me to elaborate my contextualizations. At *Noisey*, current home of the Consumer Guide I now dub Expert Witness and also where three of the obits appeared, it's different—the teen-to-twentysomething demographic of that *Vice* "vertical" turns me into a Dutch uncle reminiscing about the old days.

All three of those Robert Christgaus are the real me. Neither *B&NR* or *Noisey*, however, made it my brief to delve into the new kids the way the *Voice* once did even though Expert Witness keeps me abreast of them. So I wonder how that professional obligation would have deepened my connection to not just Beyoncé but Chance the Rapper, Taylor Swift, the Coathangers, Parquet Courts, or Heems, to name five I'd have treated to a Rock & Roll & by now. True, I did publish a 2011 *B&NR* Rock & Roll & on Heems's Das Racist that just missed the cut. But unfortunately or maybe not, you can never cram everything you'd like into a collection—sorry Sinéad O'Connor and Liz Phair, Linton Kwesi Johnson and Spring Heel Jack, Fluffy and Lily Allen, the Fugs and the Popinjays. And in the end, what felt right thematically and emotionally here often took into account the title that came to me after the deal was done and inflected the many adjustments I've made in its contents since: *Is It Still Good to Ya?*, a title copped from a key hit by the married r&b duo Ashford & Simpson that never creased top forty pop.

Dave Hickey's *Air Guitar*, Jonathan Lethem's *The Disappointment Artist*, and Marshall Berman's *Modernism in the Streets* are stealth autobiographies that I named rather than, say, Greil Marcus's *Dead Elvis* or Albert Murray's *The Omni-Americans* because autobiographical is how *Is It Still Good to Ya?* feels to me. Berman's underappreciated 2017 overview is especially pertinent not just because he was a close friend but because it came later in life than the other two—assembled after his death, it builds to a hilariously irreverent Adam and Eve excursion he was honing the morning he died. Not that I'm feeling death's approach quite yet—actuarially I'm a decent bet for ninety. But I'm old enough to be mindful of my multiplying physical incapacities and the arc of my mortality, in principle without succumbing to the escapes I've long considered matched enemies of both good rock criticism and a fully realized life: nostalgia and cynicism. That's how the "still" pertains for me at seventy-five. As for the "good to ya," well, as the prologue explains, I latched onto that hedonistic turn of phrase because it stands in contradistinction to the moralistic "good for you."

By grace of the biochemistry my parents bequeathed me, the upbringing they vouchsafed me, union-powered post-WWII prosperity, and my excellent marriage, I have such an optimistic temperament I worry that my general tone here may seem too palmy in a time when, to choose just one horrible example, the nuclear nightmare I've never thought haunted American baby boomers the way some claim is realer than at any time since 1945. My psychological luck clearly disinclines me to moon about the good old days or make my bones explaining why the end is here. But so does the music I listen to all the time, which is good for me because it's good to me. Being a seventy-five-year-old rock critic is a terrific way to keep your spirits up—so much so that undergoing the basic training described in "Ten-Step Program for Growing Better Ears" might be worth the while of any "senior" worried about his or her mojo.

One does become more weathered as one ages, which is quite different from knowing that getting weathered is in the cards. So I hope I can convince my older readers that not only is there a useful kick in vicariously accessing young musicians' recurring illusions of immortality, but also a reassurance in the growth that can ensue from their poignant, often life-affirming realizations that mortality is encroaching as some part of them always knew or feared it would. So I'd also like to convince my younger readers that by dint of disciplined exposure there's more life to be found than many of you could now dream in not just Louis Armstrong or Etta James, who I trust you know about, but, say, the Coasters, the McGarrigles, or the cultish and in your fuzzy conception almost as ancient Go-Betweens. And I'd like to convince everyone that in a horrible historical moment that may well get worse, music that's good to ya will by just that token also be good for you. As Van Morrison helped onetime rock critic Jon Landau put it in the title of a collection he published in, wow, 1972, it's too late to stop now.

Good to Ya, Not for Ya

Rock Criticism vs. the Guilty Pleasure

Rock criticism was conceived as a reproach to the idea of guilty pleasure. In fact, "reproach" and "conceive" put it too politely. "Reproach" makes it sound like we had the upper hand, so make that "attack." It was a kick in the pants, a fart in the face, a full fungu. And "conceived" makes it sound like there was something difficult or noble about a psychological necessity in a world where radical and conservative avant-gardists no less than liberal and moderate middlebrows were shouting from their varied pulpits that good art should be good for you. We who'd grown up with so-called mass culture weren't having that BS. But it would be 1978 before Ashford & Simpson put it into words from their own pulpit, an r&b-only hit called "Is It Still Good to Ya?" Forget good *for* you—art should be good *to* you.

For rock critics, in other words, pleasure is where meaning begins. A tune you hum in your head so your mind can hear it again, a beat that motorvates your body even when the main thing moving is your pulse, the slight flush that radiates from the mandible toward the ears at the right lick or turn of phrase, the virtual chuckle of amusement or amazement as that moment comes by yet again. Given our word rates, why else would we do the job? But not everyone is convinced that pleasure ensues "when you listen to music to make a deadline," as New Orleans MC Lil Wayne has put it. "You can't sit in the office with your walkman or disc player and feel this street music," he told Moke Kelekome of *Murder Dog*. "People listen to music for pleasure and writers listen because they get paid to. Some writers review albums by artists they don't like only because that was the only job they could get and they need that little $50 or whatever y'all get paid."

All too true, sometimes. But on my hustle, as Kelefa Sanneh calls our vocation, quality of product and reliability of delivery vary, just like on any other hustle. One way I maintain quality control is with letter grades, and I have no reservations about them. To those who would say quantification you rationalizer, apples and oranges you vulgarian, aesthetic judgment you authoritarian, I can only say fungu. Grading is a fun and informative exercise, not to mention a good way for a writer to get in touch with his or occasionally her feelings. But even after thirty-seven years I rarely find the calibration of opinion a simple task, and none other than Lil Wayne made it exceptionally difficult. *Tha Carter II* was the product at hand, the first post-Katrina New Orleans hip-hop album. I'd enjoyed previous Lil Wayne some, and not only had this CD generated terrific word-of-mouth, I liked the way it sounded in the middle distance. It was the next step that flummoxed me—sitting there and listening as carefully as possible to song after song, trying to ascertain how my patiently acquired somatic knowledge of the music survived the cerebrum-auriculum microscope. Did the lyrics make me queasy? Was the music more engaging than the NBA on mute? Did middle-distance pleasure hold up against the cold winds of analysis?

On Dwayne Carter's second album to be named for Nino Brown's headquarters in *New Jack City*, hooks were sticking, words sticking out. A thick-tongued, screwed-down Biggie yammered "Money on My Mind"'s title hook times seven, sometimes superimposed on another hook, Wayne's "Get money, fuck bitches." And although *Soundslam*'s Courtney Xavier hears the "August disaster debacle" in "Money on My Mind"'s triple-rhymed "New Orleans my *birth*place ya *heard* me/Where money's more important than the *person*," to me it aptly capped such lines as "Coke transactions on the phone we call it blowjob" and "Money over bitches I'm yellin it to my grave." The cocaine hustle, bloody as a way of life and commerce; the cocaine-music hustle, bloodier as a way of art and commerce. As Wayne puts it in "Weezy Baby," fourteen tracks later: "Get money, fuck bitches." Or let him expand on that: "Lead showers, black flowers/Black dresses, two hours, closed casket."

The key track is "Hit Em Up," where Wayne's "I tried talk to him" six times a chorus suggests a conciliatory mood that helped attract me to the album. Close listening exploded this fantasy—that's hit 'em up as in shoot 'em up, not as in punch 'em up, with gunshot punctuation and colorful auxiliary imagery: "Quit talkin, Ima hang you by your tongue," "Lay a nigga down in his own mess," "Start with the wrong boy, you end with a stone, boy." Unless the N.O. police are even worse at catching crooks than we think, this shoot-'em-up never happened. It's fiction, metaphor, and it's about beef, meaning an exchange of words, not jacking product or contesting turf. Beef is the special realm of what a Young Jeezy mixtape calls "Studio Gangstas"—"They doin' their job man, they actors. Shouldn't be in the bullpen, should be on TV—the big screen." Yet the song was still good to me, as seductive as the inspired Robin Thicke feature "Shooter" four tracks later, where the bullets are explicitly described as coming out of Wayne's mouth—where the bullets *are* metaphors, beat-driven, beaten-up words, Wayne's real-life weapon.

Right, beats. And let us not forget that lovely old term "flow." Because as my mind moved in and out of this music, working on a grade as I rooted forlornly for Channing Frye and fretted about EMP in its year of the guilty pleasure, I never stopped enjoying the music's shape and movement. Plus the maturation of timbre and pronunciation in a rapper who started very young—what Tom Breihan calls "the true contentment" in his voice, the way he made his drawl swing and bounce, and also his wordplay, supposedly performed from scribbled phrases rather than finalized on the page. Doesn't always work that way. Months later, Juvenile's *Reality Check* threw the same process into reverse—maturing rapper tightens shit, loses spritz. But it still bothered me that "Hit Em Up" featured an Uzi and that the Lil Wayne character used it, and disappointment undercut my pleasure. Was it therefore a guilty pleasure? At the very least it was uneasy. Instead of making my groin glow, it made my gut congest, like an extra handful of Thai peanuts.

Sad to say, this problem is of practical interest to almost nobody. Despite its popular dominance, hip-hop remains an intensely polarizing music. Few of the few people over forty who care about it can tolerate its gangsta variants, while most of its true fans—be they black or white or Latino or other, urban or suburban or rural, twelve or twenty or thirty-five—cheer Snoop Dogg and 50 Cent louder than OutKast and Kanye West. Lil Wayne, like such competing grind merchants as Atlanta's Young Jeezy and Memphis's Three 6 Mafia, is less ubiquitous because he doesn't attract many pop casuals, but all three are major hip-hop brands. And in hip-hop it is somewhere between an artistic convention and a philosophy of life that real music is street music and the street is where the realest people deal drugs. Just read Wayne's interviews, where the hard questions are about the music business, with the cocaine business taken for granted. In an economy where a majority of inner-city males drop out of high school and sixty-five percent of black high school dropouts in their twenties are unemployed, there's more factual truth to this than we who don't live in the hood want to think. But there's less than Young Jeezy wants us to think. So for many if not most hip-hop fans, drugs have a mythic cowboys-and-Indians quality. They provide the setting for, and the excuse for, safely dehumanized tales of azz-jamming sex and don't-give-a-fuck violence.

Beats, schmeats—most gangsta can be ignored because it just isn't good enough. Strong beats are no rarer than strong voices, and in themselves they're another species of virtuosity, like a Swedish metal drummer playing in 13/8. So don't let yourself be guilt-tripped—it's fine to dislike a song solely because its lyrical premise angries up your blood. Resisting such spontaneous reactions is another way of trying to appreciate art that's good for you. What isn't fine, at least not for anyone who believes popular music is a precious gateway to our shared humanity, is trashing a whole megagenre—especially one dominated by black Americans, who've been two steps ahead of white Americans so many times before. It was in that spirit that last fall I approached not just long-ago miscreant turned University of Houston undergraduate Lil Wayne but big-time Atlanta coke dealer turned mixtape cult artist turned trap star Young Jeezy and veteran grinders Three 6 Mafia. Admittedly, I was trolling for turkeys. But deciding whether they were bad was as hard as deciding whether Lil Wayne was good. With these guys, extricating pleasure from unease is pretty intimidating.

For a while Jeezy's "anthem beats," his term, had me disregarding the marketing coup of the coke-dealing snowman logo all the kids were wearing last fall, about which Jeezy chastised Kris Ex in XXL: "Show me anywhere on that shirt that says anything about narcotics. . . . Anything about racketeering, rape, prostitution, armed robbery, so and so forth—you got me? The Snowman represents"—not coke dealing, mind you, but—"'do what you love and love what you do.'" I still enjoy Jeezy's "My Hood," in which a cheerful string-synth riff bolsters his claim that the reason he quit dealing for what he calls "putting words together" wasn't money but love: "When I show up at them shows, it ain't about the money, man. I'm more excited to see the people. I'ma give them all I got, and I want them to give me the same thing." But when I listen back, "My Hood" doesn't rise above the graceless rapping and rhyming of a CD whose central selling point was what Bun B. praised in *Murder Dog* as "a certain level of street talk that had never been put down before"—that is, up-to-date underworld slang. Jeezy refers to this as "keeping the morals in the streets"; trap music, coke-dealing music, is ethical because it's, once again, real. Maybe next album, if he describes the unhappiness he's told many interviewers he never escapes like he says he will, I'll put his oeuvre under the cerebrum-auriculum microscope again. Right now I think he shoulda been a turkey.

Instead the bird I roasted was the more modest Three 6 Mafia. If the main difference between Young Jeezy and Tony Soprano is that Tony has too much taste to compare himself to Jesus, the main difference between Three 6 Mafia and Paulie Walnuts is that for Three 6 crime is a sideline. They never pretend they're not really musicians—in fact, they brag about it: "Three 6 Mafia, wild on tour/Whooping these niggas and fucking these hoes." Though they love an unfair fight, they'd rather beat your head in than blow your brains out. They dig weed and syrup not just as product but as highs. And they're too busy to pimp, so if you want some dick that'll be a dollar a pound, weigh in first please. In short, they vividly simulate the kind of real-life tough guys who make their neighbors miserable, envious, or both. Nevertheless, play their *Most Known Unknown* up against the perfectly honorable *Hustle and Flow* soundtrack and learn what hip-hoppers mean by "beats." And then recall the Oscars, where Three 6 performed a song from that film as composers. I love Dolly Parton and liked *Crash* OK, but when "It's Hard Out Here for a Pimp" won I was happier than Jon Stewart, although not Juicy J. I felt jubilant, vindicated, as if I'd never had a mean thought about Three 6 Mafia in my life. Between Juicy J and Tom Cruise, I could pick my guy.

I loved the movie and really liked the song—for its overstated, gospelized self-pity, affirmed and mocked simultaneously, and for its contextualized realism. Despite Cecil Brown's and Donald Goines's congruent arguments that pimping is an essential form of black male self-determination, and despite Frankie Lymon and Larry Williams and a young Louis Armstrong whose heart wasn't in it, to name just three, I think pimps are scum. But some scum have it hard—like the two dealers who worked my block ten-twelve hours a day during the crack epidemic, pounding the pavement with the collars of their skimpy leather jackets folded up against the chill, and then vanished, I hope to jail. But what made me so happy on Oscar night was a full fungu—a pop song sticking it up gentility's ass, the culturally uncontainable busting up the toothless liberal self-congratulation of an Oscar night that threatened to revive the noxious concept of PC even if I did like all those movies OK. Bullies sentimentalizing the exploitation of women in song—crucially, a good song, a catchy song, the recorded version of which was improved on by Three 6 in their bowdlerized witches-for-bitches Hollywood shot—were my allies in my lifelong war against art that's supposed to be good for you. In a disastrous historical moment that could generate any number of horrific outcomes, this war seems less important than it did forty or fifty years ago, but I remain attached to it. The Three 6 upset was like the White Sox sweeping the Series.

A few weeks later, my father died at ninety. It was a good death that followed a miserable senescence, and although it came as a relief for him and for his children, it was also troubling—guilt-inducing. I couldn't altogether escape the thought that by dint of great personal sacrifice I might have made his decline more bearable, nor the knowledge that his outrage at his infirmity would have rendered any such sacrifice twice as hard and half as effective. Driving to the funeral in Queens, I played Glenn Miller in tribute, and my wife could see him fox-trotting in heaven. But going out to set things up two days earlier, I chose the least likely of the CDs I'd grabbed: a post–*Carter II* mixtape subtitled "Like Father Like Son" featuring Lil Wayne, his surrogate dad Birdman, and DJ Khaled, who hyped: "This ain't no mixtape, niggaz. This is a gift, from Cash Money, for the streets." In other words, it's crude, all gangsta rhymes and killer hooks. My father didn't even know what rap was—when she was cognizant, my mom corrected him about it once. Maybe that's why I played it. Fucking thing felt so cleansing, so purposeful—so confident, so violent, so casual in its sublimated rage. Singsonging "If I don't give a fuck about you/And you don't give a fuck about me." Screwed-down "Where the cash at/Where the where the cash at." Grinning "I'm nice with the flow but a chosen few know that I'm a hustler on the low." And as I neared the funeral home, the chilling and exciting "Problem Solver": "He didn't count on no more problems I'm the problem solver/He didn't count on no more problems I'm the problem solver/He didn't count on no more problems I'm the problem solver," then—"Click, click pow, problem solved."

The appeal at that moment was about sublimating personal rage—my father's at his mortality, mine at myself and my father and our dilemma and I suppose at my own mortality too. Confidently, casually, sinuously, Lil Wayne was venting for me, and while in many of the guilty pleasures I've been running down, guilt is a detriment, here it worked like it does for people who believe in the cliche—it provided fillip, a crucial layer of zap, a sense of redeeming transgression. Although gangsta proceeds from economic oppression, this zap rarely attaches to the political rage I live with, because gangsta doesn't engage that oppression in a useful or, for the most part, insightful way. As it turns out, "Problem Solver" itself could pass as one of those battle-rhyme metaphor clusters that helped hip-hoppers of a more innocent era, before criminal credentials were a commercial plus, maintain that they only killed people symbolically. The tipoff is the *Friday the 13th* reference: "Jason Part XI I'm more scarier." Whether or not Lil Wayne has some hustle on the low, and beyond maybe some money-laundering I doubt it, even he doesn't claim he's a professional assassin like the problem solver. But you don't have to be any kind of criminal, as our laws define crime, to think life is about fucking bitches and getting money. And even more than his contempt for people who make their living fifty bucks at a time, it's the way he pumps and pimps that commonplace, more than any glorification cum trivialization of murder or cocaine, that I dislike most about Lil Wayne.

Yet in the end I have to say—I don't dislike Lil Wayne. Maybe I should, he seems like kind of a dick, but I don't. As with 50 Cent—to whom I could have devoted a related but different analysis, because every case is individual, every artist and song and response—the pleasure he's given me, disgracefully cornball though it is to put it this way, has offered me a glimpse of our shared humanity. At some level I'm one with this dick. If pleasure is where meaning begins, what this pleasure means is inextricable from the unease that comes with it. It's a moral complexity that has left me lost for words dozens of times as I've labored over this slight and manifestly incomplete analysis. And because I still don't believe in guilty pleasures, I'm committed and doomed to ponder this one and all its close relatives for the rest of my ever shortening life.

EMP Pop Conference, 2006

I History in the Making

Ten-Step Program for Growing Better Ears

1   Don't give up now.

2   Have a few drinks—smoke a joint, even.

3   At the very least, lighten up, willya?

4   Forget about soothing your savage beast.

5   Repeat three times daily: The good old days are the oldest myth in the world. Or, alternatively: Nostalgia sucks.

6   Go somewhere you think is too noisy and stay an hour. Go back.

7   Grasp this truth: Musically, all Americans are part African.

8   Attend a live performance by someone you've never seen before.

9   Play your favorite teenager's favorite album three times while doing something else. Put it away. Play it again two days later and notice what you remember.

10   Spend a week listening to James Brown's *Star Time*.

Dartmouth Alumni Magazine, 2001

Dionysus in Theory and Practice

I'll begin with a few excerpts from Robert Palmer's wonderful *Rock & Roll: An Unruly History*, which interrupts a narrative hooked to a PBS series with three essays that add up to an avant-primitivist revision of rock and roll history.

Climaxing number two, "Delinquents of Heaven, Hoodlums of Hell," is a section oddly entitled "Safety Zone," the most inspired exposition I know of the trope or claim or theory at hand, which begins: "The ancient Greeks enshrined philosophical dualism in their hierarchy of gods and myths, identifying spiritual forces or powers that embodied two basic tendencies in society and culture: the 'balanced, rational' Apollo and the 'intoxicated, irrational' Dionysus."

If this could be clearer and truer, that's nothing new. Scholars and theoreticians have always used the Greeks as a metaphor bank, imposing theoretical templates on a piecemeal historical record. Palmer's template derives from *The Birth of Tragedy*, Friedrich Nietzsche's long, murky riff on an Apollo-Dionysus polarity he copped from German romanticism. But Palmer never mentions Nietzsche. Having cited the reputable E. R. Dodds to establish that music and dance are means to, or is it blessings of, Dionysian "madness," he relies primarily on rogue ethnomusicologist Alain Daniélou, who equates the Greek wine god with the Indian phallic god, Shiva.

Palmer grants that "compared to an ancient Dionysian revel—trances, seizures, devotees tearing sacrificial animals to pieces with their bare hands and eating the meat raw—a rock and roll performance is almost tame." But he insists that in the wake of *Your Hit Parade* and *Father Knows Best*, early rock concerts became "temporary autonomous zones": "a kind of functional anarchy that manages to exist within a more or less repressive mainstream culture precisely because it is of limited duration and scope." Whereupon, in a wickedly if also lazily disruptive formal touch, he shelves scholarship and gives over half his six-page exegesis to descriptions of the Rolling Stones, not in concert, but wreaking mayhem at a Memphis hotel in 1975 and then, grayer and calmer fourteen years later, turning into "mere musicians—*professionals*." But this is OK, Palmer quickly adds; in fact, "that's the beauty of rock and roll." To be specific: "The lifestyle can be perilous, the rate of attrition remains high, but the survivors can go on practicing and perfecting their craft while the younger generation's best and brightest assume the Dionysian mantle and get on with the main program, which is liberation through ecstasy. . . . As rockers, we are heirs to one of our civilization's richest, most time-honored spiritual traditions. We must never forget our glorious Dionysian heritage."

This language is so redolent that I've now quoted it four times—including, unfortunately, in Robert Palmer's obituary. Keith Richards survived; his prophet did not. But even if you've never encountered Palmer's version, the

Dionysus theory you know about. Nietzsche's dichotomy is now boilerplate. Ruth Benedict held that whole cultures were Apollonian and Dionysian, although in the end she never described a Dionysian one. Ayn Rand, various Jungians, and endless New Agers have taken up the theme. It's proven so adaptable in the world of letters that a 1996 article in the journal of the Virginia Community College Association was called "Apollo vs Dionysus: The Only Theme Your Students Will Ever Need in Writing about Literature." And Nietzsche's full title, of course, is *The Birth of Tragedy Out of the Spirit of Music.*

The composer whose spirit Nietzsche thought uniquely worthy of the Greeks was his soon-repudiated beau ideal Wagner. But Apollo-versus-Dionysus has since been taken up by Stravinsky, Britten, and most prominently Richard Strauss—whose greatest hit was named after Nietzsche's *Also Sprach Zarathustra*—as well as analyses of Beethoven, Liszt, Bizet, on and on. It surfaces frequently in jazz commentary too. So rock has competition for the wine-bringer. But Google the name of a rock demigod plus the word "Dionysian" and you'll hit paydirt. The trick doesn't work with black artists, where who else but Jimi Hendrix is the only big winner, or with Bob Dylan, who's on record as insisting that Stagger Lee was "not some egotistical degraded existentialist dionysian idiot." But Beatles Stones Velvets Zep Patti Ramones Pistols Nirvana PJ Harvey Smashing Pumpkins—hell, why not? Tori Amos likes to throw the word around. Phish's corporate arm is called Dionysian Productions. LA's Dionysus Records has been purveying "the finest in Garage-Surf-Rockabilly-Exotica-and more" since 1984.

Rock's champion Dionysian, however, is that egotistical degraded existentialist idiot Jim Morrison, dubbed Bozo Dionysus by Lester Bangs. Morrison is said to have named his band during a bull session about *The Birth of Tragedy.* And in Arnold Shaw's *The Rock Revolution*, he sums up the history he gleaned at UCLA: "In its origin, the Greek theatre was a band of worshippers, dancing and singing on a threshing floor at the crucial agricultural seasons. Then, one day, a possessed person leaped out of the crowd and started imitating a god." This is garbled, but its dancing and singing and leaping and god act all evoke a Doors concert better than a performance of *Also Sprach Zarathustra.* Yet here's the odd thing. Not only do both Morrison and Nietzsche, with their intense commitments to different kinds of music, validate that commitment by reference to literature, but neither bothers to guess how the original Dionysian music might have sounded or, really, functioned. So I thought it might be instructive to try and find out.

To begin, say there are three Dionysuses: the Dionysus of myth, of cult, and of festival. Not that they sort out so neatly, of course—Euripides's *The Bacchae*, for example, was originally presented at one kind of Dionysian festival and purports to represent cultic practices that have since been imported big-time into the mythic record. In almost all accounts Dionysus is the son of the great god Zeus and the mortal mother Semele and gestated in Zeus's thigh after Semele was murdered. And although recent archaeological finds indicate deep Greek origins for the god, in post-archaic Greece he was universally believed to be an outsider—perhaps from Thrace, which we call Bulgaria, or Lydia or Phrygia in Asia Minor. Dionysus gathers around himself such a complicated entourage of tales and histories that ass-covering contemporary scholars find it convenient to subsume them all under the heading "god of paradox." Half human, half divine, he's the bringer of madness and the deliverer from madness, lord of masks and maenads, of the underworld and raw meat au jus; he's the phallus god who turned femme and lost his beard. And always Dionysus is the god of wine.

Leaving out lots of good stuff, that's the Dionysus of myth. In varying versions—only one of which, the Pentheus story Euripides and later René Girard made so much of, involved human sacrifice, and only one of which, the myth of Dionysus Zagreus that Nietzsche appropriated, has Christian overtones of divine suffering and rebirth—the Dionysus of myth was the god called upon in cult and celebrated in festival. Unfortunately, the cult of Dionysus was even more secretive than most cults. Palmer's man Daniélou defeats this inconvenience by positing that Dionysus was an essentially unchanged descendant of Shiva, whose jism-jetting erections are amply documented. But most settle for secondhand evidence by skeptical or hostile sources scattered over a thousand-year period. Here's Livy in Rome: "When wine, lascivious discourse, night, and the intercourse of the sexes had extinguished every sentiment of modesty, then debaucheries of every kind began to be practiced, as every person found at hand that sort of enjoyment to which he was disposed by the passion predominant in his nature." Although "the beating of cymbals and drums" is as musicological as Livy gets, Palmer would go for that. Problem is, all Livy knew for sure when he wrote it in 186 BC was that he wanted the Roman senate to ban the god then called Bacchus, as it then did. There's better info in that old muso Plato: "In a Bacchic frenzy, and enthralled beyond what is right by pleasure, they mixed lamentations with hymns and paeans with dithyrambs, imitated aulos songs with their kithara songs, and put everything together with everything else, thus unintentionally, through their stupidity, giving false witness against music, alleging that music possesses no standard of correctness, but is most correctly judged by the pleasure of the person who enjoys it, whether he is a better man or a worse."

Turn Plato's values upside down like they deserve and you have a presentiment of popular music. But "enthralled by pleasure" doesn't mean much. As with Livy, Plato's facts are secondhand at best—thirdhand is likely. And while like any good postmodern I shrink from blanket generalizations about human behavior, I'd like to suggest a tentative one, which is that the guy who didn't get invited to the party always believes the guy who did is having a ball. Historian of religion Walter Burkert is part of an antisex wing of Dionysus scholarship that includes Nietzsche. But Burkert has studied ancient cult practices as scrupulously as anyone, and he finds it impossible to "associate them with the concept of orgies." He also concludes that most if not all of Dionysus's initiates were women, usually women of means, and that after "days and days of fasting, purifications, exhaustion, apprehension, and excitement," their big debauch was the chance to wolf down some roast sacrifice. Yet Burkert does allow that for "a few special individuals" initiation could provide "a veritable change of consciousness in ecstasy" to which wine was essential, and adds that "certain kinds of music" opened up pathways to the divine. He also quotes a Christian-era source: "This is the purpose of Bacchic initiation, that the depressive anxiety of less educated people, produced by their state of life, or some misfortune, be cleared away through the melodies and dances of the ritual in a joyful and playful way."

With their trances, seizures, and gore, these initiations are as close as we're going to get to Palmer's "ancient Dionysian revel." Yet cults weren't the ancient Dionysus's main venue. Far more amenable to outside observation were uncounted festivals in rural and urban places. These were more open-ended and less fraught than initiations—more rock and roll. A festival that jumbles rural Dionysia and what was called the Anthesteria climaxes Aristophanes's *The Acharnians*, and even correcting for the playwright's comic will and dirty mind, it smells like one of those orgies Burkert can't find as Aristophanes's farmer hero calls for "dancing-girls" to grab his "rejoicing prick." We know a lot about the Anthesteria, the spring festival of new wine, because we have a thousand of the illustrated 3.2-liter jugs from which the watered wine was quaffed. These depict dance moves ranging from capers and acrobatics to mimetic set pieces, often by satyrs or men in satyr costumes, and many varieties of music-making.

As even Livy knew, the true Dionysian instrument was the drum. Greece was not a percussion culture compared to Egypt, where Osiris's celebrants were far more polyrhythmic. But the tympanon, which generated a deep thump from a single animal-skin side, always came out for Dionysus, as did giant castanets called krotala. Symbolically, however, the double-reed aulos, which used to be translated flute but had a bigger oboe sound, also ruled. Charles Keil suspects that the Macedonian dauli music he describes in *Bright Balkan Morning*, music he deems unrecordable due to its fluctuating overtones, descends from aulos-and-tympanon. The Anthesteria made room too for the panpipe, and for Apollo's ruling-class ax, the lyre. Then there was song. Remember Plato? "They mixed lamentations with hymns and paeans with dithyrambs"? Happy-sad speaks for itself, but you should know that paeans were for Apollo, more dignified than Dionysus's dithyrambs. In absolute terms we have barely an inkling of how all this sounded—certainly not the rhythms, tempos, or God knows scales. But most likely it was perceived and received more like rock and roll in 1955 or rock in 1967 than Wagner in 1872. And its social history is redolent.

Dionysus was a minor god in Homer's time. Only after 700 BC did his fame start spreading, in festival at least as much as cult. This was a grassroots movement—a grassroots movement of people who liked to party. Did it have graver meanings? Perhaps something to do with how inadequately Apollo's paeans lightened mortality's pall. Did it threaten the state? Made it nervous, maybe. Was it explicitly "versus" Apollo? It seems the Germans made that up. Did it offend bigshots and bigdomes? Plenty, but it also attracted some— most people like to party, and Dionysian partying featured big jugs and wild music. So naturally various Greek politicians proceeded to coopt it.

Shortly after 600, Cleisthenes of Sicyon cut into the authority of the Dorian nobility by transferring a local choral festival from the Dorian hero Adrastus to Dionysus. And by 500 or so, Dionysus and his dithyramb were fixtures of Athenian life, because the midcentury tyrant Peisistratus, in an end run around both the aristocracy and a potentially anarchic popular force, had by then instituted the Great Dionysia, a rival to the aristocratically controlled Pythian Games. In other words, Apollo versus Dionysus reduces to a power struggle between hereditary rulers and the populist big men who supplanted them. And before too long Dionysus's dithyramb, once what a rakish classicist calls "a merry song sung by anybody who was feeling up in the world (usually after a few jars)," came to be performed by an elaborate chorus, complete with choreography as contained and "noble" as all official dance in Greece. Pindar, the untranslatable poetic titan who was the last great spokesman of the Greek aristocracy, was one of its masters.

Before too long, the dithyrambic chorus morphed into Greek tragedy, judged the most sublime of art forms even by some Chuck Berry fans. You can read whole books about tragedy and never guess that a third of it was sung. Note, however, that tragic music was dominated by the aulos, which like Dionysus himself came to be regarded as exotic, disreputable, low-class—at best non-Greek in origin (which like Dionysus it wasn't) and for Plato and lesser snobs as a carrier of cultural contagion. Tragedy enjoyed a creative life of barely a century, but the classics continued to be performed along with the New Comedy that succeeded it. Actors toured and professionalized, and so did musicians—there were virtuoso auletes, kitharodes who wowed the crowd with runs on the concert lyre. They formed guilds that lasted for centuries. The first harbinger of the American Federation of Musicians translates as the Commonalty of the Artists Concerned With Dionysus. Perfect.

Mere musicians—*professionals*. Over a longer timespan, this is Palmer's story, an exotic music of freeing frenzy brought to heel by rationalizing exploiters, only "the younger generation's best and brightest" don't do their part. So rather than an avant-primitivist continuum we have the kind of decadence decried by, of all people, rock criticism's most distinguished classicist: Nick Tosches, a major Pindar and minor Doors fan who believes rock was formally exhausted by the late '60s. But before we get too disillusioned, let's remember that in the bargain we get tragedy, which for all its over-rated sublimity is some kind of recompense. And remember too that the Dionysian reality that got rationalized was rarely if ever as ecstatic as that postulated by Palmer or Nietzsche. Wine festivals probably didn't occasion as many rejoicing pricks as jealous playwrights and censorious legislators believed; the Dionysus who embraces death in affirmation of the collective life-force is a Nietzschean figment; the maenads who tear Pentheus limb from limb in *The Bacchae* are a Euripidean device. Nor need we regret this loss. One of the hundred reasons I wish Robert Palmer was still alive is so I could ask him how he felt when Alain Daniélou, the most extreme contemporary Dionysian of any standing, argued that the caste system is a natural way of life and a small price to pay for Shiva, whose maxims include: "Women are light-minded. They are the source of all trouble. Men who seek liberation must avoid attaching themselves to women."

Probably he'd shrug in bemused dismay. For certain rock and rollers, the program will always be liberation through ecstasy, and all the rest of us can do is thank them for creating temporary autonomous zones and hope they don't die before they get old. Early in *The Bacchae*, before Dionysus starts illing, the Asian chorus sings his praises. I don't know the tune, but the lyrics are choice:

> *These blessings he gave:*
> *laughter to the flute*
> *and the loosing of cares*
> *when the shining wine is spilled*

And later:

> *The deity, the son of Zeus*
> *in feast, in festival, delights.*
> *He loves the goddess Peace*
> *generous of good,*
> *preserver of the young.*
> *To rich and poor he gives*
> *the simple gift of wine,*
> *the gladness of the grape.*
> *But him who scoffs he hates,*
> *and him who mocks his life,*
> *the happiness of those*
> *for whom the day is blessed*
> *but doubly blessed the night;*
> *whose simple wisdom shuns the thoughts*
> *of proud, uncommon men and all*
> *their god-encroaching dreams.*
> *But what the common people do,*
> *the things that simple men believe,*
> *I too believe and do.*

EMP Pop Conference, 2003

B.E.

A Dozen Moments in the Prehistory of Rock and Roll

1227: Moon-June-Spoon Meets Death-Metal

Simply by inventing (or—here we go—cribbing from the Moors, who were writing love poetry well before they were expelled from their Provence stronghold in 973) not love but *l'amour*, love as a concept, the troubadours of Provence laid one of the foundations of rock and roll, which whatever its socially significant pretensions has always had a thing for male-and-female. They were neither effete aesthetes—this was a rough world where all men were warriors and rape was one of the commonplaces the myth of courtly love glossed over—nor the lute-strumming adventurers you dimly imagine. The itinerant singer-songwriters of the Middle Ages were called jongleurs— all-round entertainers whose etymology honors another of their skills, juggling. Jongleurs played marketplaces, fairs, the hostelries that catered to pilgrims and such, and, when they could get in, castles. Troubadours lived in castles—court poets in an era when "lyric" poetry was still sung to musical accompaniment, they were the highbrows of the secular world, upwardly mobile if not nobility themselves. Considered blasphemous by the religio-political powers that were, troubadours pretty much ended with the Albigensian crusade of the thirteenth century. So as our symbolic rock and roller we'll select Guilhem Figueira, an embattled hero of the movement's decline who "was not the man to frequent barons and respectable folk, but he was much at home with ribalds, whores, and tavern-haunters"—or so says his vida, an unauthorized bio that was as accurate as a press release. Is "In the fires of hell, Rome, you've chosen to dwell" close enough to Slayer for you?

1623: The Discovery of Natural Rhythm

"There is without doubt, no people on the earth more naturally affected to the sound of musicke than these people; which the principall persons do hold as an ornament of their state, so as when wee come to see them, their musicke will seldome be wanting," claimed Captain Richard Jobson, describing a visit he made to Gambia starting in 1620, the year after a Dutch man-of-war sold North America's first black slaves to British colonists in Jamestown. Africa's music had varied and evolved in uncounted strains and permutations for thousands of years, but this first published account in English is a benchmark, for what is rock and roll but African music as understood and controlled by white people? The intensity of African vocal technique, loud and harsh and keening by European standards, was frequently noted in the numerous reports to come, as was the "multitude of drums in various sizes." Less remarked were the underlying melodic similarities between African song and Scotch-Irish folk music, which would help Brits get into this exotic stuff. Soon Africans who could play an instrument fetched premium prices on the open market. By 1676, the governor of Cape Town owned his own slave orchestra.

1815: Sex and Beer and One-Two-Three

The Viennese were dancing fools—during the city's three-day pre-Lenten *Fasching* celebration of 1832, when its population was 400,000, 772 balls attracted 200,000 citizens. After all, this was their heritage. Vienna had produced what remains the greatest revolution in the history of social dancing—the waltz. Just like most of the court dances invented since the fifteenth century, the waltz was bred from peasant stock. But unlike any court dance, it required couples to embrace each other, and once they went that far, a lot of them went further. Already invading France and England by 1790, danced in seized monasteries by sans-culotte revolutionaries, the waltz was a scandal well before the European powers divvied up Napoleon's empire at the 1815 Congress of Vienna, where the Prince de Ligne went down in history by quipping: "Le Congrès ne marche pas—il danse." But after the Congress it became a full-fledged vogue. Once the assembled dignitaries had brought their good times home, both social dancing and popular music were permanently linked to a more carnal vision of courtship.

1843: Straight Out de Land ob Cotton

Musical miscegenation is an old story in America, where shocked reports of white teenagers dancing to black fiddlers go back to the 1690s. But though black musicians were common enough in a certain class of bar, even the freemen among them remained strictly local celebrities. Traveling white performers, on the other hand, found that to "imitate" blacks on stage guaranteed yucks. By 1832, when Thomas Dartmouth "Daddy" Rice went nationwide with "Jim Crow," a song-and-dance routine he claimed to have stolen from a crippled black stablehand, burnt cork was a staple of American showbiz. But it was not until 1843 that four musicians dubbing themselves the Virginia Minstrels formalized blackface into a full evening's diversion—minstrelsy. Playing banjo, tambourine, "bones" (castanets), and fiddle—the specialty of leader and chief composer Dan Emmett, whose "Dixie" was later appropriated as the unofficial Confederate national anthem—the Virginia Minstrels and their many imitators probably sounded something like the earliest recorded "hillbilly" music of the 1920s, only longer soon enough on sentimental ballads and parlor polish. Rendered more genteel by the addition of small pit bands and more businesslike by a burgeoning songwriting industry, the minstrel show was America's dominant popular entertainment for most of the nineteenth century. Though eventually many actual African-Americans got into the act, it remains a pungent reminder that black people and what white people make of them are two very different things.

1849: From Jim Crow to Tin Pan Alley

Stephen Collins Foster became the toast of his middle-class Pittsburgh neighborhood by performing "Jim Crow" and "Zip Coon" in amateur theatricals in 1835, when he was nine. The extent of his exposure to African-American culture is debatable, but minstrelsy he knew. A typical quasibohemian dreamer, he wasn't rebellious enough to turn minstrel himself. But as his tunes began to bring in some money, he saw a way out of his bookkeeping job. In 1849 he persuaded Firth, Pond & Co., a major New York music firm whose interests went far beyond minstrelsy, to pay him royalties at a time when songs were invariably sold outright for sums that didn't support the performers, conductors, music teachers, and dilettantes who wrote them. Thus he became America's first fulltime professional songwriter, and also the first master of its polyglot musical heritage—Irish ballads and Italian opera as well as African tinge. Foster was never altogether comfortable with his so-called Ethiopian songs ("Swanee River," "Camptown Races," "My Old Kentucky Home"), and after he moved to New York in 1853 he concentrated on parlor ballads—since they were more artistic, he figured they'd have a longer shelf life. But only "Jeanie with the Light Brown Hair" and "Old Dog Tray" were major successes, and before long the spendthrift songsmith was reduced to writing songs for hire like a common hack. As a nonperforming composer, Foster presaged the Tin Pan Alley rock and roll overthrew. He also presaged almost everything else in American pop. He died a Bowery alcoholic at thirty-seven.

1890: Dawn of the Indies

The phonograph that Thomas Edison invented in 1877 was conceived as a dictaphone and didn't work very well. Only after others developed the floating stylus and covered the cylinder Edison recorded on with wax instead of tinfoil did he merchandise his machine, with his chief target the U.S. Congress, where he believed it would soon render secretaries obsolete. Fortunately, the fate of the phonograph was in the hands of Edison's thirty regional franchisees, all of whom would have lost their shirts pursuing what Edison pumped as "the legitimate side of their business." And somewhere out there somebody came up with a money-making bastard—a coin-in-the-slot protojukebox into which rubes, children, and men about town would insert a nickel to hear tunes by Foster and John Philip Sousa. So before there was really a record business, freelance entrepreneurs with their ears in the air had given the record business a shot in the arm, which is also the story of rock and roll. And let us not forget another independent, rival inventor-entrepreneur Emile Berliner, who in 1887 patented a gramophone that recorded on discs instead of cylinders, an idea whose time soon came. Berliner always knew he was in the home entertainment business, and record collectors owe him their gratitude. Just exactly how would you store five hundred long-playing cylinders in a studio apartment?

1913: Sex and Champagne and Four-Four Animals

Vernon Castle was an English comedian with an engineering degree, Irene Foote the daughter of a physician and the granddaughter of P. T. Barnum's press agent. They married in 1911 and in 1912 lucked into a job dancing at a fashionable Paris cabaret. By this time, the turkey trot, the grizzly bear, the bunny hug, and other barroom-cum-barnyard terpsichore had made inroads in high society, and though the Castles' versions of these "nigger dances," to borrow a phrase Irene was tossing about several years later, were "considerably toned down," they created a sensation. Soon they were back in New York making up steps, first and most prominently the Castle walk, in collaboration with black composer Ford Dabney and black composer-conductor James Reese Europe. It was the waltz all over again—Western civilization going dance-mad from the top. As less stringent standards of decorum replaced the previously prescribed six-inch distance between partners, a barrier was breached. Song publishers were convinced that hits had to have a good beat, and though many a tearjerker broke the rule, the parlor ballad was finally on its way out.

1925: This Is Lou-Iss, Dolly

Well before abolition, the French-Spanish port city of New Orleans spawned a unique music colored by the African dances of Congo Square, and eventually the city's nonstop party generated the greatest musician of the twentieth century. But like Muddy Waters and his Delta progeny two decades later, he didn't make his mark until after he took the train up to Chicago. Louis Armstrong invented or at least standardized the improvised solo. His gravelly, sardonic vocal excursions cut singing loose from cornball beauty and bullshit text; his high-handed fun with pop trash prefigured postmodernist recontextualization. And though he's more closely associated with the subcategories "jazz" and "pop," rock would be unimaginable without solos or gravel or high-handed popwise fun. The year I've chosen is when he started recording as a leader, but you might want to check out the Lonnie Johnson guitar solo on 1927's "I'm Not Rough"—sounds for all the world like r&b fixing to cross over. You could also give a listen to his "Saints." Or "Hello Dolly."

1938: Les Paul Takes Lunch

As long ago as 2000 BC, when Babylonian lute players were depicted as shepherds rather than priests, the guitar was conceived as a people's instrument. Its seventeenth-century vogue was associated with dance music, its nineteenth-century vogue with romantic melody. In America, the first electric model was developed in the '20s by country guitarist Lloyd Loar, who couldn't sell it. By 1931 Rickenbacker was manufacturing an electrified Hawaiian version, followed quickly by a so-called Spanish guitar, which introduced the electromagnetic pickup. T-Bone Walker is generally credited with introducing such a guitar to blues. The first known recording is "Good Morning Blues," cut in 1938 by Count Basie sideman Eddie Durham, and it was Durham fan Charlie Christian who turned the electric guitar into a phenomenon after he joined Benny Goodman in 1939. But all of these retained the lute's acoustic resonator—its hollow body. Lifelong tinkerer Les Paul had another idea. Sometime around 1938 he fitted a railroad tie with steel strings and a pickup: "You could go out to eat and come back and the note would still be sounding. It didn't sound like a banjo or a mandolin, but like a guitar, an electric guitar. That was the sound I was after." It took another decade for Leo Fender to start manufacture, and soon the solid-body electric came to dominate pop, bestowing on a single barely trained player the aural power of a symphony orchestra. Les Paul went on to invent multitrack recording.

1940: Enter the Barbarians

ASCAP—the American Society of Composers, Authors and Publishers—was Tin Pan Alley's guild, collecting licensing fees from all manner of musical venues and promoters. It constructed favorable deals for the most powerful Broadway and Hollywood firms, treating more folkish genres with something closely akin to contempt. And though initially it resisted radio, by 1939 it earned two-thirds of its income there and was sure it could up its rates. After all, where else were broadcasters going to get the music they'd created an addiction to? But radio elected to stand and fight, chartering BMI—Broadcast Music, Inc.—to license all the songwriters ASCAP shortchanged. At first BMI concentrated on rearranging uncopyrighted songs, Foster's among them, but by the end of 1940 it had corraled the catalogues of disgruntled Tin Pan Alley oldtimer Edward B. Marks and ace talent scout Ralph Peer. Peer was credited with coining the terms "race" and "hillbilly" music for what we now call blues and country, and was the first to record both Jimmie Rodgers and the Carter Family. His Peer International not only controlled many country and blues copyrights, but had invested heavily in Latin American music, as had Marks. So when on January 1, 1941, the broadcasters let their ASCAP contract expire, radio was positioned to boost a bunch of hicks, greasers, and Negroes, many of whom couldn't even read music—and who were about to destroy the pop power brokers' monopoly forever.

1941: Afternoon of the Indies

Like Edison's phonograph, radio was first conceived as a business tool—a talking telegraph. But even in the early ham days, when would-be broadcasters would first distribute crystal sets to their neighbors, some had more poetic ideas—a San Jose buff was airing live and recorded music as early as 1909. By 1926, when there were already Tin Pan Alley songsmiths who limited their melodies to the five notes early receivers could handle, David Sarnoff, who'd first proposed a "radio music box" in 1916, had assembled the NBC network. Much of radio's allure, however, lay in the access it afforded to swank (and costly) metropolitan entertainment *as it happened*—stars live in your living room, big bands playing big hotels. Only in 1941, when the federal government—which back in 1922 had allotted the choicest frequencies to operators who promised not to broadcast records—moved to break the power of the networks, was the stage set for the small local stations whose need for cheap programming would soon transform disc jockeys into tastemaking local celebrities. And in those days, local celebrities played local music—including all the insurgent folk-pop BMI had had the luck or vision to exploit.

1947: Fix It in the Mix

Bing Crosby was no Armstrong or Sinatra, but again and again he had the right idea at the right time. In addition to linking up John McCormack and Al Jolson with the informal phrasing of the jazz artists he idolized, he had an equally inspired instinct for the gadget. Singers "crooned" throughout the '20s, and megaphone-toting Rudy Vallee was the first pop heartthrob. But it was Crosby who mastered vocal amplification by developing a style appropriate to the microphones that defined radio and recording studios— who learned to create an illusion of conversational intimacy by pretending that the mike just happened to be there when he lifted his baritone in song. Soon the floodgates were opened to a host of singers who hadn't gone through the painful rituals whereby a few lucky, hard-working individuals train their freakishly exceptional "beautiful" voices to carry in a concert hall. And eventually the Groaner hit upon an even more democratic technological angle. Frustrated by the sound quality of his half-improvised radio shows, which had to be patched together from 78-rpm master discs so they could be scheduled through four time zones, he became the first entertainer—unless Adolf Hitler counts—to exploit the fidelity and editability of the magnetic tape an enterprising Army officer had purloined from the Nazis. Musical "authenticity" would never be the same. Crosby scored well over three hundred hits even though he didn't give a paid concert between 1933 and 1976. But the rock and roll that couldn't have happened without him did him in—after 1955, his pop play was limited primarily to "White Christmas."

Details, 1992

Let's Get Busy
in Hawaiian

A Hundred Years of Ragged Beats and Cheap Tunes

The decade is a dandy organizing device—a convenient construct. Generalize a little? Why sure. The most important thing to happen to pop in the '90s was a tenfold increase in the amount of music recorded. That's the factoid bandied about, anyway—I've never seen the documentation. Even if the truth is half as much, it would add up to more hours of music than there are in a year, a symbolic threshold. No one can hear it all, folks. It's out of our control. Good. Daunting, overwhelming—but good.

The millennium, on the other hand, is a chimera—an inconceivable vastness for anyone who isn't a professional historian and almost anyone who is. No wonder the idea produces false prophets and religious manias. We know quite a bit about things that will pass for popular music in the 1100s, when troubadours roamed Provence, and the 1600s, when Europeans discovered African rhythm. But to wrap this info into a thousand-year package would be a waste of time.

In between these two accidents of the decimal system falls the century, which if it happens to be the twentieth means something in pop. This is due to the technological action that closed the nineteenth, especially the development of the phonograph. Charts going back to 1890 have been devised, but musical sound recordings really do more or less begin with the century. In Evan Eisenberg's conceit, records turn music into a thing. Of course it's also living process—often a crucially unique process. Of course it will and must continue to be created in the heat of the moment by and among musicians interacting with an audience; of course (although not so unequivocally) it will and must reflect local cultures. But now and forever music will be storable, portable, reproducible. And for those reasons it will be pervasive—in all industrialized places and many that aren't, an assumed fact of the aural environment.

Anyone can produce music—you just sing. Consuming it didn't come so easy; except at special sites like markets or churches, the consumption of music was for the privileged through most of history. But as the world urbanized, performance venues proliferated. By 1845, the minstrel circuit was organizing the young male audience that has been with pop ever since; in post-Commune France, the café-chantant drew a more self-consciously aesthetic crowd to its music hall–cabaret; and from the refined English assembly rooms to the low-life hot spots of New York's Tenderloin, public dance spaces were a fact of courtship before 1900. Songwriting for these venues was professionalized, following neither the folk pattern, in which songs were created by local celebrities who had other jobs, nor the classical one, in which composers scribbled for the aristocracy or church. As Charles Hamm emphasizes in *Yesterdays: Popular Song in America*, these new professionals often took it to the stage as well—they made their livings as performers. By 1850 sheet music was the stock in trade of publishers who targeted a genteel emerging market—namely, owners of pianos, the great status symbols of the emerging petit bourgeoisie.

Recordings didn't simply overrun all this music for the people; not until after World War II could they even be said to dominate it. But along with radio they greatly intensified its dissemination. Internationally, records are everything. The Americanization of world pop isn't simply an imposition of capitalism or the inevitable outgrowth of our irresistible Euro-Afro meld— without records, our cultural imperialism would have been far less monolithic. And here at the source they've always been learning tools for listeners and musicians both. To repeat: live performances and one-on-one interactions are crucial—as in the epochal blues culture of Clarksdale, Mississippi

(Charley Patton, Son House, Robert Johnson, Howlin' Wolf, and more) or the Benny Goodman–Eddie Condon generation of young white jazz players that emerged in Chicago at the same time, shortly after Louis Armstrong followed King Oliver up from New Orleans. But even at this point we have pathfinders like Bix Beiderbecke and Bing Crosby studying records in the boonies. And although Billie Holiday used to attend dances just to listen to the band, it was a Victrola in a whorehouse sitting room that introduced her to Bessie and Louis.

....

As the century began, operetta and minstrelsy had already spawned the powerful promotional medium of musical comedy, with the very American George M. Cohan and the very European Victor Herbert pioneering beneficiaries, and the very Jewish, very American Irving Berlin just around the corner. Demographically, Broadway's melting pot was white—African-Americans were present there primarily in the all too symbolic form of blackface. But as an artistic force if not people getting paid they were at the heart of what was called ragtime. Ragtime wasn't just the elegant piano style it's reduced to today. It was an addictive compulsion to syncopate the beat—to "rag" it, make it ragged—that was felt throughout pop, Broadway included. This rhythmic foregrounding had its counterpart in the sexualization of social dancing—black-derived "animal dances," a tango craze, and the canny commodifications of world-class society hustlers Vernon and Irene Castle.

It says something about the secondary importance of recordings before World War I that composers like Cohan and Berlin remain legendary while the era's hit artists—uptempo ballad specialist Billy Murray, barbershop harmonizers the Peerless Quartet, blackface singer-comedian Arthur Collins—are forgotten. Crucially, it was only in the '20s that record companies thought to single out the "race" and "hillbilly" markets. Besides providing access to America's most original musicians, most of whom were Negroes, this development belatedly recognized pop's rural strain, which in a drama of modernization and accommodation with worldwide parallels has been infiltrating our urban-suburban culture ever since. Combine a booming economy, an impatience with the morality of repression, some youth culture, and a few dollops of postwar alienation and it was the perfect time for blues and jazz to come into their own.

It cannot be reiterated too often that "rural" doesn't get us to the naive, untutored, not-for-profit "folk." The rural music that got recorded had a commercial purpose, and its creators were knowledgeable and shrewd. Old-timey icon Uncle Dave Macon, for instance, went into music profession-ally after his transport business failed and learned many of his songs at the Nashville hotel his family owned. And the blues—well. The blues are a lot more certainly twentieth-century than, for instance, jazz. There were plenty of black marching bands and songsters after the Civil War, but nothing like a bluesman existed before around 1890. Primitive though the twelve-bar form may appear, it was brand new, and the individualism of the blues within that form's stretched and reimagined constraints constituted an existential leap for the unreconstructed black people who played them. That individualism is intrinsic to the blues's enduring attraction. But just as intrinsic, Peter van der Merwe argues in his fascinating *Origins of the Popular Style*, has been the blues's appetite for melody—not rhythm, as is always said and also true, but melody, melody that encourages variation and hence both individual expression and the generation of "tune families," which van der Merwe be-lieves often suggest a common ancient origin for African and Celtic music.

Blues and country are still cordoned off commercially in the '20s. Sus-tained by rubes without money, they'll make their move twenty years later. But "race music" also signified "jazz," which as a loosely defined genre soon lent its deracinated name to the "age," and closely coexisted with a Tin Pan Alley then starting to peak with the harmonically ambitious pantheon com-posers of so-called classic American popular song. Since even today it's com-monplace for literate ignoramuses to claim a monopoly on artistic worth for the Berlin-Gershwin-Porter-Rodgers axis, there's a temptation to ac-cent-chu-ate the negative about musical comedy song, as do van der Merwe and Hamm. But from "Always" to "Body and Soul" to "Hello Dolly" to "Send in the Clowns" (would you believe maybe "Don't Cry for Me, Argentina"?), it stands as a titanic cultural achievement by hundreds of composers and lyri-cists whose great songs number in the thousands. And however overrated the legerdemain of their chord structures, these structures were a precondi-tion of bebop, which render them a precondition of all postwar jazz.

Defying sociological determinism as riders of formal upsurges so often do, Berlin-Gershwin-Porter-Rodgers-etc. just kept on writing songs and shows during the Great Depression. The Jazz Age, on the other hand, took a nosedive, and the record business very nearly died. By 1935, however, jazz had staged a comeback and pulled the biz back up with it, with Benny Good-man, a student of black dance bands who hired Fletcher Henderson to do his arrangements, leading the charge. The swing era quickly morphed into the big-band era and was essentially over by 1940, but it occasioned a connoisseurship barely approached in previous pop. This was the first time black singers and players attracted anything like a mass audience, and the only time in America that a predominantly instrumental music did, although fans of rock improvisers from Jimi Hendrix to Sonic Youth come close enough. As assiduously elaborated by and for an in group, swing was a subcultural dance music that presaged disco, funk, and techno. It was the first pop to inspire serious critical dialogue. Its hipper admirers evolved into the jazz aesthetes who assure the real if parlous viability of jazz as both avant-garde and institutionalized art music. It was only a moment, but a tremendously pregnant one.

....

The swift demise of swing, in which formerly peripheral singers became bigger stars than Goodman or Miller, is blamed on many things, including the musicians union and the decimation of the male youth audience by World War II, but in retrospect it was inevitable. Swing was too hard. Pop connoisseurs habitually insist on the agency, expressiveness, originality, aesthetic acuity, and progressive political thrust of the music we treasure, and we should. But chugging alongside all the effort and invention we honor has been crap we really could do without. More should be made of the supposedly bad things pop also is, and of the right of its audience to revel in them until such time as leisure is wrested from ordinary people by implacable capital or an angry God. To name names, pop is *easy* and it is *escapist*, often at its best and almost invariably at its least momentous. There's nothing so mysterious about cheap tunes. People love them because they're a stroll in the park—scenic, diverting, even surprising, without ever tempting anyone to get lost on the way home. The Castles are credited with dispatching the parlor ballad by pushing songs with a beat, but all they really did was to speed it up a little. Sentimental slow ones never go away, and sometimes they take over, especially after virtuosic energy has one of its runs; we should be thankful that their '40s comeback gave us Frank Sinatra and, less directly, Ella Fitzgerald and Nat King Cole.

By 1940, music was everywhere and runaway variety was pop's most salient and democratic virtue. Encouraged by a radio smitten with the economies of canned music as it maneuvered through publishing feuds too sordid to go into, the record industry once again marketed the rural musics of the '20s— as "country and western," which had never fully disappeared, and "rhythm and blues," an easy, escapist, exclusively African-American alternative to big-band dance music that instead of emulating the machine via arrangement

exploited it via amplification. Jazzy Western swing and jump blues notwithstanding, country and r&b mined folkish sounds. In country, a constructed
traditionalism—Bill Monroe inventing bluegrass in a cowboy hat, say—did
battle with sinful honky tonk impulses; r&b swallowed every blues trick to
hit the big city and was secularizing gospel's vocal calisthenics and ecstatic
beats before soul knew its name. True, Nashville became Tin Pan Alley soon
enough. But if Hamm is right to believe that pop belongs to the performer,
not the composer, then the triumph of the twin roots genres was a fulfillment of history rather than the betrayal of civilized standards fogeys have
whined about ever since.

Enter rock and roll, which has now prevailed in its many guises for nearly
half a century. The standard oversimplification, which declares rock the bastard child of blues and country, ignores the pop savvy of its overseers and
exaggerates the whiteness of its roots, but does serve to emphasize its proud
dependence on the modal melodies and small-group dynamics that drove
country and r&b. In addition to these essential attractions, rock privileged
three elements that had been knocking on pop's door since 1900: youth,
race, and rhythm. Pop music had always been youth music, never more than
in the '30s, but '50s teendom—enjoying an explosion of spending cash as it
resisted a resurgent nuclear-family ideology out of step with too many other
realities—was far more sure of itself than earlier youth cultures. And though
American music has always been crossbred and American culture has never
stopped being racist, the integration of pop in the '50s was far more drastic
than anything suggested by the Mills Brothers on the hit parade. Of course
whites maintained economic control and configured dozens of rock subgenres
to their preferences and expectations—often to excellent effect, too. It's even
conceivable that all of rock's radical racial metaphors were epiphenomena of
the civil rights struggle. But it's crude reductionism to charge, for instance,
that hip-hop's pop reach is blackface all over again. African-American musicians exert a status and power denied them fifty years ago.

To prove it, there's rhythm. Since minstrelsy at the latest, the basic story
of American and then world popular music had been cheap tunes getting
their beats ragged. But the tunes, arguably part African themselves, remained paramount. With rock the balance shifted—Elvis and Chuck Berry,
who had nothing on Jerry Lee Lewis and Bo Diddley, stressed and isolated
the beat as even Count Basie's riff-heavy rhythm kings had not. And it was
only ten years after Elvis that James Brown upped the ante with "Papa's Got
a Brand New Bag," which established polyrhythm as the nexus of pop musicality and jump-started a funk that motorvated not just George Clinton but

Stevie Wonder, Miles Davis, Prince, disco, a rainbow of Latin tinges, and the entire techno movement, not to mention the hip-hop fad. Still moving on up after two decades, that fad—a model of international phonographic cross-fertilization, with roots in the Caribbean as well as the South Bronx—has kicked as much ass as rock and roll itself. Before it's over, in some century or other, it threatens to stick unmitigated beatmastery and electronic sonics in the privileged place where melody and harmony have reigned since Bach.

....

Yet although African rhythm clearly deserves pride of place, rock and roll has been so much more. You don't find folk in the country because folk is an urban idea about the primitive—an idea that's been sneaking around with the vulgarities of rock and roll since before James Brown found his bag. It's folkies, whether they call themselves that or not, who are forever revitalizing outmoded musical resources they discover on old records. And bigger than that, folkies turn out to care a lot about words. Bob Dylan sold out faster than swing, and trailing behind him came a multitude of troubadours manque who turned out their own thousands of great songs—sometimes with bridges and changes attached, sometimes strophic versifying, sometimes three-chord rants, laments, or anthems. The urbane wit and commonplace succinctness prized by classic pop never died out, but rock's vernacular was more all-embracing—slangy or raunchy or obscene, earnest or enraged, confessional or hortatory, poetic or dissociative or obscure or totally meaningless. Some lyricist is recombining a personalized selection of these qualities as you read this sentence.

Where in classic pop the piano signified respectability and sold sheet music, in rock the guitar signified revolt and sold records. And where in classic pop Europe pursued pale imitations of American models alongside its own song traditions, in rock it was Brits who grasped the possibilities. Not only did the Beatles et al. show American folkies a way out of their own gentility, they took for granted the music's countercultural thrust, which was self-evident on a continent that envied and disdained Yanks more than ever. From the day they hit Hamburg, the Beatles were destined to redefine youth culture as bohemian. Nothing is ever that one-dimensional, as waves of prefab teenpop and sclerotic balladry have been proving ever since. But consider for a moment the iconography and aesthetic pretensions of that lowbrow epitome, metal. Consider the reckless hedonism, the monastic immersion in virtuosity, the long hair, the antisocial stomp, the us-against-them rhetoric. This is something unprecedented, and like hip-hop it shows no signs of going away.

The Beatles' native counterculture is long gone, of course, and with it, many old hippies would claim, rock's glory days. This smug lie was already taking shape twenty-five years ago, when it helped trigger the supposedly nihilistic but in fact stubbornly life-affirming love-hate of punk. Embracing marginality in a vacuum of imposed scarcity rather than the security of a boom, punk was the starting point for the revolving-door rock subculture called sometimes indie, sometimes alternative, sometimes late for chow. This subculture is the most articulate locus of a connoisseurship that is now a condition of pop life—although pop audiences have always been more discerning than professional discerners give them credit for, the self-conscious artiness and multimedia overkill surrounding genres both subterranean and nationwide informs shades of aesthetic discrimination it's reasonable to regard as a bit much. Alt's fling with the marketplace now officially flung, it endures much palaver about its own glory days, but shows no signs of going away either—the mean age of Sonic Youth is forty-two. As long as young people contradistinguish themselves from society and/or their elders by gathering in bars—or now also, to who knows what effect on the "local," on the Internet—it's a safe bet that there'll be music in the vicinity.

Pure populists will grouse that the musics of this subculture—these subcultures, really: some trad and some avant, some guitar and some synth, some shoegazing and some internationalist, some white and some multiculti and some black-identified and some black, some gay and some het and many feminist, some tethered to their record collections and some eager slaves of the disco round, with all combinations and possibilities left unmentioned also valid—are barely pop at all. And cultists who can be distracted from their Discmen may well agree. But they can't escape their debt to pop's history and assumptions. They are all children of the ragged beat, all acolytes of the easy and escapist no matter how abstract they get about it. It's pop at its massest that permeates—not even top-whatever radio pap, but advertising jingles and soundtracks and the Microsoft fanfare and the stuff they make you listen to on hold. Nonetheless, what's propelled pop out of anyone's control is the heedless productivity of listeners turned musicmakers, of countless individuals, coteries, and congregations putting sounds in the air and on tape. We're often told that this has been the most horrific of centuries, and in some respects that's undeniable—technology and capital are inhumane by definition. But it's not as if there haven't been paybacks—or that many aren't happy to settle for the quid pro quo. Fact is, all this music has transformed culture and even bent power relations. And one reason it's succeeded is that

that's not what it's for. It's not a way of changing the world, but of living in the world—sometimes by getting away from the world.

So let's do it. Let's get this party started quickly. Let's get physical. Let's get it on. Let's get together. Let's stick together. Let's work together. Let's dress up like cops, think of what we could do. Let's talk dirty in Hawaiian. Let's do the Freddie. Let's call the whole thing off. Let's go get stoned. Let's get lost. Let's take the long way home. Let's take a walk around the block. Let's have another cup of coffee. Let's have a tiddley at the milk bar. Let's put out the lights and go to sleep. Let's live for today. Let's fall in love. Let's spend the night together. Let's wait awhile. Let's do it again. Let's go, let's go, let's go everybody. Let's all sing like the birdies sing. Let's face the music and dance.

Village Voice, 2000

Rock Lyrics Are Poetry (Maybe)

I want to say right now that none of the categories I'm going to be using are worth much. All but a few artists resist categories; the good ones usually confound them altogether. So a term like "rock" is impossibly vague; it denotes, if anything, something historical rather than aesthetic. "Mass art" and "kitsch" are pretty vague as well. Say that mass art is intended only to divert, entertain, pacify—Mantovani, Jacqueline Susann, Muscle Beach Party. Kitsch is a more snobbish concept, and a more sophisticated product. It usually has the look of slightly out-of-date avant-garde in order to give its audience the illusion of aesthetic pleasure, whatever that is. An important distinction, I think, is that many of the craftsmen who make kitsch believe thoroughly in what they are doing. That may be true of the creators of mass art, too, but their attitude is more businesslike—they don't worry about "art," only commercial appeal.

The songwriter who sounds most like a poet is Bob Dylan. Dylan is such an idiosyncratic genius that it is perilous to imitate him—his faults, at worst annoying and at best invigorating, ruin lesser talents. But imitation is irresistible. Who can withstand *Little Sandy Review*'s Paul Nelson, who calls Dylan "the man who in every sense revolutionized modern poetry, American folk music, popular music, and the whole of modern-day thought"? Or *The Village Voice*'s Jack Newfield wandering on about "symbolic alienation . . . new plateaus for poetic, content-conscious songwriters . . . put poetry back into song . . . reworks T. S. Eliot's classic line," while serving up tidbits from Dylan's corpus, some of which don't look so tasty on a paper plate? However inoffensive "The ghost of electricity howls in the bones of her face" sounds on vinyl, it is silly without the music. Poems are read or said. Songs are sung.

"My Back Pages" is a bad poem. But it is a good song, supported by a memorable refrain. The music softens our demands, the importance of what is being said somehow overbalances the flaws, and Dylan's delivery—he sounds as if he's singing a hymn at a funeral—adds a portentous edge not present in the words alone. Because it is a good song, "My Back Pages" can be performed in other ways. The Byrds' version depends on intricate, up-tempo music that pushes the words into the background. However much they mean to Jim McGuinn, the lyrics—except for that refrain—could be gibberish and the song would still succeed. Repeat: Dylan is a songwriter, not a poet. A few of his most perfect efforts—"Don't Think Twice," or "Just Like a Woman"—are tight enough to survive on the page. But they are exceptions.

Such a rash judgment assumes that modern poets know what they're doing. It respects the tradition that runs from Ezra Pound and William Carlos Williams down to Charles Olson, Robert Creeley, and perhaps a dozen others, the tradition that regards Allen Ginsberg as a good poet, perhaps, but a wildman. Dylan's work, with its iambics, its clackety-clack rhymes and scattergun images, makes Ginsberg's look like a model of decorum. An art advances through technical innovation. Most modern American poetry assumes (and sometimes eliminates) metaphoric ability, concentrating on the use of line and rhythm to approximate (or refine) speech, the reduction of language to essentials, and "tone of voice." Dylan's only innovation is that he sings, a good way to control "tone of voice," but not enough to "revolutionize modern poetry." He may have started something just as good, but modern poetry is getting along fine, thank you.

Dylan's influence has not always been so salutary. Lennon-McCartney and Jagger-Richard would have matured without him. But had there been no Dylan to successfully combine the vulgar and the felicitous, would we now be oppressed with the kind of vague, extravagant imagery and inane philosophizing that ruins so much good music and impresses so many Kahlil Gibran fans? I doubt it.

Not much better is the self-indulgence of the Doors' Jim Morrison. "Twentieth Century-Fox," "Break on Through," "People Are Strange," and "Soul Kitchen," listed in ascending order of difficulty, all pretty much succeed. But Morrison does not stop there. He ruins "Light My Fire" with stuff like "our love becomes a funeral pyre"—what does that mean? nothing, but the good old romantic association of love and death is there, and that's all Morrison wanted—and noodles around in secondhand Freud in "The End." Morrison obviously regards "The End" as a masterwork, and his admirers agree. I wonder why. The music builds very nicely in an Oriental kind of way, but the dramatic situation is tedious stuff. I suppose it is redeemed by Morrison's histrionics and by the nebulousness that passes for depth among so many lovers of rock poetry.

....

Paul Simon's lyrics, on the other hand, are the purest, highest, and most finely wrought kitsch of our time. The lyrics I've been putting down are not necessarily easy to write—bad poetry is often carefully worked, the difference being that it's easier to perceive flaccidly—but the labor that must go into one of Simon's songs is of another order of magnitude. Melodies, harmonies, arrangements are scrupulously fitted. Each song is perfect. And says nothing.

What saddens me is that Simon obviously seems to have a lot to say to the people who buy his records. But it's a shuck. Like Kahlil Gibran, all he's really doing is scratching them where they itch, providing some temporary relief but coming nowhere near the root of the problem. Simon's content isn't modern, it's merely fashionable, and his form never jars the sensibilities. He is the only songwriter I can imagine admitting he writes about that all-American subject, the Alienation of Modern Man, in just those words. His songs have the texture of modern poetry only if modern poetry can be said to end with early Auden—Edwin Arlington Robinson is more like it. Poets don't write like Robinson anymore because his technical effects have outlived their usefulness, which was to make people see things in a new way. And even in such old-fashioned terms, what Simon does is conventional and uninspired. An example is "For Emily, Wherever I May Find Her," in which "poetic" words—"organdy," "crinoline," "juniper" (words that suggest why Simon is so partial to turn-of-the-century verse) and "beautiful" images (softer-than-the-rain, wandered-lonely-streets) are used to describe a dream girl. Simon is no dope; he knows this is all a bit corny, but that's OK because Emily is an impossible girl. Only in order for the trick to come off there has to be an ironic edge. There isn't, and "For Emily" is nothing more than a sophisticated popular song of the traditional fantasy type.

This kind of mindless craft reaches a peak in Simon's supposed master-piece, "The Dangling Conversation," which exploits all the devices you learn about in English class—alliteration, alternating concretion and abstraction, even the use of images from poetry itself, a favorite ploy of poets who don't know much of anything else—to mourn wistfully about the classic plight of self-conscious man, his Inability to Communicate. Tom Phillips of the *New York Times* has called this song "one of Paul Simon's subtlest lyrics . . . a piti-less vision of self-consciousness and isolation." I don't hear the same song, I guess, because I think Simon's voice drips self-pity from every syllable (not only in this song, either). The Mantovani strings that reinforce the lyric cap-ture its toughness perfectly. If Simon were just a touch hipper, his couple would be discussing the failure of communication as they failed to com-municate, rather than psychoanalysis or the state of the theater. But he's not.

....

It is by creating a mood that asks "Why should this mean anything?" that the so-called rock poets can really write poetry—poetry that not only says something, but says it as only rock music can. For once Marshall McLuhan's terminology tells us something: rock lyrics are a cool medium. Go ahead and mumble. Drown the voices in guitars. If somebody really wants to know what you're saying, he'll take the trouble, and in that trouble lies your art. On a crude level this permits the kind of one-to-one symbolism of pot songs like "Along Comes Mary." The recent Simon & Garfunkel hit "Fakin' It" does other things with the same idea. But the only songwriters who seem really to have mastered it are John Phillips and Lennon-McCartney.

Phillips possesses a frightening talent. Scott McKenzie's "San Francisco," catering to every prurient longing implicit in teenage America's flirtation with the hippies without ever even mentioning the secret word, is a stun-ning piece of schlock. A song like "Once Was a Time I Thought" (as if to say to Swingle Singers fans, "You thought that was hard? We can do the whole number in fifty-eight seconds") is another example of his range. You have the feeling Phillips could write a successful musical, a Frank Sinatra hit, anything that sells, if he wanted to.

Perhaps you are one of those people who plays every new LP with the treble way up and the bass way down so you can ferret out all the secret symbolic meanings right away. Personally I think that spoils the fun, and I suspect any record that permits you to do it isn't fulfilling its first func-tion, which pertains to music, or, more generally, noise. The Mamas and Papas' records are full of diversion: the contrapuntal arrangements, the idiot "yeah"s, the orchestral improvisations, the rhyme schemes ("If you're enter-taining any thought that you're gaining by causin' me all of this pain and makin' me blue") and Phillips's trick of drawing out a few words with rep-etitions and pauses. Perhaps this isn't conscious. In songs like "California Dreamin'," "Twelve Thirty," and many others, he's obviously just a good lyri-cist with a lot of tender respect for the fantasy world of pure pop highbrow critics derogate so easily. But his lyrics are rarely easy to understand. Maybe it's just me, but I wonder how many of you are aware that a minor track on the second album, "Strange Young Girls," is about LSD. No secret about it—there it is, right out in the open of the first stanza: "Walking the Strip, sweet, soft, and placid / Offering their youth on the altar of acid." But you don't notice because there's so much else to listen to.

Phillips achieves rock feel with his arrangements. The lyrics themselves are closer to traditional pop—Rodgers and Hart's "My Heart Stood Still" on the second album sounds less out of place than Bobby Freeman's "Do You Wanna Dance?" on the first. Lennon-McCartney do it with diction. Their early work is all pure rock—the songs are merely excuses for melody, beat, and sound. Occasionally it shows a flash of the subtlety to come, as in the sexual insinuation of "Please Please Me" or the psychological premise of "There's a Place." More often it is pure, meaningless sentiment, couched in the simplest possible terms. By the time of *A Hard Day's Night* the songs are more sophisticated musically, and a year later, in *Help!*, the boys are becoming pop songwriters. "Help!" itself is a perfect example. Words like "self-assured" and "insecure" are not out of rock diction, nor is the line "My independence seems to vanish in the haze." This facet of their talent has cul-minated (for the moment) in songs like "Paperback Writer," "A Little Help from My Friends," and "When I'm Sixty-Four," which show all the verbal facility of the best traditional pop and none of the sentimentality, and in de-liberate exercises like "Michelle" and "Here, There and Everywhere," which show both.

Other songs—like "Norwegian Wood," "Dr. Robert," and "Good Morn-ing, Good Morning"—are ambiguous despite an unerring justness of con-crete detail—little conundrums, different from Dylanesque surrealism because they don't fit so neatly into a literary category. Most of their mate-rial since *Rubber Soul* is characterized by a similar obliqueness. Often the Beatles' "I" is much harder to pin down than the "I" in Donovan or Jagger-Richard, a difficulty that is reinforced by their filters, their ethereal harmo-nies, and their collective public identity. This concern with angle of attack is similar to that of poets like Creeley.

Lennon and McCartney are the only rock songwriters who combine high literacy (as high as Dylan's or Simon's) with an eye for concision and a truly contemporary sense of what fits. They seem less and less inclined to limit themselves to what I have defined as rock diction, and yet they continue to succeed—the simultaneous lushness and tightness of "Lucy in the Sky with Diamonds," for instance, is extraordinary. They still get startling mileage out of the banal colloquial—think of the "oh boy" in "A Day in the Life," or the repeating qualifications in "Strawberry Fields Forever." But they have also written two songs which are purely colloquial—"She Said She Said" and "All You Need Is Love."

"She Said She Said" is at once one of the most difficult and most banal of Beatle songs. It is a concrete version of what in "The Dangling Conversation" remains abstract despite all those details, a conversation between a hung-up, self-important girl who says she knows "what it's like to be dead" and her boyfriend, who doesn't want to know. (If Simon had written it, the boy would have argued that he was the one who knew.) The song uses the same kind of words that can be found in the Beatles' quintessential early "She Loves You," yet says so much more. Its conceit, embodied in the title, is meaningless; its actuality is a kind of ironic density that no other songwriter except Dylan at his best approaches. One of its ironies is the suggestion that callow philosophizing is every bit as banal as the most primitive rock and roll.

"All You Need Is Love," deliberately written in basic English so it could be translated, makes the connection clearer by quoting from "She Loves You" while conveying the ironic message of the title. Is love all you need? What kind of love? Universal love? Love of country? Courtly love? "She Loves You" love? It's hard to tell. The song transforms rock and roll—dominant music, big beat, repeated refrain, simple diction—into something which, if not poetry, at least has a multifaceted poetic wholeness. I think it is rock poetry in the truest sense.

....

Maybe I'm being too strict. Modern poetry may be doing very well, thank you, but in terms of what it is doing for us, and even for the speech from which it derives, it looks a bit pallid. Never take the categories too seriously. It may be that the new songwriters (not poets, please) lapse artistically, indulge their little infatuations with language and ideas, and come up with a product that could be much better if handled with a little less energy and a little more caution. But energy is where it's at. And songs—even though they are only songs—may soon be more important than poems, no matter that they're easier too.

Once there were bards and the bards did something wondrous—they provided literature for the illiterate. The bards evolved into poets and the poetry which had been their means became their end. It didn't seem to matter much after a while, since everyone was literate anyway. But semiliteracy, which is where people go when they're not illiterate anymore, is in some ways a worse blight.

The new songwriters think there should be bards again and they're right, but the bardic traditions are pretty faint. Too many of them are seduced by semiliteracy—mouthing other people's ideas in other people's words. But they are bards, and that is very good. Maybe soon it will be a lot better.

Cheetah, 1967

"We Have to Deal with It"

Punk England Report

I recently spent nine days pursuing punk rock in England without once trying to contact the Sex Pistols. I just didn't have the time. The Sex Pistols are superstars, at least momentarily, and contacting superstars is more trouble than it's worth even when nothing else is happening, which was hardly the problem in London and the other English cities I visited. Anyway, secondhand contact with the Pistols was as inescapable as tales of the Weathermen used to be around the Movement in 1970.

Paranoid Backbiters

Many informed sources offered tidbits about drugs and sex, said to interest the Pistols more than they pretended, and about record producers and movie directors—Cambridge rock avant-gardist Fred Frith, a hero of Johnny

Rotten's, was in contention for the first job, while Hollywood decadent Russ Meyer, who had wanted to set Sid Vicious to fucking his (screen) mother, was on his way out of the other. But one theme overshadowed the gossip: failure. Again and again the fear was expressed that the Pistols had blown it. Having replaced bassist Glen Matlock with nonmusician Vicious in February, I was told, Rotten had deprived the band of its most gifted composer, and now a Rotten-Vicious faction was feuding with a Jones-Cook faction and with manager Malcolm McLaren. The Pistols' long-awaited album would include only three songs written since Matlock's departure and cost as much to produce as a Richard Perry extravaganza. It was even reported that the Pistols' deal with American Warners had been finalized only because McLaren and his minions had already gone through the 150,000 quid advanced them by EMI, A&M, and Virgin in England. The original strategy had been to postpone the assault on the U.S.A. Now, suddenly, it was sink-or-swim time, for the Pistols and maybe for everybody.

It's only natural for so much of the paranoid backbiting that afflicts English punk to be aimed at the Sex Pistols, who began the movement and who symbolize it not only to the outside world but to the punks themselves. Notorious antistars, dole-queue kids awash in record-biz money, nihilists who have made something of themselves, the Pistols are everything punks are supposed to be, and more—they live out the contradictions most punk musicians have barely begun to dream about. No wonder they're resented. If we are to believe that punk's future is up to the Pistols—and that is definitely the conventional wisdom—then their fall could well precipitate everyone else's. But at least the Pistols have someplace to fall from. What will be left for the others? Their picture in the papers, a self-produced record or two, perhaps a brief contract with a treacherous major, and the chance to watch a few posers make a career out of a defunct fad that once promised life.

What makes this scenario so bitter is that it proceeds from the star system punk challenges so belligerently. The English punks, with their proud concentration on the surface of things, rebel against rock royalty on the obvious ground that a pop elite cannot represent the populace. But they miss a subtler paradox: the apparent inability of most rebels to do without heroic images. When an idea turns into a movement as fast as punk did, chances are that some leadership figure is out there symbolizing away, and that if the symbol should fade or crumble the movement will find itself at a loss.

The loss would be a big one. Only ten of the twenty bands I managed to catch in my nine days played genuine punk—vocals shouted over raw, high-speed guitar chords and an inflexible beat. But within that tiny sample, three or four bands—the Clash, X-Ray Spex, the Killjoys, and perhaps the Cortinas—put on hotter shows than any I've seen from the year's newcomers at CBGB, where the infusions of energy have been provided by born-again old-timers like John Cale and Alex Chilton or improved vintage-1975 stars like Blondie and Richard Hell. What's more, punk was clearly making itself felt in the other music I saw. Weirdos like Elvis Costello and Ian Dury and Wreckless Eric do not sell out Birmingham Town Hall when the pop environment is stable. All-female French blues-rock bands like the Lous do not open major concerts if some Wardour Street money man controls the bill. Bluegrassers turned pub-rockers turned hit journeymen like the Kursaal Flyers do not dirty up their guitar sound and smash television sets on a suburban stage just because the fancy strikes them.

But if punk were to do a quick fizzle because of the Pistols, it would be more than unfortunate. It would be unfair. Johnny Rotten is an inspiration and a media focus out of a flair for self-dramatization that is coextensive with his extremism. He is typical of nothing. No matter how much he is imitated (and he was imitated by a fast-moving cult well before Glen Matlock said fuck on television and started the avalanche), he will never be a punk prototype—not because he is monumentally talented, which is beside the point, but because he comes a lot closer to genuine nihilism than often happens in the world. If he should fail, his nihilism will be at the root of his failure. It will have turned people off the Sex Pistols, and hence (in our paranoid backbiters' scenario) off punk in general. Yet no matter what you've heard, most punks are not nihilists. Bored, cynical, destructive? Well, perhaps, at least in part. But all that's been blown out of proportion as well, and nihilism is a lot further down the road.

In fact, one thing that has made English punk so attractive—both to well-wishers like me and to fulltime recruits—has been its idealism. Despite all the anti-hippie feeling, it really is Haight '67 that it most recalls—not in content, but in form. It's a new counter-culture; the sense of ferment and burgeoning group identity more than compensates for the confused sectarian squabbling, although maybe I'd be harder to please if I'd been around when hopes were highest. And in a way, it is the tragic end of hippie—not the disintegration of a generation the punks were never part of in the first place, but the way longhaired guitar assholes have continued to preach their hypocritical go-with-the-flow—that has imbued punk idealism with its saving skepticism. These kids may be naive, but they're not foolish. They know the world is a hostile place.

Having watched the Lous (enjoyed with no audible sexist remarks) and Richard Hell and the Voidoids (received with fair enthusiasm in back and moderate-plus pogoing up front) from a limited-access balcony, I decided to take my notebook down into the Clash crowd at the University of Leeds, two hundred miles north of London. The capacity of the room, which looked like an old-fashioned church rec hall only bigger, was officially 2,200; eighteen hundred tickets were sold to a crowd that appeared to break down two-to-one student-to-punk and at least nine-to-one male-to-female. Everyone was standing even though it was intermission. I'd found that as a competent New Yorker I could push to the front of most English crowds, but that was out of the question in this press, so I stood toward the back and listened to two students behind me talk like upper-class twits. Phil Spector and even some Kraftwerk came over the PA to augment the customary dub, the bass-based reggae English punks love the way early hippies loved blues. But as the wait stretched past forty-five minutes push was turning to shove up front, and I wrote with some annoyance: "an intermission worthy of Black Sabbath." That was the last time I thought of my notebook until after the Clash had finished.

The beginning I remember clearly. The band came out looking quite hale in what might almost have been store-bought punk safari gear, shirts and chinos with lots of zippers; the sole bizarre touch was the artfully tattered fishnet top on bassist Paul Simonon. Straightaway, using a conversational version of the friendly, stump-toothed, wet-mouthed, muttery snarl he sings with, Joe Strummer leaned into the mike and said, "We've come to play some of the heavy metal music you love so well." Then there was a rush of fast guitar noise and everything became an exciting blur. I remember a lot of up-and-down motion in the audience—timid bobbing to the balls of the feet in back, wild pogoing up front. I remember the twits behind me singing along. I remember thinking that it was quite good, but not mind-blowing, and going upstairs to be with my wife. I remember the entire crowd shouting along—"I'm so bored with the Yew, Ess, Ay," "White riot, wanna riot"—with no coaxing from the stage. I remember wondering how I would feel when they finally got to my favorites—"Career Opportunities," "Garageland," "Janie Jones." And I remember my mind gusting away when they did.

Before I left the States, *The Clash* had replaced the Vibrators' *Pure Mania* as my favorite U.K. punk LP. Apparently tuneless and notoriously underproduced, it was, I knew, a forbidding record, especially since the mix was dominated by Strummer's vocals, which I loved for an unmusicality others found ugly. Because of Strummer's cockney pronunciation and bad teeth, lyrics were hard to make out; my enjoyment increased markedly after I obtained a crib sheet, but I was annoyed at times by the band's more cynical me-firstisms. After seeing them, though, I stopped hedging.

Visually, the three front-liners—guitarist Mick Jones, Strummer, and Simonon, the cute one—generated a perfect, condensed punch. They occupied their far-flung locations on stage like a unit of partisans charged with some crucial beachhead—instead of roaming around to interact, the way most exciting rock groups do, they held to their posts. Yet at the same time they seemed to be having lots of fun, with Jones marching jubilantly behind his mike, Simonon executing flashy Cossack split steps in his big boots, and Strummer eventually falling to the floor in an elation that seemed entirely of the moment. It became clear that many of the bitter lyrics that had always made me laugh—"I wanna walk down any street / Looking like a creep / I don't care if I get beat up / By any kebab Greek"— were in fact intended to be funny. Also, I began to hear what was missing in the album's sound—there was a lot more guitar in the live mix, good punk guitar devoid of platitude, with Jones's terse leads clanging irrepressibly against Strummer's below-the-belt rhythm. This music lacked neither craft nor melody; it did what it set out to do with formidable verve. The songs were about as cynical as one of the football cheers they recalled, with a lot more content.

For me, the Clash are almost a return to the time when I had to see *A Hard Day's Night* before I could tell Paul from George. They are the Clash, not four guys who play in the Clash—not a star-and-support outfit or reconstituted supergroup. Drummer Nicky Headon, much the last to join, has yet to achieve his place in the gestalt, but the three front-liners form an indivisible body; their separation on stage (which isn't always absolute, I'm told) strengthens the group's structural unity. Perhaps this is simply because Simonon, the most visual of the three and one of the many punk bassists to reject Bill Wyman–style immobility, makes it impossible for Strummer and/or Jones to take over. But that it should work out this way reflects the Brit take on punk attitude, in which hippie love-in-the-sky is replaced by provisional solidarity, alliances no less potent for their suspiciousness. I feel confident that next time I see the band, Headon will have gained full partnership. That's the kind of lads they are.

Punks are so much a counter-culture that they've produced a reaction—the teddy boys, regrouping and recruiting at an amazing clip in direct response to punk's explicit contempt for the racism and dumb violence of working-class youthcult tradition. In Coventry, an auto-manufacturing city where I saw two punks pogoing to the Boomtown Rats in a disco, the teds were down to a few pathetic father-and-son pairs plus some stragglers only six or eight months ago. Now they dominate many youth clubs. The only music they'll listen to is rockabilly. Another favored pastime is beating up punks.

After the gig, about half of the eight or so groupies I'd spotted, including the one who'd been trying unsuccessfully to crack a whip backstage, were visible at the hotel. Joe was obviously proud of his catch, announcing genially: "She's a college girl. She speaks French." Then he whispered a message to me in her ear. The young woman—nervous, attentive, and dressed (like most of her sisters) in Frederick's of Hollywood support garments and *Threepenny Opera* cosmetics, translated: "*Tu ressembles à Woody Allen, mais tu as les cheveux longues.*" Later I had a talk with Mick about his hobby, which is reading; he recommended *Brighton Rock, Decline and Fall*, and his favorite, Christopher Isherwood's *Berlin Stories*. We discussed the Socialist Workers' confrontation strategy for defeating the National Front. And he told me about his mother, a former movie actress who lives in Michigan and sends him *Creem*. Recently she mailed off some song lyrics; they were, Mick sighed, "all about the desolation of living in the city with safety pins." He'd encouraged her to continue writing, though. He just advised that she try to keep things more optimistic.

Except for the Sex Pistols, the Clash are the biggest punk group in England, but that's not as impressive as American punk fans imagine. Punk is very much a minority music in England; while the Clash were not quite drawing around two thousand in Leeds, Yes was selling out six nights at London's Wembley, which seats six thousand. Anyway, to call the Clash number two is stretching it, like saying the Stones were number two in 1964, when the Hollies and Gerry and the Pacemakers were both doing better on the charts. United Artists' Stranglers have outsold CBS's Clash by far and may even pass the Pistols. But (as with Gerry and the Pacemakers) nobody takes the Stranglers seriously because (like the Hollies) they commercialize what should be a music of discovery. The Clash have status, significance, symbolic clout. They are the class of the field, defining its possibilities; most of the punk people I spoke to in England—hardly a cross-section, but an influential minority—preferred them to the Pistols. So do I.

Because its suppositions are critical and apparently pessimistic where those of Beatlemania and hippie were full of hope, punk turns ideas upside down. The Stranglers, who sing about fucking rats and assaulting women, qualify for vilification as commercial because their subject matter recapitulates the received, best-selling, megapolitical macho of heavy metal. And a revised definition of "commercial" makes for an even stranger reversal. Although the Sex Pistols definitely got there first, always the prime issue in the Beatles-Stones rivalry of the '60s, the Pistols are to the Clash what the Stones were to the Beatles in both musical strategy and general scariness. The switch is that this time the buying public prefers the Pistols/Stones. After all, in a world where nihilistic offensive-ness has become a popular option, they offer a relatively uncomplicated message dramatized by a single, visible antihero. And in that sense they're easy to sell.

It is because the Pistols are more accessible that the committed English punk tends to identify with the Clash. For him, it's simple: they're his. But for participant observers like me, it's more complicated. Say that the Pistols' negativism—passionate, closely observed, and good to dance to though it certainly is—seems a bit facile compared to the Clash's jubilantly militant en-semble aggression. Even better, say that in 1965 we loved the Beatles' ebullience but found that we wanted (and needed) the cautionary, hard-edged, rather dangerous irony of the Stones, while in 1977 we get off on the Pistols' prom-ise to tear it all down but find that the Clash help us imagine what it might be like to build it back up again. Moreover, one can imagine both participant observers and committed punks sharing in the building. But it's best to be careful with this revised version of the rock and roll "we." The solidarity it implies is so theoretical it makes the provisional solidarity among the punks themselves seem as irrevocable as Arthurian fealty.

Participant Observers and La Vie Boheme

After my crash course in English youth culture, all I'm clear about is that it's much more complicated than anything we're used to here. I don't know how many kids actually perceive all the arcane details, but some obviously do. Accustomed to rigid tracking in the schools and a class system unashamed of its name, they define subcultures for themselves; these are picked up in the popular press and thus propagated, formalized, and put to death. Yet of the six big ones—teddy boys, rockers, mods, hippies, skinheads, punks—all but the mods and rockers are still around. (Those who presume the skinheads extinct didn't just confront eighty of them marching out of a Sham 69 gig; for that matter, enclaves of rockers are said to survive in motorway cafs.) Except for the hippies, who began in America, each of these groups crystallized around the stylistic innovations of working-class teenagers, who dress just as obsessively as black and Latin kids do in this country, and a lot more regimentally. But because street fashions have some of the same sort of upward mobility in England that they do here, these uniforms are no more likely to remain purely working-class than are the subcultures they symbolize.

For the punks, this sociological fact of life is traumatic, because the punks are ideologically working-class. There was a certain ambiguous nose-thumbing in the outmoded posh of the teds' Edwardian gear, and the rockers probably resented the implicit upward mobility of the mods as much as the skinheads resented the putative classlessness of the hippies. But despite the English tradition of resenting the rich and an adolescent anti-establishment bias that alienated them from anyone with power, these groups took class as a given. No so the punks. Punks are equally scornful of the scant material rewards of welfare capitalism and the boredom that inevitably deadens what rewards there are; they're hostile to America and hate the cultural imperialism of television with a passion that elevates cliche into myth. But more than that, they place blame. Their us-against-them isn't young-against-old or hip-against-square, but a war of the deprived against the privileged.

It would be nice to say that punk's class consciousness arose spontaneously from the dole queues, council flats, and dead-end educational levels of a depressed Britain. But since most working-class kids, including those without work, don't really identify with punk, it's more accurate to credit the musicians themselves with the analysis, and in fact a lot of it has come from participant observers—semi-official theoreticians in management and journalism. Malcolm McLaren, the self-described anarchist who launched the Sex Pistols from his anti-couture boutique (called first Rock On, then Too Fast to Live, Too Young to Die, then Sex, and currently Seditionaries) understood early on how butch working-class fashion iconography might *épater le bourgeois*. Caroline Coon of *Melody Maker* and Jonh Ingham of *Sounds* (a couple at one time) perceived punk as a movement that could only occur in a deteriorating economic environment—although it combined the hoodlum-friends-outside youth politics of rock and roll with more "bolshie" counter-culture ideas. And Bernard Rhodes, an East End Jew who worked for McLaren before he began to manage the Clash, gave the music a more explicitly leftwing cast.

But especially significant, I think, was a "real" punk proficient at both journalism and music business—Mark P., who brought all this raw art and rough theory together in his Xeroxed fanzine *Sniffin' Glue* and then, with the help of rock-biz pro Miles Copeland, became the finest of the punk a&r men on his own Step-Forward label, responsible for strong singles from Chelsea, the Cortinas, and the Models. A teen genius with vanguard instincts in both music and politics, Mark P. was the East End council-flats guyser that punk legend is made of, and as near as I can tell, it was from *Sniffin' Glue* that the whole issue of class authenticity in punk, the anti-poser ethic, really took off. I did it, Mark P. said, and now you should. And so fanzines sprouted by the score, and pioneer fans organized pioneer groups like Siouxsie and the Banshees, Subway Sect, and the Slits. Outsiders became more and more suspect.

DIRTY MINDS

Jimmy Pursey of Sham 69 says he got the name off the wall of a loo; it sounds good and means nothing, he insists, specifically including fake blow job. Pete Shelley of the Buzzcocks says the name of his group came from a caption in the London entertainment weekly *Time Out*: "Get a buzz, cock" ("cock" means roughly the same thing as "fellow" in working-class slang). When I told him that many Americans took the name as a sadistic play on "buzz saw" he seemed to feel it spoke poorly for this nation.

SUPERLATIVES

To call something extraordinary in hippie argot you would say it was "far out." Among punks, the term is "over the top."

English punk bands have never pretended to be dumb. Sentimentality and intellectualism are out, but the prevailing mood encourages the (admittedly satiric) Snivelling Shits to attack "Terminal Stupid" and the (admittedly demi-commercial) Boomtown Rats to boast: "I'm gonna go somewhere where it doesn't stink / Away from the alleys, somewhere I can think." What does slip into the rhetoric, however, is the implication that Johnny Rotten or Mick Jones or Mark P. is an ordinary guyser, a bloke who goes to see bands like anybody else. Needless to say, this is nonsense. Despite the usual lemmings, loonies, and losers, the fringe people that fringe movements like punk always attract, punks tend to be bright and sensitive—they have to be, to detach themselves from the accepted belief that one's lot is one's just desert unless one manages to work one's way out of it. Nevertheless, Rotten and Jones and Mark P. are a lot more gifted than most punks—and probably than you or me.

At work here is a delusion over-twenty-fives will recall from the hippie days: the we-are-youth line. To their credit, punks don't pretend to be everybody's brothers and sisters. They savage contemporaries who don't share their self-interests—the grammar-school boys, the art students, the revitalized teds—and they savage each other with continual exhortations to cut the shit. "Try to evade reality / And now you're just a novelty," warn the Killjoys, and when punks at the Vortex cheered the news of Elvis's death—another old fart gone—Danny Baker of *Sniffin' Glue* grabbed the mike in a rage and reminded them just where they'd be without him. But like most minority groups, they take comfort in the thought that their situation is not only of central social significance, but also a source of magic powers. The notion that Everypunk can just walk off the dole queue and make great rock and roll is essential to their sense of themselves.

Behind punk's belief in its own magic is the old idea that if you live close enough to the edge of reality you gain some special grip on it. But despite the legend, their edge doesn't turn out to depend on brutal poverty. Poly Styrene, the mulatto who leads X-Ray Spex, giggles that compared to where she grew up council flats are pretty soft, and Joe Strummer jeers at the way Americans romanticize Britain's plight: "'Ey fink it's really orful over here, don't they? 'Ey fink we can't afford 'arf a pint o' beer." In fact, many punk musicians live at home and spend their meager dole or boring-job or gig money on themselves, and not all boast impeccably impecunious pedigrees. Joe Strummer has been exposed as the son of a career diplomat who was himself born working-class (as well as the former lead singer of a band of hippie squatters called the 101'ers); the parents of the Damned's Rat Scabies invited disc jockey John Peel to a sherry evening in a well-to-do London suburb, signing the engraved card "Mr. and Mrs. Scabies"; the Cortinas are middle-class boys from Bristol; Chelsea's Gene October, author of the militant "Right to Work," is reputedly of moneyed stock. So when reporters discover middle-class thrill-seekers at punk gigs, that's hardly surprising. Only because the punks themselves have made an issue of posing does such evidence appear damning to those who'd just as soon dismiss them anyway.

Perhaps the way to understand it is to say that rather than a working-class youth movement—potentially revolutionary, proto-fascist, or symptomatic of the decadence of our times—punk is a basically working-class youth bohemia that rejects both the haute bohemia of the rock elite and the hallowed bohemian myth of classlessness. Not that it's purely working-class (or purely youth, for that matter). But it gives the lie to the (basically Marxist) cliche that bohemia is petit-bourgeois. For punk, class replaces such bohemian verities as expressive sexuality and salvation through therapy/enlightenment/drugs. It is a source of identity and a means of self-realization. So the cockney accent replaces the blues voice, and disdain for luxury becomes an affirmation of fellowship with one's allies rather than a withdrawal from the economic world.

Punk doesn't want to be thought of as bohemian because bohemians are posers. But however vexed the question of their authenticity, bohemias do serve a historical function—they nurture aesthetic sensibility. Punk definitely has attracted musicians hiding arty little secrets; if Mick Jones acknowledges having gone on scholarship to art school, that unfairly discredited rock institution, can Dave Vanian be far behind? Nor is it surprising that the best punk retailer-distributor, Rough Trade, is run by Geoff Travis, an idealistic Cambridge lit grad in the boho stronghold around Portobello Road. That many entrenched (and lapsed) bohemians regard punks as mindless yobs doesn't mean half as much as the observant participation of disaffected university students, restless suburban teens, and assorted dropouts. Most of the hip folks I know could use a shot of punk, which revives the oldest bohemian tradition—artists with no visible means of support banding together against the cruel world.

Of course, most of these kids aren't artists, and they often enjoy invisible support from their parents or the state. But it's equally obvious that for talented working-class rebels denied access to Britain's scarce, narrow, and overcrowded escape routes, bohemianism—in which poverty is no bar to freedom, identity, and the pleasures of the moment—presents a way out. A recent study among the supposedly middle-class hippies of Birmingham, for instance, revealed that most of those who'd stuck with the lifestyle had working-class origins. Of course, Marxists can dismiss hippies and punks alike as lumpen because, unlike real working-class people, they're not interested in work. But it remains true that for punks class is a charged category. They have raised both their own consciousness and that of the participant observers who are now part of their movement, and it's at least conceivable that when they all grow up they'll unite to marshal their energy into a real attack on the system they detest.

I hardly expect this to happen. But I do think punk represents an advance in sensibility. Those punks who aren't direct victims of the economic rationalizations that have been wreaking drab havoc over Britain have certainly been induced to think about them a lot. The edge they all claim, their magic handle on reality, is that they're painfully familiar with powerlessness. And they want no part of it.

I'm aware that I've made the punks sound like poverty-stricken lads who only want to build a better life for themselves, and that this probably doesn't jibe with your preconceptions. What about the safety pins and dog collars, you must be wondering. What about the violence? What about the misogyny and pathological anomie? What about that groupie with the whip?

My guess is that six months from now safety pins and dog collars—but not the wonderful spikey punk hair—will be as passe as platform shoes, replaced by less disquieting concepts in costume jewelry. But the rest of the bad stuff seemed durable enough. I saw fans betoken their affection by gobbing—spitting, in thick gobs—at their idols, I saw X-Ray Spex abandon the stage to their own rampaging fans, and I saw little Kevin Roland of the Killjoys placekick one kid off the monitors without missing a beat. I witnessed numerous fistfights. I learned that punks sometimes pogo with their hands at each other's throats and embrace in holds that resemble hammerlocks. And I read both Strummer and Rotten on love. Strummer: "I can love them providing they don't come near me." Rotten: "Love is what you feel for a dog or a pussy cat. It doesn't apply to humans."

Yet none of this was anywhere near as appalling as I'd expected. I mean, I almost didn't bring my down jacket for fear someone would knife me and the feathers would all fly out, but the most antagonistic remark any punk offered in nine days was when some youngster addressed me as "guv'nor" after I declined to share my beer with him. Admittedly, I didn't spend much time with the punk on the street, and I worry that I've somehow been hoodwinked by the British music biz, which is now taking the line that punk is nothing more than teenagers venting their sociologically justified frustrations. But while I continue to find some punk music frightening, I am no longer very scared by the punks themselves. On the contrary, I consider their hostility healthy, especially given how much they've been maligned.

SYNFESIS

Poly Styrene is a plump young woman the color of a Kraft caramel who brings a pop-art kind of pop sensibility to punk. She prefers "synfetic" clothes and wears braces on her teeth. Reputedly a former reggae singer, she's vague about how she made money before X-Ray Spex. But she did tell me that her manager, Falcon Stuart, used to direct films, and I know this is true because I've seen one—*French Blue*, a rather arty and off-putting exercise in kink porn. This could make you worry about lyrics like "Bind me tie me / Chain me to the wall / I wanna be a slave to you all." But they continue: "Oh bondage up yours / Oh bondage no more." Poly says she tries to make sure her lyrics aren't obvious; they're collections of images. Her artistic aim? "I try to make people fink."

FASHION PLATE

For five minutes after we were introduced, Bernard Rhodes, the Clash's manager, subjected me to skeptical questions and comments implying that I was a poser. I held my ground, which was apparently what he wanted, because soon he was treating me to the English teen version of *Sartor Resartus*. "The differences are so subtle," he told me. "Shoelaces—you can spend half an hour deciding what shoelaces to wear." Rhodes was wearing aviator glasses, a bezippered gray cloth jacket, a Clash T-shirt, a large digital watch, jeans with rolled cuffs, chartreuse socks, and black oxfords. I didn't notice anything special about his shoelaces.

Gobbing I could do without, as could the gobbed-upon, but the pogo is a different matter. The pogo is more than oafs jumping up and down; its reputation as an idiot dance preceding a punch-up misses entirely the joy, humor, and madness of the real thing. Pogoers don't just jump—they leap, as high as they can for as long as they can, exhilarated to the point of exhaustion. The dance is very physical, with much flailing and crashing near the center, and most pogoers are male. At first they flew strictly solo, but soon couple-dancing began, and with it the stranglehold developed. It was startling to see two sixteen-year-old boys, their faces shining with sweat and glee, pretending to throttle each other in what amounted to an airborne playfight. But I hadn't encountered such joyful-looking kids at a rock concert in years. This dance did justice to something about rock and roll that all the fast steps and sexy grinds ignored—its exultant competitiveness, its aggressive fun.

Not that pogoers confine themselves to playfighting. People trip and tromp on each other and come to blows—less often than has been reported but more than at a Renaissance concert. Only who needs Renaissance concerts? This is rock and roll, and in England rock and roll—like football, only less so—has always occasioned violence. Yet there were only one or two scuffles a night at the gigs I attended, and I neither saw nor was told about anything to compare, for instance, with the Beatles' second professional engagement, where a sixteen-year-old boy was kicked to death. I would describe firecrackers at Bad Company concerts as violent, and I would describe Johnny Rotten's vocal attack as violent. But I would describe punk as rough.

It is also of course predominantly male. But this, too, must be understood in the context of England, which has produced a rock folkway without exact parallel in the States—boys bands, with their all-boy audiences. "Quo, Sab-baf, and 'Eep"—a legend you can still see on the backs of jackets—were and are boys bands; so was Mott the Hoople, the group Mick Jones used to follow around. This sort of fandom is clearly much like rooting for a football team, with the ominous difference that rock's sexual content might be more sanely absorbed in a coed environment. Jones was amused that the Clash now seemed to be a boys band, and expressed the hope that the photogenic Simonon would break the pattern via the teenybop magazines—not so much to up the band's market share as to humanize its audience.

But beyond such camaraderie there is a lot of woman-hating in English punk—not as much as is reported, once again, but more than in America. Lately the Stranglers, who can be passed off as pseudopunks, have ceded their Gold Dildo to Eater, who cannot: "Why don't you get raped / Why don't you get raped / Why don't you get raped / Go and get fucked." You can call this underclass scapegoating, you can talk about the virtues of irony, you can talk about the virtues of candor, you can even praise certain artists for exposing misogyny as the sex-fearing pathology it is. Those lyrics are still hateful.

They're not the whole story, though. On specific songs—the Sex Pistols' "Bodies," for instance—the power of the statement does, I think, justify and perhaps even necessitate the hatefulness. And there's something more important, especially if you believe, as I do, that an aggressive popular art like rock and roll is a better way to fuse righteous anger than acoustic folk songs or documentaries about the siblinghood of humankind. For coexisting with the misogyny is an unprecedented opportunity for women to make rock and roll. Mick Jones voiced the prevailing attitude: "There ought to be as many girls in bands as boys by now. But if I'm gonna like 'em, they gotta be as tough as we are." In addition to the all-female Lous and X-Ray Spex (where Poly Styrene braved the onstage pogoing of her admirers long after her male musicians beat their retreat), I ran across a bassist and two keyboard players in three other bands. That's no population explosion, but it does represent a significant increase over the number of females who played electric instruments at the Palladium in 1977—one, a punk, Patti Smith—because in punk conceptual energy does the work of chops. Not that punk women seem any more inclined to be nice little feminists than punk men.

They choose names like the Castrators and the Slits. They talk about free sex like acolytes of the Playboy Philosophy. And they believe in looking out for themselves. Says sixteen-year-old Arri Up of the Slits: "The reason there's hardly any girl rock 'n' roll stars is because most girls are not strong enough in their own minds."

I hope Arri figures out sometime just why girls have this problem, insofar as they do, and insofar as it's a problem. I also hope Joe Strummer and Johnny Rotten change their hearts and minds about love. The fervent alienation that fuels such ideas suggests an egoism and a crippled capacity for outreach that alarm me. The most encouraging note I can add is that egoism and crippled outreach are no less adolescent than idealism and a desire to reach out, and that maturing—exotic term—is basically a process of becoming aware that other people exist. Hippie romanticized youth's potential for good and foundered on its gift for evil. Punk errs in the other direction, but the good is there too, however reluctantly acknowledged, and it may develop more naturally if not too much is expected of it. The thought of punk growing up is not an altogether happy one. But I hope it does grow up, because it's going to get older regardless.

What Is to Be Done?

The word "punk" can refer to a music and/or a youth movement because the two are inseparable. Not even rockabilly or disco, and certainly not "psychedelic" rock, have enjoyed such a clear, before-and-after, cause-and-effect relationship with a support subculture. In fact, punk rock was conceived by Malcolm McLaren and Bernard Rhodes (out of the intuitions of avant-punks like Iggy and David Johansen) to inspire such a subculture. Not that it turned out exactly the way its prophets imagined—the unpredictability of talent was essential to what they wanted to instigate. Still, their ideas have had appreciable effect.

While in England I looked up pioneer punk propagandist Jonh Ingham, who was a student of mine at the California Institute of the Arts when he decided to change the spelling of his name in 1970. This precocious bit of image-building was typical of both his sharpness and his shallowness, but punk has clearly deepened him. The apolitical acidhead now wears a Marx patch, and the lines around his eyes belong to someone who's discovered passion. Not that he's so passionate anymore. For Ingham, the turning point came last January, when McLaren, instead of investing the Pistols' £40,000 settlement from EMI in a punk countereconomy, chose to expand punk—that is, his punks—on establishment capital. So it was going to come down to good groups after all, Ingham said to himself. Within months he was managing Generation X, now signed to Chrysalis.

The punk counter-economy, such as it is, was destined to arise anyway. "It was easy, it was cheap, go out and do it," sang the Desperate Bicycles, who produced their own single for £153 in March 1977, basically to show people it could be done, just as the Desperate Bicycles themselves might have learned from Australia's Saints, who scored a 1976 hit by mailing their forty-five to U.K. journalists, and Manchester's Buzzcocks. Many of these instant labels record one group exclusively, but others go on from a profitable sale—ten thousand is pretty good, twenty not unheard of—to work with others. It's likely that one or two of them—London's Deptford Fun City? Manchester's Rabid? Cambridge's Raw? Edinburgh's Zoom?—will join the worldwide trend toward specialty labels for minority popular musics. In this they will be following two somewhat older indies, Stiff and Chiswick, which although they're known here as punk labels actually cater to the rock 'n' roll discophiles who supported pub-rock.

One implication of independent production is that punk too could turn into a collectors' music, a hobby, as is brought home by such frivolous marketing devices as the twelve-inch single (saving vinyl is for hippies). But independent production doesn't reflect punk's eccentricity, or its idealism, so much as its refusal to withdraw from the economic world. It's a trick of survival, a way to prepare your own demo at a profit. Mark P.'s backer and boss at Deptford-Fun City, Miles Copeland, is typical; he has placed his managerial clients the Cortinas with CBS and is codistributing a twelve-inch with Sham 69's new label, Polydor. Copeland, the son of a CIA bigshot, calls class consciousness "England's big sickness" and used to advise Wishbone Ash how best to carry their hods; he struck me as one of the more dismaying professionals now attached to punk, but his business ideas are the norm. He describes how the Cortinas "wanted to go pro" and "wanted the strength of a major worldwide," while the Buzzcocks' manager—a twenty-four-year-old art drop-out named Richard Boon who oversaw their debut EP on New Hormones and then signed the band to UA—talks coolly about doing an album only when the time seems right. But neither can imagine a new way to get this music out there.

Not that I have any bright ideas. My first minutes with Joe Strummer were spent in praise of medium-sized halls, an article of faith with the punks now as it was with the Who and the Grateful Dead a decade ago, although it's not hard to figure out that if you sell three thousand tickets a night for a brutal three hundred nights a year you still don't play to a million people, a rather small-scale cultural crusade. Strummer went along with me—modest venues were best. But then he doubled back: "Nah, you do it too much that way and you get just like the hippies. Keep it small, keep it efnic . . ." Basically, Strummer didn't see any way to avoid turning into what he'd rebelled against. No matter how staunch his own idealism—not that he made inflated claims for it—someone would always be checking his rear for him. "People say, if you don't do that the So-and-Sos are gonna catch up. You don't wanna get behind the So-and-Sos, do ya?"

Like Jonh Ingham, I really wish it could be different, and I'm somehow disappointed with the punks for not cutting through the old masscult paradoxes. If powerlessness is your secret, shouldn't you have something more to say about power than vague plans to recycle your capital and specific promises never to own a Bentley? But in the absence of such a miracle, I agree—better the Clash than the So-and-Sos, whether the So-and-Sos are good guys like the Jam (Who-style punks-as-mods not averse to Bentleys) or the Vibrators (Velvets-style metaphysical sex on the surface and a perfect blank ambition underneath) or bad guys like the semi-fictitious Pork Dukes, who offer a record sleeve and T-shirt depicting a woman sucking off a pig, and who are rumored on excellent authority to include two moonlighting folkrockers from that apogee of rock gentility, Steeleye Span. But the very profusion of so-and-sos is positive, especially since even the so-called posers—both the Jam and the Vibrators are dismissed that way by much of punk's hard core—can make wonderful rock and roll. Punk really is a new wave—a new wave of musicians. Some of those so-and-sos are going to be playing the English rock and roll of the '80s.

Which raises two questions: one, will this rock and roll remain strictly English, and two, will it remain punk? As extraordinary as the Clash are, they'll have to do as an example. The Clash may be the greatest rock and roll band in the world, but they haven't conquered Britain yet, and if they gain a following over here—which they seem in no special hurry to do—it will be proportionally smaller. Their fierce national identification strengthens their music but narrows their American potential, because our class system is afraid to speak its name. Even if their second album, unlike their first, is picked up by American Epic or some other U.S. label, I'll be pleased if they gain enough audience to support an annual tour, perhaps inspiring some young American rocker to translate the English punk way of seeing things into terms as fiercely national as the Clash's own. But the sustenance that keeps whatever dozen English punk bands eating and recording over the next few years should come from England.

Because finally it's the sensibility that must survive—the sensibility that thinks in terms of class and means to bring home the class conflicts that underlie every one of our lives. If it comes to that, I'll even settle for hobbyists, a few genius musicians making overpriced direct-to-disc collector's items for ten thousand connoisseurs of raw power. That'll be enough to keep the word alive. As the Clash sing on—and about—"Hate & War": "And if I close my eyes / It will not go away / We have to deal with it / It is the currency." No matter how many people are resisting right now, they're going to find out eventually that these ill-mannered boys are right.

Village Voice, 1978

Rock 'n' Roller Coaster

The Music Biz on a Joyride

1. Woe Is Us

Because only those willing to suspend their disbelief in eternal youth invest any real confidence in the staying power of rock and roll, premature obituaries have been as much a tradition of the music as teen rebellion and electric guitars. Ever since the '60s—hell, the '50s—I've scoffed at them. The 1982 rumors that followed in the wake of the Great Disco Disaster of 1979 and the Bad Christmas of 1981, however, proved so persistent, pervasive, and persuasive that by the fall of that year I was half a believer myself. And though they've now vanished as utterly as Peter Frampton, that never seemed foreordained. The nadir was gloomy trend pieces in February and April of 1983 by Jay Cocks and Jim Miller of *Time* and *Newsweek*, which crystallized general unease into near panic.

Both were essentially laments for what used to be called rock culture, but Miller, who is less sentimental than Cocks, got the scoop in the process. Rather than indulge in blanket critical condemnations of a music that had afforded different kinds of success to the Police, Rick James, and X, he concentrated on dipping profits and the dubious utility of marketing strategies designed to revive them. His conclusion was grim: "Rock 'n' roll has a future all right. But whether it can ever recapture its cutting edge and resume a leading role in defining the frontiers of America's popular culture is another matter entirely."

The official explanation for the falloff in gold and platinum albums and two consecutive ten percent sales dips was the social evil of home taping, which Recording Industry Association of America president Stan Gortikov still sums up with the remarkable claim that for every record bought another is home-taped, consumer "theft" that supposedly costs the record business upwards of a billion a year. Although a suspiciously unspecific October 1983 RIAA study asserts that 425 million hours of prerecorded music were home-taped annually (1982 blank tape sales were barely half that), detached analysis of a more detailed 1982 Warner survey suggests a maximum annual loss of around $350 million, much of it absorbed by distributors and retailers. This no more accounts for a billion-dollar slump than that other slant-eyed bogeyman, videogames. Although the audiocassette industry is still fighting off proposed legislation to control record rentals and institute a hefty surcharge on blank tape sales, the no-nonsense social science theory is that the "recession-proof" music industry simply wasn't—that in tandem with the demographic dip that always awaited rock and roll as the baby boom grew up, the near depression of the early '80s was too much for it to take.

Without doubt the much-bruited Reaganomic "recovery" occasioned a mood shift that helped bring young middle-class record buyers back into the stores. But the biz earned its recession-proof rep by surviving several recessions, and I say it got beat in the latest one for the most fanciful reason of all: quality. By this I hardly mean that if only the big labels had promoted Blood Ulmer or the Human Switchboard or Southside Johnny or Black Flag, the world would now be safe for rock and roll. I've never sung that old song. But I'll settle for the answer record, "Nobody Loves You When You're Bored and Bland." One thing about cults—they do love what they like, enough to seek it out and if necessary pay a premium for it. All of the industry's payola and market research and supergroup status-mongering couldn't instill that kind of enthusiasm in the passive audience shaped by radio's cowardice and conservatism—its consultancies, its racism, its fear of tuneouts. Whatever excitement people are once again finding in music begins with content—or anyway, form/content. As bizzers like to say, it's in the grooves—or anyway, that's half the story.

So many accounts of rock and roll's recovery dwell on new technology—business analysts always prefer machines, which can be owned, to human beings, who according to enlightened capitalist theory can't. But in fact bizzers progressed with science only after clambering headlong in the opposite direction. It took years of ghetto blasters and Walkmen, both far more stimulating to the public appetite for music than high-end hi-fi, before the tape crusaders had the bright idea of lowering the price of prerecorded cassettes. A similar pattern is evident in video. Before their misreading of disco ate up all that venture capital, forward-looking record execs used to dream about producing and selling consumer videos, which five years later is still risky business. But even Warner, half of MTV's parent corporation, clearly had little inkling of the vast hype potential of the twenty-four-hour rock-video cable service. For all its infinite venality, MTV livelied up the rock audience and juiced record sales. But if the majors had been prepared with Linda Ronstadt and REO Speedwagon videos when the channel went live in 1981, it might have gone nowhere. Instead, bizzers handed the ball to appearance-obsessed, mostly British "new wave" longshots so eager to stake some of their Eurodollars on the Stateside profits all rock and rollers dream of that they came up with lots of snazzy clips.

Thus MTV was the making of such bands as Men at Work, whose debut eventually outsold both *Asia* and John Mellencamp's *American Fool* in 1982; the Stray Cats, London-trained Massapequabillies whose midline-priced compilation is now double platinum; A Flock of Seagulls, with their high-IQ haircuts and dumb hooks; and let us not forget Duran Duran. And much as I hate typing with my fingers crossed, I'm willing to venture that it won't ever be as conservative a cultural force as AOR. The circumstances that thrust it briefly into the commercial forefront of "new wave" were temporary, and that was never the whole story—the rampaging "new" heavy metal has also been a major beneficiary, as have "Puttin' on the Ritz" and Linda Ronstadt's Nelson Riddle album. But because visual information is so specific that people quickly get bored with it, the channel craves novelty by nature.

For many younger bizzers, of course, the innocent words "new music" resonate with significance, and the New Music Seminar launched by Rockpool and *Dance Music Report* in 1980 is their very own confab. The term "new music" was appropriated from the downtown minimalist avant-garde just as "new wave" was taken over from the French auteurist avant-garde, and no one knows exactly how to define it—the *Wall Street Journal* has called it "futuristic 'technopop'" and "a blend of rock, soul and reggae" in the same sentence. I'd suggest that, as with "postmodernism," the sweeping yet abjectly relative vagueness of the term signifies above all a fervent desire to deny antecedents that are in fact inescapable. Having once defined the equally amorphous "rock" as "all music derived from the energy and influence of the Beatles," I would now define "new music" as "all music deriving primarily from the energy and influence of the Ramones and the Sex Pistols." Then I would hope against hope that two qualifications were understood: first that in both cases "energy and influence" is meant sociologically rather than musically, and second that I'm making fun.

The New Music Seminar began as a mildly bohemian one-day affair in a friendly recording studio, and it was still pretty bohemian in 1982, when it attracted eleven hundred to the Sheraton Centre. In 1983 it was at the Hilton, enrollment had more than doubled, and bohemian it wasn't. "Everyone realizes that they are the future of the industry, so there is less rowdiness," opined organizer Joel Webber, and with the Police, Eddy Grant, Kajagoogoo, David Bowie, Culture Club, and Madness in the top ten, this sense of destiny was understandable. Not that some bohemian stragglers didn't hoot at the chasm between the Sex Pistols and Kajagoogoo, and not that all the skepticism about new music came from disillusioned punks—"It's our business to give the audience what they want," announced Ocean City, Maryland, deejay Brian Krysz, who clearly didn't think these New Yorkers had any idea what that might mean where he was from. But somewhere in between the old bohos and the old pros gathered a comfortable consensus that the ailing music industry had pulled itself back from the brink by finally coming to terms with the progress it had resisted so pigheadedly for so long.

One factor was missing from this analysis, however: Michael Jackson. "New music" is a very broad concept, but there's no way it subsumes Michael. The overwhelming success of *Thriller* fulfills the blockbuster fantasy that has possessed the industry ever since *Saturday Night Fever*. For years retailers argued that if only the nudniks over in production could suck people into the stores with another piece of product like that, they'd take care of the rest. And there are those who believe *Thriller* is the whole secret of the recovery. But it couldn't have happened in a vacuum. The new Anglodisco's rapprochement between the white rock audience and dance music helped make it possible.

For all its whiteskin provincialism, its defanged funk and silly soul, the new music world is in fact somewhat more open to black artists than AOR. After all, what isn't? Certainly neither Prince nor Eddy Grant could have crossed over without the white dance clubs, and while Jackson didn't need the boost, he did benefit from it. And here too MTV was crucial. Indulging its disgraceful if not unconstitutional reluctance to air black music, MTV only started airing Jackson's videos after CBS president Walter Yetnikoff threatened to withdraw CBS clips from the channel. And soon thereafter, the $200,000 production number Jackson contrived around "Beat It" turned into the channel's biggest hit ever. With MTV fallen, AOR finally jumped in, and a hit album was transformed into an unprecedented megacrossover.

The triumph of *Thriller*, in which music marketers heroically sold the new to the yearning masses, would seem to refute my brave assertion that the recovery owes more to art than it does to hype. But just like the neat binary opposition between form and content, the old hype-vs.-art polarity is a middlebrow convenience that camouflages the vulgar details of the pop process. With Michael Jackson or the Stray Cats or Culture Club, it's hard to say where art leaves off and hype begins, because all three devote unmistakable aesthetic energy to promulgating image as well as inventing music. Image promulgation is tricky business and trickier art, but after a dull gray decade of grind-it-out professionalism I'm rather enjoying the current flashstorm. My pleasure is sure to diminish as the most cunning of the young posers currently overrunning the London video industry dig in for the careerist haul. But if hype it's gotta be, I'll take mine tacky, thanks.

3. Kajagoogoomania

All descriptions of the current pop moment invoke the British Invasion hook sooner or later, so why not? But let's get one thing straight. Unless you favor the formulation in which the second British wave began Hollies-Donovan-Cream circa 1967 (making the current incursion number seven or so), the first one was more like an occupation, or an endless parade that lasted from 1964 all the way till 1977, when Malcolm McLaren set about revitalizing the troubled U.K. branch of an industry that was marching off a cliff.

Overlooking the Sex Pistols' unseemly politics, many armchair promo men professed surprise when McLaren's gambit failed to conquer America, where disco and AOR were reaching sizable new audiences. So I propose that we think of this "second" British Invasion as a reactive return to normalcy, with conveniently prepackaged Brits regaining their customary advantage in the musical balance of trade—not to beef up my pitch for American music, but to make sure all the British Invasion guff doesn't make this pop moment seem more . . . *gear* than it actually is. It's *different*, sure; times change. But it isn't Swinging London all over again.

Young music fans may be acquainted with the music of the first British Invasion, but its excitement comes to them secondhand, and while British punk was a pop moment, it was also an antipop moment, excluding potential listeners far more antagonistically than any generation gap. When it didn't put new clothes on the radical fallacy that youth is sitting out there eagerly awaiting an Alternative, it exploited the supposed truism that rock and roll thrives on shock—just outrage the Establishment and every teenager in the NATO alliance will throw money at you. It would have been wonderful if some synthesis of these ideas had reunified the pop world, and in fact it was wonderful anyway. But unity didn't ensue, because punk's antagonisms were aimed not just at the Establishment, but at the complacent or self-deluded or indifferent or just plain different rock fans who failed to get the message. Some of these converted, others got pissed off, others remained indifferent, and still others changed their minds a little. So say that Swinging London II comprises most of those who changed their minds plus many indifferents and a significant admixture of reconverted converts. And for all its backbiting, infighting, and sectarian trendiness, its pop impulse, meaning nothing more noble than its craving for commercial success, is more wholehearted, though not more idealistic, than punk's ever was.

Yet avant-garde polemicism notwithstanding, 1977 does stand as a great pop moment, and reconciliations notwithstanding, 1983 remained a dubious one. That's because 1977 held out a promise at once more radical and more realistic than that of Elvis or the Beatles or the hippies. Where the myth of rock culture had vitiated rock and roll's rebel strain by glamorizing it, punk amplified it by focusing it, and though it perceived the mechanics of hegemony and oppression clearly enough to despise '60s-style utopian folderol, it stuck by its idealism-in-the-negative. In contrast, all 1983 could offer was fifteen minutes in the limelight, or maybe three. Punk's populist strategy was to reclaim the quick hooky virtues of the then-moribund pop single, and "new music" has definitely embraced that punk idea. Thus it's also inherited two kinds of burnout—not just the no-future cynicism affected by 1977's cynosures and pennyrockets, but the flash-in-the-pan one-shotism of the pre-"rock" era. There's nothing more British Invasion about all of this than the bewildering profusion of new names on the charts. How do you sort them out? Is one of these bands really the Rolling Stones and another the Moody Blues? One the Yardbirds and another the Nashville Teens? One the Herd and another Dave Dee, Dozy, Beaky, Mick & Tich?

Nevertheless, I can't go along with McLaren, who claims that the newest Brit wave broke because American bizzers "don't want black music taking over." It's not just that McLaren is oversimplifying with an ulterior motive as usual. Nor is it that Michael J. has rendered further race war superfluous—Afrika Bambaataa and Blood Ulmer and the perennial George Clinton did great work in 1983 too, and none of them cracked MTV. My skepticism has more to do with the sometimes useful, often unavoidable, but here merely obfuscatory vagueness of the term "black music" itself. Insofar as Anglomania kept conciliatory, professional black *pop* down in a strong year for the genre, it did so on the merits; James Ingram may be a nice fellow, but Boy George has more to tell the world. And there's no reason to believe that if every fop in England were to expire of synthesizer poisoning, hard, tricky black *funk* would fill the vacuum. Both punk and funk are avantish styles that articulate megapolitan street values. Insofar as they've failed to make a serious dent in middle America, that's largely middle America's fault, and choice: hegemony is subtle and not altogether undemocratic stuff.

If this seems like a retreat from my traditionally staunch affirmative action stand, I'm sorry, but it isn't. Of course black music would be more popular if it got the exposure it's denied by the manipulatively racist market calculations of AOR and MTV. But that doesn't mean those calculations have no basis in white listeners' actual tastes—tastes that don't necessarily reduce to race, and tastes they have a right to even though they live worse for them (and sometimes they live quite well, thank you). Always craning their necks toward the next big thing, opportunists like McLaren make pop music happen, but even in the punk years there was great work from old farts like Fleetwood Mac and the Stones, oddballs like the McGarrigles and Ronnie Lane, and all the soul and funk and disco and blues and folk and country professionals who rolled merrily along as if Johnny Rotten didn't exist, which for them he didn't. More often, several promising-to-exciting things will go on at once. And then there are times that throw up no markers at all.

4. What Recovery, Exactly?

It's a distortion to label rock videos commercials; at worst they're promos, which is not the same thing, and if they borrow advertising techniques that's an inevitable consequence of their brevity, their lyric structure, and their roots in the hook aesthetic. But to excuse the directors somewhat is only to make the music look—and sound—worse. Great exceptions and pleasant surprises notwithstanding, most rock videos diminish the second-rate songs they're supposed to enhance; however circumscribed rock artists may be musically, their literary and dramatic endowments tend narrower yet. Because videos visualize lyrics and compel contemplation of the artists' mugs, they bring home how slick, stunted, smug, self-pitying, and stupid rock culture has become. Even more offensive than the racism MTV promulgates by omission is the way sexism that's only implicit in words and live performance is underlined again and again by the vaguely sadie-maisie mannequins who sing backup or play their mute roles in male jackoff and/or revenge fantasies. The clips make it all but impossible to reimagine songs you like—Billy Idol's fake-gothic misogyny and adolescent fear of commitment have ruined "White Wedding" for me forever. And of course, they replace participation with spectatorism on the physical level as well.

True, whenever I think such thoughts I remind myself that early brainwash theorists once leveled similar charges at talkies. Because pop culture evolves like anything else, there's a chance "Atomic Dog" and "Burning Down the House" and "Thriller" and "Atlantic City" and even, yes, Phil Collins's "You Can't Hurry Love" will eventually prevail, enabling rock video to escape its current box, the one with genre movies, film school dream sequences, Helmut Newton, and *Midnight Special* at the corners.

But even in this best instance the little matter of capital would make MTV one of the bad guys. Clips cost $15,000 for technically acceptable concert footage, with forty or fifty grand par for concept videos and two hundred grand not unheard of. As an accepted part of promotion, videos raise the ante for struggling artists even more inescapably than high-tech audio; eight years after the first Ramones album seemed to harbinger a new era of rock and roll access because it cost $6,400 to record, they put the game squarely back into the hands of the money boys. And while I don't buy the Mass Culture 101 fantasy of a nation of suburbanized adolescents lulled into passive consumerist pseudo-community by their television sets, I do believe that every popular form has its optimum audience size, and that rock and roll climbs above five million or so at its occasionally invigorating peril.

In the stagnant information system of AOR, MTV provided liberating, pluralistic input. But MTV's tuneout-sensitive national programming leaves even less leeway for local quirks than, well, Lee Abrams's Superstars HQ, which in October sent out a typically visionary memo warning its stations that "progressive music is out." Artists such as Elvis Costello, Graham Parker, and Joan Armatrading (as well as many heavy metal acts) had "no business

being on the radio" because the nation's tastes had turned "horizontal"—
consultant talk for top forty, music that crosses demographic boundaries,
which as CHR—Contemporary Hits Radio—is the new hot programming
idea. In New York, AOR bellwether WPLJ set tongues wagging a year ago
when it added Prince's "Little Red Corvette," and by June was playing nothing but hits, which in current radio parlance doesn't equal "rock," a term that
designated all popular music except country and disco five years ago but is
now considered too vertical.

There's something comic about this commotion—just imagine, maybe
people actually *want to listen to hit records*. But in fact the pop single had become almost theoretical during the slump—after WABC went all-talk in 1981,
New York was left without one genuine top forty station, and if it weren't for
MTV and the attendant Anglomania the format mightn't have come back at
all. And insofar as it brings down bastions of white power like WPLJ, CHR is
incontrovertibly a good thing. But this doesn't justify the eager comparisons
to the Beatlemaniac glory years I've heard from bright-eyed populists old
enough to know better. It can't, because Beatlemania's excitement was bound
up in a sense of expansive social possibility as well as artistic reach, with
rock and roll more reflection than source. In the age of Reagan, that kind of
utopian optimism is effectively dead.

Anyway, horizontal radio ain't necessarily so great for the record business. One survey indicates that for every CHR fan who buys six LPs a year
there are three AOR faithful, and while CHR isn't the cause of such deplor-
able penny-pinching (the younger, predominantly female audience it attracts has never been all that free with its music dollars), it's not helping
any. The phenomenal growth of the album market was predicated on the
passionate, committed, "vertical" myth of rock culture; pop commitments
simply aren't as all-consuming. So perhaps it shouldn't be a surprise that,
just as the slump was never as severe as the tape-obsessed doomsayers said
it was, the recovery clearly doesn't qualify as a boom. When the tally was in,
it turned out that the great slump of 1982 had generated more gold and platinum albums than the great recovery of 1983. The dollar volume of only four
megasellers—*Thriller*, *Flashdance*, Def Leppard's *Pyromania*, and the Police's
Synchronicity—probably accounted for most of the industry's total 1983 gain.

This is inauspicious, because it commits venture capital to a blockbuster
mentality. Experience has shown that blockbusters can't be predicted positively—in 1983, only *Synchronicity* wasn't a major surprise. But they can
be predicted negatively, and they will be. It's going to get even harder for

marginal artists with zero-plus platinum potential to find backing. Because make no mistake, folks, the problem is capitalism. What else did you think I've been talking about—the natural order of things?

5. Eternal Youth

I'm aware that such rhetoric is apt to exasperate many readers. Because make no mistake about this either: rock and roll is capitalist in its blood. Its excitement has always been bound up in the individualistic get-up-and-go of ambitious young men who looked around their land of plenty and decided that they deserved—hell, just plain wanted—a bigger piece, and it would never have reached its constituency or engendered its culture without the entrepreneurial derring-do of countless promoters, hustlers, petty criminals, and other small businessmen. But the most ambitious young rock and rollers are rarely as likable or as visionary as they were twenty and thirty years ago. And the derring-do of the big businessmen involved is often on a grandly international scale. Like the man says, it's a jungle out there, and for those who aspire to a musical vocation what might have seemed like a dream or a lark in 1967 or even 1977 now feels more like a go-for-broke gamble.

The alternative that attracts many gifted musicians is avant-gardism whether pop or renegade. Devolving into three-chord clamor or forging toward total cacophony, recombining roots musics or traversing alien structural, harmonic, and improvisational concepts, these artists put the limits of their acquiescence in boldface and let the fans fall where they may. Inaccessibility both formal and physical assures that their audiences won't be passive, and sometimes they make music galvanizing enough to jar loose some free-floating complacency. But by definition avant-gardists sacrifice the special political purchase of popular form—the way it speaks to and for the populace. The charm of a walking tolerance advert like Boy George or a raving idealist like U2's Bono Vox is that their refusal to make that sacrifice doesn't seem ostrichlike; rather it evinces the kind of willful provisional naivete that these days is rarer and wiser than irony. The enduring beauty and pleasure of black music from pop to rap likewise inheres in its will to keep on keeping on—nowhere are the material satisfactions of living in the U.S.A. evoked more seductively, and nowhere do they sound more earned.

Nor did punk destroy the rock faith among those it moved most directly, so that now two otherwise adverse youth populations—AOR's still sizable white male demographic and the tiny core of perhaps fifty thousand (?) postpunk clubgoers and record collectors who send their elected representatives to hoot at functions like the New Music Seminar—continue to make music the measure of things. We veterans are loath to pass the flame to either side because in rock and roll populists and avant-gardists are supposed to keep each other honest. But if that hasn't happened, the reason isn't the music's breakdown as a cultural organism so much as capitalism's breakdown as a nexus of social possibility.

To put it simply, in the present go-for-broke environment all the arts are fucked. Those popular forms that remain cheerful avoid making stringent demands on themselves, as in the rich but rather complacent neoclassicism enjoyed by many jazz musicians and Hollywood folk. Network television is network television, and while video artists are bursting with technological imperative, their visions of a public-access future are utopian folderol. Note too that video artists are rarely disdainful of rock and roll—or rather, of the capital that will be ventured if rock video opens up some. And among poets and visual artists, for instance, the punk and funk subcultures that seem so truncated to participant-observers like me are viewed as a means to the "vitality" of their fitful dreams. There's still a profusion of good rock and roll coming down, of every conceivable description in a state of continual superpluralistic international cross-fertilization. In fact, there are times when the music's somewhat shapeless quality nowadays seems almost a virtue—a metaphor redolent with democratic fecundity where the myth of the Great Artist has become a quintessential capitalist hype.

So if I conclude that the current situation still won't do, it's not because I pine for rock culture. It's because I refuse to suspend my disbelief in eternal youth. That theme has been turning sour for a decade now, but the older I get the surer I am that it carries meaning—something like what Bob Dylan called busy-being-born before life got to him. It's an idealism that might conceivably foster the kind of cross-generational alliances that have always been too rare among white Americans. Even after you factor in America's inferiority complex and dead-ass bizzers, what puts the U.K.'s young rock and rollers in the chips and ours in day jobs boils down to style, by which I do not mean haircuts. The good young rock and rollers here still partake of enough of our tattered national optimism to act as if youth rebellion is a real-life possibility, complete with a hearty fuck-you-if-you-can't-take-the-heat that as always I could do without, but also with a depth of commitment that seems to come naturally. In London, on the other hand, youth rebellion looks like a desperate game, a flamboyant, fleeting masquerade. What fascinates the new Brits about youth is that like everything else it'll betray you eventually, and for many there's a comfort in that. Expectations are such a burden these days.

It can certainly be said that like rock culture itself, eternal youth is an illusion worth discarding—that kids today are realistic and good for them. But that kind of realism is exactly what the neoconservative thrust of capitalist culture means to inculcate, and I'm against it. Of course I believe people should grow up, and yes, I think it's the better part of grace to accept the inevitable decline of body pride, the purely physical exuberance that fuels rock and roll's fabled energy. But the fact that people grow up doesn't mean they have to stop growing, and if that sounds like some Marin County bromide, well, I learned it from Chuck Berry and John Lennon and George Clinton and indirectly Karl Marx too. Only people who insist on changing themselves are liable to end up changing the world around them, and although it would be nice to think rock and roll could change the world all by itself, I've never had much use for that fallacy. All I expect from rock and roll is what rock and roll taught me to expect: more.

Village Voice, 1984 · Substantially condensed

Not My Fault, Not My Problem

Classic Rock

No no no, you've got it all wrong. Kids today, jeeze. It's like we used to say—never trust anyone under thirty. (Wasn't that it?)

I know classic rock isn't the issue, exactly. In its orthodox form, classic rock is for people who aren't quite as cool as Joe and Jo College—people who may go to college, but who don't go *away* to college, if you catch my drift. Yet somehow classic rock seems like the key concept here: art that's stood the test of time, as my professors used to put it. And although it would be deluded to claim that critics created this concept—the buying audience has never taken us that seriously—we certainly collaborated in establishing the canon. For if the early rock critics were more enamored of Chuck Berry than the typical progressive jock, and also more receptive to punk than any population group this side of Houston Street, we did play the game of vaunting our "generation"'s "artistic achievement." We celebrated pop flux, insisting—despite our distaste for if-it-feels-good-do-it, love-the-one-you're-with, hope-I-die-before-I-get-old banality—that music, like life itself, was best experienced in the present. But we couldn't resist valorizing it in the historicist terminology of the academy.

I'm not sure we had an alternative, either. As the Rock and Roll Hall of Fame wishes to remind you, *somebody* was gonna do the canonizing, and I guarantee you it wasn't us who enshrined paragons of excess Jim Morrison and Led Zeppelin—Genuine Artists though both may have been—so near the top of the heap. So we put our two cents in, plumping for *Van* Morrison, say, or Randy Newman—cultish figures who needed all the help they could get—as well as validating Hendrix and the Beatles and the Stones. We did our damnedest to absorb the shock of the new, and almost invariably caught on to future icons quicker than radio or retail. We got hip to our own history, listening beyond the hits of our youth till we got to know parallel geniuses (George Jones, Thelonious Monk), major minor artists (Wanda Jackson, the "5" Royales), and loads of great predecessors (Hank Williams, Billie Holiday, Louis Armstrong, Franz Liszt). And if none of this turned out as we would have wished, from shooting-star-of-the-week on the cover of you-name-it to the Hall of Fame, well, who ever said we ruled the world? Not us. So it seems like a good time to point out some stuff.

First of all, though we might be accused of extravagant hero worship—and for many poor souls, an audience with a rock star was a brush with the divine—there was actually another reason we hung on John Lennon's every word and scrutinized the jacket of *John Wesley Harding* until we finally discerned with our own eyes the tiny heads concealed in the leaves of that literal-looking black-and-white tree. To put it plainly, we believed these guys spoke for us. That means we felt there was an us for them to speak for, and it also means their power didn't reside solely in their personal charisma. Their power derived not just from their audience, though in these starstruck days that self-evident observation flirts with heresy, but from the imminent worldwide movement supposedly prefigured by that audience. We paid close attention to their pronouncements to find out how history was going, and sometimes to find out whether our public spokesmen were still on the bus.

Although classic rock draws its inspiration and most of its heroes from the '60s, it is a construction of the '70s. It was invented by prepunk/predisco radio programmers who knew that before they could totally commodify '60s culture they'd have to rework it—that is, selectively distort it till it threatened no one. Three crucial elements got shortchanged in the process: black people, politics, and Pop-with-a-capital-P, Pop in the Andy Warhol sense. Granted, rock's chronic inability to come to terms with any of the three made the betrayals easier. Even when Motown and Stax-Volt were getting respect, the soul artist was an exoticized Other, and in the wake of Black Power and James Brown's "Mother Popcorn," any African-American who didn't fly his or her freak flag high got frozen out of "progressive" radio. The understandable tendency of musicians to believe that music is the most important thing in the world was elevated into pseudo-political, antipolitical ideology—the aforementioned imminent worldwide movement was expected to effect its transformations not just peacefully but naturally, spontaneously, without tactics or strategy. As for Pop—well, '60s rock was a Californian faith, especially in America. It had little use for Pop irony, for its hard edges or primary colors; at its most pretentious it never fully absorbed that it was part of the entertainment business. Too bad—though the sellout would probably have been every bit as gross had it been informed by Pop's sane and distanced self-consciousness, it wouldn't have been quite as grotesque. Even if you don't much like Mick Jagger, you have to admit his sense of irony rendered him a more attractive bigshot than David Crosby or Grace Slick.

Yet for all the mistrust and bitterness that's ensued, the '60s were when the black people who are America's greatest musical asset were accepted (more than in theory, if less than in fact) as equals—when the national commitment to social integration was finally (I hope) established. We're only beginning to learn what that means, but where once rock and roll was in the forefront of the educational process, now it struggles to keep up—because in the official rock pantheon the Doors and Led Zeppelin are Great Artists while Chuck Berry and Little Richard are Primitive Forefathers and James Brown and Sly Stone are Something Else. Hippiedom and rockdom were never as radical as cliche has it, but before the '60s were over the Vietnam War was anathema throughout youth culture, and the idea of this country throwing its moral weight around had zero credibility. In case you hadn't noticed, that kind of skepticism is now again utterly marginalized, so that a war in which a hundred thousand human beings die is considered bloodless because not much of the blood was ours—so that as the attack on Iraq began, the black station in my town kept playing Sean Lennon's "Give Peace a Chance" while the AOR outlets moved on to "The Star-Spangled Banner." Meanwhile, out in Theoryland, Pop has spawned postmodernism, cough cough. And while pomo's trivial pursuits can stand to bump up against a canon now and then, for college students' pop-music aesthetic to wallow instead in AOR's dumb, received Victorian romanticism is not the kind of irony Andy had in mind.

In short, race and Pop and politics are the other half of sex and drugs and rock 'n' roll. They're half of what the '60s were about—what made the '60s dangerous, and what made them a good time to be alive. And since they're the "serious" half, to leave them out of your myth of rock as art-that-stands-the-test-of-time is to render it totally fatuous. But let me add that to attribute this transmogrification solely to the machinations of media manipulators is also fatuous. It had, as we rads like to say, a material base. All of this risk-taking cultural outreach proceeded from the two decades-plus of real prosperity that followed World War II. It would never have occurred if your average student longhair had grown up with the radical economic insecurity of parents who'd survived the Depression. Nor would it have occurred if the kid had grown up with the gnawing sense of socioeconomic contraction that was soon to afflict his or her younger siblings and offspring (including you, gentle reader). By the early '70s a whole mess of chilling effects—some material, some perceptual—were impinging on the collective confidence of my generation and everybody else's, especially as our values and aspirations were picked up and found wanting by the unluckier kids crammed toward the lower end of America's broken-runged class ladder. Not for nothing did classic rock crown the Doors' mystagogic middlebrow escapism and Led Zep's chest-thumping megalomaniac grandeur. Rhetorical self-aggrandizement that made no demands on everyday life was exactly what the times called for.

It's hard to think realistically about the future when you're young, and for all our forward-looking idealism, even the most political among us did a lousy job of figuring out how our vaunted culture was going to keep renewing itself. We really weren't much better than that tie-dyed fool John Sebastian, whose "Younger Generation" is not a song that's stood the test of time in Radioland, though I still find it touching in a Pop-ironic way. "Can I put a droplet of this new stuff on my tongue?" Sebastian imagines his unborn child (a son, of course) asking, inspiring Dad to formulate some verities: "And then I'll know that all I've learned my kid assumes / And all my deepest worries must be his cartoons." Progress along a line to infinity, the permanent cultural revolution: spontaneous, natural, automatic. How sad that it didn't turn out that way—sadder for you than for me, whether you know it or not.

I'm not naive enough to think there's much to be gained by do-gooder appeals to conscience or idealism, though in case there's a stray bleeding heart reading this, I don't mind mentioning how politically retrograde the classic-rock mindset is. The really sick thing is that as heartily as I disapprove of the establishment con that the permanent cultural revolution turned into, it does me more good than it does all the lost young people who are buying it retail. After all, how better guarantee that boomers remain in control? I almost said us boomers, only it's been a long time since I've made common cause with David Crosby—better Johnny Rotten, who didn't turn out so great either. But even so there's a sense in which my generation remains a cultural entity while John Sebastian Jr.'s generation doesn't. No wonder the old stars rule so omnipotently for their fifteen years or eons—it's been forever since the young audience they ought to be responsible to had any sense of itself as a collectivity, as opposed to a put-upon consumer group. This absence of collective consciousness is insured by the progressive fragmentation of rock marketing. The imaginative young listeners who might assume some sort of leadership role are stricken with contempt for anybody who doesn't share their taste (for indie rock, or rap, or dance music, or film, or theory, or whatever). But you'd think some smart person would grab this dilemma by the tail and twist it till it cries uncle. After all, fragmentation is itself a shared experience, a paradoxical common bond worthy of ironic exploitation.

Good luck, kids. If you (or your younger siblings) manage the trick, I'm sure I'll be confused by the details—by what's honored and what's rejected. But it'll beat being appalled by the smugness of my contemporaries and the banality of their children. And let me warn you—until it happens, I get to write more articles like this one. Only you can stop me.

Details, 1991

A Weekend in Paradise

Woodstock '94

In my job, the idea is to have fun. If you don't have fun most of the time, you're not doing your job. And if you do, you're permitted to conclude that when you don't, they're not doing their job. So one reason I attended Woodstock II was to have fun. But I never thought it would be easy.

For one thing, I had trouble finding a date, and understandably so: preliminary reports read like Monty Python fantasies. The rigidly scheduled arrivals at inaccessible parking lots in groups of not more or less than four, the severely limited egress, the bans on not just drugs and alcohol but children and coolers and, Jesus, tent stakes, and—the crowning touch—the scrip that would be the only legal tender at the overpriced concession stands made Woodstock-in-Saugerties sound like a cross between Tommy's Holiday Camp and the company store Tennessee Ernie sold his soul to. My life's companion preferred to stay in bed.

Still, I found much of the nay-saying misguided. Doing talking head duty as one of the few veterans of Woodstock '69 with a public claim to enthusiasm for Rock and Roll '94, I was dismayed when an interviewer complained that the new model was "commercial." I mean, this was rock and roll. The main reason the first festival didn't make money, if it didn't after residuals, was that the exploitation of popular music was so primitive back then. Even sillier were the whines of Catskill locals that Michael Lang and his PolyGram collaborators had purloined a sacred spirit from either a bunch of washed-up folkies at the old Max Yasgur place or the town of Woodstock. By refusing to countenance a real rock concert in a neck of the woods where the old-timers I've talked to look back on the first festival with nostalgic pride, the Sullivan County powers-that-be got the traffic jam and terrible music they deserved (although the Deadhead-style Free Festival that replaced Sid Bernstein's abandoned fiasco clearly did have a utopian-escapist magic of its own). As for the boho yokels sequestered in Woodstock-the-municipality, let me be perfectly clear. One factor above all made both Woodstock I and

Woodstock II whatever they were: size. They were big, b-i-g big. BIG. BI-fucking-IG. And they wouldn't have been that way without money, m-o-n-e-y money. Shekels. Dollars. Venture capital.

None of which is to suggest that the basic pretension of Woodstock II, which is that somehow a myth would return to life with the proper application of money, wasn't totally and permanently ridiculous. "They say history repeats itself," we in the press tent heard again and again from PolyGram's John Scher, who emerged as corporate spokesperson once the event was underway and Lang's patina of authenticity had outlived its usefulness. Yet though the conceit goes back to Thucydides, as a '60s fart I prefer Marx, who amended Hegel with "the first time as tragedy, the second as farce"—only since the original Woodstock was more like a miracle, call the follow-up a spectacle. As I told one interviewer, it's impossible to re-create your own marriage five years down the road, so how could anyone expect to re-create so much vaster a social fact? But as I also told her, that didn't mean something else fairly wondrous couldn't happen instead.

That wasn't the main reason I ended up at Woodstock II, however. The main reason was that I wanted to see the bands. Maybe somewhere in the world there's an equally vast social fact, perhaps a religious pilgrimage I'm too culture-bound to know about. But this one wouldn't have happened—wouldn't have happened once, wouldn't have happened twice—without rock and roll. The music wasn't *what* the original seekers remembered about Woodstock I, but it was *why* they were there, and as the crowds jamming the North Field at Saugerties Saturday and Sunday proved, no amount of mud or mind-boggling gestalt could distract second-generation celebrants from the cultural commodity that brought them together. Over the past twenty-five years, however, that commodity has become almost incomprehensibly more huge and various. Partly as a result of forces unleashed or catalyzed or just plain symbolized by Woodstock I, the range of available music had increased tenfold.

Newsday's Ira Robbins rightly pointed out that the bill was "solidly second-drawer. No Springsteen, no Pearl Jam, no Dead, no R.E.M., no U2, no Led Zeppelin reunion." To which one might add, no Guns N' Roses or Dr. Dre, no Elton John or Rolling Stones, no Madonna or Michael or Janet. Although the general suspicion of Woodstock II contributed to this shortfall, economics made it inevitable—most of the above-named are stadium draws capable of selling fifty thousand seats in a single city, well beyond the reach of promoters hoping to attract a mere 250,000 customers to two and then three full days of music. In 1969, there was no such thing as a stadium draw, and the only acts with the undeniable commercial-artistic cachet of the above-named were Dylan-Beatles-Stones, none of whom played Woodstock. And though in retrospect the Who and Jimi and Janis and Sly put Aerosmith and Metallica and Peter Gabriel to shame, through 1969 they had two No. 1 LPs among them, and their lifetime total was four. The long list of folkies at Woodstock I says a great deal about the provenance of American "rock" in the hippie era, and also suggests why Crosby, Stills, Nash & Young proved the festival's real commercial powerhouse. And the total lack of lineup controversy says even more about rock's focus back then. Nobody foresaw the future of Led Zeppelin or Pink Floyd, and nobody was smart enough to complain that the Velvets and the Stooges were already of far greater aesthetic and historical moment than Mountain and Jefferson Airplane. What alternatives were there? The MC5? The Mothers of Invention? Come on. Maybe we were utopians, but we didn't think we could have everything.

And then there's the most crucial difference of all. In 1969 the music was the locus of a culture that everyone believed was out there whether they were part of it or not. Going for the music meant going for the culture in a way it no longer can—the two were inextricable. Looking back to render an analysis that would have seemed pointless then, I realize I went for the culture. This wasn't because I didn't care for the acts, although I sat out Friday's rain-soaked folk bill in the commodious tent of some generous acquaintances my girlfriend and I bumped into and spent the weekend with. (Thanks again, Josh and Babette.) It was because as an unmarried twenty-seven-year-old rock critic living in a forty-five-buck-a-month apartment five blocks from the Fillmore East, I had caught most of them many times. As an overemployed fifty-two-year-old rock critic with a nine-year-old and a coop to run, I'm lucky to get out three times a month, and when I do I have alternatives galore. As a result, I hadn't seen a single one of the twenty-two acts announced as of mid July since the Neville Brothers played the Bottom Line long about 1987. For me, music is a job that's inextricable from my life. So those "two more days of peace and music"—hell, even three—sounded like they might be fun. And they were for sure, albeit not exactly in the ways I'd pictured. No two ways about it—I had a great time. Guess somebody was doing their job.

....

Ten days earlier, however, all qualms in re lineup, companionship, and totalitarianism were operative, and I had conceived a remedy: Lollapalooza IV.

Alternathink plaints about Perry Farrell's ripoff only convinced me I'd love the thing, and in 1994 the bands were L7, George Clinton, the Beastie Boys, the Breeders, A Tribe Called Quest, and Smashing Pumpkins—plus, oh well, the Boredoms and Nick Cave, but six out of eight is smoking. I was beguiled too by tales of the second stage, political tables, and interactive gewgaws. We journalists call this kind of thing a setup. It would be sheer joy to shake my fun in Michael Lang's face when his ill-laid plans went thataway. I hoped there'd be a press area to hear music from, but if not, me and Carola and Nina and our friend Marc would simply bask further back, exploring the sideshows when Nina got bored and repairing to the misting tent to cool off.

This fantasy proved seriously barmy. Maybe the August 3 Lollapalooza at Quonset State Airport in Rhode Island was merely the victim of the four-car accident that closed Route 4 and turned an hour-and-a-half trip from Boston into a four-hour crawl that cost L7 their slot and effectively reduced the number of bands we caught to four even though we saved forty-five minutes on back roads. But I think it went deeper than that. In fact, I'm ready to wonder how much effective fellow feeling a postutopian aesthetic can generate. Thank God last-minute child care reduced our party to three—at best Nina would have been the only preteen on the premises, and at worst she might have gotten hurt.

Certainly three of the sets were fine. The Breeders' rough-hewn diffidence, too raggedy a year ago, has evolved into sweet mastery of noise-tune tension, edging out toward chaos then bringing it all back home; it took just four or five brief songs for Marc, a forty-two-year-old whose appetites tend toward the blues-based and lately the African, to get inside the aesthetic. Although Clinton wasted precious minutes on a lousy white female rapper, a mediocre black female soul singer, and a lecture about drugs and the CIA, most of the P-Funk All-Stars' music was classic in the best sense—together and comfortable at its most galvanizing and up-for-the-downstroke. And the Beasties proved themselves headliners who preferred leaving early to topping the bill. But in any mass setting quality per se is never enough. You have to be able to hear it. And you have to enjoy the company.

Having left our car near the gate for a quick exit, we had plenty of chance to look the crowd over as we hoofed across a thickly weeded cement-and-asphalt parking lot. It was three-thirty at a concert announced for two, yet there was tailgating everywhere as kids downed their verboten beers. About half looked nonstraight—hair colored or braided or long or shaved or coyly unkempt, funny boots, a very few male skirts or kilts, loads of alternaband T-shirts. Between sob stories at the comp window and contraband iced tea at the frisk point, it was four before we were inside, barely in time to get bored with the Verve's second-stage feedback and discover that that dim throb over there was Quest finishing its set. After the rappers had baptized the moshers up front, the audience trod past and over our poncho. We moved up, then found ourselves packed tight for the Breeders half an hour later. They were wonderful, as I said. But sometimes the music was obscured by more immediate sensory stimuli.

At sixty or seventy-five yards from the stage we were close enough to get a good look at moshing that was willfully rough and intense for such a gentle band, and occasionally a floater would pass by. Since my body is breakable and Carola's more so, I elbowed the guy who crashed next to me for future reference, although I felt more kindly toward the girls, who were not just smaller but braver, more vulnerable—giving up their physical safety to the group, which is the theory, rather than menacing wimp standees, which was too often the male fact. Then, during a lovely "Driving on Nine," a pit opened up right in front of us, threatening a perimeter the moshers would have been happy to enlarge even if a few small young things went home with abrasions. Between eight and a dozen muscular boys, every one taller or broader than me and most both, crossed play-fighting with turf war—no fists, but plenty of hard shoves, with the requisite grins frequently forced or absent, a mark of cool rather than camaraderie. Most of them looked like frat assholes feeling their hormones, the same thing that makes dance night fight night from El Paso to Liverpool. Earlier I'd been bemused by the pit-etiquette advisories in the Beasties' free newspaper. Now I understood.

If only because the crowd never closed up, things were better for Clinton, and if half of those who stayed barely paid attention, much less danced or knew the hand signals, at least they could spy L7 boogieing on the scaffold. As the twenty-five-minute intermission ended, Marc took his camera forward for the Beasties, then quickly returned—it was too crazy up there. The set began fast and strong with "Sure Shot," and almost immediately two pits combusted spontaneously within five yards of us as everyone else pogoed. We were having too much fun to retreat. But around the end of the second song that choice was denied us as several scared-looking girls led a stampede, which we joined instantly with the help of a tall, intrepid black kid—one of two dozen I saw all day—scooping up our stuff. I shoved a few times, stumbled a few times, caught Carola once or twice; when it was over a minute later, my notes were gone and our distance from the stage had almost doubled. Musically, this made a tremendous difference—the difference between inhabiting the music and observing it. The excitement was secondhand now, and although the blanket-tossing that started up front eventually reached our depth, where we were the music was the occasion rather than the inspiration for this far friendlier physical rite.

It was after eight, so we spread our stash of Armenian food on a desolate press table slightly aft of the stage, but although we hoped to avoid Nick Cave, all too soon rampant self-expression was drowning out dinner conversation. We took our time returning, then lounged far back as the decent conventional rock and unriveting arena solos waxed and mostly waned. Occasionally the star would announce that he was about to knock our socks off, but he never came close, and around nine-twenty he started complaining in a strangely un-Australian accent. He dissed Rhode Island, he dissed the site, he told us we should "tear up the empty lot" when the show was over, he congratulated us sarcastically for attending: "There may be a bomb underneath you but you are rocking—at least you can tell your children that you came and you rocked." He pouted: "I'm sorry we suck." He rationalized: "We apologize for trapping ourselves in a vortex we can't get out of." Finally, just before ten, he advised us to drive safely and limped off to widely scattered cheers. The Quonset edition of Lollapalooza was over.

I was pissed off and deeply confused. For half an hour I'd been jeering this bad expressionist band in the expectation that soon I'd hear a good one, Smashing Pumpkins. God, I thought, that must have been some traffic jam. But when Carola asked who the female musician was, I figured it out. Nick Cave had preceded Quest—that *was* Smashing Pumpkins. How embarrassing for me—but how much more embarrassing for Billy Corgan. Carola, who isn't normally given to hyperbole, called it the worst performance she'd ever witnessed in her life. I told her she'd never seen Richie Havens.

....

Lollapalooza was no disaster, but as an event it was nothing. The security was irritating and so was the sound system. Most of the food concessions sold greasy street-fair schlock. The overtaxed sideshows closed early and the second-stage schedule was impossible to figure. We never found the misting tent. Racially, Quest and Clinton didn't make a dent. Generationally, the festival was not only uniformly young, but almost uniformly eighteen-to-twenty-five, a subset of young. And culturally it seemed fucked up— dumbass collegians seizing the symbols of the alienated contemporaries who made the scene possible in much the way carpers claim.

Also, the stampede spooked my wife, who'd been considering a date in Saugerties, and now decided I should reconnoiter first. I used to regard moshing as postutopian sublimation and complex metaphor, and I still do, but one facet of that metaphor now dominates—whilst responding poetically to these parlous times, it posits the rigidest version of rock and roll physicality extant. What makes rock and roll a youth music is above all the raw energy it demands, and moshers mean to drive off anyone who for reasons of age or gender or size or temperament can't take that energy to the limit—a limit they define. This is significant not just because a new breed of mosher became one of Woodstock II's media symbols, but because both Woodstocks were bound up in the physical demands they imposed on participants. Although these had nothing to do with the mosher ideal, I had trouble convincing Carola that smashing pumpkinheads wouldn't be a threat in Saugerties, and maybe she knew more than I did. Who would have thunk anyone would slam-dance to the Allman Brothers?

So we dealt with the demands we could foresee. I packed changes of clothes, a jacket, shorts, two hero sandwiches, two bottles of seltzer, fruit, trail mix, crackers, peanut butter and jelly, a loaf of bread, sunblock, insect repellent, a poncho, a flashlight, and (bingo) an umbrella. I purchased maps of Ulster and Greene counties. And though I'd found friends to put me up after learning the Kingston Holiday Inn wanted $340 a night, on general principles I bought a sleeping bag. Prevented by snafu from driving to the site, I found a use for my map when the shuttle driver got lost on the way from the hotel parking lot, but the congestion proved bearable—a fifteen-minute tie-up near Saugerties followed by two miles of stop-and-go. My first impression was tents everywhere—fields, hills, woods, roadsides. Some of them had stakes. John Hughes of the Fort Lauderdale *Sun-Sentinel*, an easygoing Nevilles and Allmans fan who reads me in *Playboy*, had suggested I stow my stuff with him in case I needed to share his two-person tent. So at three-forty-five we disembarked at the nexus behind the main stage, checked out the giant press tent, and found high ground in a press camping area. And soon the avantish hip-hop I couldn't believe I was half hearing drew me away.

The North Field was full but negotiable. As I shuffled past the main concession bank and picked my way laboriously to a more distant spot than I'd ever settled for at Lollapalooza, I determined that this was indeed one of my favorite live bands, Philadelphia's Goats, who finished their abrasive rock-rap to polite applause augmented by my yells. Kindly crew members hosed down a knot of moshers up front. There was a burst of deja vu as a fat, balding, clownish Wavy Gravy warned of strychnine in the white, blue, and dark green acid, pronounced the Felix the Cat and Skeleton brands "shitty," and couldn't believe what he was reading about the brown tabs with black spots: "It's . . . good? Hey, it's good!" Then came the first of many entreaties to those camped on the North Field proper, which was intended as listening space, capped by Wavy's John Lennon rewrite: "All we are saying / Is please move your tents."

Since the never-ending Blues Traveler was up and I needed to get oriented, I made my way back, passing through the gate with the laminate that was the mark of privilege in this community. At Woodstock I, where the press tent turned into a hospital, my only privileges were a lucky limo ride in with Peter Townshend and the providence of my ad hoc hosts. Here my laminate meant something—free Pepsi products and Saratoga water in the press tent, queueless phones that worked occasionally, camping close to the stage, relatively undisgusting latrines, two useful service roads—and no matter how much these advantages unbalanced my participant-observer tightrope walk, I would have been stupid (and a very atypical participant) to turn them down. I called Carola, whose knees are trickier than mine, to tell her that our jitney-and-child-care contingency plans would be ill-advised even if I could get back to the car, which seemed dubious. This was what sleeping bags were for.

An hour later I returned to a North Field that was reaching critical mass. Still learning the terrain, I was funneled onto the vehicle-clogged road between the main concessions and Ecology Village, ending up well past the camping line. Hopscotching over jammed tents and pushing slowly through impassable walkways, I encountered numerous children, plenty of mid-teens, and an enormous number of over-twenty-fives, with alternakids much sparser than at Lollapalooza. Even the college types lacked that balls-out spring-break arrogance; however much role-playing it did for the cameras, this was not a notably rowdy crowd. After twenty minutes I claimed a one-man patch of grass at the edge of a crosswise aisle, where for four hours I listened to Del Amitri, Live, James, King's X, and Sheryl Crow. The only one I might have sampled in New York was Crow, whose singer-with-backup wilted in the space, but only Del Amitri, a meaningless pop-metal outfit who were one of five PolyGram-associated acts on Friday's supposedly "cutting-edge" bill, enjoys zero word of mouth. As it turned out, James alone showed me something. But just finding out whether any songs stuck was a trip: I was touched by the way some onlooker or other always seemed ready to don this mediocre stuff like a press-on tattoo, humming Del Amitri's hit or strumming air acoustic to Crow or explaining a James lyric to an older sister-in-law up from New Mexico because her Utica-born husband had gone to Bethel when he was fifteen.

The Friday show was mostly a con. Added when ticket sales seemed ominously slow, its concept was the pseudo-alternative niche now favored for breaking acts, a subdivision of the little-of-this, little-of-that strategy that defined Woodstock II's programming as it does all current megabiz marketing. At the first Woodstock, the more naive pilgrims assumed a fundamentally homogeneous music that was the locus of a culture—a culture they were eager to share with or even absorb from their hipper, slightly older fellows (so unlike the dumbasses of Lollapalooza, who were intent on transforming its culture into their own). The run of celebrants at Woodstock II expected nothing more than bands they knew, or knew about, which in 1994 includes both Crosby, Stills & Nash and Nine Inch Nails, a bizarre Saturday-night segue that didn't produce anything like the exodus wags predicted. This-and-that was fine with these folks, who could calculate that the much-maligned $135 ticket boiled down to $3.50 a band even if there was no way you could see them all. Revolving stages kept boring intermissions to a minimum—I twice clocked the turnaround at under three minutes, about as long as it takes the Dead to start the next song. And the sound system beat Woodstock I's (and Lollapalooza's) all to shit—loud and clear at a quarter mile, with giant video screens for visuals, not the way I like to listen but a legitimate aesthetic mode nevertheless.

Still, halfway through Crow I'd had enough. I needed to talk to my wife and shoot the shit with my pals in the press tent, and Collective Soul wasn't going to stop me. It was midnight before I rejoined a much looser crowd for the dregs of Candlebox, the last band on my handout. Then, back through the gate, I heard a familiar clatter. Damn! That was "Blister in the Sun," by the announced but presumed-canceled Violent Femmes. I ran back and listened joyously to a long, animated set, often pausing to admire a vivacious teenager who was far from the only one dancing and mouthing the words. This was the first band with a serious following all day, and also the first with a signature sound. The difference was heaven. Give Gordon Gano credit—maybe he deserves a cult as much as Jonathan Richman. The Femmes played the most exciting music I heard all weekend. I've yet to meet another press person who caught it.

....

I'd been sleeping badly on the ground outside for two hours when some combination of a passing vehicle and the putatively ambient Aphex Twin woke me up. This was Ravestock, John Scher's message that sleep was for wusses, and when the volume rose I gave up and embarked on a futile search for the South Stage. Raindrops sent me racing back to the tent, where John Hughes helped me pull in my stuff. Adrenaline coursing, I grabbed my umbrella and set off down the slick entrance road, where I was refused access at the backstage gate before clambering over a pipe railing and through a breach in a cyclone fence. Onstage, two DJs were mixing loud, tribal, and fluent for an audience in the high hundreds, few of whom pretended to dance. Back at the fence, gleeful kids with bedrolls snuck in like ballplayers at a locked schoolyard. It was dawn.

PBJ for breakfast, and at the nine-thirty press conference, announcements of portajohn progress, tent struggles, overtaxed parking lots, roadblocks, an unbroken perimeter (sure), and 200,000-plus customers, most of whom seemed to be out taking the air. The foot traffic was so dense I could hardly move, and suddenly my misty memories of Woodstock I cleared: never, *never* had the bodies been this packed. It took thirty-five minutes to negotiate the half-mile route to the South Stage; the swath of grass leading down from the Craft Village concession (and camping) area was already the scene of a mud-climbing exhibition. But the South Field itself was idyllic—I was closer than at Lollapalooza, with room to lie down. Regrets to Joe Cocker, scheduled for noon in the main arena—I wanted to guard my spot for the Cranberries. A bland, overpriced curried lentil pita from a local vendor convinced me to stick to the knockwurst-sized $2.50 hot dogs and twenty-four-ounce $2 Pepsis of the Fine Host oppressors. At twelve-thirty sharp, the Irish folk-rockers began a set so tuneful and weird I never thought of leaving. That was my m.o.—to listen till I didn't want to listen, just like a real person. PolyGram's Italian rocker Zucchero assured that at two-thirty I would have no trouble reclaiming my turf for a disappointingly excellent Youssou N'Dour, who without his male dancers and singers didn't live up to the hype I'd been feeding anyone who would listen, who wouldn't have drawn like the Cranberries if he did, and who cost me Cypress Hill.

By then a bifurcation was emerging—two festivals, almost. Over in the North Field were the stars and their stalwarts, content to do the funky sardine or stand six hundred yards from the stage in a dead flat space far less ideal than Max Yasgur's rolling amphitheater. In contrast, the much smaller but never jammed South Field attracted open-minded hedonists, whose distaste for suffering often earned them better music. And of course there was migration back and forth. With the Band's comeback not even a throwback and their South Field show penciled in at two and a half hours, however, I set out for Henry Rollins via the press tent. And though there'd been sprinkles the whole gray day, that's when the real rain began—a gusty downpour that ran off the canvas roof in thick rivulets for most of an hour. In the hostile element immersed, Rollins howled and flexed through the storm like an Outward Bound poster boy—or so it appeared on the closed-circuit feed. When the rain slackened to umbrella strength, I opted for the Band after all. Avoiding the new mud on a sideline, I couldn't tell when the guest was Bob Weir and when Roger McGuinn, but everyone was sharp and loose. Eventually, though, the group's once bracing repertoire of grand old blues and personal bests seemed too predictable. On the North Field, Melissa Etheridge was into her climactic Janis Joplin routine, which to my considerable surprise she had down. Two over-thirty babes with wedding rings shimmied and grokked. I wondered whether they knew Melissa was gay. I wondered again when they both started groping a twenty-four-year-old male law student.

This Woodstock inspired volumes of dumb reporting about sex and drugs and rock and roll, always a danger when you send a generalist out to do a rock critic's job or Kennedy out to do anything. I never got close to the pits, where I'm sure clothes were often extraneous, and I don't doubt the existence of the three naked cuties who posed for five thousand snapshots. But in forty-eight hours I observed half a dozen nude men and precisely one nude woman—a lush blonde who wasn't actually nude, but wearing an open shirt, as was her well-muscled and nicely hung male companion, a very sexy image. Although I'd be sad to learn there was no fucking going on, orgiastic it wasn't. The promised searches were perfunctory, mostly verbal, but the scare worked. Muddy Evian bottles outnumbered muddy liquor bottles, beer was as much beverage as inebriant, and though there was considerable cannabis around, it was far from pervasive and never freely shared. Where at Woodstock I it took effort *not* to get stoned, here that was one option among many. Yet loose behavior remained an ideal, and my gropers had it going on. I laughed on the outside and cried on the inside when Crosby (your crazy uncle just before he burps), Stills (aging surf shop owner who likes his talent stupid), & Nash (seedy public schoolmaster well into his cups) greeted them with "Love the One You're With." Soon, however . . . well, you know. Morbid curiosity loses its charm. Craving normality, I made for the South Stage and Primus.

....

The band every kid I'd chatted up had the hots for was Nine Inch Nails, and by eight-thirty the North Field had long surpassed critical mass. Supposedly due to a sound glitch (I bet they were in a snit or applying their makeup), they came on half an hour late, the longest such delay all weekend, but they sure knew how to make an entrance—plastered with the mud that was already Woodstock's universal currency. "You miserable muddy fuckers," spat Trent Reznor, launching what should have been a set of unparalleled cacophony and aggression. Only it wasn't—half of it was dirges that gave me no reason to fight off the throng. At thirty minutes I'd listened till I didn't want to listen. Other refugees bitched bitterly when they were turned back at the laminate gate, almost breaking through—the only anger I encountered away from the stage and the press tent all weekend. Finally feeling sleep deprivation, I failed to get to the South Field until Salt-n-Pepa were over. John Hughes was flat out atop his down bag, and soon I was drifting off to the dulcet strains of Metallica, a band I don't get who sounded like the Kronos Quartet under the circumstances. At one-thirty I woke to a downpour on the rain shield of our efficient little tent and fell asleep to a rowdy Aerosmith I regretted missing. And at three-thirty I woke to World War III.

I thought it was gunshots and stayed down; John thought it was an exploding transformer and burst outside. In fact it was the ten-minute fireworks display the rowdies had capped their show with. But blessed sleep had drained from my body, and when the adrenaline didn't subside by five, I went out. Deserters who'd penetrated the laminate barrier waited for shuttles they could only hope would come. A medical guy I helped phone his parents from the thickly littered press tent claimed countless breaks and sprains in the treacherous slampits and four ODs nobody else reported. The rain had added a slippery cushion to the firmest surfaces, and past the gate the mud was much deeper. Nonsleepers and new arrivals lurched around with arms outstretched, the ubiquitous Pepsi cups their best footing. I've been phobic about mud ever since losing a shoe at a construction site as a seven-year-old, and between my wits and my laminate I was good at avoiding it, but it has a great advantage—it's drier than water, so even when you go over your shoetops you don't get soaked. And so I wandered down into the mostly empty area by the now enormous North Stage pit. Beer drinkers grossed each other out with piss tales. Two Canucks hit on a two-gal-one-guy posse just in from Poughkeepsie. A black suburban teenager in a lounge chair gave her white boyfriend a thousand-watt smile.

By now even Scher had abandoned the fable that free entries were negligible—if 300,000 attended, and it was probably more, at least a third didn't pay. Ticket-checking had been inefficient from the git, and by Saturday afternoon there was no need to crash the gate because you could walk through. Even when I came back at nine-thirty, few of those positioned up front wore the wristbands that signified official entry, and quite a few talked about driving close and hitchhiking in after midnight. This new blood kept the energy high, but also increased the spring-break quotient; for some, it seemed, this was no longer "Woodstock," just a free concert—a little of this, a little of that. CeCe Peniston's pop-gospel supergroup Sisters of Glory followed fast upon an equally glorious surprise visit from Bethel's own Country Joe McDonald, who worked up vigorous sing-along action on "Feel-Like-I'm-Fixin'-to-Die Rag" and gracefully retired. Thelma, Mavis, et al. commanded the weekend's strongest voices this side of Youssou, and I enjoyed their Sunday standards until yet another downpour drove through my umbrella-poncho combo. Back in the press tent, we were told the rain would continue all day—and that departures were overwhelming the shuttle system.

Actually, the rain would soon let up, then hold off till late, but the real person in me was worried. Nina had burst into tears when she heard my voice on the phone, and I didn't want to drive the thruway at three a.m. on coffee and good intentions. I estimated the likelihood of transcendent Dylan at one-in-five, could just barely stand to miss Porno for Pyros and the Chili Peppers, and had never figured to stay for designated closer Peter Gabriel. So when a four o'clock ride to Kingston was proffered, I decided I'd probably take it, and in the end I did. But before that, Woodstock would change, as it kept doing. Nearly three hours of Gabriel-approved WOMAD Afrofolk-pop wore out Green Day fans on the South Field, whose mood wasn't improved by Hassan Hakmoun's intense guitar weave or Wavy's grave assertion that these were "some of the best musicians in the world" when they weren't even some of the best musicians in Uganda. I spent half of this time standing on a tent-chocked hillock in the North Field listening to the Allman Brothers, who were both a revelation and utterly familiar—Warren Haynes an ace Duane substitute, Dickey Betts an ace Garcia fan, "Ramblin' Man" as hooky as "Blister in the Sun," whole band as classic as P-Funk—then tranced out against a fence to Hakmoun. But just two minutes after he finished, the stage turned and Green Day's Billy Joe shouted, "How you doin', all you rich motherfuckers?"

The Berkeley wise guys' *Dookie* is so secondhand I'd never pinned it down, and I couldn't name a song on it, but the hooks had stuck. Those fast chords were a jolt of adrenaline I wanted—somehow the punk strategy, conceived as a corrective to fuzzy Woodstock Nation vibes almost two decades ago, still sounded fresh, while the Allmans' hardly older boogie seemed timeless. Spurred on by Billy Joe—"We suggest that you throw mud, that's fine"— the pent-up kids were soon pelting their speedy antiheroes with handfuls of mud and clods of wet turf. The whole scene was exhilarating and hilarious, pure punk venting—blue-haired bassist Mike Dimt caught a clod and stuffed it in his mouth, stage-divers scampered around worried, then angry guards. But quickly it went out of control, and before Billy Joe had egged the crowd into demanding they walk off, drummer Tré Cool had lost two teeth. "Let's hear it for the earth which we're moving around so magnificently," Wavy requested pathetically. "Play hard, play fair, nobody gets hurt. These are the good old days. Thank you for sharing mud with me."

An hour and a half later, having decided that the Spin Doctors were a studio band and failed to cash in $22 worth of scrip, I was hiking the two miles to the VIP lot. When I called home from Kingston to say I'd be back by eight, Nina burst into tears again. She'd wanted to go see *The Mask*.

....

There were 300,000 stories in the not actually naked city, and mine is but one of them. It would be easier to write the definitive account of, say, Des Moines, which has the virtue of staying in one place for longer than an eyeblink. I never got to the Surreal Field or the far-side campground or the pizza whose poetry-bedecked boxes doubled so nicely as disposable seating. Beddy-bye bound, my colleagues missed my fave set of the weekend; homeward bound, I missed Dylan and the Chili Peppers, either of whom, by all reports, might (and might not) have changed the festival yet again. But at my Woodstock, even the finest '60s rock, by the Allmans and the Band, seemed ultimately unmomentous, a little of this leading only to a little of that, while new music carrying a deeper charge, like Green Day or Nine Inch Nails, threatened the post/imitation/wannabe-utopian vibe. So did alternarock's gift to Woodstock II's counterculture, the mud people the cameras made so much of, who by late Saturday were tending toward the position that anybody within reach deserved the immersion these moshers were certain defined the Woodstock experience.

Straight out of *Woodstock*-the-movie, the mud idea emerged from the pits as textbook Woodstock spectacle, and judging by the wide berth they got, the mud people never understood what it ended up meaning to most of us. By "us" I don't mean my interest groups—the laminated, most of whom were unduly appalled by the weekend's discomforts, or the many over-thirties the laminated ignored, who totaled perhaps five percent of the attendees, concentrated on the two fields' fringes. I mean the big "us"—everyone who had the unduplicable and pretty much indescribable experience of getting up in the morning crowded into a specially designed, surreally overpopulated outdoor space with the same music lovers who'd been there the night before, and who then shared the limited, manageable challenge of overcoming adversities that defeated enough celebrants to make the whole thing seem like real life.

Which it wasn't, of course. More or less as PolyGram intended, Woodstock II ended up an incalculably complex and profitable entertainment experience. "I suspect that if there were 200,000 forty-to-fifty-year-olds you wouldn't have such a mellow atmosphere," Scher boasted Saturday morning, and this meaningless hypothetical had its truth value. If only because they didn't want to ruin the movie, the young celebrants were nice to each other, keeping a lid on their aggressions however free they were with their joints, and they'll no doubt construct their own myths around an incontrovertibly wondrous event. But it's hard to imagine those myths unleashing or catalyzing or symbolizing any social forces; in fact, it's hard to imagine them competing historically with the fucked-up antiutopian struggle that is Lollapalooza, where much of the most momentous music at Woodstock II first came to prominence. These celebrants didn't believe the commodity that brought them together was the locus of a culture—at best they may have thought it was the province of a generation. Although the minuscule black population (a guesstimate two-tenths of one percent, up after the front door was opened) was probably a tiny improvement over both Woodstock I and Lollapalooza, most of the celebrants were just as glad the artist lineup represented little if any progress in the battle against racism the first Woodstock generation supposedly cared so much about, and although their range of female role models had broadened visibly since 1969, I wonder how many reflected that not one of the few women who played Saugerties had the stature of Janis Joplin or Joan Baez or the potential of the Breeders or L7. Fun was underrated in the '60s, which favored putatively permanent modes of transcendence. In the '90s, people I wish knew better are all too ready to settle for it.

....

Somehow the foursomes of fellow deserters at the thruway rest area looked wrong to me. Hey—they were clean! Most seemed to have rinsed their bare legs somewhere; even their shoes had the outer crusts knocked off. Me, I wore my mud like a badge all the way to the East Village. Carola and Nina were impressed. But my weekend was over. When I strode home from alternate-siding the car with my laminate swinging and my lower extremities still showing that good clean country dirt, not a soul looked twice.

Village Voice, 1994

Staying Alive

Postclassic Disco

Eons ago, in the strange time when punks and stoners disagreed about everything except whether disco sucked, rockist sages would complain bitterly about all the ways dance music wasn't alive. It was prefabricated, they charged—mechanical beats and studio thrills stripped of human error, with producers exerting such complete control that the so-called artists were little more than names on a label. More ecumenical souls wanted to deny these insults outright, but unfortunately, there was truth to them. The proof came whenever the latest flash made her or his pitiable attempt to cash in with a personal appearance. Without label subsidies and concerted image buildup, these were almost always solo. The norm was a brief set in a club designed for dancing during which the name on the bill attached itself to a body and emoted the words over tracks blasted from a cruddy PA. Soul has-beens and never-wases did what they could to invest this format with whatever audience skills they'd accrued on the usual hodgepodge of small stages. With the younger hitmakers, fans were grateful to be spared actual lip-synching.

Once the smarter punks sussed that disco wasn't about to take over the world, they made their peace with dance music. In some cases, in fact, they tried it themselves, and just exactly who was coopting who remains debatable. As the most insatiable rock and rollers of the time, the children of 1977 wanted it all and got plenty, so that if it was fair to say that Boy George was "like punk never happened," it was just as fair to retort that punk made glam dance-pop possible. This connection was predominantly Brit, epitomized by Scritti Politti's migration from noise-punk to tune-funk and Joy Division's rebirth as New Order. The American variant, briefly dubbed dance-oriented rock or DOR, never surpassed the B-52's, who started it.

The more significant postpunk development Stateside was a club circuit that turned human error into a consumer fetish and electric guitars into a way of life. In the Nirvana era, however, this proving ground has revealed its limits as a school for stagecraft, a concept it never much encouraged anyway. Many name "alternative" acts—think Pavement, Liz Phair, Guided by Voices, Magnetic Fields—are studio rats disinclined to look people's ears in the eye; others—think American Music Club, Jayhawks, Sebadoh—are song bands of the sort whose performances have never been all that kinesthetic, and whose human errors are usually artistic flubs as well. My worst suspicion is that "alternative"'s muddled ambivalence about success has produced a generation of art wonks emotionally and intellectually incapable of putting out for an audience—for every Belly or Green Day showing me how to hear their records there's a Spinanes or Auteurs convincing me to forget theirs.

And so one of my favorite shows of a nightclubbing year was a March date at the Academy by the declasse song band Veruca Salt. They could have been more unerring and kinesthetic, but I loved Nina and Louise's wisecracking, fondly skeptical familiarity with the assembled "Seether" fans. Accidental queens of MTV, they had half-intentionally attracted a bridge-and-tunnel crowd they weren't always sure they liked, yet they were committed to dealing with it, which was a tremendous up. Not that the scene-soaked Soul Coughing (and the unsigned Cake Like) weren't just as inspirational agitating the downtown converted at Wetlands in January. But Veruca Salt renewed my faith in the rewards of audience-mixing—my belief that, ideally, what happens at a gig should be social and popular-cultural as well as musical and subcultural. And over a recent two-week stretch, that faith was lifted heavenwards by, of all things, three dance acts.

Tricky, Moby, and M People are so dissimilar that sticking them in the same genre mainly illustrates the genre's elasticity—only insofar as it insists on its own functionality is "dance" any narrower a category than "alternative," and nowadays its functions have been expanded to include trance, repose, and, it sometimes seems, total unconsciousness. In fact, maybe what unites them is their will to deliver dance music from pure use value without undercutting its pleasure potential. In their very different ways, all three insist that their music doesn't just do something, it means something. Since unlike most creators in the dance world, which goes about its business by sucking up rivers of singles and remixes, all three apply themselves to the craft of album construction—M People's *Elegant Slumming* won Britain's Mercury Prize in 1994, and Moby's *Everything Is Wrong* and Tricky's *Maxinquaye* have been ecstatically reviewed—maybe it shouldn't have been a surprise that they also put so much into that other staple of full-fledged stardom, the tour. But surprise certainly boosted their charge. This was disco, right? So what were those *bands* doing up there?

Granted, M People sometimes used backing tracks and Moby depended on them. In the kingdom of the keyb, how could it be otherwise? What was astonishing was that Tricky—whose album is the darkest, dourest, and deepest of the three—tried to reproduce his disjunct, claustrophobic studio escape-ism with guitar-keyb-bass-drums. Not reproduce, actually—that would be impossible and Tricky knows it. Say *render*, in a soundscape long on rock guitar, with Tricky himself more forthcoming and Martine inspiring the sick fear that she may want to be Des'ree when she grows up. Tricky's show was the least successful of the three, somewhat less compelling in the packed confines of the Bank, where he headlined for an ultrahip house of dance scenesters, than preceding PJ Harvey at the Academy, where his diffident opener's cool meshed with the plusher surroundings to recall the record's mood while the rock gestalt reinforced his live sound. But either way it was smarter and more engaged than the last Pavement and Sebadoh gigs I caught, ace recording artists though both may be.

Tricky is a depressive with attitude, a complicated malcontent whose cynicism can't quash his capacity for euphoria or rebellion. Beatwise yet determinedly lo-nrg, his live shtick translates dance-music-by-association into rock-by-association. Playing Irving Plaza before Tricky came to town, Moby was something else: a rabid pessimist of the mind and politics and a raving optimist of the spirit and music who leads a revival where rock and roll, "dance," and, oh yeah, "classical" become interchangeable gateways to ecstasy. Live, the hardcore punk turned techno whiz proved the rare rock shaman who makes good on his pretensions. A blond ascetic wearing earplugs and accompanied by one white trap drummer and one white percussionist, he screamed his own lyrics and mimed those of the black divas and toasters he hires and samples. Usually he jumped around or beat drums organic and electronic, but in the middle he donned a guitar for one furious punk song and one subsatanic metal number, playing the straighter beats of both for the joyous release that was his purpose throughout. To climax he stood shirtless through a long electronic chord-crescendo as a light show played over his slight body. Martyr, messiah, universal man— Godstruck humility as human exaltation as superstar ego. His crowd was more "alternative"-looking than Tricky's, which may just mean it's getting harder to tell the ravers from the rockers, and although I never trust self-appointed saviors, the faith he manifested looked to me like an antidote to the scene's terminal irony. I just hope his presentation gets as multiculti as that of Tricky, a black male auteur who foregrounds a black female singer and fronts a white band. As political pessimists should always remember, multiculti needs all the help it can get.

Multiculturalism wasn't the only reason the most retro show of the three was my favorite, but it definitely helped. M People's U.S.-only *Elegant Slumming*, baited with extra hits from the U.K. *Northern Soul*, is a perfect disco album, an unending succession of hooky-beaty concoctions flavoring Heather Small's deep, robust, confident shout. But DJ-turned-conceptmaster Michael Pickering and musical helpmate Paul Heard seemed such studio mavens that a naive Yank would never have suspected that they and Small and their percussionist buddy Shovell had spent two years touring Europe with a full band, which on their new *Bizarre Fruit* would replace the session musicians they'd made their name with. There's a musical cost—*Bizarre Fruit* isn't mechanical *enough*. But there's also a live payback.

Although I can't attest that the well-rehearsed biracial nine-piece—two drummers, three saxophonists, four keyb players (one of whom provided only bass, two of whom were also among the saxophonists), male-female backup duo—provided that spontaneous spark humanity buffs go on about, watching them be into it sure was fun. And if Small's enthusiastic vogue-pose and bump-and-grind moves were elementary (she should try holding the mike in her left hand sometimes), I admired how she played her sexy body—navel barely exposed under a full top that revealed no cleavage, legs clad in a pedal-pusher skort. More important was the infectious everyday-people congeniality she projected. This was not a glam outfit—Pickering's sweaty midneck locks could be the worst haircut in English rock—and that was a crucial element of their charm.

Better still was the crowd—somewhere under half gay guys, many of them jammed up near the pit, augmented by loads of het couples, many unusually stable-looking. This was probably because the median age was over thirty, with the gays somewhat older than the straights. The sense you got from the grizzled out-alones who knew all the lyrics and the dressed-up dames dancing around their handbags was that M People serve the same function for old and/or loyal disco denizens as the Ramones, to choose a clear if extreme example, once did for veteran rock and rollers—they reconfirm old verities by intensifying them. Not only does disco live (a vitality that has special resonance, of course, for the style's gay fans), but it's alive in precisely the way rock puritans used to claim it wasn't, and M People get profundity points just for proving it. Pickering and Heard like to say that their songs are getting more soulful and meaningful, but the deepest meaning they have to offer is bound up in their formal commitment to what's most frivolous in classic disco—the fun positivity of Saturday night fever. That positivity provides the emotional ground on which Tricky and Moby build their more complex but not necessarily more valid meanings. And these days, rockist sages have plenty to learn from it.

Village Voice, 1995

Afternoon of the Roar

Lollapalooza '95

Living entities grow in power or they die. So no matter how revolutionary or new age or full of shit the "alternative" premise of Perry Farrell's culturally and commercially seminal Lollapalooza festival may have been, its metamorphosis into an institution was inevitable. Lollapalooza is now a recognized music-biz fixture. With a goodly push from a band called Nirvana, the long-shot aesthetic that catapulted such unlikely properties as Nine Inch Nails and Primus to platinum now powers an industry within an industry. Anyone who calls this disillusioning is a liar or a fool.

So accept the fact that Lollapalooza is no longer cool. Be glad there are scoffers out there, even if they're pumping ritual scarification or Dean Martin records—negations fertilize innovations, and if one should take root and flower, we get to put it in the salad. Meanwhile, we also get Lollapalooza. Give up on it changing your life and take it for what it is—one live music option among many, with the built-in drawbacks of any festival. Even under the worst circumstances—as I can testify as a survivor of Lollapalooza '94's notorious Quonset State Airport stop in Rhode Island—you get a hell of a big bang for your entertainment buck. The '95 bill was criticized for its college-radio predictability, cinched when Courtney Love vetoed Snoop Doggy Dogg on grounds of "sexist/racist lyrical content." But having attended many such gatherings, both Woodstocks included, I swear the last time I saw so much exciting music in one place was at the Monterey Pop

Festival in 1967, before all but a smattering of my fellow celebrants at the Meadows in Hartford were born.

I like the sound of surprise as much as the next living entity. But predictability has its uses. Hole made 1994's album of the year, Sonic Youth has amassed the deepest catalogue in Alternia, Pavement may catch up, Cypress Hill's brawny sonics and instantly recognizable hits could knock out any Beastie Boys stoner, Beck's best-selling 1994 debut remains a hoot, and Elastica's best-selling 1995 debut is sassier than anything by Sinead O'Connor, whom the English girls replaced after O'Connor sanely decided that pregnancy and heat waves don't mix. On the main stage, only aggro-metal indie tokens Jesus Lizard and ska-boy frat tokens the Mighty Mighty Bosstones were questionable. And at the show I attended, the second-stage lineup was first-rate. Having sampled about half of every act except Laika, I'd rank them Moby, Superchunk, Dambuilders, Pharcyde, Geraldine Fibbers, with only the last-named worth fleeing. And hey, Moby and Courtney both praised the Fibbers from their respective stages, so maybe I was wrong.

I mean, the free play of taste is what smorgasbords like Lollapalooza are for. Sure the show could and should have been more eclectic—I would have loved to see Naughty by Nature, Jimmie Dale Gilmore, Tuvan throat singing, or, hell, Mary J. Blige. But I was impressed by how much variation this bill made room for. Not counting the Bosstones and the hip-hoppers, every artist was an exponent of what I call The Roar—the loud, rhythmic, bone-drenching electric-guitar drone that is grunge's gift to our brains, our ear-holes, and our bodies themselves. Even techno shaman Moby, a hardcore veteran who integrates guitar into his keybs, adapted his rave version of this concept to the setting—he interpreted "Sweet Child o' Mine" as a techno song, covered "Sweet Home Alabama," and climaxed with "Purple Haze." In a sense the show was as undifferentiated as pretentious know-nothings always say rock and roll is. Yet in a blindfold test, the most casual fan would have had no appreciable trouble telling these acts' *instrumental sounds* apart.

Evolving folkie Beck fronted a piano-augmented punk band whose healthy willingness to fool around didn't prevent it from making the appropriate noises at the appropriate times. Superchunk also seemed relatively generic, but where Beck's best moments too often involved barely audible words, the Chapel Hill standard bearers regularly transcended themselves in rushing hyperdrive raveups. Both the straight-ahead Dambuilders and the expressionist Fibbers augmented their guitar onslaught with violin. And if Elastica's retro punk-pop Roared mostly by association—this was the only band propelled by its drummer, who banged with irrepressible precision—Hole's pomo grunge-pop epitomized the sonic idea: at once inescapably, sing-alongably catchy and gloriously, unkemptly clamorous, a sound bath that heightened the consciousness as it enveloped the spirit. Courtney also blathered some, natch; eventually, the vigilant Lollapalooza timekeepers pulled her plug and she was carried off by security. But don't let anyone tell you she's not a musician first. None of this melodrama—which seemed somehow expected, almost normal—was as memorable or as meaningful as the focus she applied to the songs of her life.

Hole also covered Nirvana's "Pennyroyal Tea" and the Replacements' "Unsatisfied," perfectly, and played two new songs that traded catchiness for an implosive force that recalled *In Utero* without living up to it. But Lollapalooza's unchallenged masters of the internal-tension Roar remained Pavement and Sonic Youth. Steering away from the theoretical teen anthems no one now doubts they can write, the godparents topped the show with its most avant-garde set, a clanging two-guitar barrage (three-guitar on the new songs where Kim Gordon put down her bass and strapped on a man's instrument) that evoked their symphonic mentor Glenn Branca more than anything they've sold in years. Which was gutsy, but in the wake of Pavement, also artsy.

Pavement played the epochal set that elevated the rest of the day's excellent music into what felt like a utopian fantasy, a double-barreled cornucopia always ready with a new treat on the next stage. Finally in control of their superiority complex, these arch wise guys *projected*. Steven Malkmus emptied his lungs without moving his lips, and the licks he laid on Scott Kannberg's leads combined Sonic Youth's upsetting dissonances with Elastica's sure-shot hooks. Like their records, sure, only shocking in its increased intensity—the next level an ordinary Pavement show doesn't approach.

One of alternative's coziest myths is that it's club music, naturally appreciated in close quarters by a few hundred kindred spirits. Yet except for Jesus Lizard, who I'd never seen before and will never see again, all five of Lollapalooza's main-stage Roarers showed strengths to a crowd of twelve thousand that were absent in the smaller venues where I'd caught them. This is partly because the Roar translates to giant sound systems that muck up more detailed styles—the Bosstones might have been as much fun as their dancer if we could have heard the arrangements. But I also credit the Lollapalooza concept itself, which compels overprotected cult heroes to reach out to curiosity seekers who don't know them from ABBA.

Scoffers note scornfully how indifferently many Lolla acts are received—Pavement got a good hand and deserved a standing O. But that's the way it is in the world of live music options—you pay to hear a few faves and check out the rest, as casually or ecstatically as the synergy between the band and your sensorium permits. At Lolla '95, the star attractions were Hole and—surprisingly until you thought about it with your body hair bristled by their stupendous basslines—Cypress Hill, putting out for strangely normal kids who dug their Buddha/buddah shtick. But most of the curiosity seekers were psyched for one or two other bands as well. And taken collectively this mass of consumers provided the economic base for the best nine hours of music anyone's likely to hear in America this year. Not bad for a bunch of alienated kids who don't know any better.

In several respects, we at Hartford had it lucky. The smallish crowd at the spanking new Meadows shed-and-lawn assured efficient movement, manageable toilet and concessions lines, cooling if uncool sideshow tents, and a clublike intimacy near the second stage. And the seats proved an option whose time has come at a festival that's now more about listening to music than participating in culture, because they preclude a mosh pit. At Quonset last year, the prototypical fan was a betesticled lug who endangered anyone within shoving distance. At the Meadows, the prototypical fan was a not yet glamorous girl who knew the words to every Hole song. Neither is especially, you know, alternative. But the girl is more progressive. And she's also smarter, nicer, and, yes, deeper into the music that Lollapalooza the institution served so well in 1995.

Spin, 1995

Harry Smith Makes History

Anthology of American Folk Music

The best way to understand Harry Smith's *Anthology of American Folk Music*—six vinyl LPs released as three two-record sets by Moses Asch's Folkways in 1952 and digitally remastered into an exhaustively annotated six-CD set by the federal government's Smithsonian Folkways in 1997—is to call to mind two essential concepts of '90s rock. The highfalutin one becomes ever more inevitable as rock gathers history and commentary: *canon*. The other is a fact of commercial life as labels recycle catalogue for CD purchase: *compilation*.

A canon is a definitive body of work. When Columbia University requires its minions to survey specified landmarks of Western civ or the *Spin Alternative Record Guide* names the "Top 100 Alternative Albums," canons are being posited. Because they proceed from aesthetic pleasure, canons are rich and essential repositories of wisdom and inspiration; because they presume cultural authority, canons piss people off. Although many compilations claim to be canonical, even single-artist boxes rarely are, and with multiple-artist jobs keyed to a genre or "concept," we're lucky to get decent music and glimmers of taste or sensibility; the most profitable variation, the soundtrack, is so busy throwing singles against the wall it may not even bother to pretend it's about the movie. Yet soundtracks have been canonical: *American Graffiti* for the '50s, *Dazed and Confused* for stoner AOR. When a serious reissue label like Rhino constructs its *Disco Years* series, say, it effectively reconfigures history. And on 1972's *Nuggets*, which resuscitated galvanic singles by forgotten "psychedelic" garage bands, the visionary critic-musician-compiler Lenny Kaye paved the way for punk.

Yet compared to Smith's *Anthology of American Folk Music*, *Nuggets* could be, oh, Robbins Music's funky and far-reaching overview of sex-show r&b, *Strip Jointz*. At a time when folk music encompassed Leadbelly, Woody Guthrie, tame Piedmont bluesmen, guitar-strumming fellow travelers, and many Alan Lomax field and Library of Congress recordings, Harry Smith convinced the world that it was far weirder and more exciting. The canon he established stretched back to the Middle Ages and forward to the *Titanic* and beyond, but its pivot foot was in Reconstruction, when American blacks finally became free to create an autonomously miscegenated culture that their white compatriots could miscegenate right back. Smith came at the concept not as a scared McCarthy-era progressive, but as a pioneering record collector who was also a painter, filmmaker, and legendary bohemian scrounger. Sifting through his thousands of seventy-eights, he confidently selected, astutely sequenced, and cunningly documented eighty-four sides commercially recorded between 1926 and 1932, most of them for the newly targeted "race" and "hillbilly" markets.

In Harry Smith's 1952, only twenty or twenty-five years had passed—as much time as separates us from *Nuggets*. In one form or another, some of these tunes were still widely known. Several were documented Child ballads; "John Henry," "Frankie and Johnny," and "Stagger Lee" had never left the air; Guthrie had rewritten (and copyrighted) "Washington Blues" as "Lindbergh"; "I Woke Up One Morning in May" closely resembled "On Top of Old Smokey." Yet by the testimony of the countless Northern young people whose lives were changed by the *Anthology*, including musician-annotators John Fahey, Peter Stampfel, and Dave Van Ronk, the virtuosically eccentric sound and arcanely historical content of these recordings, which Smith had chosen for variety as much as anything else, constituted a single thrilling and startling revelation. And this revelation would change American music. It would fuel the coming "folk revival" from the Kingston Trio to Joan Baez and, very definitely, Bob Dylan, and directly impact such '60s rockers as Neil Young, Jerry Garcia, and John Sebastian. It would inspire young explorers to forage the South for more seventy-eights as well as such living musicians as *Anthology* mainstays Mississippi John Hurt, Furry Lewis, Dock Boggs, and Bascom Lamar Lunsford. Traditional musicians who had escaped Smith's net or failed to make his cut would also enjoy belated careers. The bluegrass style that Bill Monroe invented in the mid-'30s spread north because Smith planted the seeds.

So is the *Anthology* that good? Of course not. Nothing that changes one person's life is going to mean as much to the next. Even the folkie faithful didn't like it all equally—different listeners took exception to different tracks, especially the dance and religious tunes Smith classified "Social Music." Anyway, much of what made the *Anthology* so remarkable—not just individual songs and sounds but Smith's commitment to overlaying the surreal on the commonplace—has been absorbed into rock, undercutting the shock factor for a vast new audience that has once again never heard a minute of this music.

Nevertheless, we're talking treasure-house here. I've long adored a few of these artists, notably John Hurt and the Memphis Jug Band. But I'd never heard two thirds of the tracks or a third of the songs, and I can't get enough of them. The remastered set—which properly devotes an entire remastered CD to each of Smith's LPs, which were so subtly structured that cramming three onto two discs would compromise the experience—makes nice archaic background music if that's your fancy. But just about every selection—my chief exceptions would be a murder ballad or two and some Cajun accordion pieces—rewards note-for-note concentration, and at least two dozen (my estimate keeps rising) pack the endlessly renewable grace, delight, surprise, and irreducibility of absolutely classic music. As I was writing this paragraph, Furry Lewis's "Kassie [Casey] Jones" came around again, its riff so fetching and lyric so unpredictable that Smith couldn't resist including both sides. And right after that up popped the Bently Boys' "Down on Pennys Farm." Just a banjo figure and some Bently or other (nobody's even sure they were from North Carolina) talking mortgage and agronomy in a sidelong singsong that manages to be doleful and sprightly at the same time. Gets me every time—in a way the next track, Delta daddy Charley Patton's "Mississippi Boll Weevil Blues," does not.

I could have chosen many other examples, or gone on longer about these—annotators Greil Marcus and Robert Cantwell have recently published major *books* that center on the *Anthology*. But since canons wouldn't be canons if they didn't piss us off, I must add a few impolite observations. The most important concerns race. Smith is rightly renowned for ignoring racial distinctions—the musical and thematic connections he draws transcend black and white (forget brown—Latinos, unlike Cajuns, are absent). In pre-Elvis and *Brown v. Board of Education* 1952, stressing the commonality of Southern music was holy work, and Smith's dumbfounding claim that it took folklorists years to figure out that John Hurt wasn't white reminds us that the struggle against stereotyping can never end (presumably, Hurt sounded too *gentle* to be the same color as Leadbelly). Yet with all Bentlys-vs.-Patton exceptions welcome, I'd say the black music here averages out a notch or two better than the white—it's less repressed, musically and sexually.

I also question Smith's weirdo bias. One reason alt types will take to the *Anthology* is that it's so quintessentially bohemian—when in doubt, Smith went for strange. He obviously had quite an ear—most of the CD era's many multiartist folk concatenations are encyclopedia-dull by comparison. And one reason his choices retain so much life is their access to the passion and originality weirdness can unleash. Prey to no ideology of cash-nexus inauthenticity, Smith insisted on commercial recordings intended for paying customers, and his tradition carriers include an Appalachian lawyer, a Hollywood cowboy, and an obscure Minnesota dance band whose semiclassical theme makes room for a snatch of "When You Wore a Tulip." But I still wonder whether some contented husband-and-wife team—with good ears, of course—couldn't concoct a radically more domestic musical image of the "folk." Maybe not—song feeds off pain, and families generate it. But comparing Legacy's *Joe Franklin Presents . . . The Roaring '20s Roar Again*, twelve terrific pop songs of canonical quality but not pretension, I suspect the balance could be shifted some.

So we needn't believe *The Anthology of American Folk Music* represents the "real" folk, much less the "real" America. It's one compelling and engrossing vision of those chimerical notions—profoundly influential rather than the Rosetta stone. It would appear, after all, that the strains of '60s rock traceable to Jimi Hendrix, Lou Reed, Smokey Robinson, Randy Newman, and the *Nuggets* collective have their proximate sources in traditions that are peripheral to these at best.

But that isn't to suggest for a moment that all those guys wouldn't love the shit out of this set.

Spin, 1997

Getting Their Hands Dirty

Michael Azerrad's Our Band Could Be Your Life

Before I'm overcome by the niggles, let me give Michael Azerrad's *Our Band Could Be Your Life* its well-earned thumbs-up. Here's my rave: While reading this five-hundred-page history of '80s indie-rock, I only resorted to something lighter to avoid putting my back out. All thirteen profiles are page-turners. Azerrad has done so much interviewing that the material will be fresh even for those whose lives these bands were. Though he does "concentrate on the bands' stories rather than their music," his unhedged critical judgments make the stories mean-not-be. And if you accept his precondition that only pure indie acts qualify, it's hard to argue with his choices: Black Flag, Minutemen, Mission of Burma, Minor Threat, Hüsker Dü, Replacements, Sonic Youth, Butthole Surfers, Big Black, Dinosaur Jr., Fugazi, Mudhoney, and Beat Happening. Right, I'll take Meat Puppets, Feelies, Pylon, Camper Van Beethoven, and others over half of them. But except maybe for Camper Van, epitomes of a "college rock" Azerrad references without going into, I'd never claim my faves were as relevant, symbolic, or influential as Azerrad's.

That's only if you accept his precondition, however. And while indies-only may seem a reasonable parameter in a history of indie-rock, note that in the other excellent book on the subject, *Route 666: On the Road to Nirvana*, Gina Arnold links her attraction to R.E.M. to their "independent label." Hmmph, says Azerrad—the eight I.R.S. longforms R.E.M. put out before selling their souls to Warner were "manufactured and distributed by A&M (which in turn had a business relationship with RCA) and later, MCA." Well OK then, although you could also say the Herb Alpert–cofounded A&M was a prototype of artist-owned labels like Black Flag's SST, where five of Azerrad's thirteen bands tarried. And like Mission of Burma's Ace of Hearts, I.R.S. was the love child of an artistic hustler with money, although Richard Harte was a lot shorter on hustle than I.R.S.'s Miles Copeland, whose current Ark 21 imprint has no business relationship with any major known to me. That's why Copeland hooked up with A&M, where he'd already placed his brother's band, the Police—just as punkzine publisher turned label head Bob Biggs took Slash to Warner for a quick cash-in that by Azerrad's rules disqualifies X, the Blasters, and Los Lobos.

From the early '80s, in other words, the majors heedlessly compromised indie-rock's indieness. The music so besmirched tended to be rootsy, like the Blasters and Los Lobos, or at least melodic, like Hüsker Dü and the Replacements, both of whom quickly abandoned the indie cause for Warner—which, since corporations do incorporate individuals, mainly meant a&r goddess Karin Berg and Sire mastermind Seymour Stein, respectively. So Azerrad avoids "relatively conventional" bands like R.E.M., who as it happens provide the spiritual impetus for Arnold's book, a sanely euphoric celebration of a counterculture published in halcyon 1993. His indie-rockers, Azerrad says, "just made sure they weren't part of the problem and fought the good fight, knowing they'd never prevail." And if prevailing wasn't their thing anyway—those who enjoyed the kind of good fight Saturday night's all right for, like the visionary Ian MacKaye, were protecting their own prerogatives rather than challenging someone else's—neither was making nice. All the bands that meet Azerrad's criteria except the childishly contrarian Beat Happening are committed to guitar noise if not rooted in hardcore punk. They're also overwhelmingly male, and they sound that way.

In part because my vinyl chops have seen better days and in part because my fondness for piledrivers exceeds that of my loved ones, I hadn't heard most of these bands in a while, and was surprised at how much getting used to they required. Not that the guitar is dead or anything, but indie-rock as Azerrad defines it generated a much narrower soundscape than we thought

a decade ago. For the most part, though, the judgments I made then hold. I
still prefer Hüsker Dü's *Metal Circus* and *New Day Rising* and sold-out *Candy
Apple Grey* to the grand but ill-recorded sprawl of *Zen Arcade*. I still think
Black Flag made one classic and some compendia. I still prefer Big Black's
piledriving *Songs About Fucking* to its pneumatic *Atomizer*—not only does
it have harder beats and mock tunes, it doesn't have "Jordan, Minnesota,"
based on a totally groundless right-wing child-care scare that Albini believed
proved "everyone in the world was as perverse as you could imagine them
being." I still enjoy the Butthole Surfers' joke EPs and then vacate the van (up
by there the police station will be fine, thanks). I still admire Minor Threat
and Fugazi from the distance they impose. I still think J Mascis is the guitar-
god equivalent of Sir Mix-a-Lot. I still want to fix Calvin Johnson up with
a dominatrix who won't let him come. I like the Replacements a little less
(Paul Westerberg is such a banal adult that his brattiness has aged poorly)
and Mission of Burma a little more (via Sonic Youth's tunings, I think). In
mourning for D. Boon, I overrated the Minutemen's *3-Way Tie for Last*, but
I underrated *Double Nickels on the Dime* when he was alive. I owe Azerrad
for Mudhoney's *Superfuzz Bigmuff*, but he owes me for Mudhoney's *Every
Good Boy Deserves Fudge*. And at this moment in history I love Sonic Youth
to pieces. Even *Confusion Is Sex* gives me a buzz.

Beyond guitars and once again skipping Beat Happening—who serve as
exception that proves the rule, representing the female principle and lo-fi
purism on the road around Nirvana—what unites this body of powerful
music is anger. The anger mutates, and with a few bands, like the passive-
aggressive Dinosaur Jr., it's well-sublimated. But rage is what gives the music
its "edge," as they say, and if blaming it on testosterone would be foolish, cred-
iting it as an attack on social injustice would be utter poppycock. Best just attribute it to the individualism in extremis that has always fueled bohemia—
you know, bad attitude.

The storyteller in Azerrad can't resist how impossible his protagonists
were. Tough, brave, ready to suffer for their art, all that—for months and
years, most of these guys risked starvation in penury severe enough to silence
any carping about middle-class slumming, especially given Azerrad's eye for
interclass (and intraclass) advantage. But that doesn't mean they weren't also
impossible. Greg Ginn was a driven ascetic, J Mascis a lazy asshole. Steve
Albini was Steve Albini (always), Henry Rollins Henry Rollins (as of 1984,
estimates Azerrad, kindly). Ian MacKaye was a control freak disguised as
a ragged-trousered philanthropist, Gibby Haynes an M.B.A. disguised as an
avant-gardist, Calvin Johnson a billygoat disguised as a pussycat. Beyond

Mission of Burma, prematurely departed due to tinnitus, and the Minutemen, ditto due to death, every band here that didn't own a label fucked over friends who did, only sometimes the friends got there first. The cavalcade of egos redefines the concept of the nice guy—D. Boon and Mike Watt debating ideology till they come to blows, for instance, or Thurston Moore & Associates reinvesting specie from their favor bank to become the godfathers of indie.

Azerrad's gift is detail, not overview. Scan his introduction and conclusion and you might never get to the good stuff. So although he unflinchingly specifies the failings as well as the virtues of the indie labels he chronicles, he seems unaware that majors also differ from each other. And although chronology compels him to outline the disappearance of explicit politics from the scene, he can't shake the bromide that "the indie underground reclaimed rock's standing as the sound of a rebellious youth culture founded on deep and far-reaching beliefs"—beliefs that, unsurprisingly, he neglects to articulate. Better if, like Gina Arnold, he'd put himself into the book, describing the hopes, passions, alienations, and disillusions of a fandom that for some manly reason he never fully admits. Indie was a bohemia, like punk and hippie and beat before it—only note how each is more bound up in the business of music than its predecessor. The history of bohemia is full of promoters and self-expressers set on turning art into rent. But the bohemia Azerrad describes is unprecedented in its penchant for entrepreneurship—from small-time impresarios to subsistence road warriors, everybody gets their hands dirty selling music. What he leaves out is who it's sold to—the complex social relationships between seller and buyer that created a new counterculture where, especially toward the bottom of the pyramid, one would often change one into the other. Instead Azerrad falls into the oldest bohemian cliche—the belief that utopia stopped short when yours ended.

On the other hand, what can you expect of E-popping ignoramuses with no idea who (Black Flag guitarist and SST bossman) Greg Ginn even is? Seeking CDs to make my listening easier, I asked a clerk at Other Music where I might find Mudhoney and the Minutemen. He racked his brain briefly, then ventured that the Minutemen might be over there. He pointed to a bin displaying prominent index cards for the Kinks and Neil Young. I had much better luck at Tower.

Village Voice, 2001

A Month on the Town

In the sixty-fifth year of my life on this planet, I went out to see live music every night (or day) of June. The main reason I conceived this project, which many considered nuts, was that I wasn't liking enough new guitar bands. So my professional purpose was to encounter young musicians in their natural habitat. But since the idea of going out is to have fun, I wasn't rigid about this. In thirty days I caught all or most of fifty-two acts and bits of nine others. To start, here are a few things that happened in New York in June—not always the best, but worth remembering.

- A teenage Be Your Own Pet fan danced on the Knitting Factory stage with a basketball under his T-shirt to simulate pregnancy.

- Andrew Geller of the Isles uttered the lyric "We should stop breathing." Or was that "breeding"?

- The art-damaged Excepter wore costumes: curly sombrero, boating outfit.

- CocoRosie's Sierra Casady came out in white shaman paint and white headdress.

- Inspired by such new lyrics as "Got to be real now baby," the !!! crowd at Northsix shouted clever sayings like "Chk-chk-chk rocks!"

- Aging Twilight Singer Greg Dulli reached over an adoring twentysomething in kerchief and glasses to pull a more glamorous girl from the second rank onto the stage.

- CocoRosie, !!!, and the Twilight Singers all had African-American friends do cameo vocals. Nervous, guys?

- 64-year-old Memphis legend Jim Dickinson said, "You've made an old fat man happy" three times in an hour-long set.

- 6?-year-old primal folkie Baby Gramps said, "Moving right along" and then "Got a little number for you" eight times between his third and fourth songs.

- 68-year-old modal folkie Peter Stampfel performed a song about raw sewage engulfing a Hawaiian multiplex while he was there on vacation.

- On the same Friday night, twin titans Ornette Coleman and Chuck Berry played eight o'clock shows fifteen blocks apart. At seventy-six and seventy-nine, they were minding their bedtimes.

- 6?-year-old primal folkie Baby Gramps cadged a bed for the night from the stage of the Lakeside Lounge.

- Nellie McKay autographed a Van Gogh print for the Joe's Pub patron who knew that Paul McCartney wrote "When I'm 64" at sixteen. "Can you write 'To Renee'?" the patron asked. "Is there an accent on that?" Nellie wondered.

- Chloe Sevigny caught Sonic Youth at CBGB. Thurston's mom was in the pit.

- A bunch of guys at the Bowery Ballroom established that the ugliest word in the English language, when chanted in unison, is "Jux."

- Tapes 'n Tapes' Jeremy Hanson earned his sixteen-bar drum solo.

- A twenty-minute Dungen song deserved its ten-minute flute solo.

- The unknown Pterodactyl repeated the same climactic six-note riff for six minutes (at least—it was underway when I arrived). This was so much better than that flute solo.

- Morningwood's Chantal Claret licked the Warsaw microphone and later her bazongas, which she claimed tasted like peaches. Bet they actually tasted like sweat and cologne—unless she meant they tasted like Peaches.'

- A short, slightly stout person in red ski sweater, red ski mask, and black shades lectured Warsaw indie-rockers on the virtues of family and the rigors of touring. Then she removed her mask, turned into an Ape, and pumped organized noise from a Farfisa facsimile for forty minutes.

- James McMurtry got pin-drop silence for an a capella rendering of the second half of "Holiday"—until some dame started arguing with the Bowery doorman. McMurtry's motto bears repeating: "We tour so we can make albums. We make albums so we can tour."

....

"'Live Music Is Better' bumper stickers should be issued," joshed Neil Young in 1980's "Union Man," which he has performed in public precisely once. Two visionary musicologists honor this dictum: Charles Keil, adept of participatory discrepancy, and Christopher Small, who believes all music celebrates the intricacy of relationship. For surprise-craving jazz fans, spirit-feeling gospel fans, and house-rocking blues fans, the primacy of the unique, unduplicatable musical event is a truism. The gig is the sacred ritual of indie rock.

Note, however, that all these music lovers like it live for different reasons. Contingency fan Keil treasures the marginal miss, contingency fan Small the magic mesh. Jazz locates inspiration in the mortal musician, gospel in the celestial divine—while blues fans, not unlike indie fans, romanticize the grotty, beer-soaked venue itself. Where blues fans differ from indie fans—and always have, even down at the crossroads—is that they regard musicians as means to a party, and the party as the goal. Indie fans aren't so sure about parties—or anything else, except maybe their favorite band that month. At their best, they're music obsessives, combining all of the above. At their worst, they're one-upping self-seekers who wouldn't know a good band if it played their student union for three bucks with proper ID. Either way they regard the venue as the crucible of their developing values and personalities.

This process now has its own theorist: indie kid turned bizzer turned anthropologist Wendy Fonarow, whose *Empire of Dirt* proved a stimulating 'tween-set read. Fonarow did her formal research in Britain in 1993 and 1994, and some things have changed—moshing has declined, the guitar relinquished its absolute dominance. But the basic pattern, in which indie is more temporary identity marker than aesthetic commitment, is depressingly stable. The best of Fonarow's many concepts divides venues into three zones. Zone One is the pit, crammed with the youngest, maddest, and most physical fans. Zone Three is the back or the bar, where what the Brits call liggers yap through sets—bizzers, musicians, scenesters, casuals. Also, Fonarow claims, journalists—but not me, or any other rock critic I know. I've been a Zone Two guy since stand-up shows became the norm thirty years ago.

The reason, obviously, is aesthetic. Zone Two is the best place to hear music—and see it, and feel it. Its sensations fill you without overwhelming you. Keil is right about participatory discrepancy—part of live music's excitement is the way it transfigures tiny failures of synchronicity. But this counts for more in the musics Keil loves—jazz, blues, polka—than in rock per se. I go to shows to get a fuller sense of the artist and to augment my experience of the music with other people's cheers and pheronomes. And I go to concentrate, focus, immerse. Invariably I find myself registering new details and making new connections. Usually I have a good time, and every once in a while I luck into an epiphany. I'm a record guy, always will be. But records can't match the exhilaration of the best gigs. You walk home prepared to live forever.

Somewhere nearby you'll find a good-to-bad order-of-preference for thirty-two lead acts (twice I doubled up). The details of the order will surprise some—they certainly did me. But let me emphasize the numbers: eleven great, thirteen good, eight bad. Three quarters of the time, twenty-four out of thirty-two, I returned home from my nutty mission feeling better than when I left. My writing suffered the loss of night hours. The two movies I got to were music docs. Toward the end I really began to miss my wife. And I had a ball.

....

The month began with two bands whose profiles had intrigued me more than their CDs: Afghan Whig prime minister Greg Dulli's white-soul Twilight Singers and the Cherokee-hippie Casady sisters' CocoRosie. The mark of the letch is on Dulli, whose black attire lacks only the waistcoat his ample bay window requires, yet there's fascination in his endangered self-assurance. The ambisexual CocoRosie—prattling model-vocalist Bianca and preening opera-trained harpist Sierra, plus a human beatbox and a shifting cast of bit players—are much more original. Slotting them freak-folk is cheap. But citing Yma Sumac and the Cocteau Twins won't enlighten young admirers who compare Bianca to Billie Holiday because nobody can stop them. Though it seemed an up when CocoRosie quoted Lil Kim's "Eat my pussy right," it was really just a relief—my enjoyment dimmed once I imagined how much deeper an actual hip-hop groove would have been.

Saturday I did some true indie-rock spelunking at the Merc with Nick Sylvester pick Stylofone, an entertaining T-shirted g-g-b-d slotted twixt the overweening button-shirted g-g-b-d Isles and the nondescript hoodies-and-T's g-k-b-d Lions & Tigers. Stylofone have one dynamite gimmick: doubled guitar leads on every

Sara Tavares

Dungen

Morningwood

....

OPENERS GOOD-TO-BAD

Robbie Fulks

Yo La Tengo

Brother Ali

Camu Tao

Gamelan Galak Tika

Flashy Python and the Body Snatchers

Nils Lofgren

Gavin DeGraw

Ian Hunter

Cage

Apes

Garland Jeffreys

Mountain High

Cannibal Ox

Tall Firs

Ryan Adams

Figurines

Rock Kills Kid

Lonesome Doves

Isles

....

TAIL ENDS/BEGINNINGS GOOD-TO-BAD

Pterodactyl

Cataract Camp

Kultur Shock

Man Man

Pink Mountaintops

hook, executed with joyous arena-rock everything-old-is-new. Go see them—but don't expect their DIY EP to shake your sternum or hippocampus. Especially at home volume, records are song-dependent that way, like Tapes 'n Tapes' buzzed-and-bizzed DIY *The Loon*, a disappointment after I admired how the quartet deployed space and dynamics whilst goofing off and going wild at the Bowery. But sometimes records work the other way. I loved how unironically Beirut blasted Kocani Orkestar's "Siki, Siki Baba"—but not their stiff marches, conservatory violins, or parlor vocals. Then I got the album and Zach Condon's lyricism melted my hard old heart. When next our paths cross, I bet I think Beirut are beautiful.

The synth fulminations of Sylvester fave Excepter were why I made the mistake of skipping Sylvester fave Tokyo Police Club, and the main thing I got from the Liars and Dungen was never again. Hoping to put friendly faces on likable CDs, I was carried, wearied, and revolted, respectively, by the drone-prone Black Angels, Brit-hit Futureheads, and lad-mag Morning-wood. Still, the Black Angels' alt-trad groove fit alt-trad Southpaw so comfortably they made the win column easily. So did Northsix heroes !!!, whose drum circles are never hypnotic enough on record, and Dismem-berment Plan graduate Travis Morrison, who proved that the stupid zero *Pitchfork* gave his solo debut couldn't stop him from doing what he does better than *Pitchfork* does what it does. And so, certainly, did Nash-ville teens Be Your Own Pet, who performed the eter-nal miracle of young people pretending their heads are exploding before a "16-and-older" Knitting Factory crowd utilizing fake PG-17 IDs. But Jonas Stein's twisty chops and Jemima Pearl's flailed blonde do didn't make up for their narrow young sonics. So I walked out slightly less sold on their album. The kids walked out flushed, high.

Beirut, !!!, and Be Your Own Pet mounted the kind of hot gigs where the passions of the pit radiate out into Zone Two—the indie ideal, at once communal and exclusive. The Arctic Monkeys started like that three years ago, building word-of-mouth with free demos, till now there's nothing exclusive about them, nor communal if by communal you mean as small as Northsix. But I got more fellow feeling and a better high out of their big square Roseland crowd. The smart money claims, plausibly, that the band's Brit provincialism will cost them Coldplay numbers Stateside, but these bridge-and-tunnel concertgoers were beyond that. Mouthing the lyrics the Arctic Monkeys are one of the few bands to post, they were aesthetes, relating to the songs as songs, with "image" secondary. Just standing there and playing their songs in the classic indie manner—an ethos long since eroded by avant-garde theatrics and populist carnivalesque—the Arctic Monkeys locked down their scrawny sound, pushed the tunes halfway, and got their party started.

Gogol Bordello are less cool about their carnivalesque, for good reason—carnival is the essence of their being. For ninety minutes at Irving Plaza they kicked out the jams, and the rabble they roused roused me. By last November's Gypsy Festival, where they put on an even bigger and longer show, their drum-surfing encore was legendary. This time, watching two dozen willing hands hold the giant parade drum aloft as Pamela Racine and Eugene Hutz clambered on, I recalled the heyday of the New York Dolls, when I assumed unthinkingly that this gift would always be mine. It should be no surprise to anyone that I loved loved loved their show. But next time they interrupt their perpetual world tour, you go catch it anyway.

I just wish I'd memorized their lyrics.

....

With their micro labels and long history on the local circuit, Gogol Bordello are indie rock, but they're also the odd band out so far. It isn't that they're mostly immigrants, or that they're not really a guitar band. It's

Gogol Bordello

!!!

Robbie Fulks

Rock Kills Kid

Be Your Own Pet

Beirut

BEST COSTUMERY

Ornette Coleman

Gamelan Galak Tika

CocoRosie

Rock Kills Kid

Apes

Twilight Singers

Nomi

Gogol Bordello

Excepter

Baby Gramps

BEST SHOWPERSONSHIP

Gogol Bordello

Robert Plant

Les Ambassadeurs du Manding

Nellie McKay

Mr. Lif

Romano Drom

Brother Ali

Stylofone

CocoRosie

Apes

Baby Gramps

that they're O-L-D old: graybeard violinist, middle-aged accordionist, haggard human dynamo (self-proclaimed Chernobyl survivor Hutz, who I fear could keel over any time). This also goes for their audience, which while mostly under thirty was strikingly mixed agewise. I'd cherished the simple hope that Be Your Own Pet and some tyros to be named later would give me a new lease on ye olde vitality. But generational details kept butting in as I followed my druthers.

I caught roughly eight old headliners, at least three older than I am. Five of these were tops by me, only one a floppola, and even he offered unique entertainment: saxophonist Anthony Braxton, who summoned a hundred tubas to open River to River's free Bang on a Can Marathon and got maybe sixty-five. What a spectacle—shiny and dull, pristine and dented, tarnished and in one case rusted, white and nickel-colored and brassy gold, and if there were two alike they were far apart. But gradually a fascinating piece about timbre and volume, with ambient aircraft comping sharp-pitched against the prevailing rumble, became a minimalist endurance contest. "Couldn't they produce a different type of sound?" asked a young professional woman taking the Financial Center air at a table near me. "More celebratory—faster, maybe?"

Sixteen years Braxton's senior, Ornette Coleman did just that. By now his alto sax is as dulcet as a French horn, and in a sonic innovation that shamed Excepter's synth foofaraw the night before, he set a bowed bass to stating tenor themes on ballads. His blue silk suit was smooth too. But when the moment came for the new-thing chestnut "Turnaround," he ripped Carnegie Hall up. At the other end of the old scale—only two of them are fifty yet—Sonic Youth sounded equally beautiful playing *Rather Ripped* in order. You can say it was just that I knew it by heart, but I was critical enough to notice "Turquoise Boy" meandering. The indie-rock godparents encored with Kim singing the twenty-two-year-old "Shaking Hell." That ripped CBGB up.

Take my word, younguns—age seldom sorts out neatly. "Can you fathom that I do this for a living? Forty-two years," boasted fedora-sporting, braided-bearded National steel whiz Baby Gramps directly after dedicating "Dream a Little Dream of Me" to Cass Elliot and shortly after declaring himself an "honorary teenager" in lieu of actually performing "You Can Throw Me in Jail but You Can't Stop My Face from Breaking Out." Yet Gramps's eccentric virtuosity and old-as-the-hills laugh lines reminded me of no one so much as twenty-one-year-old Nellie McKay. Both even did Dylan imitations. Difference was, McKay had better songs, jokes too—where Gramps is a wonder, she's already a substantial artist. Also in the wonder category is onetime Stones piano man Jim Dickinson, only he's straddled generations since before he produced the Replacements—and proved it by encoring with something from Big Star's *Third*, also his record. Like Gramps, Dickinson is a songster who knows blues, but where Gramps is a genre crank, Dickinson just shares a lingua franca with his backing band, a/k/a the North Mississippi Allstars—one of his tradder production credits, but hey, they're his sons. Of the few guitar solos I heard (though they're less verboten now than in Fonarow's period), Luther Dickinson's slide work was up there with Lee Ranaldo's avantisms. But when the tireless Peter Stampfel sought a similar injection from seventeen-year-old Walker Shepard, son of Stampfel's old bandmate Sam, the kid didn't have his parts down, and it hurt. Stampfel's set was never more vital than on Dylan's "I Want You," when the senior partner followed a whispered "I want you" with an intense, high-breaking "so bad."

Although I encountered many accomplished young musicians, including some I hated (will Rock Kills Kid rock Kills kids?), execution counts for more with artists who are old enough to have learned how—the longer one devotes oneself to music, the larger music per se looms in one's identity quest. Enter the unheralded local Ambassadeurs du Manding at comfortable little Lava Gina, who rather than providing the pleasant evening I anticipated sent my wife and me home prepared to explore Avenue C forever. Led by veteran guitarist Mamady Kouyaté, once a cog in Guinea's Orchestra Bembeya National, the four Africans and four non-Africans delighted a small crowd ranging in age from at most twenty-eight to at least sixty-four by integrating Senegalese and Congolese concepts of continuous flow. They also outplayed the rest of June not counting Ornette and Sonic Youth. The youngish, non-African trap and conga drummers were slightly tentative. An older non-African got his balafon on. Kouyaté outshone every guitarist I've named. And the singers were nonpareil: rich-burred old muezzin baritone and then this glorious young tenor in black do-rag, gold chain, and white xl T. One of his jobs, performed with shameless and efficient grace, was to get the banquettes dancing. Guess where I was sitting.

Lest anyone smell world-music exoticism, I'll add that I walked out on be-dreaded beauty Sara Tavares soon after she told us her rain song would end Cape Verde's endless drought. And despite the fat guy who got a bassy thrum out of a milk can and slapped his feet when he danced, I preferred Brooklyn's Beirut to Hungary's Romano Drom.

....

I wonder whether the Ambassadeurs' tenor raps. I also wonder whether Buck 65 raps, though it would have helped if V2 had released *Secret House Against the World*—he gave me one after his Summerstage set, and now his ambitious new songs make sense. But other alt-rappers kept the faith. The old-school party ethic gets a lot of ribbing, which was justified at the Bowery Ballroom's agonized Def Jux showcase, where the crowd was not only ninety-five percent white but ninety percent male: Saturday night and nobody getting laid. Then Mr. Lif called them "party people" anyway and sustained the illusion until prolonged prestidigitation by DJ Big Whiz interrupted his flow.

Lif has one of the best left hands in the business, a hand you can imagine caressing a butt cheek, and musically I enjoyed him as much as Ornette first half. At Irving Plaza nine days later, Brother Ali had a crowd. "It's a spiritual thing to party together, like going to church," he told this much more sexually integrated gathering, who obediently shouted "Huh!" whenever he said "Shut this motherfucker down." Atmosphere's Slug, masterful after years on the road he reports have eaten up his soul, took up where Ali left off, the audience as electric as !!!'s or the Arctic Monkeys' only more united. But after forty minutes he brought on a full band for "God Loves Ugly"—a righteous move, sure, only quickly the crowd deflated, as if the firepower onstage rendered their energy irrelevant. "Live Music Takes Many Forms" bumper stickers should be issued.

Many many. I attended June 24's Arthur Lee benefit at the Beacon out of respect for the uncrowned black king of psychedelic pop and organizer Steve Weitzman. Old artists yes, oldies artists no—if you crave Nils Lofgren's ebullience or Ian Hunter's acerbity, check out Grin and Mott the Hoople and issue "Recorded Music Is a Blessing" bumper stickers. Clap Your Hands Say Yeah lead guy Alec Ounsworth was fab on Love's "Andmoreagain" and a Dylany original. Gavin DeGraw was cute. Yo La Tengo unearthed a glorious Lee obscurity as I knew they would: an American Four garage rocker called

"Lucy Baines." (Sound familiar? Just add Johnson.) Hunter made "All the Young Dudes" a sing-along. Lofgren's long, flashy solo sounded new again. And talented asshole Ryan Adams, who refused to work with Weitzman's pickup band, explained his choice of material as follows: "Of course I would have liked to play Love songs, but some of you may know that it's not in my repertoire to, um, oh never mind . . ." Play anything you didn't write, oh poet of a zillion songs? Asshole.

But the big-ticket house, which wasn't full, had come for Robert Plant. Plant owns any room he enters. He could have fobbed off three Loves, three Zeps, a solo promo, and "Danny Boy." Instead he spent two days with the pickup band, rehearsing a set that honored Lee personally and culturally. The Zeps were early, the Loves exquisite. "For What It's Worth" led to a Hunter-assisted Everlys tune (the Elderly Brothers, Weitzman called them) and "Can't Help Falling in Love." Highlighted was "Hey Joe"—a perfect Zep-Love link, misogyny and all. And into the middle of a psychedelic fantasia Plant inserted "Nature Boy," an inspired evocation of Arthur Lee the L.A. eccentric even if you didn't know its composer was an L.A. longhair when there were no longhairs and its hit version a turning point for black pop pathfinder Nat Cole. At fifty-seven, Plant no longer had his high end. But because the music was new and the occasion felt, he was singing fresh. This wasn't the somewhat automatic mastery of great Springsteen or Stones. It was a lesson in charisma full of near misses and intricate meshes, the most life-affirming thing I witnessed all month. My daughter and I battled the rain at one-thirty a.m. just as if we weren't exhausted.

....

Les Ambassadeurs and Robert Plant astonished on successive nights. Then there was a letdown. Dragging myself to Warsaw after a bad car day in Queens was righted by a delicious dinner in Chinatown, all I really wanted to do was stay home, play records, read Fonarow, and make out. One reason my wife attended all of my top five shows except the one our favorite Zeppelin fan grabbed is that Gogol Bordello, Sonic Youth, and Ornette Coleman were sure shots. But I wouldn't have loved Les Ambassadeurs so freely without Carola. I wouldn't have had anyone to dance with, or to watch dancing alone with a song in my heart.

Fonarow believes the indie-rock identity quest is structured to end with marriage. For her, Zone Two represents a period of reflective aestheticism easing the passage from the adolescent breakout of the pit to the homebound responsibilities of capitalist adulthood. For anyone who remains sentient, however, the identity quest never ends, and music can always be part of it. It's just that in a good marriage your identity is tied up with another person's. My wife attended eight of the thirty-two shows all told—quite a few. Both of us wanted and needed it.

But that final week I was on my lonesome till June 30 yoked two very alt alt-country bards in their forties—Robbie Fulks, a honky-tonk postmodernist proud to entertain "the world capital of secularism and rationality, all right," and the now Cleveland-based Amy Rigby, one of the best in the world at forty-seven, playing South Street Seaport for free in intermittent rain to 150 people. Maybe I would have liked the Futureheads more if I hadn't skipped "Dancing with Joey Ramone" to see them. Carola stayed downtown. She tells me that the woman who kept feeding her friends in front of us vaulted onstage to sing backup on "All I Want." Her name was Sarah and it was a special birthday. Cheered Rigby: "Forty years old and she can still storm a barricade."

Carola got home after I did. She was elated.

U.S. and Them

Are American Pop (and Semi-Pop) Still Exceptional?
And by the Way, Does That Make Them Better?

As exploited most recently by student radical turned Cold War liberal turned Hoover Institution conservative Seymour Martin Lipset, who named a book after it, American exceptionalism got large as part of the anti-Soviet ideology of the nascent American studies movement in the early '50s. To quote two modern scholars, its central assumption is "American culture conceived as a unified whole," or "a homogeneous American mind." But in fact American studies goes back to the '30s—to the unjustly neglected popular culture historian Constance Rourke, the pioneering racial analysts Carey McWilliams and Oliver Cox—and the phrase "American exceptionalism" originated with leftists who wanted to know why we didn't have working-class movements like they did in Europe. Beyond the answers that became standard—the frontier, prosperity, ethnic division—Popular Front scholar Michael Denning unearths one from the forgotten socialist Leon Samson, who believed that Americanism as a belief system pre-empted socialism because its shibboleths—"democracy, liberty, opportunity"—were as enticing as socialism.

It's no wonder American exceptionalism, like pluralism and pragmatism, could be coopted by capitalist frontmen doing business as antitotalitarian freedom fighters. As rock critics know well, capitalism can coopt almost anything. But although I'm sure American studies was a CIA plot, the plot worked because the idea filled a hole. In the instance that impressed me most, the honors program designed to prepare this scholarship boy for the literary priesthood at Dartmouth surveyed the English classics from Chaucer to Hardy while requiring not a single course in American literature.

From abstract expressionism to *Moby Dick*, native art got respect in the '50s. But American cultural life had also been transformed by an influx of European refugees all too aware of how relentlessly Hitler exploited a radio they blamed on a "culture industry" they blamed on the United States. Traumatically uprooted, most of them were overwhelmed and offended by America, though not even Adorno put it as baldly as his rightwing coequal Ernest van den Haag: "Why is Brooklyn, so much bigger and richer, so much more literate and educated—and with more leisure—so much less productive culturally than was Florence?" In addition, Anglophilia still pervaded literary studies, where many fretted along with *Partisan Review*'s Philip Rahv, who in a famous 1938 essay divided American novelists into two camps, each incapable of "that mature control which permits the balance of impulse with sensitiveness, of natural power with philosophical depth": "palefaces" for depth and sensitiveness, naturally, and, specializing in impulse and natural power, "redskins."

A striking choice of metaphor. Maybe Rahv was scared of Hollywood. Or maybe he was sidestepping what's always made America most exceptional of all, to its incalculable benefit and disgrace. *Moby Dick* turns on two interracial relationships, *Huckleberry Finn* on one; a black-white polarity powered *Birth of a Nation*, *The Jazz Singer*, *Gone with the Wind*. And black-and-white has been the storyline of American music since minstrelsy—assuming that you grant white people a share of the agency. After careful consideration, I do. American music was polyglot and that's big—British folk and English genteel, Irish and Italian and German and last but not least Jewish, plus

Spanish slash Latin slash Caribbean. It was democratic, too—by the 1850s "music for the millions," designating a melodically and emotionally direct product that had thrived since at least the 1820s, was a catchphrase. And however much this music trafficked in loneliness, morbid sentimentality, and home sweet home, it also radiated an optimism born of "democracy, liberty, opportunity"—which must have been a white optimism, since for black Americans its preconditions didn't exist.

But with the democracy, liberty, and opportunity of white Americans underwritten by chattel slavery, we're already on shaky ground, especially since, as far as most admirers are concerned, the optimism of American music isn't about the frontier or prosperity or the permeability of the American class system—it's about black people. Maybe "Oh! Susannah" was literally stolen from some plantation, maybe it was a polkafied gloss on William Dempster's "The May Queen," or maybe, as I prefer, it was the impure, multi-determined product of Stephen Foster's conflicted experience and imagination. Don't matter, because it was understood, perhaps even by the many blacks who sang it, as an expression of the African-American capacity for the transcendence we call fun. And while this was clearly a racist construction in the 1840s minstrel show, where faux darkies doing the walkaround were inventing American show business, by the 1890s at the latest it was a conscious African-American aesthetic that whites adapted with gradually increasing sensitivity and skill.

Albert Murray often cites Constance Rourke's conceit that the American was one-third Yankee, one-third backwoodsman or Indian ("redskin"), and one-third Negro, just as Stanley Crouch often cites Carl Jung's observation that "white Americans walked, talked, and laughed like Negroes, while Africans usually think of Negro Americans as dark-skinned white people." Both are passionate about a proposition Murray goes so far as to italicize: "American culture, even in its most rigidly segregated precincts, is patently and irrevocably composite. It is, regardless of all the hysterical protestations of those who would have it otherwise, incontestably mulatto." Murray's no radical, and a prog in a bad mood could slot that idea as an Africanization of the melting pot myth. But in fact Murray has always been a propagandist for difference not just in America but in Afro-America—difference in hairstyle, skintone, mindset. Not all strains of American exceptionalism are coextensive with simplistic notions of "American culture conceived as a unified whole" or a "homogeneous American mind."

The melting pot is a metaphor in which different metals liquefy to form a stronger alloy. For most of us here, that metaphor is over. A replacement beloved of rock critics is the African-American gumbo, that Caribbean-inflected creation of blended flavor and complex texture that leaves larger constituents recognizably whole, and then there's the olio, which is what minstrels called the segment where one variety act followed another willy-nilly. Some sort of gumbo or olio is what became of American studies, now a stronghold of articulated difference and identity politics. And a similar fate has befallen the oldest rock and roll creation myth—the blues-and-country-had-a-baby theory. It was always partial, always about the adoration of rockabilly, about Elvis and Buddy Holly and just for luck Chuck Berry but not Little Richard or Bo Diddley or the Coasters or your favorite doowop group, and pretty soon not Frankie Avalon or the Beach Boys or the Byrds. These days, it's cited uncritically only by musical neocons who deploy the so-called roots genres against the beat-based, the arty, the newfangled, the young, and actually existing black people; or, worse, by those committed to a "rock" that after a bracing immersion in the tarpit redounds primarily to bands of white youths bearing guitars and proud of themselves for liking Jimi Hendrix.

Obviously, the great virtue of blues-and-country-had-a-baby is that it's mulatto. Although it's as American exceptionalist as can be, claiming the American South as the cradle of world popular music, it's also a reproof to all the overviews of the national character whose default American was white—until the civil rights movement forced a paradigm shift. The theory's draw-backs are (a) that its biracialism is too bi, ceding whites a dubious parity and (b) that it ignores two important white precincts: the music business rock and roll rebelled against but didn't defeat or reject, and the bohemia that by 1960 would spark a very different paradigm shift that soon had American folkies following the lead of such English art students as John Lennon, Keith Richards, Pete Townshend, and Eric Burdon.

I wouldn't think of minimizing American music's black-and-white story-line. But I do want to emphasize what in the '60s me and my contemporaries didn't really know or want to know, which is that it didn't begin with Elvis and Chuck. It goes back to young white dancers caught jigging to slave fiddlers in 1690, to minstrelsy and Foster and the integrated Five Points music joint Dickens described in *American Notes*, to Vernon and Irene Castle taking distribution on James Reese Europe's foxtrot, to the many visionary and/or compromised and/or exploitative racial interactions of the so-called Jazz

Age and Swing Era. Rock and roll was merely a major stage in a vexed process that has never progressed in a straight line toward utopia.

In a way, that's also true of the closely related factor I want to emphasize instead: rhythm. Rhythm isn't exclusive to Africans. But that doesn't mean "Oh! Susannah" didn't lilt more infectiously than the Paris hit "Cellarius Polka Quadrille," and throughout the twentieth century African-American rhythms continually gained crossover play while gathering internal complexity and power. In rock and roll the crucial change involves foregrounding. 'Tis oft said that rock and roll worked the upbeat, which it did. But there are many rock and roll beats, and the reason Alan Freed called all of them "the big beat" wasn't that Fats Domino's "The Big Beat" drove harder than Count Basie's "One O'Clock Jump," which it didn't, but that the beat looms so large within early rock and roll's individual compositions, arrangements, recordings, whatever. There's less there to distract from the bodywork at hand—less harmony, less melody, less virtuosity, less content.

Few doubt that rhythm's pop primacy has African origins, but many would deny that they need be African-American—especially U.S. African-American, because the great exception to musical American exceptionalism is the Caribbean. The music of New Orleans, symbolic birthplace of jazz and maybe funk too, is steeped in Haiti and especially Cuba—what Jelly Roll Morton called "the Spanish tinge." Cuba had at least as drastic an effect on African pop as American r&b did. Jamaica jump-started hip-hop in the Bronx shortly before Bob Marley turned reggae into the music of the world's oppressed. And so forth.

Nevertheless, the special history of blacks in the U.S. has generated some formal advantages. Start with Peter van der Merwe's unorthodox argument that structural congruences between African and British folk musics are the great melodic resource of blues, which he believes thrived as much on tune as beat—to which I'd add my own guess that it was American democracy, personified by a poor-white population much denser in the American South than in any Caribbean place, that gave the congruences a fair chance to come together. Moreover, as African-American bluesmen fabricated a cultural identity from memory and oppression, omni-American songsters, minstrels, and composers for hire accessed the melodic resources of what even without them would have been the world's most multicultural music—and the industry developed to diffuse it. Nor did it hurt that American blacks spoke English. Finally, downpressed though they were, African-Americans were also the world's most affluent black population, with unparalleled access, comparatively speaking, to technology, education, and—comparatively speaking—prosperity.

The two other factors also flourished here. Late nineteenth-century Britain had its professional songwriters, as well as a music-hall circuit as lively as vaudeville. But even before the ragtime boom, British songs never traveled as well as their hard-hitting, hard-sold Tin Pan Alley counterparts, and then it was time for Kern and Berlin and Gershwin and Porter and beyond—a beyond that continued into the rock and roll era with the Brill Building and its outposts in L.A., Nashville, now Atlanta. And authenticity, an animating myth in Europe since folk songs were called popular ballads, has always had extra kick in America. In the form of a marketable sincerity that was pop's stock in trade, it was less about origins than unmediated openness of expression. When we grew a folk music movement of our own, sincerity continued to fill in for authenticity, with dire effects corrected by British example—by the reflexive irony of pop bohemians who never kidded themselves that they could become American, much less African-American, and invented their own style of fun pretending to try.

Why should the music I've just abstracted for purposes of argument—altogether omitting such matters as youth, rock and roll's prime identity marker—sweep the world? Obviously there are sociological and economic factors, and I don't dismiss either. But just for fun, let me throw out a more reckless suggestion. Let me pretend that it swept the world because it sounded good.

....

In what is clearly a matter of taste, I feel obliged to call in a food theorist—a pioneer, Sidney Mintz. In *Sweetness and Power: The Place of Sugar in Modern History*, Mintz emphasizes that refined sugar didn't sweep the world merely because people liked sweet and white sugar was the most effective sweet ever devised. But he does recognize "an underlying hominid predisposition toward sweetness." And he's so appalled by the political, economic, nutritional, and gastronomic consequences of that predisposition in England that he momentarily abandons the anthropological open-mindedness he lives by: "The less conspicuous roles of sugar in French and Chinese cuisines," he writes, "may have something to do with their excellence. It is not necessarily a mischievous question to ask whether sugar damaged English cooking, or whether English cooking in the seventeenth century had more *need* of sugar than French." Amazing—a fervent cultural relativist granting the intrinsic attraction of certain flavors, setting some cuisines above others.

In a footnote Mintz hems and haws about how his generalization applies to "sophisticated persons in the West," so I'll hedge too—I only feel comfortable universalizing into the industrialized world. But anyone who's ever giggled at the famous *Saturday Night Live* joke about the *Voyager* space probe—the one where NASA equips the probe with the Declaration of Independence and the Gettysburg Address and musical samples from Gregorian chant to Beethoven to Chuck Berry and the first message from the outer galaxies is "Send more Chuck Berry"—will permit me to wonder whether rock and roll had intrinsic attractions too. Some fresh way of configuring melody to rhythm, first of all. But in addition, perhaps, expressive usages that make rock and roll's values—you know, rebel youth, universal prosperity, untrammeled sexuality—signify on a sensory as well as a conceptual level: getting loud in public, flaunting your accent, expressing your animal nature. It's even possible that in its size and regional diversity, America was uniquely equipped to transform into music a principle now self-evident: that before you try to speak globally you should act locally.

If I seem to speculate too wildly here, I apologize—asked to go out on a limb, I figured I'd better float a notion or two to keep me aloft. Most of us accept the common-sense idea that American music is exceptional, at least in its blues-based forms, and that this helped it go global, and many would dissent from the British claim that rock has been Anglo-American since the Beatles. But nobody thinks this exceptionalism continues uncompromised today. Acting locally, young musicians worldwide have grabbed, stolen, distorted, misprised, and pirated what they wanted and figured out how to get their booty across, to small audiences they know firsthand and bigger ones they can only infer or imagine. That's how Elvis and Chuck did it, and nobody who takes rock and roll to heart could want it any other way.

For twenty-five years I've been an avid fan of Afropop, regarding which I long ago adopted the rule of thumb that Africans who imitated American or European forms were doomed to competence if that, while those who seized them stood a chance of going over the top. But I've also fallen for non-American artists whose music displays far fewer similarities to rock and roll than Franco's or Youssou N'Dour's. This appetite for so-called world music sets me apart from most mainstream rock critics. Narrow-mindedness camouflaged as specialization is one reason journalists aver themselves weary of pop—or, more often, bitch that it's played out. Critically, my experience tells me this is a lie. However much it does or doesn't mean culturally, the music is there. Spending fourteen hours a day listening to it is my definition of nice work if you can get it, and it wouldn't be such a great job if there weren't always more avenues opening up, more small geniuses and cultural byways revealing themselves. In that wide-open context, however, I continue to make an exception of America, notably in two very different genres: hip-hop and indie rock.

Hip-hop's worldwide influence is inarguable—it has clearly replaced reggae as an international language of protest as well as injecting its usages into pop music of every provenance and description. What is arguable is first, whether hip-hop is by that very token American any longer, and second, whether the rise in an increasingly multiracial Europe of the beat-based genre I'll call techno doesn't render hip-hop extraneous. To me the first question seems silly. I've heard compelling hip-hop from France, South Africa, even Greenland. But except in the border realm of trip-hop, the beats of world hip-hop are elementary, smooth, and predictable even when they're highly effective. I'm not just comparing RZA and Timbaland and Organized Noize; I'm talking white guys who can walk that walk, from underground mixmaster El-P to pop superstar Eminem. A paradigm shift could happen tomorrow somewhere—maybe it already has. But hip-hop will likely resemble jazz, which African-Americans continue to dominate musically while the rest of the world chips in.

Techno's claims are not silly. Internationally, electronic dance music is as major a development as hip-hop or for that matter teenpop, now blamed on the American culture industry even though it's based on a European model and was test-marketed there. Techno can be simplistic, if that's bad, all volume and beat. But it's a hotbed of predominantly instrumental innovation and abstraction with an audience ready to follow its every move. Cipher-created, DJ-manipulated, site-specific, multi-versioned, it challenges established patterns of music consumption, and its failure to break out of its subculture here is widely regarded in Europe as proof that Americans are square. If I confess that I've generally found it more interesting to think about than listen to, that's not a critical judgment—not quite. But whether you trace popular music to the industrialized 1850s or the banquet rooms of ancient Egypt, it's always been about songs. Techno is not about songs. It's a longshot flirting with an absurdity to pretend that right on time for the millennium, human beings will suddenly abandon songs. If rhythm is destined to dominate the formal future of music, a plausible surmise, then the rhythm music that understands song form is hip-hop—a verbally explosive music from the nation that's always had a leg up on pop song.

Indie-rock is a more personal matter. The guitar band lacks song's aura of eternity; you'd think it had outlived its allotted time. But since it hasn't, we

can't assume it's obsolete. Pop pundits did a lot of that in 1990, when supposedly not a single rock album topped the *Billboard* chart, and a year later here
comes Nirvana. I don't see any Nirvanas lurking around. But just in case I'll
observe that techno tends to tempt whiz kids away from the guitar option
in England. And I'll also observe that most exceptions, from the pop Pulp
to the postpunk Clinic to the roots-it-says Gomez, do what English bands
have done since the '60s, only more self-regardingly and less educationally—
conceptualize, keep their aesthetic distance. They're in it but not of it, by
choice; they're formalists. In America, where indie sometimes seems like a
synonym for "ironic," the myth of authenticity nevertheless holds sway, so
that some kind of unmediated openness of expression is achieved even by
angular wise guys Pavement and gender-bending hobbyists Imperial Teen.
Moreover, the indie circuit, with its infrastructure of hometown bigshots
and rumors in a van, epitomizes act-locally think-globally, branching out
from the bohemia that rock first drew on and now catalyzes. Bands keep
coming, and the bohemia picks up freshmen every year. College rock, some
still call it.

With forty-eight hours of new music recorded every day, the biggest
drawback of these last generalizations is that my chance of inducing others
to share the experience that grounds them is zero. The destiny of American
hip-hop is manifest no matter how much it's misprised overseas; the destiny
of Amerindie guitar is marginal no matter how many bands tour Europe.
Statuswise, it's less than marginal. Since the dawn of cultural studies, college
rock has never gotten much respect from college teachers, bound up in their
own authenticity myths. And the cachet of U.S. bands has been dipping in
Europe since *Sgt. Pepper* or ELP or David Bowie or the Sex Pistols or Culture
Club or Culture Beat or Afrobeat or ska or zouk or acid house or the Gipsy
Kings or Radiohead or the Bulgarian State Radio and Television Female
Vocal Choir. Our moment is over, and none too soon. We're agents of cultural imperialism as well as the other kind. I have a rule of thumb about that,
too. Any Third World artist wants to attack U.S. imperialism, I listen. When
our silent partners in capitalist depradation render such critiques, however,
I assume turf war. Boeuf bourguignon—yum. MC Solaar—for domestic consumption only.

But this isn't reasoned analysis—just words. Having argued from the historical basics, I've slipped back to where critics live—the realm of taste, sensibility,
rhetoric. While continuing to adduce ideas and risk Latinate polysyllables,
I've made jokes, generalized irresponsibly, gone for the occasional epigram,
slanged around, and indulged in other bits of playful demagoguery. If the

structuralism wars convinced me of anything, it wasn't to distrust language, but rather, I'm afraid, what I pretty much knew already—that language is very nearly all human beings have, that there's no right way to control it, that it's best deployed with love, respect, cunning, and a wild eye. Rock criticism, some of us still call that writerly, public-intellectual approach to pop in this country. The hope is that in matters of taste, style matters. The hope is that if I can't prove what I'm saying is true, which I can't, I can at least induce some of you to think, Hey, he's not such a tight-ass. Maybe I was too hard on Pavement. Or, alternatively, He's not a total philistine. Maybe I should try to hear Pavement sometime.

EMP Pop Conference, 2002

What I Listen
For in Music

People often wonder what I listen for in music, and maybe some other kind of critic could offer answers. Maybe someone trained in sonata-allegro procedure has the discipline to ignore transient pleasures and proceed immediately to structure. Maybe someone who reads music can establish stringent criteria of melodic originality. Maybe someone with perfect pitch applies that standard, poor uptight soul. But like most pop fans, I don't have such fancy equipment at my command. So I don't listen for anything. I just try to make sure that music I like finds me.

For most Americans, this happens on the radio—or, more deceptively because their eyes get in the way, on MTV and the like. Many critics relate to ordinary consumers by continuing to use radio or television that way at times. I don't. I just keep my CD changer filled morning till night, usually—too often, my family reminds me—with recent product. Working from past performance and hearsay and hunches and the charts and what other reviewers say, I process dozens of records a day, many for a second or fifth or tenth time. At the outset I focus in on details only when the music demands it—a rare but treasured occurrence. More often, I wait until I catch myself reacting to a newly imprinted snatch of melody, moving my body or mind to a groove, enjoying a funny rhyme or pithy turn of phrase, humming along, lying in bed with a song I can't pin down ringing in my head.

These are real, renewable satisfactions, and however narrow sonata-allegro connoisseurs may consider them, they touch more worlds than anyone can hope to comprehend. For as long as there's been a popular music industry, its glue has been melody, usually in the foreshortened form called tune. Pop listeners demand tune. But insofar as pop is American music, it's African-inflected music, and most of its key innovations have been rhythmic. So one secret of accessing new pop worlds is to get inside new beats, which can be work—it took me years to truly hear funk-period James Brown, who has proven such a crucial pop source that his beats now sound as natural as the quicksilver bebop phrases that once dismayed swing fans. The other secret is never to forget that the beautiful always mirrors the human, or that being human means manipulating technology. Today, only hopeless fogeys regard punk as ugly or disco as mechanical. In the '70s, both calumnies were philistine cliches.

The immediate reward for letting pop musicians find you—rock and rollers above all, but also folk jokers and country balladeers and hip-hop heroes and African seekers and techno whiz kids and many others—is lotsa fun and lotsa art, all mushed together like they should be. And waiting beyond are the musicians themselves, not as they "really" are, but as they create themselves in music. I've gotten to know quite a few over the years.

Borders Magazine, 1998

II A Great Tradition

Pops as Pop

Louis Armstrong

Like millions of other Americans, I was fortunate enough to witness a Louis Armstrong show once, in the winter of 1959. A college freshman too young to have seen much live jazz, I strode home babbling happily about a concert where the only songs I recall recognizing were "Muskrat Ramble" and "Mack the Knife." Back at the dorm, however, a sophomore called me on my naivete. Armstrong was corny, I was informed, and it must have sunk in, because the next time I listened seriously to Louis Armstrong was in 1975, when Gary Giddins got evangelical about the Smithsonian's canonizing *Louis Armstrong and Earl Hines 1928*.

Giddins's work on Armstrong—particularly his gorgeous 1988 polemic *Satchmo*—initiated the phase of Armstrong appreciation that doesn't worry overmuch about corny. Inspired by Terry Teachout's *Pops* to dare an Armstrong piece of my own, I would ordinarily have peppered Gary with requests for context—I edited him for decades and we remain good friends. But recognizing that he has a horse in this race, I haven't phoned or emailed him since I got Teachout's book. Giddins can scarcely be ignored in what follows. But this one's on me.

Since *Satchmo* is biographical criticism rather than a full biography, *Pops* will remain the definitive Armstrong bio until somebody tops it, which somebody should. Its major competitors, jazz specialist James Lincoln Collier's 1983 *Louis Armstrong: An American Genius* and popular historian Laurence Bergreen's 1997 *Louis Armstrong: An Extravagant Life*, have their uses. But Bergreen loves cheap color and doesn't have much to say about music, and while Collier can be good on the recordings he admires, he doesn't admire enough of them, cultivating a supercilious streak that's doubly unbecoming in such a flat-footed stylist. Both Collier and Bergreen devote the great bulk of their books to the pre–World War II period, although Armstrong lived from 1901 to 1971 and toured till the year he died.

Like Gunther Schuller and many older jazz critics, and also like that sophomore, Collier finds so little "genius" in Armstrong's later music that these proportions make a kind of sense. But in Bergreen they're ludicrous unless he believes hanging with prostitutes and gangsters makes a musician more "extravagant" than dinners with royalty and audiences with the pope. Leaving ample room for Armstrong's impoverished New Orleans boyhood, Chicago and its Hot Five and Seven sessions, the thug-ridden compromises of the big-band '30s, and a long postwar career as an American icon leading the pared-down All-Stars, Teachout's 382-page text reaches 1938 with a 150 to go because he fully respects Armstrong's life and artistic choices. "He was born poor, died rich, and never hurt anyone along the way," said Duke Ellington. "I know of no man for whom I had more admiration and respect," said Bing Crosby. No matter how drastically you believe Armstrong's music deteriorated, he deserves to be chronicled in toto.

Beyond his musical brilliance, what Teachout loves most about Armstrong is his positive attitude. "Never wear the trouble in your face," King Oliver taught him, and without soft-pedaling how hard it was to grow up black and poor in America, Armstrong brought joy wherever he played—intelligent joy, accomplished joy, freewheeling joy, comic joy, sardonic joy. Where Collier magnifies his supposed personal insecurities into a condescending excuse for his supposed artistic timidity, Teachout assumes the obvious: anyone who could rise from Jane Alley in New Orleans to Fate Marable's riverboat band, never mind worldwide fame, commanded a courage few humans ever approach and an ambition few can comprehend. Yet where Giddins risks hagiography for purposes of argument, Teachout doesn't understate this very good man's flaws: his chronic resentments and sporadic rages, his daily gage, his philosophy of philandering, and the terrible credo that united him with the notorious manager Joe Glaser: "Always have a *White Man* (who like you) and can + will put his Hand on your shoulder and say—'This is "My" Nigger' and, Can't Nobody Harm Ya."

Clear, balanced, accurate, fast-flowing, and musically informed though it is, *Pops* is based on secondary sources. Especially since these include previously unmined scholarship and archives, this seems a reasonable biographical method—the novice can start with *Satchmo*, which Teachout praises warmly, then move on to *Pops* for more detail. In a sheaf of raves dismayingly short on new ideas, the only significant objection to Teachout's bookcraft I've found, by David Schiff in the *Nation*, is there to finesse a bigger and uglier issue: what to do when the definitive biography of an African-American hero is written by a vocal neocon whose signature outlets are *Commentary* and the *Wall Street Journal*. Post-*Satchmo* especially, many left-leaning critics are fans of Armstrong's late music—Gene Santoro and Bob Blumen-

thal, to name just two, might have written excellent bios. But Teachout got
there first with something to prove.

....

Emphasizing Armstrong's positivity is fine—keep ya head up, as Tupac put
it. But when Teachout intones that Armstrong "returned love for hatred and
sought salvation in work," he sure does sound like a white polemicist with
dibs on the black role model of his dreams. So hypersensitive to identity
politics that he even spars with sometime conservative Stanley Crouch,
Teachout writes sparingly about African-American artists, especially for
someone who once supported himself as a jazz bassist. Of the fifty-nine
essays in his 2005 *A Terry Teachout Reader*, twenty concern music, eleven
vernacular music, and three African-American music: an essay denying that
jazz is fundamentally African-American, an essay denying that Duke Ellington is a great composer, and 2001's "Louis Armstrong, Eminent Victorian,"
wherein are contained the seeds of *Pops*.

Teachout has the major critical virtue of liking what he likes palpably
and unpretentiously, and—mindful of the cred factor—makes an effort
to transcend ideology. Sure, he's inordinately fond of Whit Stillman and
John P. Marquand. But he also feels such lefties as Aaron Copland, John
Sayles, and Jerome Robbins, and his forthright embrace of popular culture
plainly proceeds from his Missouri upbringing and his own pleasure. As a
left populist skeptical of academic postmodernism and avant-garde obscu-
rantism who stopped dissing the middlebrow mindset decades ago, I often
sympathize. But I doubt that would prevent him from slotting me as one of
those "middlebrow-hating radicals of the Sixties" with a "propensity to deny
the existence of meaningful distinctions between high and popular culture."

I'm not, but let me go on. Of course there are meaningful distinctions
between high culture and popular culture. The important question, which
the word "meaningful" skirts, is whether those distinctions are *qualitative*—
whether what Teachout once terms "indisputable greatness" can accrue to
both, and hence whether it can accrue to Armstrong. And from his Ellington essay, which dismisses Ellington's suites on structural grounds and assumes that Ives's and Copland's mastery of longer forms guarantees their
artistic superiority, I infer that no mere songwriter gets to enter Teachout's
greatness derby—and no mere improviser either. "West End Blues" may be
an "immortal" work in which Armstrong can be observed "descending ma-
jestically from the firmament." But apparently all that means is that he was
a hell of a miniaturist.

To me, this way of seeing things is suspiciously undemocratic. One meaningful distinction between high and popular culture is that there's way more good popular culture—because its standards of quality are more forgiving, because sobriety isn't its default mode, because there's so damn much of it. Since there's so damn much of it, and a lot of that is terrible, it rewards connoisseurship. But its strengths are quantity and variety—democracy.

From this perspective, Armstrong is overwhelming. For years my Armstrong listening was confined to three box sets, a best-of, and an Ella Fitzgerald record: the definitive, four-disc, eighty-one-track, disgracefully out-of-print *Portrait of the Artist as a Young Man*, which I'm still plumbing after sixteen years; the four-disc, eighty-nine-track *Complete Hot Five and Hot Seven Recordings*, which includes twenty-nine *Portrait* keepers; the three-disc, sixty-track *Louis Armstrong: An American Icon*, relaxed 1946–68 material; *Ella and Louis*, which I pull before any Sinatra when I feel like some standards; and the budget *16 Most Requested Songs*, which I play more than any of them. But recently I've been listening with pleasure to half a dozen more—some collectors' items, others a click away: *The Great Summit with Duke Ellington*, the All-Stars-debuting *Complete Town Hall Concert*, the remakes-with-narrative *Satchmo: A Musical Autobiography*, the George Avakian concepts *Satch Plays Fats* and *Louis Armstrong Plays W. C. Handy*, and the gloriously redundant four-disc *California Concerts*. There's more. But these'll probably hold me till I die.

This music is longer on Armstrong's corny/iconic period than on his canonical '20s. Even Teachout, eleven of whose thirty "key recordings" are post–World War II, also lists eleven from 1923–29. They're inconsistent, but at their best the Hot Fives and Sevens are indisputable, although always bear in mind what Smithsonian annotator J. R. Taylor concludes regarding three vivid but contradictory musicological analyses of the eleven-second cadenza to "West End Blues": "The subtle ambiguity of Armstrong's rhythm has—significantly—so far defied descriptive consensus." The only consensus is that rhythm comes first. Armstrong couldn't have invented swing (could he?), but he manifested it so irresistibly that every jazz musician became his imitator, and you'll know it when you hear it. Moreover, that's just the beginning. There's almost as much praise for the clarion unflappability of his trumpet sound, compromised though it soon was by the split lip he held off for forty years; for singing that exhibited, through a rough timbre almost as prophetic as his swing, what Schuller swore were "all the nuances, inflections, and natural ease of his trumpet playing"; and for his devotion to melody, admired no less by Collier the stickler than by Teachout the cheerleader.

Reading description after insightful description, however, I was reminded that jazz critics care more about good solos than good records. Thus they ignore many Hot Fives and Sevens altogether and zone in on the extraordinary elsewhere; thus they neglect Armstrong's raucous shout on the shamelessly simplistic "Georgia Bo Bo" and pretend that Lonnie Johnson's guitar occupies the same universe as the leader's trumpet on "Savoy Blues." My two favorites are well-loved: "Heebie Jeebies" and "West End Blues." But jazzbos, ever appalled by the pop market's thralldom to the demon novelty, attribute "Heebie Jeebies"'s sales breakthrough solely to Armstrong's first scatted vocal. Having just had the theme echo in my head for weeks, I say the tune is the hook, tricked up nicely by the scat and augmented by a shamelessly simplistic lyric. And on "West End Blues," often deemed the greatest record of the twentieth century, Fred Robinson's trombone is generally insulted or ignored, meaning the greatest record etc. includes twelve embarrassing bars—thirty seconds of bad music! Giddins, bless him, believes this "sober trombone solo squired by woodblocks" is integral to a "sensationally varied performance." I myself am certain "West End Blues" wouldn't be nearly as sublime without Robinson's slow walk to the corner store. I'm also partial to the woodblocks.

....

The canonical Armstrong was a singer as well as a player. His singing spread his fame and enlarged his influence, but the playing is what got him canonized, because jazz improvisation is what the canonizers value. So it's not too big a stretch to suggest that as much as his comedy, a free-flowing gift that had its uncomfortable moments, it was his singing that made the canonizers decide he'd gone corny on them. Giddins distinguishes between the young artist-as-entertainer and the older entertainer-as-artist, and although I don't think art and entertainment bifurcate so easily, the difference is clear: the entertainer-as-artist was primarily a singer, master of three or four dozen songs and interpreter of many others. As such, he made more good records in his late period than with the Hot Fives and Sevens. They just weren't as influential.

Armstrong wasn't blackmailed into this. "Singing was more *into* my Blood, than the trumpet," Teachout quotes him as saying, and I say his singing was as remarkable as his playing—only Holiday and Sinatra top him, no rock and rollers at all. "Interpreter" doesn't get it—most of the time, he didn't examine the meaning of a lyric so much as explore the potential of a melody. His shifting rhythms, assured slurs, and unstable note values don't undermine the material, they play with it—fondly, kindly, ebulliently, confidently. Nor did this vocal emphasis, which predates the All-Stars, turn his trumpet into a high-profile accessory of the Satchmo image—as his embouchure slackened, he compensated with a pensive, nuanced economy that Wynton Marsalis reports is harder to replicate than his early virtuosity.

....

All these factors were well in place as of that concert in 1959. Just a kid, I got the ebullience, missed the subtlety, and did a poor job of arguing my case. Insofar as the show taught me anything about jazz, it was by motivating me to play catch-up with my dormmate. Yet the memory never left me—a memory not of jazz or pop, art or entertainment, but of Louis Armstrong himself, a great good man we lesser mortals are still getting our minds around.

Barnes & Noble Review, 2010

Not So Misterioso

Thelonious Monk

Some scenes from my youth. Forgive me.

November 1959, say. Four or five of us sit around the medium-fi record player in Dartmouth's College Hall. Sandy Lattimore, poet son of classicist Richmond and the guy who dubbed me Xgau, is spinning Thelonious Monk's *Misterioso*, recorded live at the Five Spot on Cooper Square in 1958. The special source of Sandy's beaming, chortling delight is Johnny Griffin's tenor solo on "In Walked Bud," which fifty years later remains this fireman's son's favorite five minutes of recorded music.

June 1960. At eighteen, I am old enough to go to bars in NYC. I celebrate abstemiously in the cheap seats of the Jazz Gallery on St. Mark's Place, where the bill is shared—you could look it up—by the Thelonious Monk Quartet and the John Coltrane Quartet. I see Monk many times here. Charlie Rouse always plays tenor, with Monk comping and dancing.

July 1960, as I recall. A British salesman at Sam Goody's advises *Brilliant Corners* over *Misterioso*. Objectively, he's right. I all but memorize *Brilliant Corners*. But in the end I prefer *Misterioso*.

September–October 1964. The Jazz Gallery has folded and the Termini brothers have moved the Five Spot up to the corner of Third and St. Marks. A friend with a nearby sublet spends late evenings outside the club's open windows, listening to Monk. Sometimes we park ourselves on the garbage cans in the St. Marks Hotel next door. Once or twice I pay the minimum inside. Still Charlie Rouse on tenor.

....

I caught Monk live after that, but it stopped being so personal. He was beginning to dry up and rock was beginning to flower; also, I had a girlfriend who countered my impolite distaste for folk music with an impolite distaste for jazz. Only then, two years before Monk disappeared to spend his last six years in silent seclusion, editing Gary Giddins at *The Village Voice* got me back into jazz. A girlfriend who liked jazz helped as well. Monk's "Tea for Two" was on our wedding tape, and *Misterioso* proved a lifetime companion. One could even say Monk is my favorite artist. I have myself.

Yet beyond a few Consumer Guide entries, I never wrote about him. I am a music critic and proud of it. But my formal command of music is minimal, and much of what goes on in jazz composition and improvisation is over my head. In their superb new *Jazz*, Gary Giddins and Scott DeVeaux put an old animadversion gently: "Only by penetrating deeper into the music, to the point where you listen like a musician, can you penetrate jazz's most rewarding mysteries." For a critic whose operative conceit is that he's a fan, this truism can be discouraging. So I perked up when editor Rob van der Bliek introduced the two musicological essays that top off *The Thelonious Monk Reader* by observing: "Verbal descriptions relying on metaphor and imagery have often been more successful in conveying Monk's musical ideas."

Monk has many devout fans and millions of admirers. Among post–World War II jazzmen, his mythic stature is topped only by that of Miles Davis and John Coltrane—Ornette Coleman, Sonny Rollins, and even Charlie Parker don't quite match up. Yet his literature is scant. Published in 2001, van der Bliek's useful collection is already out of print, as are thoughtful studies, translated from the poetic French and the klutzy German respectively, by Laurent de Wilde and Thomas Fitterling. Still available is Leslie Gourse's sketchy, digressive, ill-written 1997 *Straight, No Chaser*, which at least draws on a few interviews with Monk's family, as de Wilde and Fitterling do not. But it's blown away by Robin D. G. Kelley's big, invaluable new biography.

Kelley is a history professor who's written or co-written many books on African-American radicalism. But as a defender of gangsta rap who's serious enough about the piano to own a baby grand, he's not poaching when he turns to music. The meticulously researched *Thelonious Monk: The Life and Times of an American Original* plods some, especially toward the end—Kelley can write, but isn't great at motorvating narrative. Nevertheless, he performs the essential and gratifying task of transforming a deliberately enigmatic eccentric—"I like to stand out, man. I'm not one of the crowd"—into a warm, familiar, flesh-and-blood presence.

Kelley emphasizes that the chapeau-sporting genius who wrote "Nutty" was at bottom a devoted husband and father rooted in a social network dating back to his childhood on West 63rd Street in Manhattan, where he moved from North Carolina at age four in 1922. There Monk lived—except for two teen years in a gospel roadshow and a few sojourns with relatives in the Bronx—until he retreated to the Weehawken home of Baroness Nica de Koenigswater in 1976 and embarked upon his farewell silence. Monk was close to his extended family and a generous friend to many musicians, especially his protege Bud Powell, who eclipsed him for a time—and whose heroin Monk once took the rap for, sacrificing his cabaret card and much of his livelihood for six years in the '50s.

Monk's genius wouldn't have come down to us without the nurturance of three women: his wife Nellie, his patron Nica, and his indulgent, indomitable mother Barbara. But unlike Powell or Parker, he wasn't a sponge—he gave back plenty. Capable of trancing out at the piano for days when perfecting a musical idea, he was also capable of taking care of his two kids when Nellie had to work some job she was too smart for. He was a straight shooter as well as an eccentric. But Kelley also details many bizarre episodes as well as freakouts kicked off by the deaths of people he loved. He's candid about Monk's heavy drinking and lifelong reliance on recreational and prescription drugs. And he explores exactly what kind of nutty he was. Kelley's diagnosis: bipolarism exacerbated by drug use, especially the Thorazine-amphetamine cocktails administered by the Beatles' "Dr. Robert," last name Freymann.

....

While establishing that Monk was observant, widely informed, and often articulate—as opposed to the "emotional and intuitive man, possessing a child's vision of the world" Lewis Lapham fabricated in a typical 1964 profile—Kelley never forgets that he lived above all for music. I wish there was a money shot—a few pages summing up Kelley's phenomenally knowledgeable overview of that music. And many of his observations were anticipated by such critics as, among others, André Hodeir, Martin Williams, and Scott DeVeaux, whose essays in van der Bliek's collection I found especially helpful. Nevertheless, a thorough and compelling picture of Monk the musician does emerge.

Neither self-taught nor formally trained, Monk knew classical music but was immersed in jazz and Tin Pan Alley. He was very much a New York musician and learned a lot, often firsthand, from such Harlem masters as James P. Johnson and Willie "The Lion" Smith, whose boogie strode where Southerners like Cow Cow Davenport and Speckled Red rollicked. For several years house pianist at the bebop hotbed Minton's, he got props from Bird and sometimes Diz, though not as many as he thought he deserved. But he was never the true bebopper Kelley sums up as "running substitute chord changes at breakneck speed." He didn't record as a leader until 1947, when he was almost thirty and Parker and Gillespie were almost famous.

Short-lived in its quicksilver can-you-top-this? phase, bebop was a seismic music that forever opened jazz improvisation to the mold-breaking ingenuity of jazz soloists. But Monk's historical association with the style made his tremendous durability harder to hear. Next to Duke Ellington, Giddins and DeVeaux note, Monk is "the most widely performed of all jazz composers"—based on only seventy copyrights where Ellington notched two thousand plus. He was a hell of a piano player. But as Whitney Balliett put it in the most famous Monk sentence ever written (which Kelley fails to cite): "His improvisations were molten Monk compositions, and his compositions were frozen Monk improvisations." Maybe the whole-tone scales he loved sounded weird; maybe they still do. But because he was such a diligent composer, the structural underpinnings of his music are always there to comfort anyone willing to meet it halfway.

Because Monk liked to take things slow, it's easy to miss how strong he swings at first—many bassists and drummers did miss it, until he explained. But his pulse is always there doing its work. Similarly, the hallmark of Monk's simpler tunes ("Misterioso," "Bemsha Swing," the easy-listening "'Round Midnight") as well as his mind-twisters ("Little Rootie Tootie," "Trinkle, Tinkle," the impossible "Brilliant Corners") is their dissonances, a/k/a harmonies, often augmented by the disquieting silences built into their phrasing. But by now we've learned how pleasurable those tunes are anyway. Proud of his innovations, Monk didn't identify as a traditionalist. But rhythmically and melodically, one reason he sounded so wiggy, so strenuous, so difficult was that he was committed to honoring the best of the past as he told the world how he felt now.

Nowhere is this clearer than in the way this great composer treated pop songs, usually solo or trio but sometimes with horns—to my ears, "Smoke Gets in Your Eyes" in 1954 and "Lulu's Back in Town" in 1964 rank with his most extraordinary group recordings. According to Kelley, Monk seldom tossed these tunes off, often working them out note by note beforehand. Still, the standard mandarin view is that jazzmen resent the standards they're expected to cover and so plot to undermine what British Monk fan Michael James, who I guess never met Nellie, called "the dogma which puts forward a partnership between man and woman as the guarantee of a blissful existence."

Thus Kelley diminishes as merely "hilarious" the same "Smoke Gets in Your Eyes" Martin Williams considers "a recomposition" that strips the Jerome Kern perennial to "its implicit beauty." And thus Williams disparages the notion that Monk would consider playing his first "Tea for Two" "in a corny, ricky-tick style" even though the *Criss-Cross* version seven years later moves slyly in just that direction. As DeVeaux observes, Monk's "affinity for the popular songs he grew up with" is probably "more deeply embedded in jazz as a whole than its most ardent champions might care to admit." But it ran even deeper in Monk himself.

....

So Monk was less "avant-garde" than his scales and structures made him seem. He was an entertainer, too—when he finally began gigging regularly at forty, the little dances he did as his musicians soloed definitely brought in the hoi polloi. But when I look back at myself as the rock critic I had no idea I would become, I still ask myself why I was so drawn to Monk at first, and why I returned so readily when I was ready.

For sure I dug those dances too, but as part of something that is often said but seldom explored. Monk was funny. Really funny—as funny as Bob Dylan or the Ramones. Yet that too was part of something bigger—a knowing, affectionate nod to the variegations of human interaction and imagination that his sense of beauty encompassed. What I treasured most when I saw him live, even more than his tunes and his solos, was his comping—the sharp, sour, wickedly timed notes, chords, and elbow smashes he'd lay atop riveting solos by saxophonists who had struggled for weeks first to learn his heads and then to improvise off their melodies rather than their chords as he insisted. Although there's plenty of humor in cutting contests, this joshing synergy has few parallels in any music I know. As Johnny Griffin told Kelley: "His music, with him comping, is so overwhelming, like it's almost like you're trying to break out of a room made of marshmallows."

Monk's tunes weren't sweet like marshmallows, but they sure were sticky, and one function of his comps was to point players back to the molten core indicated by the title on the setlist. Monk's painstaking compositions, reworked standards, and insistence that his sidemen learn his book by ear so they wouldn't be tempted by the changes—all bespeak a committed melodicism that an eighteen-year-old jazz fan destined to spend his life listening to pop songs must have felt even when he lost the melody himself (which he still does sometimes). As Balliett put it in a quip closely related to the famous one: "His improvisations were ingenious attempts to disguise his love of melody." Of course he re-revised as he felt the moment demanded, occasionally with satiric intent. But I didn't nominate his "Tea for Two" for my wedding tape because I thought he was mocking domestic intimacy. I nominated it because I sensed he knew how to adjust to its ups and downs a lot better than Victor Youmans—or Art Tatum. And also because he was willing to grant the happy couple a catchy tune even so.

Ah yes, Art Tatum. In my view, the anti-Monk. Griffin recalls the night when Monk executed "a Tatumesque run on the piano and my eyeballs and my ears almost fell off of my head," only to hear Monk add, "But I don't need that." Maybe, although listening to Monk's indelicate recorded arpeggios up against Tatum's or Powell's, I wonder how long he could have sustained or varied that run and understand why speed-addled beboppers dissed his chops. What there's no maybe about is that Monk didn't need speed. His bent notes and unlikely fingerings evinced a technique few other pianists dreamed of, and he had power.

Monk's strength in the lower regions of the piano is well understood— Ellington once introduced him as "the baddest left hand in the history of jazz." But jazz chroniclers never seem to mention the singular muscularity of his two-handed attack. Some players—Kenny Barron and Cecil Taylor are two I've found—emulate that muscularity on Monk covers, but even acolytes like Barry Harris and Fred Hersch cultivate a lighter touch overall. Though there must be others, the only album-length exception I know in postwar jazz is by none other than Duke Ellington: his late great Ray Brown collaboration *This One's for Blanton*. But go back to Albert Ammons and Pete Johnson, Willie "The Lion" Smith and Cow Cow Davenport, or fast-forward to any number of rock-era players—Professor Longhair! Jerry Lee Lewis! hell, Elton John!—and you've got a contest on your hands.

No wonder the future rock critic loved Thelonious Monk. He played loud.

....

One benefit of finally writing a Monk piece is that I got to spend a month with the core of his catalogue: his work for Blue Note (1947–52 plus the 1957 Carnegie Coltrane concert), Prestige (1953–54), Riverside (1955–61), and Columbia (1962–68). I'll play most of it again with relish, although there are more posthumous live albums than any nonspecialist needs. But I can make a few observations other nonspecialists may find useful.

1 Most (not all) of the thirty-nine tracks on the two Blue Note *Genius of Modern Music* discs are precious, including the alternate takes (available in more profusion on more expensive collections). But if one stuck to the thirteen on 2005's once budget-priced, now out-of-print *The Very Best*, one would have something like what the title promises.

2 Monk was never recorded more acutely than on Prestige. *Thelonious Monk Trio*, with drumming by both Art Blakey and Max Roach, is his finest showcase as a composer, and not only does *Thelonious Monk/Sonny Rollins* feature Rollins, so does the one just called *Monk*. Boo-yah.

3 There are too many Riversides, and the leadoff album of Ellington covers with which Orrin Keepnews convinced the jazz public that Thelly was a regular guy is too respectful. But *Brilliant Corners* and *Misterioso* (slightly less conclusive bonus tracks included) really do represent a peak, *Thelonious Monk with John Coltrane* is a wonder (don't miss 'Trane on "Trinkle, Tinkle"), *Mulligan Meets Monk* relaxes without ever going soft, *Monk's Music* bends four horns to his will, and *Thelonious Himself*, his first solo album, is probably his best, although some argue sanely for the posthumous Columbia comp. After that there are lesser good ones and some dicey stuff. I am not a fan of the underrehearsed Town Hall "orchestra."

4 John Wilson fairly complained that Monk was "more placid" with tenor man Charlie Rouse, the only saxophonist on the Columbias and the only saxophonist I ever saw him with. But I'll keep playing *Criss-Cross*, *Monk's Dream*, *It's Monk's Time*, and *Monk.* anyway. Maybe even *Underground*.

5   Why wouldn't a person buy *Thelonious Monk Quartet with John Coltrane at Carnegie Hall?*

6   Although it's drawn largely from keepers recommended above, I feel fortunate to own a gorgeously intelligent Monk compilation called *The Art of the Ballad.* Most of the others I can do without.

7   On Tom Moon's say-so a year ago, I purchased Carmen McRae's *Carmen Sings Monk.* The lyrics vary. The performances invariably turn Monk lyrical.

....

Monk played with many titans. Coltrane and Rollins, whew; Mulligan, no slouch; Coleman Hawkins, always a fan; Gillespie, Parker, and Davis, wary bosses. But when Monk took on Coltrane or Rollins or even Mulligan, it wasn't just Monk's record anymore—their voices remained very much their own. So because Monk's songs evolved in his mind and practice, there was an advantage in entrusting them to Charlie Rouse, who came to know Monk's music like no one else.

Rouse was so unfazed by Monk's provocations that you had to root for him, but his own records never take off. He needed Monk's guidelines. Mustering a breathy sound with plenty of grit and body to it, he specialized in down-to-earth solos and sensible ripostes to the big man's outlandish suggestions. I prefer the studio albums featuring Rouse, meaning those Columbias, to the inevitable glut of catalogue-stuffing live ones (try *Monk in France* first), especially because Monk's gigs settled into the half-magnanimous, half-lazy pattern of giving his rhythm players solo room on nearly every number; over many sets, I grew to resent drummer Frankie Dunlop far more than his in-grained swing and subtle shuffles deserved. But all we have of Johnny Griffin's time with Monk is two live albums—*Misterioso* and the less intense *Thelonious in Action.* Never mind *At the Five Spot*, which boils them down to one disc—you need the outtakes. A faster, sharper, and more forceful player than Rouse who's less distinct than the titans, Griffin is my favorite Monk saxophonist.

What's odd about the pairing is that the young Griffin wasn't a ballad guy, while Monk's watchword was "it's really harder to play slow than it is to play fast." Monk prevails, natch, but not without compromise—his Griffin band ups the pace just enough to warm a rock and roller's fundament. Or maybe it's Griffin's irrepressibility making it seem that way, like when he takes off on *Misterioso*'s "Blues Five Spot," with Monk comping cordially for a while before the entire band lays out and lets him loop-de-loop on his own for forty-five seconds. Like every soloist, Griffin had his tricks, mannerisms, and pet phrases. Listening hard, I hear tiny elements of the solo I've so long adored in between 2:21 and 2:52 of *Thelonious in Action*'s "Evidence," and plenty more in his four-minute workout on that album's "In Walked Bud." But let me praise my beloved.

On *Misterioso*, Griffin's "In Walked Bud" solo starts less than a minute in, after a slightly fractured eight-bar piano intro and thirty-two bars of AABA by the quartet. Although Griffin follows the song's structure obediently throughout, he obscures the theme posthaste, and when it diddybops back toward familiarity for a couple of bars festoons it with the first of many high wails. Griffin's tone is mostly smooth and Monk's comping mostly support-ive as a melody more Griffin than Monk yet still "In Walked Bud" saunters and dips and stutter-steps and soars and unrolls till Monk lays out at around 3:00. Then, boom, Griffin goes crazy. Phrasing double- and then triple-speed toward the top of his register while signalling intermittent slowdowns with low r&b honks and blats, he works fast-moderate-fast as if extending a God-touched Sam "The Man" Taylor break toward an infinity lasting three minutes and twenty-one seconds. Monk yells or grunts approval at 3:42, 4:35, 5:38. But at 6:21 he takes over, tweaking an all but straight A theme that he shifts between his playful right hand and his sardonic left for two min-utes. After Ahmed Abdul-Malik wastes a minute twenty on a bass solo, Roy Haynes elicits more of the tune from his trap set than Griffin granted on his sax before the ensemble bids us a loose, energetic unison farewell. Cut immediately to two minutes of solo "Just a Gigolo," a lugubrious chestnut Monk recorded six times and counting. One needs some certainty in life.

Gazing steely-eyed at this solo, which I recognize is not a certifiable peak of Western civilization, I suspect that what really got and gets me about it is r&b elements that were rarely if ever so blatant in Griffin's work as a leader—coexisting here with intimations of free jazz. Somehow Monk, who except for that gospel roadshow was jazz and pop through and through and never gave Or-nette much respect, brought the r&b and the free out in Griffin in what sounds like youthful defiance even if it wasn't. And somehow Monk excitedly vocalizes his approval before restoring his own deeply satisfying order-in-disorder two different ways. No one now questions the musicality of that order. But the gen-erosity of spirit that precedes and nurtures it often goes unremarked. Kelley's vision of Monk's life should make his generosity easier to perceive. But as I'm sure Kelley would insist, it's on record for anyone with ears to hear.

First Lady

Billie Holiday

As with Frank Sinatra, as with Aretha Franklin, as with Elvis Presley, as with George Jones, as with Nat King Cole, as with Sarah Vaughan, as with Johnny Cash, as with Al Green, as with Kurt Cobain, as with—unfortunately, but it must be said—Snoop Dogg, coming to terms with Billie Holiday means penetrating an unfathomable mystery: her voice. To one extent or another this holds for most good singers, and my list—while politely making room for Vaughan and her gravitas in addition to the odious Dogg—is limited by age, happenstance, and personal bias as well as the need to stop somewhere. For instance, it excludes the "classical" tradition, whereas Roland Barthes's seminal 1972 essay "The Grain of the Voice" was inspired by lieder specialist Dietrich Fischer-Dieskau, who Barthes reported "reigns more or less un-challenged over the recording of vocal music," as if Billie Holiday, Frank Sinatra, and for that matter Edith Piaf had never existed. Nevertheless, it is in popular music, so much less stringent as to technical standards and so much more invested in performer mystique, that grain reigns.

That Billie Holiday was blessed with an extraordinary instrument isn't immediately apparent even to those who admire her. As Henry Pleasants put it, she had "a meager voice—small, hoarse at the bottom and thinly shrill on top, with top and bottom never very far apart." And what little she had she wrecked. When I discovered her in 1959, she had died a few months earlier at forty-three, so like most of my contemporaries, I formed my bond with the Holiday rock critic Carol Cooper calls "our lady of perpetual suffering." By the mid-1950s, her timbre often cracked and her melodies sometimes staggered, especially on off-label live recordings like the one I bought. If you'd asked me why I liked her, I would have cited her ability to contain pain (only then I would have made the verb a bald and inaccurate "express"), her sly improvisations (which often prove less radical than that truism implies), and her "swing," a concept that like "flow" in hip-hop covers up a myriad of inexactitudes—Holiday's time in particular is a wonder that resists analysis as unflappably as her sound. These were and continue to be the standard answers, and they're all essential to her matchless achievement. But they don't nearly explain her fascination.

Julia Blackburn's fascination with Billie Holiday began when she was fourteen, at a party thrown by her mother that featured two prostitutes and two people dancing around with their clothes off and an old man giving her the eye and her mother giving the old man the eye. Blackburn "escaped to a far corner" and spent the night playing a 1975 compilation called *A Billie Holiday Memorial*—most of it from the 1930s, the finale from the lush, lost 1958 *Lady in Satin*. Next day she bought the LP, which she's kept ever since. A quarter of a century later, still entranced by "the way her voice could chase out my fears," Blackburn decided to write a book about Holiday. The author of two well-regarded novels and several works of history, she elected to focus not on Holiday's voice but on her life, which for many feels like the closest thing they can get to it. So she contracted with promoter Toby Byron to examine the Linda Kuehl archive: a trove of taped interviews, laborious and sometimes inaccurate transcripts of those tapes, documents, artifacts, and slivers of biography previously accessed by Holiday chroniclers Robert O'Meally and Donald Clarke, although Blackburn is the first to examine more than the transcripts. Kuehl assembled this material over many years. Her plan to write a definitive biography died when she committed suicide in 1979.

Strangely, Blackburn couldn't write a biography either. Instead, in something like desperation, she assembled portraits of Kuehl's interviewees, and these, added together in all their contradictory subjectivity, constitute a portrait of Holiday she's titled *With Billie*. Fortunately, the ploy worked. *With Billie* is a compelling and intelligent book, less in its exposition than in the way it's conceived and assembled. But so are O'Meally's coffee-table "biographical essay" *Lady Day* and Clarke's biography *Wishing on the Moon* and Farah Jasmine Griffin's 2001 *If You Can't Be Free, Be a Mystery: In Search of Billie Holiday*, written without Kuehl because Griffin couldn't afford the fee. All are worth reading, and that is a credit to Holiday's profundity—she's inexhaustible.

Lady Day is where to start. O'Meally, a professor of jazz studies and African-American literature at Columbia, concentrates on music and musters the sanest and fullest overview, detailed and perceptive critically and sympathetic psychologically; he never brushes past her personal faults because he believes they're subsumed by her aesthetic virtues. Pop historian Clarke brings immense factual resources to bear on the most complete picture of Holiday we have. But he's a militant middlebrow, and his confident assertions regarding Holiday's sexuality—she was a "masochist," he avers in a more clinical tone than he has any right to—tempt one to reciprocate ("male

chauvinist" who likes the ladies more than they like him). Griffin's polemi-
cally black feminist perspective is far less mechanistic than Angela Davis's

in *Blues Legacies and Black Feminism*, and welcome in a field of discourse where, as recently as 1997, Leslie Gourse's *The Billie Holiday Companion* included among its twenty-five contributors just one African-American and two women, including Gourse herself. Griffin is both open-minded and hardheaded, as when she observes that the widely disparaged Diana Ross vehicle *Lady Sings the Blues*, based in theory on *Lady Sings the Blues*, Holiday's notoriously inaccurate 1956 as-told-to with William Dufty, inspired a boom in Holiday scholarship extending well beyond the works just cited, thus vastly enriching our understanding of Holiday and her art.

Blackburn's principal contribution to that understanding is a sense of who Holiday's friends were. The interviews about her Baltimore girlhood constitute an oral history of a 1920s ghetto, not such an easy thing to come by; the later materials, which predominate, do the same for the jazz life, which is better documented, and also the sporting life, which is less so. But it's the sum of the documentation that's so impressive. Billie Holiday was a difficult, profane, and sometimes imperious woman. She was a junkie and an alcoholic; she had sex with many men and women; she was hot-tempered and ready to clock anyone who gave her grief. Yet the love emanating from these interviews flows never-ending. Holiday wasn't just adored by her fans, she was adored by her friends and colleagues, and the paucity of backbiting is a clue to her greatness. Most artists are selfish as a way of life, and Holiday would always take what was offered her, especially if it would get her high. But she was also great fun to be around, certainly up till her miserable end and often then, and generous by nature, by which I mean something less showy and manipulative than the impulsive largesse of a Presley or Sinatra. She attracted her circle not with her power or charisma but with her spirit.

To Blackburn's credit, the sporting lifers come through as remarkable individuals: the stepfather who cherished Billie and the stepmother who envied her; the dancer who was her mother's confidant and the good-time girl who was her pharmacist's wife; the pimp and the madam; the two comedians and the five pianists; the white Southern bisexual woman who froze her out and the white Southern homosexual man who propped her up; John Levy the Good who played bass as opposed to John Levy the Evil who played her; the mousy secretary and the slick lawyer who shared her last days; the narc who busted her and still thought he was her friend. Holiday's last husband, Louis McKay, is captured in a brutal taped phone call, and Blackburn adds to Kuehl's roster portraits of spaced-out sweetheart Lester Young and

people-collecting bitch Tallulah Bankhead. She also goes on about the irra-
tionality of U.S. narcotics policy, although she argues cogently that Holiday's
heroin addiction was less severe than myth would have it—she seemed to
kick at will, and even the chief witness for the prosecution, accompanist Carl
Drinkard, who clearly wanted to believe Holiday was as hopeless a junkie as
he was, allows that unlike him she didn't shoot up to get straight: "It was not
just to keep from getting sick; she actually enjoyed using drugs." Although
many claimed she was only happy singing (and many claimed she didn't believe she could sing), Blackburn's Holiday is a woman who enjoyed a lot of
things. As O'Meally concludes, she chose very young to reject the straight
world, and she had a ball doing it.

"People don't think I like laughing. They don't think I lead any kind of
normal life," Holiday complained. And she had a right. By 1957 or so, Holiday's circumstances were bleak. She'd lost friends, she hated McKay as she'd
come to hate all the other toughs who'd turned her on, and with no manager
and an unearned reputation as a no-show, she wasn't getting enough club
work, although Norman Granz had been overseeing some of her greatest
sessions. But as Blackburn and Griffin insist, our lady of perpetual suffering was a reductive sensationalization based on her 1947 heroin conviction,
which was probably a setup. Not that Holiday resisted the cliche the way she
might have. Her autobiography cashed in on her notoriety, and because hard
living—especially alcohol—had roughed up her instrument and sapped her
sass, her late recordings often foreground her pain. Nevertheless, musically
and personally, the transmutation of suffering was never all or even most
of what Billie Holiday was about. Coming up when I did, I used to share
O'Meally's view that the late recordings old-timers disparage were markedly
superior to the music of her twenties—in O'Meally's words, "more nuanced
and evocative." But listening intensively I've come to feel not that their vocal
attractions are somehow lacking, because her voice almost always comes
through, but that they don't laugh enough—even if, as O'Meally makes clear,
they laugh more than I could once discern.

An illegitimate child shunned by the striving family that never fully accepted her, Holiday was a bad girl on principle. She was singing for money
before she left Baltimore at thirteen, but for much of her adolescence she
also worked as a prostitute. The scant evidence is tantalizingly complex,
but from Blackburn and the others it would seem that these two vocations
overlapped—that the pimps and players she liked to hang with dug her
because she could sing, because she took no shit, and because she was a real
party girl, none of which meant she didn't need to earn cash on her back.

Speaking from the naive perspective of someone who's never known or patronized a prostitute, I connect this to the mystery of Holiday's voice—a voice that gives its most exquisite pleasure by taking pleasure, just as what defines a quality hooker is her ability to convince her johns that they get her hot (and who knows, maybe sometimes they do). There's something so casually delighted yet so hip and cool about Holiday's timing, tone, and timbre—so willing, yet so impossible to fool.

The willing part wasn't merely a function of Holiday's soft-edged croon but of her musical attitude. It's invariably said that Holiday torpedoes the banality of the Tin Pan Alley dross she was compelled to sing in the 1930s by transforming the songs' melodies, and one way O'Meally argues for the late work is by laying out how extreme these revisions became. But as Clarke points out, many of the songs were expertly crafted, and as O'Meally emphasizes, Holiday was generally given several to choose from. Moreover, the assumption that to reconceive a melody is to improve it is among other things a rejection of the satisfying structural certitudes in which pop composers specialize—a rejection, that is, of the square world in which things resolve almost but not quite as you'd dreamed. In the 1930s, when she was an optimistic kid—before she turned twenty-five in 1940, she'd already put in stints with Count Basie and Artie Shaw and altered the course of her career by starting to sing (and climax her sets with) Abel Meeropol's anti-lynching song-poem "Strange Fruit"—Holiday showed a more nuanced sense of how to keep her johns coming back for more.

Compilations are the efficient way to access a singer in history, and Columbia has assembled a bunch of fine ones, starting with *Lady Day: The Best of Billie Holiday* and *A Fine Romance,* which cherrypicks her sides with Lester Young on tenor. But dip anywhere into the ten-CD *Lady Day: The Complete Billie Holiday on Columbia 1933–1944*—the outtakes, the air checks, the near crap, anywhere—and you will hear first of all not one of the twentieth century's consummate jazz artists but a dynamite pop singer. Zoom in whenever the fancy strikes you and Holiday will certainly be personalizing the tune with her compliant cunning as she enunciates the lyric in her crystalline drawl. Usually the lyric will be faring better than all the accounts of how she undercuts moon-June cliches would have you believe, and usually the tune will be the thing yet not the thing, a crucial pop mode that long preceded Holiday. But definitely there will be art going on, and definitely it will make your mind go pitter-pat. Lose concentration, however, and your aesthetic emotions will still get a proper workout. Massaged by the unfathomable, they'll give it up to background music.

Please don't think I'm trying to drag Billie Holiday by the gardenia into some quotidian realm she long ago transcended. Every realm is hers, and every good thing people say about her is true. I've learned to love the 1940s Deccas, wish their strings and big bands had gained her the hits she coveted, and I adore the Verves. *The Lady in Autumn* set is the pinnacle of her jazz artistry—evocative and nuanced, breath of my youth and intimation of my mortality. Yet it too shows off Holiday's capacity to give pleasure by taking pleasure. In the 1950s, with narcotics and inebriants eating away at her immense vitality and John Levy the Evil replaced by Big Handsome Spousal Abuser Louis McKay, it's hard to say whether she was an old working girl whose skills had become second nature or a dedicated artist whose best self emerged in song. Probably both, and whatever the explanation, her spirit remains a gift to anyone who'll let it in.

But her spirit couldn't have soared or penetrated without her voice. Throughout her life this was a feel-good voice, easy to listen to in the sense that 1930s guys used to say a doll was easy to look at. Early on its signal virtue is that despite the thinness Pleasants is right to cite, it's also round, firm, even plump and gorgeous—which by an odd coincidence is pretty much how people recall her beauty in those days. Later on it's started to sag, that burnished glow coarsened some. Yet what's underneath the skin—the nerve endings, the musculature, the living flesh itself—remains intact. And always it remains a mystery.

The Nation, 2005

Folksinger, Wordslinger, Start Me a Song

Woody Guthrie

It's a credit to the mythmakers of the Woody Guthrie revival that they've never claimed their hero was the proletarian everyman he sold himself as. Not that they had much choice—well before Guthrie was inducted into the Rock and Roll Hall of Fame in 1988, Joe Klein's *Woody Guthrie: A Life* had fondly but firmly debunked the thank-God-I'm-a-country-boy aw-shucksism the folksinger had devised as an image-conscious man of the people. The son of a small-time Oklahoma real estate man whose luck ran out long before the Depression, Guthrie fit a downwardly mobile mold that turns out misfits like child abuse. He had the gift of optimism, but he knew more spiritual darkness than he let on, and he never resolved his internal conflict between principled collectivism and ragged individualism. He drank too much, he was always chasing skirt, he hit the road at the drop of a hint, and he was possessed by a creative drive so feverish that he left what Dave Marsh estimates as three-quarters of a million unpublished words, including hundreds of unnotated lyrics—mostly from the '40s, when his second wife Marjorie was tracking his outpourings, with many more gone. Yet for all his advocates' eagerness to promulgate Guthrie's political vision, they're decent and aware enough to understand that there's no future for a politics that ignores unseemly complexities.

There remains, however, an unseemly complexity often evaded: his music as music. When the Rock Hall organized its first American Music Masters symposium around Guthrie in 1996, the admirers charged with addressing his leftism or his drawings mentioned that music incidentally if at all. Ace compiler Jeff Place detailed Guthrie's recording history while all but ignoring his singing and playing. And the Hall of Fame guy stuck with specifying his impact on rock and roll (Lennon? Marley? please) found himself in the same pickle as the Smithsonian guy who felt compelled to equate his musical reach with Ellington's, Elvis's, Dylan's—claims so grand they verge on the absurd.

As it happens, music was one interest among many for the young Woody—his biography lacks that signal moment when the hero obtains his first guitar and isn't seen again until he's mastered a bunch of chords. Instead he was a deft cartoonist and draftsman who earned his keep as a sign-painter and specialized in comedy with a local trio where he played mandolin because his buddy was the superior guitarist. And then there were words per se. The author of a lost adolescent psychology treatise who grew up to generate daily columns for the Communist press while pursuing his musical career in L.A. and most fruitfully New York, Woody Guthrie loved language above all else. His writing was pithy, airy, lyrical, acerbic, waggish, imagistic—so word-drunk, in fact, that it didn't always connect up. Not to worry, he insisted reassuringly: "There's no trick of creating words to set to music once you realize that the word is the music and the people is the song." Having long signed his letters "True as the average," he was persuaded by Alan Lomax to churn out the less-true-than-average and therefore mythic autobiography *Bound for Glory* in 1940. Yet he insisted: "I ain't a writer. I want that understood. I'm just a little one-cylinder guitar picker."

For sure Guthrie warn't much of a musician. Proudly inconsistent though he was, never did he claim to pick on two cylinders. His vocal understatement was so far south of catchy that his recordings benefited inordinately when his negligible sidekick Cisco Houston pitched in, and although he liked to argue that the simple old tunes were best because they were the ones folks wanted to hear, he showed small ability to concoct a simple new tune out of them, as has always been folk and pop practice. This is why it's so dubious to equate him with Dylan, who took his ideas so much further—it's like equating King Oliver with Louis Armstrong because Armstrong learned so much from Oliver. Smithsonian Folkways' *The Asch Recordings*, which collects all four of Jeff Place's meticulous reissues in one tidy box, is a fascinating and well-conceived overview of an American artist who surpasses, say, his mutual appreciator John Steinbeck. Just don't imagine it's a one-man *Anthology of American Folk Music*.

Sure Guthrie was influenced by Jimmie Rodgers and Blind Lemon Jefferson and all the songs his crazy doomed mama knew. And when he hit the road, sure he took his guitar. But we see him clearer when we look beyond music for an immediate forebear: fellow Okie Will Rogers. This deeply affable part-Cherokee, like Guthrie a newspaper columnist as well as a performer, became a superstar saying things like "I never met a man I didn't like," "This country is here on account of the real common sense of the Big Normal Majority," and "Don't gamble. Take all your savings and buy some good stock and hold it till it goes up, then sell it. If it don't go up, don't buy it." Guthrie loved him, as he loved Charlie Chaplin, whose impishness he also absorbed; the goofy hayseed he played on the L.A. radio shows where he got his start worked off Rogers's shtick. And though many other '30s entertainers—including Bing Crosby, chief among the "sissy-voiced" jukebox lotharios Guthrie railed against—also drew on Rogers, none of them told friends that the men they most admired were Jesus and Will Rogers, much less named their firstborn sons after him.

But in part because Guthrie carried that guitar, he was never circumscribed by Rogers's model, and he outgrew it. While no conservative, Rogers specialized in a folksy humanism that was pretty soft—Guthrie met plenty of men he didn't like, most of them moneyed. Soon the trouble he saw—and suffered—on his escapes from the Dust Bowl had engendered a radicalism brought to fruition by the analysis and community of the Communist Party's Popular Front. And that wasn't all the CP provided. Especially once he came east, it also gave Guthrie an outlet and an audience for language the way he liked it, language that honored the actually existing plainspeech of the folks whose voices he knew so much better than such perceived rivals as Walt Whitman and Carl Sandburg, touched unpredictably with a word-play so fanciful at times that it prefigured the dementia of the Huntington's chorea that would destroy him. And like Whitman and Sandburg, like Joe Hill and Robert Frost too, but also like all the matinee idols and pop stars he considered enemies of the people, Guthrie chose to project those words through a cunningly fabricated public persona, so that the denim-clad ramblin' man he epitomized ended up inspiring road-dog rockers who've barely heard of him.

No one understood this more profoundly than shape-shifting fame-gamer Bob Dylan, who was as taken with *Bound for Glory* as with any of Guthrie's recordings. It's probably fair to say that without Dylan, Guthrie would have had little impact on rock and roll, and that as it stands he's had plenty. Some of his ideas would have lived on because they weren't exclusive to him—the ramblin' man, the recycled folk melody, the vocal deadpan Wilfred Mellers called his "monody of deprivation," which has lots of relatives in folk and country. But it was the Bob Dylan of a dozen voices who proved once and for all how musical logocentrism could be. Guthrie was a page writer of some distinction. But it was in song—in doggerel shot through with the ordinary, often tuneless yet touched by the natural rhythms and casual eloquence that will rise to the surface of people's speech for as long as they talk to each other—that he found his artistic calling. It was Dylan, however, who took that calling to the next level, convincing rock and roll that popular song's immemorial tradition of ambitious dreamers scribbling verses could go anywhere it wanted. It was Dylan who opened the floodgates to species of poetry good and bad that had more precedents in Guthrie's wilder flights than in the well-honed bon mots of Broadway's highest brows.

I don't want to overstate Guthrie's musical limitations. Alan Lomax praised his "low, harsh voice with velvet at the edges, the syllables beautifully enunciated"—what another folklorist called his "lemon juice voice," Western rather than Southern. And in *Chronicles*, Dylan himself went all out: "There was so much intensity, and his voice was like a stiletto. He was like none of the other singers I ever heard, and neither were his songs. His mannerisms, the way things rolled off his tongue, it just knocked me down." But for this listener Guthrie's recordings will always be too sere, most moving when his monody intensifies his contained rage, especially on political tracts like "Philadelphia Lawyer" and the harrowing "1913 Massacre," or reflects his simple delight, especially on kiddie ditties like "Hanukkah Dance" and the all-American "Car Song." The people's tune stock can only take a fella so far. Struggling to think of an actively lovely Guthrie melody, I came up with "Deportees," then learned that it was concocted by a schoolteacher named Martin Hoffman, who set Guthrie's 1948 poem to music in 1958, two years after its author's hospitalization in Greystone.

With "Deportees," there's a sense in which the word became music after all, and also a sense in which Martin Hoffman, who I hope got his royalties, prefigured Woody Guthrie's musical heyday—namely, the twenty-first century. Starting in 1998 with *Mermaid Avenue*, fifteen lyrics from the archive brought to melodic life by gawky Billy Bragg and adaptable Wilco, Guthrie's words have inspired a musicality attributable to divine intervention if not superhuman language on albums not just by Bragg and Wilco but by the post-Orthodox Klezmatics, the alt-pop Jonatha Brooke, session bassist Rob Wasserman, and leftish bluegrass vet Del McCoury. Part of the miracle is in the songsmithing, as with the direct melodies Guthrie's simple stanzas get out of the normally prissy Brooke. But in Bragg and Wilco's two collections it's also about band sound and rock and roll attitude—the hang-loose irreverence of "Walt Whitman's Niece," the edgy rancor of "Feed of Man," the Child-ballad conjure of "Way Over Yonder in the Minor Key." And equally momentous are the Klezmatics' two Guthrie albums, which with an essential boost from Lorin Sklamberg's lithe, caring tenor situate Guthrie in the New York of his peak, where the aw-shucks Okie made his home and sharpened his wits among Jews, marrying one and consorting musically and politically with hundreds of others. In that New York, he truly became a proletarian everyman—hustling, agitating, thinking, trying to love.

Village Voice, 2000 · Substantially updated and revised

Caring the Hard Way

Frank Sinatra: 1915–1998

Like Elvis Presley, who he despised, and who he outlived by two decades on each end before he died May 14, Frank Sinatra was the only child of a strong mother who preferred him to her handsome, ineffectual husband. Both were macho-vulnerable sex symbols who bought the affections of syco-phants and innocent bystanders with consumer goods and medical treat-ment. But Sinatra was a much classier guy than Elvis, and a much bigger prick. An early crusader for racial tolerance and a key supporter of JFK, he played apartheid-era Sun City and was so turned on by power that he ended up fawning over Ronald Reagan, whom he'd once jeered. Although his con-quests included Marilyn Monroe, Elizabeth Taylor, Judy Garland, Lauren Bacall, Mia Farrow, and the love of his life, Ava Gardner, he also went to bed with a dumbfounding profusion of starlets and prostitutes, not to mention the Mafia. And one more thing—he was the greatest singer of the twentieth century.

Sinatra's voice went through five periods. With Tommy Dorsey on RCA in the early '40s, the sensual sweetness of his baritone made bobby-soxers swoon, but there was uncommon substance there—he was a male inge-nue with character. Without a band crowding him, he got to elaborate this audience-friendly complexity through his teen-idol years on Columbia, but without a band challenging him, he turned into "The Voice," his most physi-cally capable and artistically uninspired persona. From 1948 to 1953, an un-disciplined movie career, a crazed love life, and booze in the fast lane taxed his instrument and his musical resolve. Only after he won an Oscar for *From Here to Eternity* did he have the confidence to invent the Capitol Sinatra. Pushing forty, his baritone lower and a human touch rougher but far more knowing technically and emotionally, he sculpted selected standards and custom-designed specialties into an image of mature, civilized cool that hit the '50s almost as powerfully as Elvis's rebellious vulgarity. On the label he founded, Reprise, he stopped aging gracefully, overextending his genius and privilege through the '60s, which threw him for a loop. Despite numerous superb recordings and increasingly heroic fame, his music never came all the way back. Finally, the erosion of his voice betrayed his technique. Stake too much on physical prowess and old age will whup you good.

Although the philistines for whom Sinatra represents all that is good and holy and tragically past in American pop claim that his taste in arrangers was as exquisite as his taste in shirts, in fact he transmuted most of the timebound professionals he hired the way Elvis transmuted the Jordanaires. But when the arranger was Nelson Riddle, the alchemy was built-in. Like Al Green and Willie Mitchell perfecting soul as its moment ended, Sinatra and Riddle ignored rock and roll to bring to fruition everything that had been happening in their world since big bands put vocalists up front. Instrumentally, the great Capitol albums—*Songs for Swingin' Lovers*, *In the Wee Small Hours*, many more—tailor and accessorize the material with jazz, pop, and classical colors and rhythms while exposing it to Sinatra's vast musical intelligence. Though calculated to the nth, the arrangements sound natural, inevitable—just like the vocals, which were both meticulously studied and subject to last-millisecond shading and beat play. Every note is obviously under his control even when it isn't precisely the one the composer intended. Yet the minute adjustments that led early nay-sayers to accuse Sinatra of singing off-key humanize his awesome attentiveness and command, as do the textured hints of pain that sneak into the timing or finish or timbre or microtonal contour of crucial notes in almost every line he sings. He never makes a mistake, and at the same time he's plainly intimate with failure. His perfection is so total it has room for error. No wonder women fell into bed with him.

Sinatra earned the hold he exerted on the women of his generation. Broads swooned as his intricate emotional specificity created a romantic illusion that in the short run could unlock the door to untold pleasure—while he was singing to them, they could be sure he cared. But this worked better in art than in life—in the long run, which was sometimes measured in hours, he wore many of his literal conquests out. As for his male fans, they were in on the con even though they were rarely good enough for it, quickly discarding women they'd never attended to properly in the first place. It's no surprise that among the post-Presley young he gets a lot more guys than gals. The gals have other ways to get off now—provisional romance is one thrill among many rather than the precondition of any thrill at all. The guys, on the other hand, admire Sinatra because he personified a style and an era in which guys still held all the big cards. And they admire the way he made gross material acquisitiveness seem classy instead of just classbound.

So better to stick to the music, where his compulsive upward mobility never undercut his common touch. Sinatra was renowned for a breath control that evoked both operatic bel canto and Dorsey's trombone, fueling the long phrases that made his singing so magically conversational. But though he was even more legendary for studying lyrics like scripts, those who respect rather than adore classic Tin Pan Alley are more deeply touched by his colloquial ease than his dramatic skill. Sinatra enunciated his words with a casual sophistication that defined his notion of class. But underneath there was always Hoboken, in all its immigrant insularity and street swagger. Where most American pop was spawned from the liquids of African-inflected Southern speech, Sinatra's home idiom was harsh, urban, learned the hard way. And after that it was naturalized and nationalized—bent and weathered by jazz, crispened and universalized by pop. No one better conveyed the worldly wisdom of Cole Porter and Sammy Cahn. But Sinatra's pleasure came in even smaller packages than verse-chorus-bridge. With every phrase, he turned English into American and American into music.

Details, 1998

Like Ringing a Bell

Chuck Berry: 1926–2017

"While no individual can be said to have invented rock and roll," hedged the Rock and Roll Hall of Fame upon inducting Chuck Berry into its 1986 freshman class along with Elvis Presley, Little Richard, Jerry Lee Lewis, Buddy Holly, Fats Domino, and others, "Chuck Berry came the closest of any single figure to being the one who put all the essential pieces together." And of course, the hedge was justified by many factors, among them Presley's pre-eminence and the equally momentous although not purely rock and roll innovations of classmates Ray Charles and James Brown. But now that the man has died—on March 18, unexpectedly, at ninety—let's get real. Chuck Berry did in fact invent rock and roll. Of course similar musics would have sprung up without him. Elvis was Elvis before he ever heard of Chuck Berry. Charles's soul vocals and Brown's everything-is-a-drum were innovations equally profound. Bo Diddley was a snazzier guitarist. Doowop and New Orleans were moving right along. Et cetera. But none of this would have been as rich or seminal without him.

After all, it was Chuck Berry who had the stones and the cultural ambition to sing as if the color of his skin wasn't a thing. Mixing crystalline enunciation with a bad-boy timbre devoid of melisma and burr, he took aim at both the country audience he coveted and the white teenagers he saw coming. Nor did teen anthems like "Rock and Roll Music," "Sweet Little Sixteen," and "School Day" merely play to the kids Elvis had transformed into the next big market. With his instinct for the historical moment, alertness to his fans' folkways, matchless verbal facility, acute autobiographical recall, and delight in America's unprecedented prosperity, Berry played a major role in the invention of teendom itself—in augmenting a generation's self-awareness and turning it into a subculture. He also established rock and roll as a songwriter's medium. Some in his cohort wrote a fair amount, others barely at all. But it was Berry in particular who presaged Buddy Holly, the '50s' second great-songwriter-cum-great-performer. Between them they established the artistic template of '60s rock, where self-written material was a prerequisite. And with the '60s in the mix, consider Chuck Berry's guitar.

Caveats again. Elvis fetishized an instrument that Scotty Moore could actually play, Carl Perkins was a master, and Bo Diddley—not much of a hit-maker but always a legend—was a protean virtuoso. Each guitarist imprinted himself on history, Bo especially. But Chuck Berry was the wellspring as a player and a showman. The two-stringed "Chuck Berry lick" was really many closely related licks. As Gregory Sandow specified thirty years ago, different songs' "fanfares" were distinct—"Maybellene"'s car horn, "School Day"'s school bell, "Roll Over Beethoven"'s minisolo, "Too Much Monkey Business"'s jangling telephone. And although you can discern earlier versions of that lick in T-Bone Walker and Louis Jordan sideman Carl Hogan, it was Berry who had the ears, gall, and imagination to amp a few stray note clusters into a whole music, integrating Ike Turner–style guitar-based r&b and neater country-style picking into a new electric sound that changed everything. For the very different styles of George Harrison and Keith Richards—of, you know, the Beatles and the Stones—Berry's guitar was foundational, and soon there wasn't a rock guitarist anywhere who wasn't imitating his shit. Contrary as always, Bob Dylan was more taken with his groove— the rhythm of "Too Much Monkey Business," he's said, was where he got

"Subterranean Homesick Blues." Chuck Berry: inventor of rock and roll, lodestone of the "rock" rock and roll generated.

Although Charles Edward Anderson Berry got fairly rich remaking the world, which he always claimed was the main idea, he never became a tycoon although or because he was a skinflint who demanded cash payment before he'd join his pickup band onstage. And while key in establishing unalloyed democratic fun as rock and roll's core value, he was too cantankerous to fully enjoy his genius. Born October 18, 1926, which made this mythologist of teen the oldest of the rock and roll originals, he was raised in a lower-middle-class black St. Louis neighborhood by solid, hard-working, musical parents—one sister trained to be an opera singer. Chuck was also musical and hard-working—he won a guitar competition in high school, married for life in 1948, and was supporting a family of four as of 1952. But his bad-boy voice wasn't merely an act. An absurd crime spree involving a fake gun earned him the first of three prison bids in 1944, long before he and pianist Johnnie Johnson hit Chess Records and unleashed "Maybellene" in 1955.

Then ensued what the first of his uncountable greatest hits collections dubbed Chuck Berry's golden decade. But "golden" is poetic license, and so is "decade." Berry was a major star from 1955 to 1959 as well as a reliable concert draw through the high '60s and well after. But though the aforementioned teen anthems as well as the guitar-hero foundation myth "Johnny B. Goode" all went pop top ten in the '50s, not one topped the singles chart. Fact is, all his '50s hits did somewhat better r&b, where he also scored such canonical coups as "Too Much Monkey Business." And in the Beatlemania-fueled 1964 comeback that followed his second prison term, the warmly African-American but also patriotic "Promised Land," a history of the Freedom Rides so subtle few figured it out at the time, didn't make top forty.

That second imprisonment—involving a fourteen-year-old girl he had reason to believe was decisively older and always denied having sex with (but with Chuck Berry you never know)—was a turning point. The first trial was so racist it was disallowed, the second merely subtler about it. But that doesn't mean Berry was innocent, because he was always a very bad boy—cf. the 1986 autobiography replete with bangable blondes, written during the 1979 tax evasion stint where all those cash payments caught up with him, or the 1989 lawsuit alleging that he'd installed peeping cameras in the ladies room of a restaurant he owned, which he escaped with a $1.5-million class action settlement plus a suspended marijuana sentence. Or consider the Keith Richards–instigated 1987 Taylor Hackford documentary *Hail! Hail! Rock 'n' Roll*, which Berry, presented with a once-in-a-lifetime publicity coup, sabotaged by overamping his guitar and demanding extra cash up front. Many stars age poorly, but the fairest guess is that the musically race-less Berry was deeply embittered by an American racism that remained in force despite his breakthroughs—and also a rather unpleasant kind of perv.

Yet although Chuck Berry both missed out on and misused too much of the fun he established as an aesthetic value, the art with which he achieved that transmutation was always playful—sly sometimes, in fact often, but de-void of the meanness that marred his personal interactions, plus he was a funny guy. And for millions if not billions of people, that fun continues to inhere in music that has remained indelible. But Chuck Berry is loved first and foremost as a lyricist, and as a writer I second that emotion.

With no prodding from anyone who's entered the public record, Chuck Berry savored and materially enriched a disreputable dialect of American English. Although he had no particular place to go and never ever learned to read or write so well, he took the message and he wrote it on the wall, and soon the folks dancing got all shook up. From coinages like "motorvating" and "coolerator" to phraseology like "any old way you choose it" and "cam-paign shouting like a Southern diplomat," he was a master of the American demotic, and even after that decisive second prison term, he started back doing the things he used to do. Check out the late diptych "Tulane"/"Have Mercy Judge," a made-up true crime story about a pot dealer who sings the best blues Chuck Berry ever wrote after he gets caught—and turns it into the best love song he ever wrote as well. It's only just that very late in life he not only won Sweden's Polar Music Prize but shared the first PEN songwriting award with Leonard Cohen.

Chuck Berry cut down hard on touring a decade ago. Yet when he turned ninety he announced that in 2017 he'd go on the road to support his first new album in thirty-eight years. For quite a while now it's seemed passing strange that four of the teen heroes in the Hall of Fame's freshman class—Berry, Lewis, Domino, and Little Richard—were living long enough to be knocking on immortality's door. One explanation is that their musical gifts were powered by a pitch of vitality known to few humans. So be sure to check out that new album. It's called *Chuck*.

Billboard, 2017

Unnaturals

The Coasters with No Strings Attached

Most of us treasure pop moments—junctures in time when it seemed that every week brought a new revelation. I was in love with AM radio as well as my girlfriend for most of 1966, and will never forget that spell in 1977 when Bleecker Bob was hawking a new piece of punk every week. But for me, May 1957 was even bigger. In the wake of the Diamonds' "Little Darlin'" and the Dell Vikings' glorious "Come Go with Me," and preceding the August onset of Buddy Holly, May was when we first heard the Everly Brothers' "Bye Bye Love" and Ricky Nelson's record debut and—at least as striking as either—Johnny Mathis's "Wonderful Wonderful." It was also when the Coasters' "Searchin'" blew all of these away.

Jerry Leiber was some lyricist, but the impact was sonic: four mixed-down, oddly harmonized, bass-repressed "Gonna find her"s over Mike Stoller's alley piano leading to the classic Billy Guy vocal. For me at fifteen and even now, that vocal came from nowhere. I can find rough parallels in the Clyde McPhatter of "Honey Love" or the Wynonie Harris of "I Like My Baby's Pudding," in Louis Jordan's ability to sound so delighted with a lyric that he's gonna bust out laughing any second. But those are stretches. The fact is that the singer Guy most resembles is either Jerry Leiber himself—Atlantic sachem Jerry Wexler once claimed that "Billy Guy was a surrogate for Jerry's interpretations"—or Guy's neighbor and discoverer Carl Gardner. Guy's big, clear baritone, so wet its growl is a gargle, shaded at whim into rasp or drawl or slur or even lisp and rose without warning into the slam-dunk falsetto of "Bulldog Drummond." Neither Leiber's intense break on "That Is Rock & Roll" nor his throwaway finale on *50 Coastin' Classics* shows such pipes or timing. But Gardner, though a tenor, still sings "Searchin'" for a living. He was the backbone of the Coasters before they knew their name and took as many leads as Guy in their heyday. It was Gardner, for instance, who lost sleep over the beribboned sex object of "Searchin'"'s B side, "Young Blood," which broke top forty the same week.

That's right, two Coasters songs at once. May 13, Ricky Sings Fats; May 20, Coastermania. Young rock and rollers didn't then know "Down in Mexico" or "Turtle Dovin'" or Leiber and Stoller's productions with the Robins, as the West Coasters were called before half of them migrated from L.A. to New York and Atco Records: for comic social criticism, "Framed," sung by bass man Bobby Nunn; for comic social unrest, "There's a Riot Goin' On," sung by very special guest bass man and future "Louie Louie" composer Richard Berry; and for the premise of a nostalgia-pandering Broadway revue, Gardner's "Smokey Joe's Cafe." So the thrill of their greatest record was pretty hot, and "Young Blood" made it hotter. Bill Millar—whose 1975 biography, along with Claus Rohnisch's well-tended website, is the main source of Coasters facts—has gone so far as to brand it pedophilic: a song about "middle-aged blacks who relished the idea of importuning adolescent girls in the street." A survey of contemporaries of both sexes has failed to locate anyone who recalls taking it that way; two male hipsters who played in racially integrated bands assumed twentysomethings hitting on a teen queen, but most heard kids coming on to other kids, and several shared my initial misapprehension that the Coasters themselves were the young bloods.

Who knew how old they were? Even those lucky enough to catch their live show couldn't tell that Gardner and replacement bass man Dub Jones were both twenty-nine while Guy was twenty-one and Cornel Gunter only nineteen. What we did know was that—on the major hits "Searchin'," "Young Blood," "Yakety Yak," "Charlie Brown," "Along Came Jones," and "Poison Ivy"—they were *representing* not "middle-aged blacks" but teenagers, and not black teenagers but teenagers who happened to be black. If anything seemed old about them, it was the popular culture references "Searchin'" supposedly introduced to rock and roll discourse. With the saving exception of *Dragnet*'s Sgt. Friday, the detectives Guy invoked—Sam Spade, Charlie Chan, Boston Blackie, Bulldog Drummond himself—were staples of Jerry Leiber's '40s youth known to the teen audience from old movies on television or radio shows remembered barely if at all. Like Eddie Cantor and Ed Wynn on *The Colgate Comedy Hour*, "Searchin'" taught high school students that pop culture had a history as surely as Shakespeare and *Silas Marner*.

This was an early instance of vernacular intellectuals' urge to certify as popular their own formative influences—always already dated, like the "cherry red '53" of Chuck Berry's 1964 "You Never Can Tell," or the alt-country on NPR. In the Coasters' "The Shadow Knows," the radio sleuth of the title solves cases television heroes Marshall Dillon and Wyatt Earp can't. One wonders as well how current the black-cultural references Leiber fed the Coasters were—references submerged in the hits but integral to low-life succès d'estimes from "Smokey Joe's Café" to "Idol with the Golden Head" to "D. W. Washburn" as well as the 1960 tour de force "Shoppin' for Clothes." As May 1957 became history, pop music's chroniclers worried about this. In 1970 Charlie Gillett argued that the "indolent and stupid" stereotype implied by Dub Jones's "deep, 'fool' voice" was a tradition of black-on-black comedy, but by 1972 he'd reconsidered: "The trouble with most of Leiber and Stoller's songs is that they describe improbable or incongruous situations and get too many of their laughs from making black clowns out of the singers." Millar lets Johnny Otis, who still thinks he's owed royalties on "Hound Dog," complain at length that Leiber and Stoller "dwelled entirely on a sort of street society." And in 1989, Coasters fan Dave Marsh regretfully concluded that the Coasters' "subtleties and universality" had been "overwhelmed" by "a climate in which covert race-baiting runs the country, from the streets of New York and Los Angeles to our political campaigns."

I had thought scrutinizing such claims might tease out the Coasters' affinities with minstrelsy, but the claims didn't survive much scrutiny. The Game, Condoleezza Rice—these are black people whose role-playing white people have a right to find morally noxious. Not the Coasters, who as per Gillett extend a black comedic tradition—which as Gillett doesn't mention traces back to minstrelsy because show business does. And now Gillett has re-reconsidered: "I was writing before Richard Pryor and Eddie Murphy, before hip-hoppers turned everything on its head in terms of presenting black life in songs, and before Quentin Tarantino start[ed] writing 'nigger' into his scripts for both white and black characters to say," he wrote me. Marsh specifically denies that the Coasters invited racist interpretation in the '50s. And two crucial African-American critics are fans: Mel Watkins, whose history of African-American comedy singles out "Shoppin' for Clothes," which "received scant notice outside the black community," and Nelson George, who gives credit for the Coasters' "deft vignettes" to "two young Jewish men [who] grew up around blacks"—which they did, Leiber as a ghetto grocer's son, Stoller in the kind of family that sent their kids to interracial camps, both as blues and jazz fans who joined black and Pachuco social clubs, respectively, in their teens. So maybe it's time to reclaim the subtleties and universality of an artistic entity specializing in what Leiber once called "the joke that the poor tell on themselves," an entity Greil Marcus reduced to eight words in 1979: "Stepin Fetchit as advance man for black revolt." The Coasters don't get enough respect.

Unlike Chuck Berry, Little Richard, Buddy Holly, and the Everlys, the Coasters were not Rock and Roll Hall of Fame charter members—they had to wait a year for the 1987 batch, which also included Ricky Nelson, Clyde McPhatter, Louis Jordan, and Leiber and Stoller. Nor has their star risen since—not compared to such fellow '87s as B. B. King, Bo Diddley, Aretha Franklin, and Marvin Gaye. It doesn't help that they were comedians—funny never gets respect, because it doesn't give it. And their body of major work isn't large, although neither is Little Richard's or Buddy Holly's, or in any obvious way seminal. The deep reason racial anxieties cut into their status is that they don't seem like primal creators. They permit no fantasy of the natural. The problem is less content than structure—the calculation of the whole project. The Coasters are seen as producers' puppets, like the Monkees or 'N Sync—not only did Leiber plot out every line, Stoller wrote King Curtis's sax breaks. That the concept had white men pulling black men's strings is merely an additional drawback.

As someone who retches quietly at the idea that Stax-Volt was a lost biracial utopia, I refuse to sentimentalize Leiber and Stoller. They were so gifted that their signature product proved inimitable—unlike "Love Me" or "I (Who Have Nothing)" or their other major stroke of genius, the violins they added to the Drifters' "There Goes My Baby," which someone else would have thought of sooner or later, which the Robins tried to get out of RCA in goddamn 1953, but which as a matter of actual historical development was a decisive mutation in the evolution of r&b. But they were also, Leiber especially, incorrigible wise-asses and aspiring aesthetes, hipsters who quit r&b in the late '60s and produced little of interest thereafter. Nevertheless, to disrespect the Coasters is to set exceedingly high standards of racially integrated art. As Nelson George avers and even Johnny Otis allows, Leiber and Stoller wrote their songs from within a black culture they knew intimately and observed acutely—not all of black culture, as if anyone could do that, but the part of it that generated the music they loved most. Inflected by Leiber's incipient pretensions, incongruous associations, and love of radio, that intimacy underpinned even the teenified "Yakety Yak" and "Charlie Brown." And it was turned into music by four strong black men. Eight Coasters all told recorded between 1956 and 1968. But there were just four hitmaking Coasters from 1957 to 1961: Carl Gardner, Billy Guy, Cornel Gunter, and Dub Jones.

Only Gardner is still alive, and only Gardner has left a substantial record—an unpublished autobiography. But the others are clear enough in outline. Bass man Jones was shy and religious yet made for comedy. He first displayed his depth with the Cadets, who anticipated the Coasters' shtick with the 1956 novelty "Stranded in the Jungle," a James Johnson-Ernestine

Smith composition recommended to students of racial stereotyping. Jones quit in 1967 after he contracted fear of flying and was replaced by the title character in Johnny Cymbal's "Mr. Bass Man," Ronnie Bright. Texan-born Guy teamed with a Chicano partner in a successful L.A. comic duo called Bip and Bop when he was just eighteen, and was enlisted by Gardner, who knew him from the block. Endowed with timing and imagination as well as that baritone, he often devised his own deliveries, adapting or overruling Leiber. By the time he was scared half to death by the same airplane incident as Jones, he'd made several solo stabs, and for a while he reportedly earned a living doing blue material in Vegas lounges. Cornel Gunter was an out gay who was built like a prizefighter and served as the Coasters' muscle when things got rough on the road. As the group's best-trained singer, he often corrected the others when they forgot their harmonies, and eventually wrote some voicings himself—on "Shoppin' for Clothes," for instance. He left to back Dinah Washington in 1961 and after she fired him formed the first fake Coasters. Gunter was a notorious liar. No one knows why he was shot to death in Las Vegas in 1990.

As with most musicians, the bulk of the Coasters' niggardly income came in on the road, where their comic polish was hell to follow. Leiber and Stoller never witnessed a Coasters show until well into the '60s and contributed nothing to their routines, which Guy and Gunter usually invented. Not very puppetlike. This wasn't a George Martin–Beatles or Quincy Jones–Michael Jackson situation where the operator with the educated line of patter gets credit for the genius of his social inferiors. Leiber and Stoller were the creators here. The group was their concept, the members their material; Stoller's piano was the linchpin of the Coasters' superb interracial studio bands. But even in the studio Guy and Gunter were collaborators, not stooges. And Guy and Gunter weren't the guys with the big ideas—Carl Gardner was.

If Leiber and Stoller imposed their ideas on anyone, it was Gardner, who will nevertheless celebrate fifty years as a Coaster in November. From a family of self-described "house niggers" in Tyler, Texas—one sister sang opera in New York for a while—Gardner writes in that unpublished autobiography that he learned early on how to get ahead by catering to white people. A born-again Christian now, he once followed Malcolm X into Islam, and he remains a bitter critic of white racism. Gardner moved to L.A. at twenty-five to become a big-band singer. But, he reports, when Robins-Coasters manager Lester Sill told him, "'Either you sing these particular tunes, Carl, or we just have to forget it,' I says, 'O.K. money's first' so I took this group thing." Gardner made side money, although less than the other Robins, as a pimp—one white girl, one black. He's angry to this day that Leiber and Stoller broke their promise to bill the post-Robins "Carl Gardner and the Coasters," not least because it might have simplified all those trademark-infringement suits in the '80s and '90s. Live he was Zeppo, the straight man and romantic lead, and although he dismisses the notion that the Coasters' songs "depicted blacks as ignorant and superstitious," he never gave up his pop dreams. In 1960, with the Coasters' six top-ten hits behind them, he got Leiber and Stoller to let them do a standards album. *One by One* was cut in two days to specially prepared orchestral tapes. As Gardner brags, his rapt, pellucid attack does "Satin Doll" proud, although I doubt Atlantic buried it so he wouldn't do a Ben E. King and go solo, which is his theory. But to my ear, Cornell Gunter is the star of the set, lisp and all.

Gardner's is the familiar saga of a star impoverished by changing fashion, greedy management, and callous royalty disbursement. He obsesses on the parade of fake Coasters—Gunter had some, Guy had some, Nunn had some, an ex-Robin who was never in the Coasters had some, their relatives had some—and overestimates the moneys due him at least as wildly as WEA underestimates them. But late in life he married a woman who rebuilt his career, and he is one of the rare oldies acts who doesn't cater to white people by performing other artists' hits—his DVD offers no "Blue Moon" or "Get a Job," just a "Stormy Monday." If in his perfect world he would have been a big-band singer, he settled for organ-and-horns r&b when he recorded his first solo album at sixty-eight, and at sixty-eight his tenor was too shot to handle "I'll Be Seeing You" or "Don't Let the Sun Catch You Crying."

In all this, Gardner shares much with Leiber and Stoller. Some of the Coasters' greatest records were created after "Poison Ivy" became their last top ten in 1959. Neither "Run Red Run," a minor hit about a monkey who learns to play poker and steals his teacher's car, nor its r&b-charting B side "What About Us," a joke that the poor tell on the rich, quite earns Greil Marcus's "Stepin Fetchit drops his mask, and pulls a gun," but they were pretty redolent. Stoller judges the tent-show fantasy "Little Egypt" "the epitome of the comic playlets." "Bad Detective," "Soul Pad," "Down Home Girl," and "D. W. Washburn" weren't au courant, but have aged well. It's likely one reason "Searchin'" has such irresistible life is that, according to Leiber, it was recorded in the final nine minutes of a four-hour session with the board gone haywire like some Chess mess, making it the sloppiest but also most spontaneous thing Leiber and Stoller ever recorded at Atlantic. And anyone troubled by the unprimality of the pair's control-freak side should compare "Shoppin' for Clothes" to the looser Kent Harris record it appropriated, because its precision tells—it's so much sharper and more developed, so much funnier, maybe even so much truer. Curtis Mayfield listened and learned; the Beatles' rendition of "Searchin'" was why George Martin signed them. Yet as the hits dried up, Leiber and Stoller—who back in 1958 had told *Time* magazine: "Kids nine to fourteen make up our market, we're tired of writing rock 'n' roll, but we can't stop"—decided to stop. Carl Gardner had his pop dreams, and they had their art dreams. There was Peggy Lee's "Is That All There Is?" Then there was that Joan Morris and William Bolcom album—"Either a different, more conservative kind of art," John Rockwell observed in 1978, or "inflated and pretentious overreaching on the part of songwriters who should have stuck with simpler forms."

Fact is, both Leiber and Stoller and Carl Gardner were best when, as Leiber described his ideal pianist in "That Is Rock & Roll," they played "between the cracks." Is the monkey in "Run Red Run" Nat Turner or John Muhammad—or J. Fred Muggs? Is the protagonist of the Coasters' crudest hit sneaking a cigarette or setting a trash-can fire? "Charlie Brown"'s crap game is a cheap move, a big fat slice of watermelon foisted on Dub Jones's Charlie—who, whatever his vocal affect, is no more black than Dub Jones's Salty Sam, the six-reeler villain bedeviled by a white-on-white cliche who shares Dub's surname in "Along Came Jones." At worst, Charlie is a trouble-making goof-off who happens to be black, a small-time teen hero whose "Why's everybody always pickin' on me" is as universal as his slow walk. Once he's out there, of course, he's ripe for reinterpretation. In my life, "Charlie Brown" provided the beat to which a Vermont tent-show queen—white, weary, with a scar on her tummy and no rubies in sight—gave me my first disquieting glimpse of vulva.

There really is a street society, and whatever its limitations, in the '50s it was a crucial corrective to postwar fantasies of domesticity. Its African-American variant lured Carl Gardner the sometime pimp as well as Jerry Leiber the sometime slummer. It is to the credit of all those who created the Coasters, black and white, that their version of that society deployed racial stereotypes with the purpose of muddling them, turning them into jokes that have no end—because that's so much more bearable than a tragedy that has no end. We know, because the tragedy is far from over.

EMP Pop Conference, 2005

Black Elvis

Sam Cooke

I note with interest that Peter Guralnick has taken over rock history's Sam Cooke concession. It's Guralnick who annotated the specially re-mastered thirty-track centerpiece of Abkco's new Cooke campaign, the career-spanning *Portrait of a Legend 1951–1964*, as well as 2001's progress-proving *Keep Movin' On*, the remastered *Sam Cooke at the Copa*, and others. He also scripted Abkco's seventy-minute biographical DVD *Legend*, and his ink-and-paper biography should appear in 2004. Guralnick being award-winning Elvis biographer Guralnick, I assume his book will supplant Daniel Wolff's authoritative 1995 *You Send Me*—whatever our procedural disagreements, he is a dogged researcher and an engrossing storyteller. Some will hope he ties up the loose ends of Cooke's ugly death in 1964, when he was shot by a motel manager after being robbed by a prostitute, but I want dirt on Guralnick's quondam business associate, Abkco acronymsake Allen B. Klein. I also wonder whether this principled resister of critical fancy will venture any Presley analogies. Wolff doesn't, and neither, Lord knows, does Arthur Kempton, who bases a long section of his eccentric new r&b history *Boogaloo* on Wolff's work. But listening to Cooke as I read Wolff and Kempton, I found the similarities inescapable.

Wolff does observe that Cooke's appeal to black teenagers paralleled Elvis's appeal to white ones, which is fundamental, although the equivalence wasn't precise—where Elvis impressed male fans as well as arousing the girls, Cooke was pure heartthrob. He was just nineteen in 1951, when he replaced thirty-four-year-old Rebert Harris in the Soul Stirrers after Harris had forged them into the definitive gospel quartet. Not until 1953 did he conquer the churches by devising his so-called yodel—the casually fluttered high note that surfaced pop on "You Send Me" in 1957. Yet from the first, other Soul Stirrers noticed that even when he was outsung, which was often, the crowd flocked to this handsome, polite, well-groomed high school graduate: "They like the boy. You can't help but people like him!" And from the first he was attracting females much younger than the church ladies it was gospel's mission to transport.

For many admirers, Cooke's gospel phase, which lasted almost as long as his pop career, sets a standard. Hyperbolic sage-entrepreneur Jerry Wexler, who once called Cooke "the best singer who ever lived, no contest," supposedly (I don't believe it) refuses to listen to his pop records. Kempton prefers Cooke's gospel work—"the only emotional content he could rely on to give his singing more depth, honesty, and coloration than he could otherwise provide"—without pretending it approaches that of Rebert Harris, Julius Cheeks, Archie Brownlee, or others Wexler doesn't mention. Among the rock-oriented, it's a truism that in his final years, culminating with the magnificent "A Change Is Gonna Come," Cooke was returning to the rough authenticity of the Southern church, promising newer and greater triumphs in the soul years up the road as he read through his extensive black-history library and explicitly embraced the civil rights movement. But this judgment misses what was most profound about Sam Cooke: his shallowness.

Take Cooke's 1955 live version of the self-penned gospel hit "Nearer to Thee," which climaxes Specialty's three-disc *Sam Cooke with the Soul Stirrers*. His voice generating the grit he normally left to hard lead Paul Foster, Cooke whips up cathartic release in a classic performance whose excitement is nonetheless generic; Cheeks achieved something similar every night without trying so hard. In contrast, "You Send Me"—an all but lyricless song I heartily disliked as a fifteen-year-old and don't love now—was something never heard before. It was the B side of a major-key cover of "Summertime" because no one credited the commercial potential of a record that delivered nothing but Cooke's naked voice—its lucid calm, built-in smile, and mildly melismatic whoa-oh-oh-oh-oh-oh-oh. Backup singers so white they make Presley's Jordanaires seem hep rendered the dumb concoction even weirder by accentuating the likelihood that this wimp was a Negro. Flipped instantly by r&b jocks, it was a chart-topping pop smash nationwide.

Professionally—until he ran up against Klein, who put himself in control of the holding company supposedly set up to keep RCA away from his client's money—Cooke was a prodigy. He produced himself, owned his own publishing, started a successful label, and earned top dollar on the road. Thus it computes for Kempton to observe that he "was cautious in his art so that he might be daring in the conception of his life"—Cooke's much-bruited songwriting ability, Kempton complains, was good mostly for "facile ditties." But in the end this misses the point almost as thoroughly as encomia to his unalloyed genius. One writer who grasps the paradox is Stephan Talty, who in a striking *First of the Month* essay calls "You Send Me" "a masterpiece of nothingness," identifies the secret of Cooke's gospel singing as joy without reverence, and devotes more than four hundred words to "Chain Gang," which everyone knows is one of the strangest pop records of all time: a black-history buff moved by Georgia convicts to purloin their sound and banalize their longing for freedom. "Who else but Cooke," Talty asks, "could see this tableau, the prisoners chanting in a call-and-response pattern as old as slavery itself, and think 'Top 40 hit'?"

If there's an answer to this question, it's Elvis Presley. Not specifically—he didn't have that much racial chutzpah. But he did have that much omnivorousness. Talty sees Presley as Cooke's obverse—"If Elvis channeled gospel depths (and thus black history) through the voice of a Southern white boy, Cooke claimed the other half of the bargain"—and if that formulation seems blurry, it's probably because the truth is too close to focus on. These were matched teen idols who craved universal acceptance and universal power. They were also dreamboats with gorgeous voices and studious manners who got more ass than Casanova. The few others who dared aim so high lacked either the right charisma (Bobby Darin, Paul Anka) or true pop touch (Jackie Wilson).

The very real differences between the two went well beyond skin color. Songwriter Cooke was much more intellectual and inquisitive, while Presley was the natural rocker (better dancer, too). Cooke also aspired to sophistication when the moment was right, proving far readier to cosset a moneyed adult audience at the Copa than Elvis was in Vegas six years later—by which time his earliest fans were moneyed adults themselves. But although close comparison reveals more melodrama in Presley's singing, the two shared something new—a vocal transparency that came across naive and unpremeditated. Their songs, especially the slower ones, were so simple-minded, melodically as well as lyrically, that pop connoisseurs still dismiss them as witless and banal. Sometimes I do too—but not without recognizing the aesthetic audacity their witlessness required.

In part their leap owed the fluid class structure of an America never so prosperous before or since. It was the right time for poor boys to prevail without kowtowing. But mostly it was about teenagers. Cooke and Presley made their pop moves just as American teenagers were making theirs. No matter how lowest-common-denominator the guidelines in the songwriting handbooks Cooke studied and quoted, Tin Pan Alley never conceived an audience whose mean age was fifteen. It never tried to make the world sing along to sentiments so blissfully uncomplicated they could stimulate vaginal secretions in listeners who'd barely begun to menstruate. And like it or not this was a wondrous thing. To my way of hearing, the assiduously rehearsed tightness and musicality of Cooke's Copa set boils down to schlock—handcrafted schlock, like most schlock that goes over, but imbued with complacency when all is said and sung. In contrast, the silly likes of "Cupid" and "Only Sixteen" reach out to the disempowered as surely as "Touch the Hem of His Garment" and "Nearer to Thee." Without question teen disempowerment is temporary—more privileged than it knows, and as a result unrealistically hopeful. But the confluence remains inspirational nonetheless.

Since I've never been a pubescent female, and don't happen to be one of those deeply touched by the physical reality of Cooke's epochal voice, my personal connection to this aesthetic achievement will always be compromised. But I'm awed by it. Unlike Talty, who in a telling omission never mentions "A Change Is Gonna Come," I don't feel betrayed by Cooke's inevitable abandonment of his grandest pop dream; I blame the pains of business, the righteousness of the civil rights movement, the ennui of the pussy quest, the swimming-pool death of his one-year-old son, and age. When he regaled an all-black r&b audience at Miami's Harlem Square Club with hard-edged revvings of hits suitable and not, it was hardly what Talty brands "his biggest sham." But it also wasn't a birthright finally reclaimed. And neither was "A Change Is Gonna Come," which while consciously informed by both blues and gospel was sparked by his envious respect for "Blowin' in the Wind."

Like most of America, Cooke first encountered Bob Dylan's best-known song in the summer of 1963 via the Peter, Paul & Mary hit. Anodyne though that rendition was, it proved a radical radio breakthrough that established Dylan commercially—one that Wolff reports impressed Cooke not as "folk poetry" but as proof you could "address civil rights *and* go to #2 on the pop charts." Cooke recorded it under challenging circumstances—just after the 1964 Chaney-Goodman-Schwerner murders in a swankly swinging version designed to climax October's Copa album. Wolff deems this performance both a "protest" ("too many people have died") and a "reassurance" (the finger-snapping beat); I deem it unlistenable. But either way it was obliterated a few months later when Klein and RCA marketed Cooke's murder by releasing "Shake" with an "A Change Is Gonna Come" B side he'd cut a full year before. "Shake" went top ten. The flip became a modest hit and a revered standard.

Cooke's string-suffused production is an eccentric and elaborate thing, clearly enunciated atop calculated drawl and gravel, underpinning French horn, kettledrum, and tympani accents with an Earl Palmer pulse. Otis Redding, who idolized Cooke, put straight Stax-Volt readings of both "Shake" and "Change" on *Otis Blue* nine months later; Aretha Franklin, who crushed out on him, lavished her piano all over the song to climax her *I Never Loved a Man* album (and in 1968 released a magical version of "You Send Me" that somehow embodied how it moved her as a fully sexualized fifteen-year-old). Both covers are major, both prophetic. Both are a minute longer than Cooke's. But neither is as bold. Although his arrangement is arguably a compromise, his talk of getting knocked down and run out of downtown by a "brother" you just know isn't a racial brother undermines that effect. And his admission that he doesn't know what's "beyond the sky" casts doubt on the faith that was supposedly the bedrock of who he was.

It's said that one reason Sam Cooke sat on "A Change Is Gonna Come" is that it scared him, and that rings true. He couldn't have repeated it any more than he could have repeated "You Send Me"—strokes like that are unrepeatable. I have no idea whether he would have politicized soul music, gone Vegas, or both, and neither did he. But I'm certain he would have kept on addressing his times and his heritage with a complexity his simplicity comprehended.

Village Voice, 2003 · Expanded and revised

Tough Love

Etta James

Etta James's death at seventy-three on January 20 was not a surprise. Her leukemia had been declared incurable in December; her dementia was ongoing; her kidneys were bad. The gastric bypass surgery that put the four-hundred-pound singer back on her feet in 2002 had long since proved more dangerous than promised. And though none of the many laudatory obits mentioned it, there was also her liver, which having soldiered through decades of heroin, alcohol, cocaine, and painkiller addiction, must have been ready for a rest.

Prepared by these hard facts for the inevitable sales uptick—James even appeared briefly toward the top of the Rhapsody streaming site after she died, though never as high as Adele, who has said James inspired her to become a singer—Universal asked ace compiler Andy McKaie to prepare a four-CD set to supplant or supplement 2000's excellent three-CD *The Chess Box*. This he achieved by adding nine tracks from 1954–58 and twenty-two from 1977–2007 while subtracting nineteen from James's Chess/Argo/Cadet years, 1960–76. Because the new arrangement respects James's extraordinary longevity, *Heart & Soul: A Retrospective* would appear to be where to catch up with this essential artist you may well have ignored. But it's not like those omitted Chess tracks would waste your time. Even before she died, they kept sounding better, just like the five years we'd always thought Aretha Franklin threw away at Columbia. Great voices get more precious with the years.

Great voices are also difficult to describe, so much so that obituaries seldom try, although Peter Keepnews recalled a few useful words from Jon Pareles in the *Times*: "a huge range, a multiplicity of tones and vast reserves of volume." All true, and relevant, but if range and volume did the trick there'd be great voices by the thousand—it's in those unspecified tones that the vocal "grain" resides. Preliminarily, say that James, who began recording at fifteen, was often girlish and always not, and that her jailbait clarity coexisted readily with her big-mama grit. Combined with her range, volume, and knack for drama, those contradictions rendered her a sing-the-phone-book original, which served her well with the generic r&b ditties of her pre-Chess teens and also in her fifties and sixties, when she turned out some twenty rather miraculous if hit-or-miss albums. That she should have recorded effectively for so long, from 1955 till 2012—leukemia and dementia notwithstanding, her 2011 farewell, *The Dreamer*, is more hit than miss—puts her in a class with Ray Charles, Johnny Cash, and James Brown, slightly older artists who unlike James never identified as rock and roll or targeted teenagers. She wasn't merely "influential."

More than their contemporaries, all four '50s lifers survived harrowing childhoods: extreme poverty, very young and/or absent mothers, prostitution in everyday life, brothers dying before their eyes. Born at the tail end of the Depression, Jamesetta Hawkins was the best off economically and also biracial. But what really set her apart was that she wasn't southern or "downhome"—she grew up in Los Angeles and San Francisco, and her family was from Omaha. Raised till she was twelve by a nurturing stepmother who suffered the last of multiple strokes under James's care, young Jamesetta then shuttled between her footloose party-girl mother, her self-possessed hooker aunt, and a working-class uncle who was the family's rock. Musical from infancy, she was taught to sing by the gay choirmaster of a big-time Baptist church and always enjoyed LGBTQ support. No showbiz life is square. But not many girls go pro at fourteen the way James did. She was one hip chick, and like her biological mother's beloved Billie Holiday, she surveyed the options her upbringing posited and made up her mind to be bad.

All this I gather from one of David Ritz's finest r&b as-told-tos, James's 1995 autobiography, *Rage to Survive*. Not that every memory is factual or every date verified—Ritz's calling is to help artists tell the story they want to tell, not research it for them. But James's chosen story is rich in insight as well as incident. The players in her private life are worth meeting, and the artist sketches are revealing whether their subjects are well-chronicled like Sam Cooke, Jackie Wilson, Sly Stone, and Ike and Tina Turner, cult heroes like Allen Toussaint and Esther Phillips, or all too undocumented like Jesse Belvin, Richard Berry, Johnny Guitar Watson, Larry Williams, and doowop headman turned world-beating producer-bizzer Harvey Fuqua, the first and far from worst of the many users James loved more than they loved her. Moreover, the dysfunction tales—the hyperextended family, the "crafty grafty men," the copping and chiseling and arrests and incarcerations and rehabs and millions down the toilet—don't dominate the music. If anything, they help us understand it.

Musically, James was all shook up. Church-trained at the behest of her godly stepmother, she never sang in church again after her stepfather tried to take over her nascent gospel career when she was ten, although she happily cashed a check for a gospel album once. Her jazz-sophisticate mother warned Guitar Slim–blasting Jamesetta that she'd "wind up in a bucket of blood," which sounded fine to a mouthy hellion who "adored" jazz but resented its "discipline, being exactly in tune, working out complex harmonies and subtle rhythms." Convinced that the r&b she dove into with pals like Watson and Williams was the real rock and roll—and still outraged that Georgia Gibbs got to bowdlerize her 1955 "The Wallflower" into the crossover smash "Dance with Me Henry"—she nonetheless pays selected white musicians compliments so astute I feel sure she means them: Janis Joplin, who idolized and imitated her; Randy Newman, whose songs Joplin's producer Gabriel Mekler gave her; the Rolling Stones, who in 1978 judged her "wildass enough" to open for "the most intense fans I've ever seen"; Stevie Ray Vaughan, credited by James with instigating an '80s blues revival that improved her paydays.

James was hardly the only African-American singer with such a broad frame of reference. Because musicians tend to be interested in music for some reason, it happens all the time. But few have taken so much stuff so deep or mastered it so variously. James's street-tough come-hither and wronged desolation, her hunger and relish, reflected the girlish-yet-not tension built into her physical voice and also—shaped as she was by both shrewd demimondaines and solid citizens—her psychological makeup. This was an observant, cynical, highly intelligent woman who lived as much for the fun of it as for the love she craved and the dark nights she got for her trouble. She made many friends and took no guff. And in the course of her very long career she mixed r&b, rock, soul, pop, blues, and eventually even jazz.

In a lifelong pattern, James recorded plenty in the '50s whether she had hits or not, writing a few songs (including "W.O.M.A.N.," when she was seventeen) and leaving a legacy summed up by Virgin's *The Essential Modern Records Collection* but well-represented on the *Heart & Soul* box. Hear especially the revealing texts "Crazy Feeling," better known as "Do Something Crazy," and the Etta-penned, Little Richard–influenced eHarmony application "Tough Lover": "He can make you laugh, he can make you cry / He's so tough he'll make Venus come alive / He can do anything that he wants to do / He'll step on Jesse James's blue suede shoes" (and Etta James's too, bet on it). Thus she proved one of two female heroes of the rock and roll '50s. Ruth Brown and LaVern Baker were experienced nightclub singers who never grokked the teen thing; Esther Phillips got hooked on junk so fast she was out of commission from 1954 to 1962. James's only competition also started recording at fifteen but was otherwise her diametrical opposite: the classically trained Catholic schoolgirl Arlene Smith of the Chantels, a grave teen angel who later studied at Juilliard and became a schoolteacher while James did something crazy and then something crazier.

As indicated in the absurd Leonard Chess biopic *Cadillac Records*, where Beyoncé plays an OD-sex scene that never happened more soulfully than she sings "Stop the Wedding," James then became Chess's most reliable '60s hitmaker, scoring one of the great teen makeout anthems with 1960's "A Sunday Kind of Love." But despite all the obit talk of how she crossed over by turning the minor Tin Pan Alley chestnut "At Last" into Barack Obama's theme song, that one never broke top forty—James's biggest pop-chart successes were "Pushover" in 1963 and "Tell Mama" in 1968, and neither got to twenty. Much more than the soul-identified Curtis Mayfield, Wilson Pickett, Gladys Knight, or Aretha Franklin, she remained r&b-specific as "r&b" itself became a temporarily outmoded concept. This reflected both her tough sound and her blues label—Chess a&r chief Ralph Bass lacked the pop instincts and connections of Motown and Atlantic. When he finally sent James down to Muscle Shoals, where Pickett had found so much success, she recorded the hit Janis Joplin latched onto, "Tell Mama," which she admired technically but found wanting as ideology: "I didn't like being cast in the role of the Great Earth Mother, the gal you come to for comfort and easy sex."

In Muscle Shoals James formed a lasting musical relationship with keyboardist Barry Beckett, who was producing her as late as 1996. And she did good work in this vein, always when she covered Otis Redding and sometimes too on her two albums with the controlling yet irresistible Jerry Wexler. To my ear, however, that soul groove seems too friendly and civilized for someone who learned to sing in church but never went back, and perhaps unintuitive for a non-southerner. Not that I was any more skeptical at the time than, for instance, Janis Joplin. On the contrary, it was Joplin's man Mekler moving in on James that seemed dubious to me—why foist Randy Newman on the "Tell Mama" gal? But now James's choir-powered, bitterly sacrilegious reading of Newman's "God's Song" seems like her truest recording, and his calmly incendiary "Let's Burn Down the Cornfield" captures her badness well. "Feeling Lowdown," where Mekler set her to moaning miserably over jazz chords for three minutes, is also a coup.

Post-Chess, James's catalogue is a morass. I was surprised to learn, for instance, that she'd done an album with Toussaint in 1980, and when I located it was equally surprised to learn how mediocre it is. Unfortunately, her best late-period producer, Private Music's John Snyder, was not Universalaffiliated, which is presumably one reason the standards albums he did with her—the finest the Billie Holiday tributes *Mystery Lady* and *Blue Gardenia*—get short shrift on *Heart & Soul*. But given the box's title we can also assume a desire to showcase James as Queen of Soul II, a mistake not just for musical reasons but because the melodrama built into the concept tends to overwhelm both her brains and her disruptive impulses. James was right to distrust jazz as a tough teen—its veneer of class wasn't for her. But early on at Chess she was assigned the likes of "At Last," "Stormy Weather," and "These Foolish Things." And without ever turning a cocktail lounge into a bucket of blood, she claimed these ballads by roughing them up like a drunk in a china shop—a mouthy, sexy kid brazening through. Redoing Billie forty or fifty years later, she's gained polish, savvy, wisdom, pain. But she's still rough. By never letting her palpable respect smooth over her well-weathered prerogatives, she maps peaks and valleys in this sacrosanct territory beyond the emotional ken of Madeleine Peyroux or even Carmen McRae.

All of which is to regretfully suggest that Etta James is a little too deep to catch up with via a single career-spanning box. There's no easy route—why should there be? *The Chess Box, The Essential Modern Records Collection*, and one or two of the Snyders would be my best advice. Or if you're feeling skint you could limit Chess to the budget *Millennium Collection* and nose around for those Mekler tracks.

And then there's *The Dreamer*, with her co-producing sons on bass and drums. By January 10 I'd concluded sadly that it didn't click somehow. By January 30 I couldn't get enough of "Groove Me" and "Cigarettes and Coffee" and had come to terms with her patently unautobiographical claim to have been "born and raised in the boondocks." Great voices get even more precious when you know they're gone.

Barnes & Noble Review, 2012

The Excitement! The Terror!

Miles Davis's '70s

Miles Davis's '70s—beginning with the widely admired modal shifts of 1969's *In a Silent Way* and ending with the widely disparaged funk sprawl of 1976's *Agharta*—are the most incompletely understood period in the recording career of any major jazz musician. This is mainly because the job of understanding jazz musicians falls to jazz critics, who until very recently were neither inclined nor equipped to put much heart or mind into such recondite records. For if this music is any good at all, it's not good the way jazz is supposed to be good. Altogether lacking in that casually hyperintelligent aura of smart guys sitting around talking to each other that is the great legacy of bebop, it offers little sustained improvisation and less brilliant composition. Like the distantly respectable "free jazz," it's not arranged, it

does nothing with harmony, and doesn't swing properly; it table-hops and races to nowhere and spaces out staring at the ceiling. But unlike "free jazz," this music was electric, beat-heavy, and marketed to kids—and thus obviously worthy of suspicion if not contempt.

And then there is the little matter of fusion, many of whose perpetrators passed through Miles's '70s bands. Fusion has its loyalists, and in acid jazz its revivalists, and thus also its ideologues; like lounge at a more egotistical level of virtuosity, it lives off the tight and the tasty, and these days some contrarians dig it for that. But statuswise it's still stuck between Emerson, Lake & Palmer and Hamilton, Joe Frank & Reynolds. This is a music whose saving grace is mystagogy, as on Rhino's depressing *Jazz Fusion Vol. 1*, where early selections from Tony Williams and Larry Coryell (no Mahavishnu?) generate a forthrightly phony rock grandeur that's soon left behind by cute schlock—Chick Corea was bad enough without Flora Purim's oh-oh-ohs. Yet if these be the children of Miles, one peculiarity must be noted—pretty good or very bad, their fusion doesn't sound much like Dad's. Without the hint of a doubt, they all compose, they all arrange, and they all solo to beat the band.

In the wake of his abstract-to-wan post-*E.S.P.* music, I was pro electric Miles, especially the early and late studio albums—*In a Silent Way* and *Jack Johnson*, *Get Up With It* and *Agharta*. But I also found him daunting, particularly on the three live double-LPs Columbia and Teo Macero unloaded between the fall of 1970 and the spring of 1973. I mean, was there anyone who didn't? Presumably the young potheads who bought the tickets were impressed enough to lie back and enjoy it, faking orgasm if perchance they should fail to achieve same. But reading the liner notes from saxophonists Gary Bartz and Dave Liebman that Columbia commissioned for its quintuple reissue—three originally U.S.-available live double-CDs (*Miles Davis at Fillmore, In Concert: Live at Philharmonic Hall,* and *Live-Evil*) plus two import-onlys (*Black Beauty* from the Fillmore West 1970 and *Dark Magus* from Carnegie Hall 1974)—you get the sense that Davis's musicians created in a state of excitement closely akin to existential terror. That may be the music's greatest strength, but it's also one reason many found it offputting at first. Anyway, it wasn't until 1980 that I got up the nerve to write about most of these albums—and discovered that except for *At Fillmore*, which I thought meandered overmuch, they were (a) all rather good and (b) all rather different.

On the one hand, this is a unique body of music. You want to hear '70s Miles, you don't pull out Mahavishnu's *Inner Mounting Flame* or Tony Williams's

Emergency!, two rather good early fusion albums by Davis U. summa cum laudes. Only Miles sounds like Miles, even back in April 1970, when *Black Beauty* preserved an inkling of why the jazz-rock idea seemed so auspicious before it found form in flash and filigree. Wailing through "Directions" or blasting the blues from out "Miles Runs the Voodoo Down," Corea's keybs sound more audacious and grounded than they ever will again, with an uncommonly muscular Miles challenging his facility and fledgling soprano whiz Steve Grossman mimicking it, and beyond a few dollops of needless noodle, Jack DeJohnette keeps the troops in order, injecting more notes and accents than Ginger Baker on double amphetamines into a beat that rocks. Yet this unique sound is evolving fast. Still nominally beholden to theme-and-variation, *Black Beauty* is soloists' music, and as such the corniest electric Miles on record. Just two months later, on *Miles Davis at Fillmore*, the formula is breaking down. Like all '70s Miles, *At Fillmore* is more inviting in the wake of ambient techno than it was in 1970 or 1980, but like most ambient techno it fails to cull the mesmerizing from the soothing from the boring. Moreover, several of its high points are provided by some of the most Milesian solos of this era, and that is not what the era was for.

One reason jazz old-timers dismiss '70s Miles is that the bands aren't stellar. Here he is, bossman of Coltrane and Cannonball, Hancock and Shorter, and suddenly the best he can do for self-starting sidemen is John McLaughlin, Keith Jarrett, and Jack DeJohnette. Solo, the likes of Corea, Mtume, and Michael Henderson all proved abnormally schlocky, and Sonny Fortune, who came on very late, was as near as Miles got to a name saxophonist. *Live-Evil*, out for Christmas 1971 after the definitive McLaughlin showcase *Jack Johnson* slipped past in April, flaunts this development. Tweaked by Macero like most of Davis's '70s albums, it arrays five contained, seductive early-1970 studio tracks featuring recent old-guardists Herbie Hancock, Wayne Shorter, and Joe Zawinul against four long jams—all from Davis's December 19, 1970, gig at the Cellar Door in Chocolate City, all anchored by Michael Henderson. Davis's first exclusively electric bassist, Henderson was only a Motown session man, and his vocals could make a fella love George Benson, but he was a supple and responsive player—along with Macero, Miles's key collaborator in the '70s. On *Live-Evil* McLaughlin plays the blues, Jarrett gets funky, and Henderson is the devil who makes them do it. By *In Concert*, almost two years later, Henderson is the sole survivor from the more talented prior band—although, crucially, Al Foster pushes like DeJohnette with less excess motion. The result is the purest jazz-funk record ever—not as quick or tricky as James Brown, but more richly layered, riffs and drones and wah-wahs and tunelets and weird noises and shifting key centers snaking along on a sexually solicitous, subtly indomitable pulse.

Saxophonist Liebman has described all too revealingly what it was like for the young cats plucked up into these bands: "Somehow, he would get you to play in a manner that in most cases you would never do again." To me, that seems like the secret—less what these close-enough-for-funk subgeniuses played than the single palpitating organism their playing turned them into. Regularly abandoning his trumpet for atmospheric organ, Miles the guru-manipulator shifted gears at will, orchestrating moods and settings to subjugate individual musical inspirations to the life of an ensemble that would have been nothing without them. No arrangements, little composition, and not many solos either, because at any moment a player could find himself swallowed up or left to fly off on his own. Kept the kids on their toes.

Harsher and dreamier than *In Concert*, louder and sweeter than *Agharta* or *Pangaea*, *Dark Magus* both culminates and casts doubt on this aesthetic. There's still that sense of an autonomous life-form that has evolved away from the intimate articulations of the small-group species. Yet this specimen is bifurcated, like jazz-rock again. If you want a true fusion you listen to some funk, which subsumes both in a new conception, albeit one that privileges rock; here the two elements are left distinct and recognizable. Liebman is good for wild-to-mellow jazz input that's solidified by a Coltranesque house call from Azar Lawrence, and for rock there are three guitarists: Reggie Lucas and Dominique Gaumont wah-riffing the rhythm as Chess session man and cult hero Pete Cosey launches his own wah-wah-inflected noise into the arena-rock stratosphere. The beat belongs jointly to Henderson and Foster. And Miles is Miles whether blasting out clarion notes or letting his Yamaha drench the scene.

Recondite once, this music seems almost natural now, which is not to say it ever was or can be pop. That takes more than electrification and street-smart jacket cartoons—maybe covering Cyndi Lauper and cheering on the fleet-fingered folderol of Mike Stern the way '80s Miles did. Rather it was what avant-garde's supposed to be—so far ahead of its time that eventually, like for instance in this soundscaping epoch, it feels right as rain. It was and remains its own place, a world apart from unmoored jazz experiments and dilatory rock jams then and the most humanistic electronica now. In the '70s this was because Miles admired the rhythmic commitment of such black coequals as Sly and Hendrix. In the '90s it's because his most arbitrary-seeming whims and conceptualizations nurtured a living organism. Does that mean there was no other way to achieve the same end, or that no similar end can match it? Of course not. But that was how Miles did it, and there is no longer the slightest question that it will endure.

Village Voice, 1997

Sister, Oh Sister

Kate & Anna McGarrigle

Released in 1976 and 1977, when the marginal movements of punk and disco were revolutionizing popular music, Kate and Anna McGarrigle's *Kate & Anna McGarrigle* and *Dancer with Bruised Knees* are cult records. The McGarrigles were folkies who will never become iconic the way the Ramones and *Saturday Night Fever* soon did. But neither were they obscure: when Kate died of cancer early last year, the tributes flooded in like she was Marlene Dietrich. It helped that Kate's son with Loudon Wainwright III, Rufus Wainwright, is more famous than either of his parents. It also helped that the McGarrigles hailed from Canada, which promotes its artists like the national assets they are. But the main reason is the two albums themselves. Cult records they are. Classics they also are.

Though the McGarrigles ended up recording less music than I'd hoped in 1976, there's enough, and most of it will endure. But the first two albums are indelible—since 1980, I've revisited them more often than any of my punk-era faves except maybe *Rocket to Russia*. In part it's the material, in part something subtler, as came clear when I somewhat apprehensively test-played the bonus disc of *Tell My Sister*, Nonesuch's handsome, economical reissue of the two classics. Only Dylanologists and smitten fanboys need the detritus that fills most bonus discs. But that wasn't how this one felt even though half of its twenty-one songs were also available on the two accompanying albums—in what must be, given how I've been raving, definitive interpretations. I appreciated the previously unheard material, especially a lost masterpiece about the almost carefree pleasures of a hippie August called "Saratoga

Summer Song." But mostly the bonus disc succeeds for the same reasons I'm always introjecting these records into my musically oversaturated home life.

I've called the McGarrigles folkies, a mildly belittling characterization that seems fairer than ever now that I've read the Dane Lanken coffee-table book *Kate and Anna McGarrigle: Songs and Stories*. But as is invariably pointed out, Kate and Anna were domestic folkies. They made piano-and-accordion music not guitar music, parlor music not campfire music, stay-at-home music not on-the-road music; rather than pretty or gorgeous or powerful, their voices were just beautiful, in a proudly plain way. Products of a household where everybody sang, they meshed perfectly with the give-and-take sociability of chopping vegetables and reading in bed.

Produced by the astute folk-rock impresario Joe Boyd, the McGarrigles' classic albums built a bridge between Canada and California, where folk music had been profitably homogenized by the likes of Jackson Browne and Linda Ronstadt, who named her 1974 breakthrough album after Anna's "Heart Like a Wheel." From the debut's opening track, Kate's "Kiss and Say Goodbye," Boyd goes for a more casual feel than Peter Asher could have countenanced for Ronstadt—Steve Gadd pokey, Bobby Keys laid-back. Nevertheless, parlors seldom come equipped with trap sets and saxophone honchos, and when a full band and Anna's harmonies rev up around Kate's ebullient "And I don't know where it's coming from / But I want to kiss you till my mouth gets numb," we who love this record recognize a representation of the casual—and the ecstatic. The bonus-disc demo is very different— solo with clunkier piano, only then toward the climax Anna's harmonies sidle in, and soon a guitar is quietly kibitzing. The song is so good, as I know because Boyd softened me up, that right now I prefer the bare-bones conversation of this truly living-room version (which was recorded in a studio).

I understand why most McGarrigles fans swear by the debut, which listens easy without ever going soft or making room for a merely good song. Topping even Anna's "My Town" and "Heart Like a Wheel" and her own "Mendocino" and "Tell My Sister," Kate's Loudon farewell "Go Leave," taken solo with guitar, is regarded by some sachems of sorrow as the most bereft breakup song ever recorded; although it's perfectly written—the disarming six-word opening, the enjambed "aching"-"breaking," the intrusion of the blunt "stalling" three lines from the end—quoting even a couplet would do a disservice to its power as music. Nevertheless, my own beloved has always been *Dancer with Bruised Knees*, where the McGarrigles perfected their aesthetic. Although a few of the debut's Stateside session heavies reappear, most of the music comes from the evolving crew of Montreal folkies the sisters started hanging with as teenagers. These include Dawson College philosophy prof Chaim Tannenbaum on harmonica, mandolin, recorder, and backing vocals as well as trumpeter-vocalist Dane Lanken, a journalist already encountered above as an author and thought of by many as Mr. Anna McGarrigle.

What I love so hard about this lovely, homely album is that it doesn't listen so easy. It risks an austerity that rings as true in eat-the-poor 2011 as it did in high-punk 1977. Its melodies run deeper, its beats are less swinging even with jazzmen on five tracks, and it risks the cognitive dissonance of three songs in French that won't sound so quaint to Anglophones who work out the translations. Admittedly, I'm smitten with Kate's "Walking Song," about taking a stroll with your life's companion, which my wife and I have been putting on each other's mixtapes since I turned forty, and for "First Born," about a privileged kind of son who could be Rufus, Loudon, or even me. But my thematic preferences don't stop me from admiring how the album ends with two songs about circling back to zero without your life's companion, one by Anna called "Kitty Come Home" and one by Kitty herself.

Kate was the motivator, declares Anna, born fourteen months earlier on December 4, 1944. Kate taught herself banjo and blues; Kate set out for New York with a singing partner who ended up producing Laurie Anderson; Kate made away with Loudon Wainwright's fickle heart; Kate urged her big sister to write songs because she needed the material. Without Kate, Anna swears, she's retiring. And although I hope she keeps writing, there's common sense to this pledge, not because Kate's somewhat fuller voice and bigger songs rendered her musically dominant, as to some slight extent they did, but because if Anna had died first, Kate would have been hard-pressed to go on alone as well.

Their signature trick, after all, was that singular synthesis of timbre and intonation, nature and nurture, that has raised up the harmony of so many siblings. But harmonizing families aren't all alike—consanguinity didn't help the Osmonds all that much. The McGarrigles were blessed in addition by their long immersion in the Celtic mysteries of French-Canadian song and the contrarian intelligence of their eccentric close harmonies. This intelligence also inflected the physical cast of their voices. They're female, and Anna's voice especially has a courageous fragility about it, so their male admirers can't resist calling them sweet. But to me they always seemed tart, sharp, wry, nearly prim. They seemed sexier that way, too.

Which brings us, by the back door, to the even bigger reason the sisters needed each other artistically: to complete their domestic arrangement, which combined two radically different households and spanned four generations.

Lanken outlines a childhood in which both grandfathers were music-mad, one as an impresario-performer and the other as a fan. Musicales at their childhood home in the modest ski town of Saint-Sauveur featured Stephen Foster, pre-WWI chestnuts from a songbook Kate committed to memory, thirteen senior Francophone siblings with their own specialty numbers, and not two but three singing McGarrigle sisters—the eldest, Jane, produced the duo's fifth album and has joined in occasionally onstage. But then Kate and Anna's parents took an apartment in Montreal, and soon the two sisters had joined a shifting folkie menage. Locally renowned as the Mountain City Four even though there were sometimes eight of them, this collective went worldwide on *Dancer with Bruised Knees*.

The McGarrigles were younger than most of their cohort, and female in the pre-feminist bohemia of 1962, when women weren't supposed to know blues like Kate or even paint in a garret like Anna. Yet long before their fame they were anything but marginal in their little community, which migrated from living room to living room, including one in Saint-Sauveur. Most of this I know from Lanken, who narrates via text and caption until Kate and Anna start getting serious press in 1976, at which point *Songs and Stories* turns into a generous clip file augmented by many more captions (the snap-shots are exquisite throughout). But left out of this scrapbook is a piece I love from *Ms.* magazine. Poetically, it was written by my own sister, Georgia Christgau, and it examines ideas of family—as do the transcriptions of un-published interviews with the sisters and their mother that Georgia dug out of her files when I solicited her recollections.

Interviewed separately, Kate and Anna each applied the word "incestu-ous" to their crew, and they weren't just being metaphorical; Kate told Geor-gia that Dane was the only man at a get-together that she'd never made love with—and that love was invariably involved. Anyone who thought "I want to kiss you till my mouth gets numb" was not imagery one ordinarily associ-ates with parlor music should understand that this was no ordinary parlor. I believe Kate about the love part—by then she'd known these people fifteen years, time to love quite a few fellow spirits if you're young enough. In her ac-count, those affairs were in the past, and far from generating the resentments and rivalries you might suspect, they instead guaranteed her an extra portion of the "love and concern" Anna promised in "Kitty Come Home." Georgia, who found herself pouring out her own life story the day she hit Montreal, concluded that "intimacy is all Kate and Anna are really comfortable with."

The McGarrigles were at home in an exceptionally complex domestic arrangement that melded an extended family of amateur musicians with a floating collective of semi-professional ones. Either formation had the makings of a minefield riddled with repression or one-upmanship. But the McGarrigles' formations avoided such perils. They allowed you to feel what you felt and tolerated your mistakes when you were proving what you had to prove. It was a perfect environment for intimacy, meaning not just candor but all the improvements on the low-concept "heartfelt" and "natural" that surface in the appreciations Lanken has assembled: "strangely unsentimental," "translucently undramatic," "unselfconsciously reflective," "poignant and playful," "temperate, forthright and cheerful," and just "civilizing."

What none of this richly deserved praise suggests—though it's hardly a secret: the title song of the album Jane produced, *Love Over and Over*, makes a point of it—is that neither Anna with her long, private marriage nor Kate with her foreshortened, defining one has ever written a love song. I don't mean a heartbreak song—*Kate & Anna McGarrigle* is among other things a heartbreak album. Nor do I mean a sex song—Kate's begin with "Kiss and Say Goodbye," in which the goodbye has the last word, and culminate with "Talk About It," a fifty-year-old's invitation to bed that promises, "We can talk about it in the morning / It'll come / It always does." There are even mother-love songs, crowned by Kate's translucent "Babies If I Didn't Have You." Appreciations of their life's companion, no. Appreciations of their month's companion, ditto.

Although some of the McGarrigles' more benighted admirers consider this a virtue, I think it's a failing, one as conducive to cult status as their acuity and reserve. But given their strange unsentimentality, it's a forgivable failing, because as anybody knows, it's easier to write a credible heartbreak song than a credible heart song. Anyway, there's a major exception, one so unsentimental you can forget it's there: the aforementioned "Walking Song." It's wistful, imagined—Kate's vision of a Loudon, let's just say, ready to spend days hiking and talking, hopefully in Canada but Mexico would do. "Be my lover or be my friend," she proposes, or implores. This was an early song, and the available evidence suggests she never got her wish. So together with her sister she completed a circle of love that served as a substitute. And together with her sister she gave it to us. That's love too. In a way, all the McGarrigles' songs are love songs.

Barnes & Noble Review, 2011

Two Pieces About
the Ramones

1. Ramone

I remember the early releases as hand-written, but on the one in my files only the gig dates are: "Appearing at Performance Studios 23 East 20th Street, Friday April 11 9 P.M. Also C.B.G.B.'s 315 Bowery + Bleeker Monday + Tuesday April 14 + 15 11 P.M." The text is typed and photocopied. Its first paragraph reads: "The Ramones are not an oldies group, they are not a glitter group, they don't play boogie music and they don't play the blues. The Ramones are an original Rock and Roll group of 1975, and their songs are brief, to the point and every one a potential hit single. Contact Tome Erdelyi, Loudmouth Productions," it goes on, with a Forest Hills address and two phone numbers, a "BR 5-" and a "777." The latter was a Manhattan exchange, the former a Queens; no 718—it was that long ago. Appended were lyrics to six songs, starting with "I Don't Care" and "I Don't Want to Go Down to the Basement."

I think it was that Tuesday that my wife and I went to CB's with *Voice* critic Tom Johnson, laconic explicator of Reich and Glass and the "one-note music" of Rhys Chatham, after Tom had lured us to the Kitchen. The twenty or so patrons included Danny Fields at the bar in back. Soon the Ramones played thirteen songs in twenty-four minutes or whatever it was, and among the converts was Johnson, who had little interest in pop but lots in minimalism. For me, it was life-changing. These four inept-sounding geeks had figured out what the Stooges had done wrong—the expressionistic stuff, the long and the slow and the chaos-for-its-own-sake. Over the next four years I would see the Ramones more than I've ever seen any band (even the Grateful Dead!). But having followed the tragic trajectory of the life-changing New York Dolls, I wasn't optimistic about "potential hit singles." The Ramones were obviously aesthetes one way or another, and in rock and roll, aesthetes rarely conquer the world.

Of course, the Ramones never did—as hitmakers. In 1994, two years before they finally broke up, the 1988 *Ramones Mania* comp went gold, and maybe eventually the remastered and bonused-up *Ramones* or *Rocket to Russia* will join it. Because of course, they have now been inducted into the Rock and Roll Hall of Fame. Because of course, they did conquer the world, if changing rock and roll utterly counts. And somewhere in between they gained and/or created a following far closer to the idealized rock and roll audience they'd imagined than anyone knew existed.

Starting with their names and costumes—yes, costumes: Dee Dee was bitching about the prescribed look long before he quit in 1989 and refused to wear leather to the Hall of Fame induction—the Ramones strove to convince fans they were all alike. Even today it's like they were all alienated and nothing else mattered. But of course, they were far from alike. Johnny was the son of a construction worker, Dee Dee an army brat in Germany until his mom got them out; both probably felt outclassed in a Forest Hills where there were loads of families like Joey's, whose divorced parents owned a trucking company and an art gallery, and who was Jewish, hence higher in the Forest Hills pecking order. And Tommy's background is murky. He escaped Hungary with his otherwise unchronicled family in 1956, started a high school band with Johnny, liked Bunuel, worked in some vague capacity on Jimi Hendrix's *Band of Gypsys*, ran the performance space where the Ramones took shape, and managed them before stepping in as self-taught drummer. Most bios give his birthdate as 1952, within a year of the others; some say 1949, which makes more sense, and not just because eighteen is young for a Hendrix credit. He seemed more mature. He was the businessman, the promoter, the conceptualizer, the guy who declared them "an original Rock and Roll group of 1975."

Tendencies crisscrossed. Joey and Dee Dee were the head cases, and also the songwriters. Dee Dee and Tommy romanticized America from a European perspective; Tommy and Johnny romanticized fuckups and kept their shit together. Around 1981, Johnny stole Joey's girl, a secret bond and disastrous rift. But although all four were formalists, surly prole Johnny and stoned wildman Dee Dee were instinctive if not compulsive about it, while Tommy and Joey maintained some semblance of aesthetic distance from the rock and roll ideal Johnny and Dee Dee represented—a distance they could make something of because they knew the ideal from the inside. Musically, the four groundbreaking neoprimitives split into the same pairs. Dee Dee amplified the Dolls' one-note basslines into a barrage that underpinned Johnny's from-the-wrist downstrum to create the band's sound. But the deepest innovator in this rhythm band with tunes on top was Tommy and his brand new beat: "Tommy basically played eighth-notes across, with the 'one' on the bass and the 'two' on the snare, constant eighth-notes on the high-hat. Playing fast with eighth-notes constantly—a lot of people try it, but they get sloppy and can't keep up." And since, as ten thousand hardcore bands soon proved, the beat would have gone nowhere without the tunes, the weirdo who sang them ended up defining the band's emotional identity as opposed to its sonic signature.

The trained drummer whose analysis I just quoted is Marky Ramone, who joined in 1978 after Tommy had had it with touring, left eventually for a four-year detox, and returned. Tommy geared his acute taste to his limited technique, playing no fills or rolls and hardly any accents—he was a little guy with small sticks and a light touch, and his quick forcebeat propels and permeates *Ramones, Ramones Leave Home*, and *Rocket to Russia.* Marky admired and replicated Tommy's groove. But he'd played metal before hooking up with Richard Hell and had a show drummer's chops, and his muscular sound and well-chosen flourishes helped galvanize the community of brainy anti-intellectuals, postpunk losers, and assorted hitters brought together by the Ramones' hard work, word-of-mouth, and faith in what they'd wrought. He was the link between the punk they'd invented and the good old hard rock they believed it to be—as well as a sign that they were the road band God made them rather than the radio band of their pop dreams.

Which leaves Joey where? Where he was to begin with—as one of the strangest singers ever to mount a stage, only now there are a quarter million fans believing it or not. There's no better way to grasp what a shock the Ramones' sound was than to realize that, in the reams of celebration piled on *Ramones*, Joey's vocals went almost entirely unremarked. Granted, it didn't help that his singing is indescribable. "Affected" is too mild, "cartoonlike" redundant. Garbled? Gargled? Strangled? Unhinged Jewish beanpole's dream of Mick Jagger? The Small Faces? The Nashville Teens? Had he merely forgotten his Sudafed? Here were nincompoops by the thousand whining about how cliched the Ramones' *chords* were when emanating from Joey's tonsils was a sound unlike any ever heard on earth. If the voice came from anywhere, it was from rock and roll itself—that was its only frame of reference. But it was anything but inhuman. In fact, although this wasn't instantly clear, its freak vulnerability was living proof that the Ramones loved cretins, pinheads, lobotomies, and glue sniffers. And its Daffy Duck mannerisms were why their hippie-baiting patriotism and playful little Nazi references, while sure to be taken the wrong way and not altogether unrepresentative of Johnny's philosophy of life, never actually seemed threatening.

In 1981, I opined that in future centuries 1981's *Pleasant Dreams* would sound pretty much like *Ramones Leave Home*. In 2002, however, the first four albums are clearly not just classic but sui generis, which with Marky on board for *Road to Ruin* I attribute to a remarkably long-lived initial songburst. But there were many good albums and important songs after that, and what holds them together is less Johnny's sound than Joey's sensibility, although his writing declined after he got his heart broke. Spurred by Marky, the son of a left-leaning longshoreman-turned-lawyer, Joey emerged—the signal was "The KKK Took My Baby Away," which preceded "Bonzo Goes to Bitburg" by four years—as a staunchly unelitist, no-BS version of the bohemian liberal his background would suggest. He joined Artists United Against Apartheid. He supported Rock the Vote. He did a Jerry Brown benefit. He got saner. He stopped drinking. He became a patron of the rock and roll arts.

And then he died, and everyone was so sad that Lucinda Williams, for Pete's sake, sent "2 Kool 2 Be 4-Gotten" out to him from Roseland, and in no time the Ramones were elected to the Hall of Fame, and only Tommy mentioned him at the induction, and *Don't Worry About Me* came out. He'd been recording his solo debut forever with Eighth (or Ninth) Ramone Daniel Rey; Marky's on half of it, also a Dictator and a Del-Lord and the keyb honcho from Loser's Lounge. Joey can't outpower the Ramones-qua-Ramones gestaltwise, and *Don't Worry About Me* probably isn't as good as 1992's *Mondo Bizarro*, much less 1984's *Too Tough to Die*. But it sure beats most other late Ramones albums, which it resembles without benefit of Johnny's downstrum for the reason just cited—in their postclassic, touring-icons period, which (I repeat) was far more productive musically than that otherwise accurate characterization suggests, Joey was the identity marker. Despite the persistence of Johnny's scowl-and-chop and Dee Dee's wart hogs and cretin families, and despite the hitters they were finally attracting, a certain softness rose to the surface. It had always been there, but as the songs departed from their strictures and Joey gargled more emotively, it got bigger, undercutting what was already a play toughness—call it tuffness, as physically enthralling as any hard rock without the menace—with shows of feeling that at times were almost coy and girly.

I give you *Don't Worry About Me*. It isn't a lot softer than the pop experiments of *Pleasant Dreams* or the '60s memories of *Acid Eaters*, but it's less punk and more rock, like the Dictators and the Del-Lords. "Venting (It's a Different World Today)" continues the tradition of "Bonzo" and "Censorshit"—less sharply worded, more warmly expressed. "Mr. Punchy" and "Like a Drug I Never Did Before" assure us that in some essential part of himself Joey is as screwed up as ever. The praise songs "Maria Bartiromo" and "Searching for Something" are direct descendants of "Sheena Is a Punk Rocker" except that neither the investment guru nor the recovering crackhead needs the Ramones. And at the end, Joey didn't either.

There's no point pretending that any of this good-to-better material would mean as much if he hadn't died. But give him credit for having the chutzpah and formal smarts to play that hand high-low. Like everything here, the title track, a failed-love plaint framed as a message from the grave, could have stayed on the record if Joey had beaten lymphoma. A bigger winner is the lovably embarrassing Louis Armstrong corndog "It's a Wonderful World," stiffened by the punkest attack on the record and doubly credible from a mortally ill man. Similarly, the straightforward music and chin-up sentiments of "I Got Knocked Down (But I'll Get Up)," precisely the content his enfeeblement called for, would have remained so if in fact he had gotten up. But they're doubly poignant because he didn't.

On *Too Tough to Die*, which nobody is forever but the Ramones remained for much longer than anybody gave them, Joey sings a Dee Dee song called "I'm Not Afraid of Life." The Ramones all earned that boast. Joey's earning it at this moment.

Village Voice, 2002

....

2. Road to Ruin

The most vivid figure in Michael Gramaglia and Jim Fields's *End of the Century* was the least articulate and most archetypal of the Ramones: Johnny, the right-wing prole whose hard-ass sense of style the others nutballed and softened and accelerated and above all imitated. We felt we knew Joey the singer, Dee Dee the hophead, Tommy the conceptualizer. Whether beating out his chords or glowering at assholes, taciturn Johnny was far less distinct. But throughout this thorough, moving, long-awaited documentary he talks more than Legs McNeil in an accent outlanders will oversimplify as New York and connoisseurs of Queens English will pin down as Ridgewood or Middle Village. It's an accent steeped in working-class repression—the accent of white men who think being in touch with your feelings is for fags.

In exchanges that had me cackling and wincing at the same time, Johnny makes clear that he's no fag—when he finds himself "caring" after Joey dies, he's so bewildered that he examines himself for "weakness." Granted, the two barely spoke once Johnny became the KKK who stole Joey's baby away—and then made an honest woman of her in a union that's lasted decades. But for a third of Joey's foreshortened lifetime they remained Ramones anyway, through five years of Marky rehab followed by seven of eager CJ replacing the one and only Dee Dee. Johnny and Dee Dee defined the Ramones where Joey and Tommy interpreted them. But Johnny and Joey kept them going start to finish. While they were never again as primal or superb as on the four '70s albums they sped through, they recorded loads of fine music thereafter—much of which Johnny hated, but gabba gabba hey. No matter how pissed off he was, he never let up on the downstrum. Exciting and absolutely right though their '70s sets always were, the film establishes that they kept the faith live till the end, lifted by Joey's goofy dedication and powered by the chords Johnny thrashed out like they were why he was alive. As unyielding in his aesthetic principles as he was in everything else, this reactionary was an avant-gardist in spite of himself.

"Opposites attract and all that crap," shrugs Joey, who emerges as somewhat vaguer and more distant than we who loved him from a distance believed. Maybe this is unfair to a shy compulsive who was mortally ill when shooting began. But for four guys who pretended they were all the same, they sure had their differences—and for four guys who got famous acting stoopid, they sure are intelligent. Although he's aged badly and will soon OD, Dee Dee's down-to-earth off-the-wall partakes of the same charm he radiates in the many welcome and miraculous archival clips. But Johnny's analysis carries the film. Of course they didn't get along—they were a rock group. And Johnny understands with surpassing clarity that a rock group is infinitely bigger than its members—a work of art requiring species of creativity and endurance geniuses operating alone can barely fathom.

Village Voice, 2004

Nevermore

Nirvana

The recorded legacy of Nirvana is ungodly small—three studio albums, the first of which cost $606.17 to make, plus one miscellany and two posthumously released live CDs. Given the exploitations that might well have ensued after Kurt Cobain killed himself in April of 1994, we should be grateful that the band's catalogue hasn't been stuffed with one of those four-CD boxes of redundant concert tapes that now diminish Jimi Hendrix, the Monkees, and the Doors. This discretion has been good for the band's image, and for our fond memories. There the six titles are on the shelf. Each sounds different from the others, and each sounds at least as vital today as it did when Nirvana was a historical force rather than a historical anomaly. Taken as a unit, Nirvana's albums are living proof of the subtlety and variety of what conventional musicology still regards as a crude, undeveloped genre.

Although the three members of Nirvana—Cobain, Krist Novoselic, and Dave Grohl—looked like hippie-manque undesirables, their cultural identification was punk, and in 1991, fifteen years after the Sex Pistols turned the British music business upside down, they stormed American pop with it. But they worked hard and long before that. In a new biography of Cobain, *Heavier Than Heaven*, Charles R. Cross dates the band's first gig to a March 1987 house party in Raymond, Washington, a nowhere logging town thirty minutes south of Aberdeen, the nowhere logging town of the then twenty-year-old Cobain. That's four-and-a-half years before Nirvana broke through with their second album, the cunningly produced major-label debut *Nevermind*. It's also eighty-seven pages into the text, which reaches its midpoint before *Nevermind* is released in 1991. While this structure inevitably shortchanges the achievement of Nirvana itself, it's a crucial source of the book's considerable power. Cross asserts his compulsion to ask "questions concerning spirituality, the role of madness in artistic genius, the ravages of drug abuse on a soul"; the drug details are especially wrenching. But what emerges far more emphatically is the life story of someone who never grew up, someone whose maturation was half done before he was twenty-one, someone who extracted art from a perpetual adolescence that was over much too soon.

Many American kids have it worse than Kurt Cobain, and quite a few survive just fine. His family was never fully middle-class, never deep poor. He was well-loved until his parents divorced when he was nine and not so badly treated after that; his mother was self-involved, his father uncommunicative and somewhat authoritarian, but neither was abusive. When Cobain was seven, he was briefly diagnosed as hyperactive and underwent a three-month course of Ritalin he claimed set up his later drug use. He was gifted in the visual arts, where he was encouraged by a paternal grandmother whose hobby was carving Norman Rockwell images on the caps of mushrooms with toothpicks, and in music, where his model was his mother's guitar-strumming kid sister.

Unfortunately, he had other family models as well—two paternal great-uncles and a maternal great-grandfather killed themselves. Cobain boasted to classmates that he had "suicide genes"; at the very least, something in his constitution predisposed him to take his misfortunes hard. Once a popular boy, he was a full-fledged stoner by his freshman year in high school, and he never graduated. Lazy, petulant, and depressed, he fought with both parents, living away from home intermittently. When he was seventeen, his mother kicked him out of the house after she interrupted him in the process of losing his virginity.

Cross underpins his story with assiduous interviewing—the partygoers at that first Raymond gig, for instance, are good for a riotous short chapter. He also gained access to Cobain's drawings, journals, and numerous un-sent letters. One conclusion of his research is that Cobain didn't just dream of becoming a rock star—a hypothesis the schismatics who squabble over Nirvana's heritage still argue about—but that he worked at it, too. A gui-tar teacher recalls that Cobain studied longer and more seriously than he wanted to admit to an audience he'd introduced to punk's just-do-it ethos, and among Cobain's writings are the texts of imaginary interviews, which include lines that showed up in real ones.

The work Cross put into augmenting the already plentiful evidence of Cobain's attraction to stardom served his own prejudices; in addition to ed-iting the Seattle music paper *The Rocket* from 1986—well before the local independent-label culture from which Nirvana was to emerge gained no-table profile or clout—until it folded in 2000, Cross worked with the widely circulated Springsteen fanzine *Backstreets*. Unlike the indie-rock ideologues Cobain so admired, Cross doesn't believe rock's aesthetic value stands in inverse proportion to its mass appeal. Neither do I, but his argument might have been sharpened if he'd spent more time with the opposition: people like Calvin Johnson, the doyen of indie-rock in Olympia, Washington, where Cobain moved to live with his first serious girlfriend; Tobi Vail, the riot-grrrl theorist who became Cobain's second girlfriend; Steve Albini, who produced *Nevermind*'s follow-up, the raw, cold, edgy *In Utero*; and Bruce Pavitt and Jonathan Poneman, the owners of Nirvana's first label, Seattle-based Sub Pop.

Jump-started by the contagious alienation anthem "Smells Like Teen Spirit," *Nevermind* went on to sell more than ten million copies, transforming Cobain into the first class-crossing rock idol of substance since Bruce Springsteen discovered barbells. Sloppy, malnourished, lank-haired, a self-proclaimed "negative creep" with beautiful eyes and a vocal attack that stylized adolescent angst as cannily as Billie Holiday's stylized the sophisticated kind, Cobain stands apart from the long line of rock's outsider heroes. He had little of the self-regard of Mick Jagger, Alice Cooper, Johnny Rotten, or Michael Stipe, and none of their vanity, clothes sense, or theatrical savoir-faire. Yet neither was he a symbolic Everyman in the manner of Springsteen, John Fogerty, or Garth Brooks. He seemed like every born loser who ever failed gym—a geek you could get wasted with, a shy guy whose cuteness cried out for mothering, an arty weirdo with a common touch. So for two or three years, until the act of abandonment that was his suicide, he gave a generation of losers a hero who felt like a loser even in success—as opposed to a hero whose triumph they could only admire, emulate, envy. And thus he turned the barely self-sustaining concatenation of tendencies called "indie" into a hot genre called "alternative." Finally, some dreamed, ordinary fans would outgrow their craving for star power. And if not that, maybe idiosyncratic cottage industrialists like Sonic Youth (who helped hook up Nirvana's major label deal) and the Meat Puppets (belatedly introduced to the outside world on Nirvana's 1993 MTV *Unplugged*) would get the audience base they deserved.

Cobain's ability to galvanize the young was the economic motor of the alt-rock bubble. The teen appeal of Sonic Youth (arty New Yorkers who imbued bizarre tunings and deadpan singing with pop pleasure) and the Meat Puppets (spaced-out Arizonans whose uncanny tunecraft won them a major-label deal well before Nirvana broke) was considerably narrower. But both bands were capable of reaching old punks, even old hippies who didn't get all gooey over Crosby, Stills & Nash. And here's the best part—Nirvana reached them too. Ten years after *Nevermind* was released, to merely acknowledge its power as a generational artifact is to stick it on a shelf and forget about it. It wasn't just teenagers who loved Nirvana—it was everyone who cared about rock and roll. The band's moment is long gone. Its music isn't.

Of course the mystique remains, and of course new teenagers discern something ineffably simpatico in Cobain's voice. But music is what has moved millions of copies of *Nevermind* since Cobain died, and what Cross inadvertently shortchanges. Familiar now with Cobain's extraordinary gift, we can hear it loud and clear on the 1989 debut album, *Bleach,* where his gigantic, goofy, bass-playing buddy Krist Novoselic adds drollery to the band's chaotic irreverence. But only with the 1990 entrance of the robust, songful, head-bustingly hyperactive drummer Dave Grohl did Nirvana turn into a great band.

The conscious nakedness of Cobain's singing was key; in the studio, he pushed and shaped his white-boy burr to extremes rarely sustainable for more than a few vocals per day. Yet he's never sung more movingly than on the mellow, one-take *MTV Unplugged,* and the sharp cracks and forlorn howls on the carefully constructed live recording *From the Muddy Banks of the Wishkah* broaden our access to a sufferer who regularly veered beyond the outer reaches of self-control. Moreover, everything else on the records mitigates the pain of the voice—not just the melodies, which stick in the ears with a consistency few bands have equalled, but Cobain's guitar, riff-based no matter how furiously it tests the riffs' limits, and the lyrics he pulled together from years of notebook poetry, which even when morbid or opaque almost always break into tenderness, wit, illumination. Novoselic provides solidity, certainty, and comfort, while Grohl revs and flails with an irrepressibility that repolarizes any negative charge Cobain has left pending. Throughout, punk minimalism redeems arena excess in a delicately shaded show of sonic force. Cobain was set on suicide, especially toward the end; as Cross points out, five of the six cover songs he chose for *MTV Unplugged* intimate death. But his music subsumed such impulses as surely as sonata-allegro procedure leads the hero home—subsumed them courageously, explicitly, and with the unmistakable message that existential struggle was at least as real for hippies-manques from nowhere as for Woody Allen or Jean-Paul Sartre.

Cobain's music conquered and he didn't. The last half of *Heavier Than Heaven* is the agonizing story of how he got the fulfillment he wanted and hated it more than the frustration he'd known. Cross dates Cobain's heroin addiction (as well as many of the best songs on *Nevermind*) to his breakup with Tobi Vail in late 1990, when a character named "heroine" began appearing in his journal. In the next year and a half he achieved fame and fortune and married the love of his life—Courtney Love, of L.A.-based quasi-riot-grrrl

Hole, a dream mate for one of the rare rock stars whose predilections were monogamous. Yet neither consummation would curb his need for chemical escape.

Some blame his abrasive, attention-grabbing wife for his drug abuse; she was so despised by some of his fans that early on there were rumors she'd killed him. Although Love clearly cooperated with Cross, he doesn't seem to be her stooge. His accounts of the child-rearing arrangements for Frances Bean, the daughter she had with Cobain, are highly uncomplimentary, and he notes that she "indiscriminately ingested" every drug her friends brought round after Cobain's death. Just because Cross is straightforward about Love's many faults, he's convincing when he argues that Cobain dragged Love, who no one would call abstemious, into using more dope than she would have on her own, and that, by the way, she contributed more to his music than he did to hers. The official version of Cobain's heroin addiction described it as off-and-on, spurred by chronic stomach pain. Cross establishes that this story was a cover-up. Cobain was a big-time junkie for all but a few stray weeks of his season in the public eye, including almost all his time with the daughter he loved. He was a frequent near-OD before he died, and if the rifle that killed him had misfired, the hit of heroin he'd just injected might well have done the job instead. By shooting himself, however, he clarified his intentions. Kurt Cobain was bound for oblivion. How lucky we are that he made six records before he got there.

New Yorker, 2001

A Long Short Story

The Go-Betweens

Eleven years after they finally attained major-label status with their sixth and formerly final album, *16 Lovers Lane*, the Go-Betweens' *The Friends of Rachel Worth* arrives bearing Robert Vickers's tiny, arty, economically self-sufficient Jetset brand. Yet in America, where their cult was always less substantial than in Europe or their Australian homeland, chances are excellent the new Jetset release will outsell the old Capitol one, because the band's U.S. base has grown steadily since it ceased to exist. All of their '80s albums are now in print on Beggars Banquet, three for the first time stateside. And with the songs and sounds out there—stirred by word-of-mouth, Robert Forster and Grant McLennan's many solo and occasional collaborative efforts, and the indelibility of the work itself—more new fans sign on every year than old ones check out.

Juicing the story of this great postpunk reunion are the even greater postgrunge DIY-ers Sleater-Kinney, whose cheerleading after a San Francisco gig was what set Grant and Robert to recording together again. Although in their subtle way the Go-Betweens were and remain as crucially male-female as X or Sonic Youth, the two bands weren't an obvious match, not just because Sleater-Kinney are natural militants while the Go-Betweens are cultivated noncombatants, but because their respective musics sound it. So although the album was recorded in Portland with all three S-K members aboard, it makes sense that frontwomen Corin Tucker and/or Carrie Brownstein cameo on only two tracks. The regular is drum dynamo Janet Weiss, who replaces the legendary Lindy Morrison. Adele Pickvance fills the bass slot long occupied by label head Vickers. And Weiss's ex-lifemate Sam Coomes plays keyboards—just as he does as Weiss's bandmate in yet another of her projects, the postdomestic Quasi.

Sonically, the Go-Betweens don't resemble Quasi—the Coomes-Weiss duo is much wilder and much whinier. But the two share a modest sense of scale. Where in the '80s, the Go-Betweens still aimed to become stars, they're cult bands focused on small songs about manageable subjects. Sleater-Kinney sound as if they want the world and they want it now; the Go-Betweens sound as if they want breakfast but could probably hold out till lunch. Even with the serious pop fans who haunt alt shops and specialized Internet sites, they're not an automatic sell. I've played them for people who've loved them right off—musically, before registering more than a few words. But they can be hard to explain to the convinced ecstatics and habitual malcontents who constitute so much of their theoretical audience.

There's no denying that the Go-Betweens are a bookish taste—if you're bored by the literary, you won't get 'em. But rather than lyric poets, as I once thought, Forster and McLennan are better conceived as short-story writers, with the concreteness and forward motion of voices and music compensating for their imagistic technique and low word count. To quote their signature line—from "As Long as That," way back on 1984's *Before Hollywood*—they've "got a feeling, sounds like a fact," and that's how their songs work. They don't go in for the old-fashioned tales that folk-identified bards like John Prine spin so well. But at their most fragmentary, the Go-Betweens are far more representational than Sonic Youth or even X, Pavement or even Sleater-Kinney. So to me they seem pretty firmly in the modern short-story tradition, the one invented by their fellow interloper from down under Katherine Mansfield as much as anyone—and attenuated to near intangibility in the *New Yorker* and elsewhere by writers convinced, unlike Mansfield then or the Go-Betweens now, that the quality of one's narrative art is in no way diminished by the narrowness of the milieu where it is situated.

Here it might be objected that the Go-Betweens never spread their net very wide. But at least their characters don't know the Metro-North schedule by heart. Coming from Brisbane has been terrific for their frame of reference, as has touring on the cheap and living all over the world among artistic types respected enough to keep their heads up. And a decisive plus has been their self-image as pop professionals, required by definition to deal in love songs. Not even McLennan, much the more relationship-centered of the two, shies away from other subjects—the band's first stone classic, his "Cattle and Cane," nails with typical tenderness another pop staple, a young man's nostalgia for his lost youth. But romance has been good to both of them in any case, and vice versa. Litterateurs rarely do love as much, and popsters rarely do it as well.

The Go-Betweens' romantic complaints abjure bile, raw self-pity, and the kind of wimp vulnerability gumsuckers with guitars have manipulated to their own ends since Cat Stevens was an infidel. They're analytic, they're bemused, they're amusing, they're emotional within bounds, they're as kind as they should be or a little kinder, they're sharp-tongued when it's called for, and often enough they're, well, loving—all of which is rendered more approachable by the flat thoughtfulness of their voices and tunes and more complex by the well-worked intricacy of their arrangements and song structures. Beneath the surface, at a level far from unreadable but appropriately personal, this music isn't so much about love as it is a model of love's preconditions. It has no equal in pop, and also no equal of any note in the contemporary short story, where convention commonly confuses darkness of worldview with depth of purpose.

None of this is likely to attract ecstatics or malcontents, I know, but perhaps it clarifies what's at stake for the band's fans, whose devotion mystifies outsiders. If you can't find Capitol's career-defining *1978–1990* and its glorious non-LP add-ons, let me simply point out that they've never made a bad album and recommend the consensus oeuvre-topper *Tallulah*, followed closely by the consensus runner-up It Depends. *The Friends of Rachel Worth* definitely crowds into this second echelon. But as is only to be expected after eleven years, it doesn't quite mesh the way the Go-Betweens' true band records did. Lacking that sense of fills and figures stumbled upon over long performance histories and instantly integrated into the act not because they were brilliant, which these nonvirtuosos rarely were, but because they felt right, it seems somewhat one-dimensional musically; especially on McLennan's songs, there's the same singer-with-backup expediency that straitened his solo CDs, two of which surpassed any of Forster's on sheer tune power anyway. And near as one can tell, neither Pickvance nor—surprisingly, since she's such a powerhouse—Weiss provides the kind of subliminal cross-gender input with which steadfast drummer Lindy Morrison and, on the last two albums, mercurial cellist-and-such Amanda Brown always riled the band.

One can't be sure in part because, for some timespan or other, Morrison and Brown's inputs were romantic as well as musical, which ultimately contributed as much to the group's breakup as the marketplace's unfeeling demolition of their star fantasies. A decade on, apparently, neither couple is talking. So although what's happened in between is murky, one is tempted to wonder whether Pickvance (or the female drummer from across the sea who'll replace Weiss on tour) is Grant's girlfriend. Certainly the new lyrics suggest that the two old partners' life-paths have diverged. Robert is reliably reported to be happily married in Germany, a union presumably joined after the two years of seclusion sketched drolly in "German Farmhouse," one of four Forster songs here that aren't about love. These are the catchiest and most fetching tracks on the album, taking up surfing dreams, a fond and funny envoi to Patti Smith, and a life-swapping fable that when you think about it may be a love song after all. Comparatively, McLennan's five songs seem unevolved, conjuring the image of a single inamorata—willful, entrancing, a mystery lady brewing love and loss.

This femme fatale cum idée fixe may merely be an artistic creation, of course, or a conflation of my imagination; to some extent she no doubt is. But as an old fan, I catch myself thinking, He's forty-two now—why doesn't he find himself a nice librarian? I remember too how surging McLennan melodies like "Right Here" and "Streets of Our Town" would launch whole Go-Betweens albums into a dimension *The Friends of Rachel Worth* never approaches. And then, to refresh my memory, I play McLennan's finest solo album, 1995's *Horsebreaker Star*. I note and very much enjoy how smartly the hooks circle by on their appointed rounds, far more accomplished in their pop professionalism than the songs on *Rachel Worth*. I wonder how many of these clear-cut little gems sprang from his own life, how many from friends or snatches of conversation or his considerable craft. And then my changer takes me to "Magic in Here," the McLennan title that leads the new album. The arrangement is a touch expedient, as I said. But that's relative to old Go-Betweens. Relative to *Horsebreaker Star*, it's quirky and homemade and riddled with pitfalls. "Lovers lie around on tangled knots," McLennan sings, describing a dock, and his life, and, of course, this music. It's a Go-Betweens album. It's like nothing else. Except, perhaps, love.

Village Voice, 2000

Generation Gaps

The Spice Girls

I went to see the Spice Girls for the drugs, and I did not score. Since concentrated doses of first-crop estrogen will turn any household into a tilt-a-whirl, it figured that in ambient collective form this uncontrolled substance would make Madison Square Garden levitate. How could I miss an event that seemed sure to attract ten thousand twelve-year-old females to the Basketball Court of Broken Dreams?

But as it turned out, my thirteen-year-old date, who rates the Spice Girls seven on a scale where the Backstreet Boys represent nine-point-five, was one of the rare attendees targeted by the zit-strip, leg-razor, and lip-wetter ads that filled the preshow video screens. The modal age may have been ten, but there were more fans under than over. The standard configuration was a mother shepherding several little girls, and minors unaccompanied by adults were just about nonexistent.

What we have here, in greatly accelerated form, is the Michael Jackson Slide: the tendency of all pop phenomena to lose teen cachet as younger kids catch on. Which is yet another reason it's so shallow for the rock hipoisie to pump the Spice Girls as pure pop. I mean, do TV aesthetes call Barney the new Pee-wee Herman? I'm not claiming they're awful. "Wannabe" is a classic, there's a winning sweetness to the necking guideline "Stop" ("I need somebody with the human touch"), and such prefab butt-twitchers as "Spice Up Your Life" and the concert-opening "If You Can't Dance" are crafty enough for anyone but alternadrones and sixteen-year-old boys. But Michael Jackson the Spice Girls are not.

At least not as musicians, dancers, or writers. Icons, maybe. But the Slide isn't helping—I bet Ginger quit because she wanted no part of a kiddie ghetto that teen advisories like "Stop" address as inaccurately as a tampon commercial. The concert was fun. The very integrated six-man (you expected six-girl?) band whomped, the very integrated Spice Boys dance troupe leapt, and Girls/Boys race-mixing was hearteningly thorough, as was inevitable with the Boys split three black, two white, one Asian. Baby covered "Baby Love" with her nice warm burr; Scary and Sporty covered "Sisters Are Doin' It for Themselves" with their nice tough rock. And "Naked" was *performed naked*, Girls straddling turned-around chairs whose triangular backs hid bathing-suit parts.

But for this audience, the Spice Girls weren't models of female adolescent autonomy. They were teen dreams for children whose mothers were looking over their shoulders. Which may be why they closed by topping "Wannabe" and "Spice Up Your Life" with, what a stroke, "Mama," as snapshots and home movies of the Girls as girls looped behind them. I would have found it even more moving if I was my date's mama. After that stroke, the encored "Viva Forever" and "Never Give Up on the Good Times" were letdowns. But the true show-closer, "We Are Family," wasn't. All over the arena, sisters little and big were singing it for themselves.

Spin, 1998

Ooh, That Sound

The Backstreet Boys

There is a sound that looms large in rock mythology from Elvis and Beatles documentaries, yet is seldom heard live. It's the sound of thousands of barely pubescent females screaming for their heroes, their white knights, their dreamboats. The finest thing one can say about the Backstreet Boys is that—unlike their forerunners, the New Kids on the Block—they are worthy of this ecstatic, not-quite-knowing, supernally high sound.

The Backstreet Boys are five ambitious Tampa lads who after four years of hard work are world-famous. Now eighteen to twenty-six, they can actually sing and dance even if they ain't Boyz II Men, and their quadruple-platinum U.S. debut is lit up by at least two pop classics: "Quit Playin' Games (With My Heart)," the most lissome of their many vulnerable ballads, and the uptempo summer smash "Everybody (Backstreet's Back)." At Radio City Music Hall July 17, the former was deployed to prove that they can too play their own instruments, albeit less smoothly than their predictably expert and integrated band. Brian, the guilefully sincere one with the heart condition and the good voice, manned percussion and sang lead.

Unlike Boyz II Men, the Backstreets rarely flaunt their crotches, relegating occasional bump-and-grind gestures to punky-rappy rebels AJ and Howie B. Wimpy, sure, but also age-appropriate for a pre-explicit core audience. That's one reason the climax is so exciting. It's encore time, "Everybody"'s rockin', and the girls know what's coming. Dreamboat Nick, eighteen and blondly handsome, will ask his world, "Am I sexual?" Close your eyes and love it—there's that sound again. Yes, yes, five thousand times yes.

Rolling Stone, July 1998

Tear the Sky Off
the Mother

'N Sync

At Philadelphia's Spectrum last July, 'N Sync's No Strings Attached Tour felt like the end of teenpop utopia: cameras confiscated, hand-painted signs seized at the door ("the boys will see them backstage"), and no pretense that music mattered in a show that was all skits and costume changes. But two subsequent televised stadium cameos by the group—soul-perfect World Series "Star-Spangled Banner," sure-footed Super Bowl "Walk This Way"—aroused one's hopes. And at Giants Stadium in New Jersey June 3, a crucial problem with the earlier indoor show was clear even before the boys had danced down the two-hundred-foot runway from midfield staging area to stage proper: nowhere with a roof can hold what 'N Sync has become.

The Pop Odyssey Tour's many nonmusical accoutrements improve drastically on last year's—hurray for the toy show, the art-directed plays on the word "pop," the b&w flick with a not-yet-discernibly-cynical Justin doing a respectable Chaplin, and, especially, the regular returns to the staging area, giving fans in the stands something closer to the access they craved. But access is a chimera in all megavenues, and said fans—among whom, parents and kiddies aside, teenaged girls outnumbered teenaged boys by at least fifty-to-one—already had something no one gets in an arena: sky's-the-limit grandeur and the relaxed if illusory freedom of the open air.

Of course there was music too, and even the unfamiliar songs from the upcoming *Celebrity* album sounded fine, although one wishes "Celebrity" itself wasn't a dig at gold-digging. Fact is, combining a half-black band that knows its funk with guys who can negotiate our national anthem, the entire 'N Sync oeuvre is beginning to sound classic like Coke—even "No Strings Attached"; even, Lord, "God Must Have Spent a Little More Time on You." Bland, sure— let's not be silly. But also inevitable, historic, somehow wonderful.

Rolling Stone, 2001

The World Is His Boudoir

Prince

So the superlover leads you into his storied boudoir, details the delights about to unfold, and then commands you to play with yourself while he answers his e-mail. Two hours later he returns. You're pissed, frustrated, chafed. Do you give him a piece of your mind and split? Or lie back and enjoy it?

If the superlover is the Artist Who Once Wrote "1999" and you paid seventy-five dollars to see him celebrate Good Friday at Irving Plaza with funk legends Larry Graham (Sly, Graham Central Station) and Chaka Khan (Rufus, her fine fat self), you shrug and get down. Starting an announced one a.m. show at ten of three, the Artist instantly gave up the requisite funk, although most of the songs readily identifiable by name originated with Sly and Rufus. A fit fifty-one, Graham sang strong and tore it up on bass. Khan played keyboards and sang harmony, then wailed and scatted through a three-song, half-hour lead stint. Both, we learned, have albums due on the Artist's NPG label. Fancy that.

The Artist saved himself for an encore that lasted as long as the set. A multipartite, unidentified jam that seemed to be called "Mad Sex" (not "Bad Sex," surely) preceded a third Sly tune, "I Want to Take You Higher," which climaxed with disoriented extra-special guest George Benson scaring up a chicken-scratch solo that was neither fish nor fowl. Then Doug E. Fresh shouted "Who rocks the hardest? / The Artist rocks the hardest" over vamps appropriated from P-Funk, Chuck Brown, Fresh's own "The Show," and the Artist himself. It was five a.m., yet barely a soul left the building before the last whomp was through. I know, because I was near the door, checking.

Rolling Stone, 1998

Two Pieces About
Aretha Franklin

1. Queen of Pop

Between March 1967, and July 1968, Aretha Franklin began her long stay at Atlantic Records with four classic soul albums: *I Never Loved a Man the Way I Love You, Aretha Arrives, Lady Soul,* and *Aretha Now.* This burst of glory is hardly unparalleled. Beatles-Dylan-Stones erupted just as prolifically, as would Al Green and P-Funk in the '70s. Only with Aretha, however, has the eruption been declared an aesthetic standard by self-appointed soul connoisseurs, most of them white. Even today she's sometimes accused of abandoning her gritty muse when she strays from the path charted by Jerry Wexler's taste in rhythmic stomp and catchy songs.

Yet although it was unquestionably those Atlantic LPs that turned Aretha into the queen of all she surveyed, there was nothing ineluctable about her meld with the white Muscle Shoals session players who defined her deep-South phase. If this middle-class Detroit matron had a natural music, a conceit her omnivorous career eats for breakfast, it was the gospel she grew up singing in her famous father's church and first recorded for Chess at fourteen. Hosannas to Wexler for bringing her to Muscle Shoals—and then bringing Muscle Shoals to New York, where "Respect," "Think," "A Natural Woman," and the rest were actually cut. But by the early '70s he was overseeing the intimately lowdown *Spirit in the Dark* and the airily ambitious *Young, Gifted and Black,* two rather different records that rank with any Aretha beyond the titanic *Never Loved a Man* itself. And soon, despite the renown of the gospel and live albums that are beyond the scope of this discussion, he wisely concluded that his greatest artist needed "fresh production input"—which Atlantic proved unable to provide.

So in 1980, Aretha chose a new corporate mentor: Arista's Clive Davis. While cultivating the artist-friendly aura that has enabled him to woo and faithfully support such prestige properties as Aretha Franklin, Patti Smith, and the Grateful Dead, Davis has also been the crassest of hit men, regularly torpedoing music that hasn't achieved perfect knowledge of the lowest common denominator, and Aretha's eight '80s albums for Arista aren't above the hokey, the shallow, or the lame. But with the possible exception of the Curtis Mayfield-overseen *Sparkle*, all of them are more felt and focused than her non-Wexler Atlantics. In addition to two meticulous singer's records produced by Luther Vandross, there's *Love All the Hurt Away*, just about the only time old Atlantic concertmeister Arif Mardin ever got Aretha right, and *Who's Zoomin' Who?*, just about the only time young fusioneer Narada Michael Walden ever got anything right. As a result, *Greatest Hits 1980–1994*—which due to Arista's artist-hostile deletion policy is now the only place one can purchase most of this music—smokes the fourth disc of Rhino's *Queen of Soul: The Atlantic Recordings*. After *Young, Gifted and Black*, even her bravest '70s pop—Mardin's elaborate orchestrations, the overblown 1973 mismatch with Quincy Jones—was a polite compromise with evolving fashions no one involved understood. On Arista, her style is "urban contemporary," no apologies. She's going for the gold, and it suits her.

In the '90s, however, Aretha disappeared as a recording artist. The records had been headed downhill since the great one-dimensional whoop of 1985's *Who's Zoomin' Who?*; 1991's *What You See Is What You Sweat* could have sent her into seclusion on the ineptness of its title alone. Aretha's absence since then—which effectively turned her into a historical figure—is reason to mistrust the eager hype surrounding her new *A Rose Is Still a Rose*. So please believe me when I urge you not to be so damn popwise. Big chillskis may find the new record airless or cyborgian or whatever stupid stuff middle-aged people say about drum synthesizers, but for the open-eared it should stand as permanent proof of the vitality and adaptability of Aretha Franklin's amazing grace.

Aretha's no greater than James Brown or Ray Charles, but she's crucially different. Alone among such peers, not to mention mere contemporaries like Deep South shouter Wilson Pickett or r&b-schooled lounge pros Patti LaBelle and Gladys Knight, the Queen of Soul is totally at home with up-to-the-minute black pop. That's true whether the producer is Jermaine Dupri, Dallas Austin, Lauryn Hill, Puffy Combs, Daryl Simmons, Michael J. Powell, the unsinkable Narada Michael Walden, or Aretha herself, each credited with at least one of the eleven new songs, or Walden, Vandross, Mardin, and all the others who got a crack at her in the '80s. So in the end, the achievement of *A Rose Is Still a Rose* is as much cultural as personal. Of course she comes in and takes over this new-jack r&b, which builds off hip-hop the way her funk lite did off disco. She always does when she's on. But she also sits back and takes strength from it.

Remarkably, *A Rose Is Still a Rose* does its excellent work without Baby-face, an obvious match whose notable Aretha tracks on *1980–1994* and *Waiting to Exhale* wouldn't be fiftieth percentile here. The procession of standouts includes Simmons's "In the Morning," disintegrating over and over into a mournful "I don't wanna be the other woman"; Aretha's virtuosic "The Woman," inarticulate in its wronged pain until she moans and scats the coda into a show of the pride she brushed by in the second verse; the uncountable rhythm tracks of Combs's apparently simple (and apparently unsampled) "Never Leave You Again"; Austin's long-suffering yet somehow jaunty "I'll Dip," on which Aretha sings barely a scrap of the written melody, improvising the verse and embellishing a chorus hook stated by a multitracked Debra Killings; and Hill's equally impressive title cut, whose unaffected big-sisterhood underpins Aretha's most credible feminist outreach ever. None of these songs aspires to the declarative tunes and pungent phrases of the soul era. Like so much recent r&b, they're atmospheric, with minimal lyrics and hooks that catch only after repeated exposure, and the range of studio help would seem extreme even in hip-hop, where the too-many-cooks strategy first developed for divas like Tina Turner and Aretha herself has become de rigueur. Yet rather than wandering or pogo-sticking, the record plays seamlessly—she varies producers the way Wexler did songwriters when he was running the show.

Although the success of this approach does definitely owe the cohesive sensibility of the new r&b, which can be cautiously samey, earning its own accusations of soul betrayed, it has its upside in dedicated craft and sweet emotion—from Babyface and Boyz II Men to the pop-hop of Puffy and the Fugees, a woman-fed insistence that music isn't just phony street hustles and black CNN. But at its heart, of course, is Aretha Franklin's voice—not just the instrument, which is losing its high end the way aging voices usually do, but what she does with it. It doesn't need saying that this voice is at the core of Aretha's virtually universal appeal—does even Rex Reed, who once called her "probably the worst ballad singer I've ever heard," deny her now? Its power is so ineffable, however, that no one has ever satisfactorily described it in words. One reason the sentimental myths that identify her solely with soul grit, gospel exaltation, and the big beat hold such sway is that they at least make surface sense.

I'm not about to penetrate this mystery here. But I am going to note the obvious—that however misguided other artists' upward gentility may be, Aretha does it right. For three decades now nothing has been beyond her reach. Of course she fumbles sometimes—too often. But existentially, she's in command. In fact, as she proved with her Grammy opera stint, there's nothing she does right that she doesn't also do her way. When she's on, what defines her magic is that she's in the music but not of it. All her great performances, even "Who's Zoomin' Who?" and "Freeway of Love," are infused with suffering, and from "Ain't No Way" to "In the Morning," all her suffering is infused with joy. While Jerry Wexler provided the means, it was her father's colleague Martin Luther King who showed her the way. Great Godamighty, she's free at last. And no sentient human can resist that freedom.

Village Voice, 1998

....

2. Familiar and Fabulous

In 1998, *A Rose Is Still a Rose* proved what it set out to prove: that alone among her soul peers, Aretha Franklin could skin, fry, and suck the marrow from contemporary r&b. Her more homogeneous new multi-produced *So Damn Happy* also proves what it sets out to prove: that Aretha Franklin's voice subsumes petty stylistic details, especially in a moment when so much r&b goes for the lush timbres and hook-defying swoops and melismas that dominate her mature style. But on the Radio City stop of her supposed farewell tour, she proved something bigger. R&b—kid stuff. Queen of soul— what else you got? Aretha Franklin was as large as any pop singer you can name. Larger.

This is not a stupid joke about her weight, although her recent willingness to be fat in public says all we need know about why she's so damn happy. It's a statement of fact about her presence. Neil Young? Bob Dylan? In-the-house Bette Midler? Titans and vital artists all. But they don't fill a room like Aretha Franklin. When she grumped about how Streisand would have "a chalice of water" onstage and she couldn't even find a handkerchief, some descried temperament, but she was merely marking her territory. Maybe Streisand, or in olden days Sinatra or Umm Kulthum, can claim comparable impact. Me, I'll wait till John Lennon comes back from the dead. That might be a contest.

Audacity, not spectacle, was key. Anybody with the cash can hire a thirty-two-piece orchestra including two tambourine players, a bank of local cellists and violinists, and a Hammond organ. But the unlikelihood that an aggregation so grand would decline the emoluments of a synthesizer was exceeded only by the unlikelihood of her opener—not some Atlantic classic or signature piece from her two-decades-plus Arista run, but "Won't Be Long," a negligible r&b-styled number that rocketed to not quite seventy-five on the pop chart in 1961 as her debut single for Columbia, where her girl-woman explorations had so much more grace than we used to think. What was more unlikely still was that it sounded both familiar and fabulous.

What a commanding, magnanimous show. Not just "Try a Little Tenderness" and the impressionistic Johnny Mercer–Hoagy Carmichael flight she never got to do on Sullivan but also the unnecessary young dance troupe booty-popping to "Hot in Herre," which you knew she fell in love with on the radio while cooking up some chicken (when the song resurfaced unexpectedly from the PA later, bet money she had steps ready). The gospel showpiece featuring a young rev from her father's church with stronger, less epochal pipes. The way she went out on a vamp-till-done from the faux classic "Freeway of Love," during which she introduced Ahmet Ertegun, her gownmaker, several publicists, and others too numerous to mention. The way she took her wig off when she wanted to let her hair down. Not just "Respect" and "Think" and "Chain of Fools" but also the single and then the title track from *So Damn Happy*, which sounded, exactly, both familiar and fabulous.

And of course her voice, always her voice, all over the glorious concert, all over the sturdy album. Deeper, yet undiminished. The world still awaits musicological analysis of its miracles, so metaphors will have to do. Chocolate mousse cut with liqueur—here Drambuie, there Grand Marnier, when it kicks Crème de Cacao. No, my wife says, something simpler—chess pie, as they call pecan pie without the pecans, or your mother's cooking, 'cause you know there'll always be more. Sexflesh, I think to myself, Jimi Hendrix's earhole or Sheena Easton's sugar walls. Metaphorically, I mean it—no aphrodisia implied. The reality Franklin accesses is spiritual, philosophical, metaphysical—the essence of pleasure in all its incomprehensible immediacy. There's pain in there, can't live without it. But that's for completeness's sake. Like a rose, which when it pricks is still a rose. And so damn happy about it.

Village Voice, 2003

Two Pieces About Bob Dylan

1. Dylan Back: World Goes On

Last year *Spy* did an amusing item graphing "Dylan is back" claims, often in precisely those terms, all the way to 1968. The same fiddle-faddle greeted not only 1970's winsome *New Morning* and 1975's well-remembered *Blood on the Tracks* and 1989's widely heralded *Oh Mercy*, but many tours and just about every other album the man put some effort into. So naturally the news that *Under the Red Sky* would feature such sidemen as Al Kooper and Stevie Ray Vaughan got the treatment as well—until the rumormongers heard the actual record, which met with the mixed-to-contemptuous response I keep at the ready for all new Dylan projects. Only this time a dis won't cut it for me. To my astonishment, I think *Under the Red Sky* is Dylan's best album in fifteen years, a record that may even signal a ridiculously belated if not totally meaningless return to form. Oh Lordy—Dylan is back.

Can't be, of course—there's nowhere for him to come back to. Although he's not as far gone as John Lennon, his moment is, and that's the fantasy beneath the fiddle-faddle—the rock star as cultural hero, the weathervane to tell "us" which way the wind blows, the messenger who can change the world. Dylan's iconic clout has proven more durable than I would have guessed: watching a house full of scruffy professionals cheer the October 15 opening of his five-night stand at the Beacon, I was reminded of none other than the universal icon, Elvis Presley himself. But that cuts both ways. Like Elvis, Dylan is faced with the insuperable problem of living up to the memory of a time when, for reasons of history mistakenly attributed to mere genius, he embodied the dreams of a "generation." Always preternaturally media-hip, he's ridden this dilemma with more creative grace than Elvis, keeping at it for close to three decades now where Elvis barely lasted two. But for fifteen years he's been a bad joke more often than not—*Renaldo and Clara*, the religious conversions, the crank politics, horrendous product like *Street-Legal* and *Down in the Groove*.

Live, he's stuck to the same strategy ever since the 1974 rebirth commemo-rated on *Before the Flood*, performing a motley assortment of classics and not-classics with lyrics intact and music damaged, and ever since 1975's ramshackle Rolling Thunder Revue the reinterpretations have been miss-or-hit. I say this as someone who stopped going to his concerts after *Street-Legal*, three live albums ago now, and never gave it a thought. For five minutes at the Beacon— the fanfare cum antiwar dig of a three-guitar "Marine's Hymn" intro leading into a hard, tight "Rainy Day Women"—I wondered if maybe I'd been missing something, but I got over it after the second song, when I turned to one of the three *Rolling Stone* critics nearby and shouted, "What was that?" "'Mas-ters of War,'" he grinned. Darn it, I'd almost guessed—the refrain had the right cadence. Unfortunately, the arrangement had steamrollered the not-so-intact lyrics as well as the melody, and for anyone who doesn't have a hundred best-loved Dylan songs on instant recall, it was unrecognizable. No wonder the West Pointers he'd regaled with it the night before had just sat there.

And so it went. A band featuring *Saturday Night Live*'s G. E. Smith and anchored by veteran East Coast session drummer Christopher Parker played hippie songs at postpunk tempos, often yoking them to immemorial rock-r&b readymades. "Shelter from the Storm" mounted "Bristol Stomp," "Watching the River Flow" was tailed as usual by "Dust My Broom," and neither ben-efited from the comparison. After an acoustic set that topped an overwrought "Don't Think Twice" with its loud-mouthed big brother "It Ain't Me Babe"— both of them still women songs, not audience songs—the lyrics got clearer. But the big cheers came after the titles, when everybody figured out what they were hearing. Although a raving postmodernist might crow about decon-structive revitalization or some such, it's my middlebrow conclusion that Dylan's anti-iconic compulsion to throw melodies out the window creates a musically meaningless ritual—that far from teaching his loyal over-thirtys a lesson about change, it panders to a nostalgia of brute physical proximity, no bet-ter in the end than choked-up reminiscence or middle-aged longing. Dylan has written a shitload of great songs, and he'll never ruin them all. Good. I'm more impressed with the Stones' hyperprofessionalism anyway.

Live, that is—for both acts, the studio is now a separate realm. No longer will some sparely postfolk *John Wesley Harding* parry a baroque *Sgt. Pepper* for a subculture that has never seen its hero make a foolish move. Their rec-ords are prestige product, not cultural bellwethers, and while the Stones pro-mote theirs, Dylan treats his recording career with the same fine disregard as the rest of his music. At the Beacon, the only teaser from his new album was the title tune, which was a highlight, and not merely because—like the other '80s selections, almost every one (even *Down in the Groove*'s "Silvio") a pleasant surprise—it still had the tune it was born with. It was a highlight because out of nowhere Dylan has started making good records again. I remain suspicious of the hushed emotion, weary wisdom, and new-age "maturity" of 1989's Daniel Lanois–produced *Oh Mercy*. But it gives up a lot of beautiful songs, and there's no point denying the commitment signified by its intensity of craft. And then there are the Traveling Wilburys, a superstar joke almost as liberating as it wanted to be, whose first album had Dylan's spontaneous wit and is-it-rolling-Bob? serendipity all over it. On the brand new *Vol. 3*, they sound more like a band; Jeff Lynne and George Harrison make contributions every bit as welcome and unlikely as "Inside Out," a casual jeremiad about things turning yellow that bears Dylan's oddball mark. That's three memorable albums since late '88. And I contend that the Was Bros.–produced *Under the Red Sky* is the best.

History being history, I don't expect or even hope to convince my "generation" of this, much less the world. In fact, I wouldn't swear Dylan agrees with me—supposedly, he hates *The Basement Tapes*, so what does he know? As has been charged, *Under the Red Sky*'s lyrics do seem somewhat more obscure and sloppy than *Oh Mercy*'s. But Dylan has been obscure-and-sloppy since whenever—the anomaly is *Oh Mercy*'s "focused" writing, to quote *Stone* quoting Lanois, who you can bet identifies with the bitterly ironic "Political World" and the fatally unironic "Disease of Conceit" (and understands "Man in the Long Black Coat" better than ordinary mortals). *Under the Red Sky*, on the other hand, aims frankly for the evocative. It's fabulistic, biblical— kind of like *John Wesley Harding*.

But in these postpunk times, one rarely loves a record on literary grounds. Let Dylan protect the words and fuck with the music—Don Was has his own program, and where with Bonnie Raitt and the B-52's his command of the megapop groove forced a respectful homogenization, with Dylan it produces an apotheosis. Though Dylan has known great rhythm sections, his seminal rock records were cut with Nashville cats on drums—Kenny Buttrey when he was lucky, nonentities when he wasn't. But setting the pace on *Under the Red Sky* is J. C. Mellencamp's secret weapon, Kenny Aronoff. Musically, this ain't *John Wesley Harding*, it's *Highway 61 Revisited* revisited, more on the power of its rock-r&b readymades than of Kooper's lonely "Like a Rolling Stone" rip. But the tempos are postpunk like it oughta be, with Aronoff's sprints and shuffles grooving ahead like '60s folk-rock never did. Gives the fables more oomph.

They're strengthened by the workout, and since I'm a realist as well as an oomph man, I also treasure their moments of overpowering literalness. When Dylan barks, "They said it was the land of milk and honey / Now they say it's the land of money / Who'd ever thought they could make that stick?," I credit his outrage without forgetting his royalty statements. When he moans, "Takes too much skill / Takes too much will," I believe he's gritted his teeth through the bad patches of a long-term sexual relationship even while suspecting that for him the long term is still measured in months. And when he thanks his honey for that cup of tea, I melt. But in the end I value *Under the Red Sky* most for what it is—an album where narrative metaphor is an adaptive mechanism, allowing Dylan to inhabit a "mature" pessimism he's figured out isn't the meaning of life.

When he's on top of his dilemma, Dylan insists that he's no prophet, so the unjudgmental equanimity of this record is a boon. It doesn't scold or complain—its sole foray into megapolitical cliche, "TV Talkin' Time," is put in the mouth of some other crank, a Hyde Park haranguer (and has been praised by reviewers for its outspoken criticism of modern media). Yet the lyrics are bleak even though they're also, as he phrased it in USA *Today*, "intentionally broad and short, so you can draw all kinds of conclusions." Dylan seems depressed above all about eco-collapse—about the disappearance of the landscape he grew up with. In "10,000 Men," it's a war out there; in "2 X 2," men and women march blindly into a stolen tomorrow; in "Cat's in the Well," "the world's being slaughtered" and "may the Lord have mercy on us all." The love songs are pained and gnomic—the gorgeous "Born in Time" wouldn't parse even if he'd relieved it of the sloppy-to-obscure "You married young just like your ma." The title track is a cyberpunk folk song in which getting baked in a pie surrenders its accrued nursery-rhyme innocence to the grisly realism it began with. Even "Wiggle Wiggle," Dylan's way of encouraging whoever's listening to show some life, winds up with the wiggler vomiting fire.

Through it all, though, the sweetness of Dylan's tone does him proud. Apocalyptic though that blood red sky may also be, he's crafted an affectionate elegy for a human race forced to live in a diminished world. Likely it's not a return to anything—Dylan is most representative of his "generation" in his compulsion to move on. But for a man who long ago announced that he couldn't change the world, it's an honorable place to stop off for a while.

Village Voice 1990

2. Secrets of the Sphinx

In the spring of 1997, shortly before he almost died, Bob Dylan recorded *Time Out of Mind*, which upon its September release became his most widely hailed album since 1975's *Blood on the Tracks*. Later that fall—before it was too late, you might say—he was presented with two lifetime achievement awards: the lucrative Dorothy and Lillian Gish Prize and later the prestigious Kennedy Center Honor. He even made the cover of *Newsweek* like Bruce Springsteen before him. A public recluse was a celebrity again.

Of course, Dylan hasn't been a true recluse since *Blood on the Tracks*— just an enigma. *Time Out of Mind* is only his second self-composed album of the '90s after nine in the '80s, but he tours a hundred nights a year, with the reward of a cross-generational cult that mushroomed when Jerry Garcia passed on—a cult for whom his boomer aura is secondary to his ongoing trek through Americana. Availability hasn't made him any more knowable, however; notoriously, he just plays his music and gets out of there. For Dylan, always prophetic in his aversion to the role model role, this is ideal— he makes loads of money as a working musician, recording and performing whatever he feels like, while avoiding all the burdens of stardom except fame itself. "There's nothing to say so I'm not going to say anything," he mumbled when he materialized, a jowly wraith with a bodyguard, to receive his Gish in October. "I wish she was still here. I'd loved to have made a movie with her. And I feel very fortunate to receive this and I'm not sure what I've done to deserve it but I'm going to try to keep on doing it." That was his entire speech—quite a long one, for a sphinx.

So for Dylan, the December 1 show at the fifteen-hundred-capacity Irving Plaza was basically just another gig. If it was deemed historic by the reawakened bigshots in attendance, that wasn't because it was a benefit (all proceeds to Harlem's Hale House) or "intimate" (Dylan's normal Manhattan venue is the three-thousand-seat Beacon). It was because an epochal artist had almost died, put out a rather good album, and received a lot of awards— had reentered history, a/k/a the limelight.

And while many professed themselves transported, I'm just impressed that the show was one of my top dozen of 1997—not up to Sleater-Kinney or Ornette Coleman, but on a par with Pavement, Cachao, John Prine. Although Dylanheads, who chalk up new live songs like birdwatchers spotting rare flycatchers, knowledgeably and even excitedly discuss the evolving procession of anonymous studio pros who fill his bands, I say new guitarist Larry Campbell and old pedal steel player Bucky Baxter, new drummer

David Kempner and old bassist Tony Garnier are all just backing musicians, and backing musicians are called that because they know how to stay out of the way; I missed organist Augie Meyers, an occasional solo artist who is, with the obvious exception, the strongest voice on *Time Out of Mind*. In theory the kind of skilled journeymen Dylan goes for are at least good for a great groove, but Dylan is too chameleonlike for anything quite that satisfying. He wants many different grooves played with competent fervor, and that's what he got.

Having brushed a blistering "Maggie's Farm" with the merest hint of finger-snapping swing ("for . . . Maggie's"), Dylan also took "Tonight I'll Be Staying Here with You" a tad lounge—twice he steered "I can hear that whistle blowin'" between a sob and a blubber, only to dry off his timbre for "See that station-master too." But this illusion vanished as he went spooky-lonesome on "Cold Irons Bound," the first of four new songs scattered about in Dylan's version of a promo blitz. The heads loved this subtle number; casuals like me preferred the catchier "'Til I Fell in Love with You," though it seemed kind of quiet for a set-closer, and the stark encore "Love Sick." Also among the sixteen selections were "Rainy Day Women" and "Highway 61," the '80s rocker "Silvio" (a live staple that rocked harder at the Beacon in 1990), the Reverend Gary Davis's "Cocaine" and the Stanley Brothers' "White Dove," the callow "Ramona" transformed into a lovely Mexican waltz, and two from *Blood on the Tracks*: a stuck-inside-of-Memphis "You're a Big Girl Now" and, oh yes, "Tangled Up in Blue."

The heads are weary of this one, but as a song it doesn't quit, and it occasioned the most thrilling music of the night, as Dylan worried a four-note phrase on his acoustic guitar into a medium-long solo of notable momentum and detail. On acoustic, Dylan played like he sang, wobbling and cracking but always rich, eccentric, perversely intelligent; it's as if when Jerry died he transubstantiated his old-timey thoughtfulness over to Dylan in exchange for two or three fingertips. On electric, unfortunately, the leader's blues-rock cliches were often indistinguishable from his sideman's. But whatever he's doing he's going to keep on doing it. Others may attend his next New York shows to revisit their youths, or glimpse eternal life. I just want to find out whether he ever borrowed that spoonful of sugar from Eric Clapton.

Spin, 1998

Ain't Dead Yet

Holy Modal Rounders

And in all fairness, i must give an urgent WARNING about
Weber. He steals any money or drugs he can get his hands
on. Religiously. Be warned.

Or so said walking songbook Peter Stampfel's notes to 1975's *Alleged in Their Own Time*, the Holy Modal Rounders' first album for Rounder, the folk label that had been named after them five years before. In 1979, though, he rejoined Steve Weber for *Going Nowhere Fast*, which was released in 1981, when his old partner came in from Oregon to play a few dates and record a never-released double-LP. After that, an acerbically dried-out Stampfel would occasionally remember him with a rendition of "Lonely Junkie": "My past is a bummer / My future's a drag / I live for the moment / And the moment is scag." Yet there they were at the Bottom Line last Friday for a reunion engineered by Chicago's Dysfunctionells.

The fifty-seven-year-old Stampfel looked his age and acted fourteen—even more manic than usual. Weber, who is fifty-two, looked between sixty and ninety and acted as if all things considered he was very glad he'd returned from the dead. A very skinny six-five, hair and beard completely white, he could have been a moonshining geezer out of *Barney Google*, an effect heightened considerably by the fact that he had no teeth. Seated throughout, his guitar more fluent than his vocals, he was all arms, legs, and attitude. When Stampfel sang one he didn't know, he threw up his hands and shouted, "I feel so useless!"; when a Dysfunctionell joshed about a "Theme from Exodus" encore, Weber misheard him and muttered, "Excellence is completely out of my grasp." But he never stopped hamming up a set that included his "Sea of Love" and "Chitlin Cookin' Time in Cheatham County" as well as a "Flop Eared Mule" the two oldsters transformed into both "Ain't Dead Yet" and "Over the Hill." Many stayed for the second show.

Weber had cadged a pint of vodka backstage and seemed calmer. Early on he wandered through a lament about the pills his girl went on after rehab that messed up her period and now he can't make her come, but she still tastes good yum yum. "I made that up on the spot," he told us. "The wet spot," Stampfel chimed in. "The G spot!" Weber crowed.

Village Voice, 1996

How to Survive on an Apple Pie Diet

John Prine

John Prine and Iris DeMent were seated across from each other at a table for eight in Michael's on West 55th Street. Here BMI had convened a small party to celebrate George Strait's conversion of the obscure Prine copyright "I Just Want to Dance with You" into a hit that paid Prine's hospital bills while he fought off cancer of the neck in 1998. Prine is a genially impish guy who wears his grayish-black hair in a long crew cut. He looks his age whether it's fifty-five, as he told me, or fifty-two, as the books say, but like so many musicians he doesn't act it. He has a storyteller's memory, conjuring details from years back about anything, and without claiming a monopoly or even seeming immodest, he did most of the talking. Among the topics I recall: Prine's collaborator on the Strait song, obsessive Australian-Nashvillian craftsman Roger Cook; God d/b/a Sam Phillips threatening to kick Prine's ass all the way to the Houston clinic that saved his life; a bar for midgets on Roosevelt Road in Chicago; Prine's forthcoming Billy Bob Thornton movie, *Daddy and Them*, which generated the title song of his DeMent-heavy duet cover album, *In Spite of Ourselves*; how to roast pork with German wine; regaining forty lost pounds on an apple pie diet; Prine and his late buddy Steve Goodman's Kris Kristofferson–brokered courtship by Atlantic's Jerry Wexler and Buddah's Neil Bogart, making them the first Chicago artists ever to sign with a major without emigrating first; and—the only time he actually boasted—his skill at buying shoes for his third wife, Fiona.

Early on Prine pulled out snapshots of his two preschool boys—"Irish twins" born ten months apart who were honored guests at their parents' wedding. They're his first kids, and he's officially hooked. Knowing that happy marriages have taken the piss and vinegar out of many songwriters, he mused about how he would cope—"I could become a peeping Tom and write about the neighbors." But although "In Spite of Ourselves" is his only new song in three years, he's too glad to be alive to let that worry him—in 1992, he predicted that the Grammy-winning *The Missing Years* might be his last album, only to produce the even better *Lost Dogs and Mixed Blessings* in 1995. Before long the conversation moved on to Prine's dad, a frequenter of country-music bars who for an extra fifty bucks a month served as president of his machinists' local and always planned to take his boys back to Kentucky. This impossible dream inspired Prine's "Paradise," and Prine told how his father first listened to the acetate from the next room, so it would sound like it was on a jukebox. He died young, at fifty-six, shortly after losing a union election.

I glanced over at DeMent, who had silently pumped her fist at the news that Prine's dad was a union man. To my astonishment, she was trying to wipe tears from her eyes without making a fuss. The guy from BMI leaned over and quietly asked if she was OK. Yes, she nodded, then murmured, "It was just such a moving story." A minute later, she entered the conversation. What she wanted to know was how old Prine was when he realized he was something special. She posed the question in several versions, and Prine listened up good. But without wasting any false modesty, he never really answered. This wasn't something he worried about either.

Afterwards Prine walked DeMent down Fifth Avenue to go watch themselves on Conan O'Brien, where the powers that be had liked "In Spite of Ourselves" so much they didn't bleep out the dirty words. At home, I watched too. Unfortunately for TV purposes, Prine's voice was less mellifluous than ever. Throat radiation can do that to you.

....

If DeMent had seemed a bit fragile at Michael's, at Town Hall two nights later she bounced out like a trouper, proudly displaying her red thrift-store heels over the footlights. At thirty-eight, the late-blooming DeMent has grown into the role thrust upon her by her big, high, Holiness-steeped soprano. But she's in the middle of a divorce, and the songs aren't coming—her unaccompanied thirty-minute set included only one that postdated 1996's *The Way I Should*. Her speaking voice was an octave lower than the one she sang in. Introducing one of the several songs she's written about her late father, she told how she'd cried at dinner.

DeMent's performance proved that power doesn't always require speed. But half an hour later, Prine burst onstage with rockabilly-looking guitarist Jason Wilbur and balding bassist David Jacques, launched the "Blow Up Your TV" chorus of the time-tested "Spanish Pipedream," and took over. Even before his voice loosened up he was lit, radiantly explaining why he was "really glad to be here tonight." He'd become a medium for the glow I'd heard him describe Tuesday—the glow that surrounds the things of this world after you've beaten a command to leave it.

Making things glow has always been a Prine specialty anyway. Even at the beginning, he wasn't the "protest" singer he's still said to be: blowing up your TV was a prelude to throwing away your newspaper, eating lots of peaches, and finding Jesus on your own. When the *Rolling Stone Encyclopedia* praises his depictions of "white proletarian America," I wonder whether the writer grew up in a world so rarefied it lacked frying pans, slippers, umbrellas, knick-knack shelves, and four-way stop signs, to name a few of the everyday objects that figure on the four terrific albums that got the young Prine not far enough between 1971 and 1975. Prine is like Bobbie Ann Mason, or early Barry Levinson, or a Nashville songwriter going for quality (which in fact is what he's become). I'd call him an American realist except that often he's also an American humorist, which brings out his omnipresent surrealism—associative leaps from an imagination that's known a normal life's complement of consciousness enhancers, although Prine cut down on his drinking years ago. His realism, his surrealism, and his laugh lines all shoulder the fundamentally celebratory function of language in love—especially language born from the spirit of music. Prine's adoration of the turned cliche ("Some day you'll own a home / That's as big as a house") and the newly minted idiom (lovemaking as "the land of the lost surprise") transfigures even such oppressed proletarians as Donald and Lydia masturbating in two different worlds, or the isolated old wife of "Angel from Montgomery," although not the Vietnam junkie of "Sam Stone," which as Prine's best-known song has always made him seem more maudlin than he is.

I could quote Prine's houseful of first-rate work forever, make you wish you knew him by heart the way I did when he brought out "Grandpa Was a Carpenter" at Town Hall, which had me singing "Voted for Eisenhower / 'Cause Lincoln won the war" on the first chorus. He performed for two hours without sinking below "Sam Stone," an exceedingly well-written piece, and there were plenty more where those came from—Rhino's *Great Days* comp barely falters for forty-one tracks, and after that you can go back to *Sweet Revenge* or *Common Sense*, to name just two. Yet between 1980's *Storm Windows* and 1992's *The Missing Years*, the quality flagged—his only selection from the period wasn't "I Just Want to Dance with You" but the withering "Unwed Fathers," written with Bobby Braddock, one of the many songsmiths and sidemen who've revved his tune sense since he got to Nashville. Prine's fondness for Braddock types is one reason the novelties and cheating songs of *In Spite of Ourselves* are a perfect way for him to keep his hand in until his muse feels as glad to be alive as he does. The other is that he doesn't have to sing so much. His soft-burred drawl is real lovable once you get to know it, but that doesn't mean Trisha Yearwood and Emmylou Harris and Dolores Keane and Lucinda Williams and Fiona Prine and creaky old Connie Smith and Melba Montgomery aren't welcome additions to his soundscape.

Yet with all due respect, Iris DeMent cuts every one of these ladies. Her four tracks on *In Spite of Ourselves* include two all-time George Jones gems: Braddock's beyond-cornball Tammy feature "(We're Not) The Jet Set" ("We're the old Chevro-let set") and the impossible "Let's Invite Them Over," which had George and Melba spouse-swapping up on the c&w charts in 1964. DeMent joined Prine about an hour into his set; reticent on "Milwaukee Here I Come," she picked up steam on "Jet Set" and an eye-rolling "Let's Invite Them Over" and owned Yearwood's part on "When Two Worlds Collide." Then it was time for "In Spite of Ourselves," where her first verse begins, "He ain't got laid in a month of Sundays / Caught him once and he was sniffin' my undies." DeMent is rightly known as a good girl. The few sexual references in her writing are indirect. But she sang those lines with an unflappable gusto worthy of Loretta Lynn or Belle Starr and topped Prine throughout, as she was meant to. A good portion of the standing O at the end was for her.

"In Spite of Ourselves," in which a husband and wife who love each other to death paint wildly disparate pictures of their marriage, is the comic masterpiece of someone whose family ways have left his bodily fluids intact. Prine and the band immediately obliterated it with a loud blues and two 1995 copyrights, including the surreal history of a wrecked marriage "Lake Marie," a mostly recited flag-waver that's climaxed his shows since he put it out. It must be daunting for a songwriter in a dry spell to witness such an endless catalogue unfold from the wings, even one who almost stole the show.

Returning for the encore, DeMent was subdued on "Unwed Fathers" and "So Sad," then perked up on "Paradise," with all its evocations of father, struggle, and a transformed past. It was just a show. She'd established that when she kicked up her heels. But in this kind of music the show feeds off direct emotion—the vivid joy and complex regrets of people with a new lease on life, people who cry at dinner. Together, John Prine and Iris DeMent had established that too.

Village Voice, 1999

The Unflashiest

Willie Nelson

At sixty-five, Willie Nelson is an icon. His headband-and-pigtails could be trademarked if it was in him to bother, and neither his IRS run-in nor his adventures in the marijuana trade will stop the man who toked up on the roof of Carter's White House from receiving his Kennedy Center honor this December—no doubt with more enthusiasm than his immediate predecessor in this modest coup, his longtime Columbia labelmate Bob Dylan. However suspect, this analogy goes a long way. True, Dylan was promulgating his songs as a youthcult avatar while the older man was still hewing to the Nashville system of selling "Four Walls" to Faron Young and "Crazy" to Patsy Cline, finally cracking the hit parade with a cover of "Blue Eyes Crying in the Rain" after fifteen years of major publishing bucks and failed record deals. But as Nelson entertained a solidly middle-class crowd at Newark's New Jersey Performing Arts Center a few weeks ago, what came clear was the overriding link between these two great American songwriters: both now earn their livings, and find reason for living, as road musicians. Maybe if Nelson has a near-death experience someone will notice.

The irritation in my tone is not meant to imply that Dylan is unworthy. On some objective level, he's probably more "important" than Nelson. But not by much—they're *both* titans, definitely in the same league. Live and on record, I've gotten even more from Willie than from a resurgent Bob in recent years. So I'm impatient with the cultural politics that transform one icon into a symbol of eternal life and the other into a has-been. Admittedly, I was long derelict myself—until a 1996 Supper Club show timed to his finest recent album, the Island debut *Spirit*, I'd never seen Nelson, and so was astonished by what was in many respects a standard set. An hour in, figuring he was about done, I chortled to my wife that he was going to exit without playing one song from the record he was supposedly promoting. Just then he ambled into an instrumental I dimly recognized: the lead cut from *Spirit*, which he proceeded to run through in its entirety and in order, the whole album from beginning to end. Then he went on as usual. All told, Nelson and his companionable little four-piece played for two hours and forty minutes that night, performing some fifty-two songs. It was wonderful. It was also, as I told my diary, "the unflashiest music I've ever seen in my life."

Understandably, the standard bios all strike the same chords: Nashville and then outlawism, annual Fourth of July shindig and then Farm Aid, concept albums and then off-the-cuff collaborations, the unplanned windfall of his 1978 classic-pop masterpiece *Stardust*. Whether or not they note Nelson's stint on bass for Ray Price (taught himself overnight, the *Virgin Encyclopedia* adds), all they have to say about his guitar is that he plays one. They talk up his "starker, more modern" writing, so much "more complex technically than the usual country tune," while treading gingerly around the "weather-beaten directness" of his "parched, grainy" or "dry, wry voice." But in concert it's different.

The first thing you notice is that he's some guitarist. Famously, at least to his fans, his customized Martin has two holes, one cut by the luthier, the other worn in by his pick. Its sound is resonantly gorgeous, and the chords he gets from it have no parallel in country—he has a way of timing a dissonant comp so that the beat stumbles in a precise-seeming parallel to the chord's harmonic effect. His single lines are just as adroit and unpredictable, and once you acclimate to his musicianship, you start really hearing his singing, which beyond all that parched stuff is loud, flexible, strong. Nelson's midrange is so nasal that it diverts attention from his phenomenal breath control, and though he doesn't lift into high tenor as readily as when he was forty, he still glides at will into a powerful baritone that locates the true source of his voice deep in his thorax. What makes this harder to remember is that his records hardly seem sung at all—they register as half-spoken. Like all his music, the off-beat phrasing that pigeonholed him as uncommercial until he fled Nashville in 1970 is distantly informed by jazz, but the effect he intends is antivirtuosic. He's going for the intimate clarity of one-on-one conversation.

That's the secret of his unflash: he's an adept of the natural. Amazingly, the band that backed him in Newark—guitarist-vocalist Jody Payne, harmonica heartthrob Mickey Raphael, bass man Bee Spears, percussionist Billy English, drummer Paul English (his kit a snare on a packing case), and older sister Bobbie Nelson playing piano as if she'd learned from the saloon scenes in a hundred Westerns although in fact she doodles Mozart in her spare time—has been with him since 1972. These are not the crack shots Dylan likes to hire—they're just Willie's friends, and 150 nights a year they play together like water seeking its own level. They were on for two hours and thirty-eight songs—one every three minutes, bang bang bang. Both nights the simplicity of the presentation had a devotional aura. Not that there was anything mystical or sanctimonious about a bunch of old buddies playing a bunch of old songs. But live, Nelson makes it his discipline to avoid not just pretension but metaphor. In an artist who willingly keyed 1981's *Somewhere Over the Rainbow* to E. Y. Harburg's dreamy kitsch and 1993's Don Was–produced showcase *Across the Borderline* to Paul Simon's filigreed "American Tune," the basic-English literalness of the set list amounted to a statement of aesthetic principle—or at least an entertainment strategy. In Newark, Nelson's mostly instrumental Cole Porter selection was the elegantly laconic "Night and Day." "City of New Orleans" and "Pancho and Lefty" seemed positively Shakespearian in their narrative detail.

Nelson has cut lots of rock material, but "City of New Orleans" is as close as I've seen him get live; although he has a Jamaican album in the can and correctly credits producer Booker T. Jones as the hidden genius of *Stardust*, the only African-American song he performed—both nights—was Kokomo Arnold's "Milk Cow Blues." "What I do for a living is to get people to feeling good," he declares on the jacket of his out-of-print autobiography, and this he achieves with instantly recognizable country and pop touchstones whose meaning can't be mistaken: "All of Me" and "Blue Skies," "My Bucket's Got a Hole in It" and "Rolling in My Sweet Baby's Arms," "Working Man Blues" and "Georgia on My Mind." If other people's copyrights outnumbered Nelson's two-to-one at his shows, the model for their simplicity was still the bare-bones diction and subtle musicality of "Crazy" and "Funny How Time Slips Away," of "Night Life" and "Me and Paul"—and of *Spirit*, buoyed by new songs, suffused with his guitar, and defined by a drumless variant of his road band.

It is widely believed by people who've barely listened to Nelson's '90s albums—and since he's bedded down with at least six labels since Columbia ditched him in 1993, this clueless group includes almost everyone outside his fan club—that they aren't much good. But in fact the quality has picked up plenty since that played-out relationship ended. Nelson will never write a "Funny How Time Slips Away" again, but neither will anyone else. In fact, most would be happy to match the rejects he pulled out of a steamer trunk for the new Daniel Lanois–produced showcase *Teatro*, especially the infinitely hummable "Everywhere I Go," which celebrates either a memory or a harmonica. And on *Spirit*, the likes of "I'm Not Trying to Forget You Anymore" and "Too Sick to Pray" break Nelson's New Age-ish vow to abjure songs "that can put you into a self-perpetuating mood of negative thinking"—only to be turned around by the likes of "I Guess I've Come to Live Here in Your Eyes" and the inspirational "We Don't Run," performed at the Supper Club as a singalong devoid of all exhortation and cheerleading. *Spirit* certainly deserves canonical status as much as the overinflated *Red Headed Stranger*.

And to get down to cases, I also prefer it to another artist's Daniel Lanois–produced showcase: *Time Out of Mind*. Because if Bob Dylan seeks to capture what Greil Marcus has dubbed "the old, weird America," then Willie Nelson is after the enduring, commonplace America. One is as great a mystery as the other.

III Millennium

Music from a
Desert Storm

Vestigial since WLIR lost its charm, my tuner got stuck up on a file cabinet to make room for the CD changer I bought last June, but the afternoon of January 15 I connected fourteen feet of cable and punched some buttons. WBAI segued from Stevie Wonder's MLK tribute to something Arab before fading into an ecological teach-in. WNEW's Scott Muni looked disco tuneout in the eye and gave us Marvin Gaye's "What's Going On," followed by Lenny & Sean's "Give Peace a Chance," Stevie Ray's "Tick Tock," "Eve of Destruction," "The Unknown Soldier," and "hopes for peace to our soldiers in the Persian Gulf." On WBLS that night, Vaughn Harper also sent out "What's Going On," then backed a Dick Gregory routine about "puttin' the capitalists behind the United States Constitution" with Bob Thompson's soul-jazz "All in Love Is Fair," a title worth pondering. Later Champagne spun a whole side of the *What's Going On* album and Jarreau & Crawford's "Imagine" while listeners sent "smooth moves to all their loved ones in the Gulf." What kind of storm are Vaughn and Champagne into? Not a desert storm, that's for sure. A quiet storm, sisters and brothers, a quiet storm.

In the exhausting anxiety of the calm before, I needed radio to tell me I was part of a demographic wider than WBAI's. On January 15, it did. And I'm still tuning in. As news of the first bombs hit, Frankie Crocker delivered an enraged, choked-up "no blood for oil" rap, and in general "urban" BLS has been staunch—behind "Give Peace a Chance" while "rock" NEW pairs it with "I Won't Back Down" and the BBC bans it altogether. But that's no surprise—as I learned from BLS, blacks oppose the war in the polls even now. The surprise is that the pop stations are more unlistenable than ever—Z-100, which refused to air "Nothing Compares 2 U" during its 1990 countdown, displays "The Star-Spangled Banner" daily—while the boring old progs at NEW keep coming up with stuff, like when night man Dasher speculated on what else we could do with a billion a day in between Grand Funk Railroad's "Closer to Home" and a bone-crunching brag about the offensive capabilities of the Giant defense. So conventional music media may be of some use in a censored war. Score one for rock and roll.

But remember that even in the '60s, the music wasn't as oppositional as some now believe. With a tip of the cap to the Doors' "Unknown Soldier," getting requests and still a mess, the era's antiwar songs usually came from folkies, sometimes in folk-rock drag—Peter Paul & Mary, Donovan, Phil Ochs, Country Joe, and Bob Dylan, who wrote "Masters of War" as a rock and roller in folkie drag and kept his politics to himself for the entire Vietnam period. Arriving in 1969, the deliberately soft and general "Give Peace a Chance" failed to excite older activists—it was a teen hymn, favored by pink-cheeked newcomers to the protest-march scene. Never reluctant to exploit hippie retro-nuevo, Lenny Kravitz has yoked a '60s aura that seems both militant and warmly idealistic in secondhand retrospect to Sean Lennon's tougher, more specific rewrite, and good for him. The new "Give Peace a Chance" is an anthem where Randy Newman's compulsively subtle "Lines in the Sand" is only a work of art, and Sean's hopes for peace, unlike those of the supposedly nonpartisan remix of Styx's genuinely nonpartisan "Show Me the Way," aren't compromised by the working assumption that George Bush is a sincere statesman confronting a mad beast. (As of now, by the way, both the Newman, an Americana-style pop song, and the Styx mix—which features Gulf dedications and Congressional rodomontade and originated with Knoxville DJ Ray Edwards, not A&M—are radio-only.) And among ordinary potential protesters, smoothly noncommittal moves hit home hardest. Despite its lucky "You can reach me by caravan / Cross the desert like an Arab man," Oleta Adams's big black-pop request "Get Here" is summed up by its bereft title, while Bette Midler's platinum "From a Distance," a profoundly ambivalent song that made a pass at encompassing every contradiction of faith and compassion in Nanci Griffiths's austere 1987 version, implies in this context that incomprehensible wars are better understood close up.

When I say these songs hit home, I mean they hit home here at home. How music functions among GIs in Saudi Arabia is harder to determine—there's no gauging the accuracy of scattered reports this early in the news blitz. "All we are saying / Is kick Saddam's ass," rewrite some grunts on CNN, and the *Boston Globe's* Colin Nickerson reports that the soundtrack of the Kuwaiti front comes straight out the '60s. Nickerson believes that *Platoon*, *Apocalypse Now*, and *Full Metal Jacket* are why he's been hearing Hendrix, Joplin, "The End," "A Hard Rain's A-Gonna Fall," and even Edwin Starr's "War" blasting out of boomboxes on, that's right, Armed Forces Radio. Declares a reformed rap fan: "We grunts are the mean green machine that's gonna make that King Saddam wish he never was born to breath. We need real war music from the war movies." This may not seem to jibe with Public

Enemy's claim that "a lot of brothers walking around in the fine sand of the 'Middle East' have adopted 'Black Steel in the Hour of Chaos' as their marching song, according to the letters we've been getting." But I doubt that every uniformed African-American goes over to the other man's music the minute he gets off the boat. Rap has long since established that in the teeth of kill-or-be-killed there's a tonic pleasure to be had from sick jokes and horror stories about your bad dream of a world. If the Doors can steel a recruit against hard rain someplace where there's not enough water to take a shower, why not PE? Why not both?

Public Enemy? On Armed Forces Radio? Well, maybe not—when I phoned Sergeant Major Bob Nelson, our program director in Saudi Arabia, the only rapper he cited was M.C. Hammer. But somehow I doubt teetotaling non-smoker Nelson, who says he would no more permit sex or Christmas carols in the Saudis' house than booze or cigarettes in his own, could name too many others—when he reports that the Navy station in Al-Jubayl likes "harder" stuff, he means "more country and staunch patriotic" songs, like Lee Greenwood's "God Bless the U.S.A." Nelson denies rumors that his network, often the best source of rap and metal near woebegone Stateside base towns, has run into flak in Saudi Arabia's urban centers, where decadent American culture can now be plucked out of the air by any unformed youth with a radio. Life during wartime means fifty percent of his programming is news, but during music hours American requests rule—from Creedence to Guns N' Roses, he boasted, with lots of overseas dedications, slow love songs, and those inescapable favorites "We Are the Champions" and "Born in the U.S.A."

And if requests aren't respected, the ubiquitous audiocassette is there to compete with the airwaves, airwaves like it does on the streets of Anytown, USA. Not just in the sand, either—Prong and Suicidal Tendencies were big in one reconnaissance plane, I'm told, while a recent report that bomber pilots were mixing Van Halen with radio communications in combat has alarmed U.S. Central Command. That's just the risk you take with a hiply equipped army. Recruits were urged to bring Walkmen, Sony has donated more, and those so improvident as to embark for war without personalized music can take advantage of various giveaway programs. Many labels have proffered product, and shortly before Christmas CBS solicited public cooperation by offering a dollar discount for each consumer donation—store-bought cassettes only, no parental guidance stickers, and remove inlay pinups please. The Tapes for Troops program founded by Baskin-Robbins distributor Bill Frank (c/o VFW, 239 Rubber Avenue, Naugatuck, Connecticut 06670) will accept homemade cassettes as well. Frank told *Billboard* he was inspired by a newscast that "showed guys over there listening to Saudi music, snake charmer music. I thought it would be nice to send them some good tapes."

....

Well, yes. What American in his or her right mind would settle for snake charmer music with Public Enemy and Lee Greenwood there to evoke a home that seems so impossibly sweet from a distance? I'm not being sarcastic—however hard Franco and Mahlathini hit my pleasure center, I think it's puritanical to claim that art should be good for you, and I've always resisted the world-beat propaganda that it's every fan's duty to extend his or her international boundaries. You like what you like, and although I'm proof that such an effort can extend the boundaries of your pleasure center, the strange scales and heavy verbal emphasis of Islamic musical cultures from Morocco to Pakistan have never done the trick for me. A smattering of rai, a few sub-Saharans, the first Najma LP, that's about it—five Umm Kulthum albums later, I still haven't gotten the point, and in the Arab world, Umm Kulthum was Elvis and Frank Sinatra combined. So just say I've had a breakthrough. My account of war music's other half draws on library research and two dozen interviews with scholars and music professionals (many of them Arabs of varying national origins who preferred—sanely, with the FBI and its brethren on the loose—to remain anonymous). Especially given the necessary generalization level, I doubt it's as accurate as I'd like. But it's as accurate as I can make it. It's a start. I wish I didn't believe I'll need it five years from now.

Since 1904, when recording began there, Arab pop's commercial center has been Cairo, although Beirut did pose a challenge in the '60s and '70s until circumstances intervened. Through its music and film industries, which are closely related—most singers were also movie stars—Egyptian culture and dialect came to pervade the Arab world. Although the pop-classical dichotomy makes less sense in that world than in Europe (or India, or Iran), a syncretic genre called "Arab song" or "ughniyah" arrived at a common denominator. While striving for a typically catchy pop simplicity of lyric and melody, ughniyah abandons Arab music's distinctive three-quarter tones to accommodate louder, more resonant Western string sections. Each country has its own stars, who tend toward their own modes, rhythms, and dialects, but slight variations on the Cairo sound have dominated Arab popular music since World War II. Around the death of Nasser in 1970, however, less ornate and conservative folk-based musics (structurally and culturally similar to rock and roll, I'd guess, although few volunteered the comparison) began to come up. Like the funk-tinged Algerian rai that's best-known here, the defiantly working-class shaabi and rebellious young al jeel showcased on David Lodge's *Yalla: Hitlist Egypt* synthesize Western and indigenous elements—Nubian and Bedouin rhythms and folklore, input from Libyan refugees, prominent roles for traditional flutes, cymbals, tambourines, and drums as well as synth and electric bass.

Somewhat less blatant in its modernization than these subcultural styles, more orchestral yet more danceable than ughniyah, is "the Gulf sound," said to be the most commercially potent trend in Arab pop. Different observers cite different influences—Indian movie soundtracks, Bahrainian pearl-diver music, Omani trade ties to East Africa, the intricate handclaps of North Africa. Everyone agrees, however, that the charge has been led by singers from, of all places, Kuwait. Because it favors more puritanical strains of Islam, which eschew all music, the Arab peninsula has few classical or liturgical musical traditions to popularize, and so the Gulf sound's indigenous input springs from lower on the class scale than Cairo's. But it's also crucial that modern Kuwait is wealthy enough to afford experimental leisure and hedonistic enough to permit it—that it has plenty of recording studios, although soon enough the stars move on to Cairo and its string players. According to BBC's Julian May, it was before a live audience in Cairo last fall that the biggest Kuwaiti singer, Abdullah Roueshid, introduced an Egyptian-composed song about Kuwait called "Alla Homma La Ertarag." Soon the entire house was weeping.

Arab pop is a music of romantic travail, of love and loss. Although a strong punning tradition makes for scandalous double and triple meanings in small-scale live performance, our democratic ally Mubarak censors recordings vigorously—no sex, no religion, no politics. In wartime, however, safe topicality booms—paeans to Nasser in 1967, assertions of Arab pride in 1973, songs of national pain during the Lebanese tragedy. Instead of mourning a lost love in "Alla Homma La Ertarag" (which leads side two of the *Al Layla Al Mohamadia* compilation, available from New York's flagship Arab record store, Brooklyn's Rashid Sales), Roueshid mourned his lost nation with an astonishing funereal intensity, and he got the monster hit he deserved. The martial resistance music created in Cairo to be smuggled into Kuwait is nowhere near as rousing. But while the song's popularity proves that some ordinary Arabs oppose the Iraqis, many don't. There are vague reports of signals, calls, and marches emanating from Baghdad as a prelude to war, of an agitprop record called "Allah Akbar." Every day Iraqi radio transmitters beam Nasser songs by the late Egyptian matinee idol Abdul Haleem Hafiz all the way to Cairo, where the notion that Saddam is Nasser's pan-Arab successor has plenty of takers—anti-Mubarak puns are plentiful in folkloric settings. And Paris's huge Algerian population has made an underground smash out of an ughniyah-style anti-American praisesong called "Saddam Saddam," which has been banned by our democratic allies in the French government.

"Saddam Saddam" is more heard about than heard—I'm still not sure whether it's a record or a video, and I don't know the artist's name. But I'm certain it's by an Algerian rather than an Iraqi, and this is no surprise—Iraqi pop rarely travels, although there's more to it than accounts of the society's Orwellian horrors suggest. Iraq has its ughniyah stars—I now own a Bahrain-recorded tape by Hussein Naameh, who gazes warmly out from the inset card like a Julio wannabee and sounds blandly indistinguishable from anything else you might hear while eating falafel on St. Marks Place. Cassettes are sold on the street as they are all over the Arab world—Sting and Bob Marley and maybe even Bon Jovi (although such ecumenicism is presumably impossible now) as well as Hussein Naameh and Umm Kulthum. It's fair to assume that political censorship is absolute, but Iraq has been more tolerant than Egypt, say, in sexual and religious matters. There are venues catering to Kurds and Bedouins and Chaldeans and displaced peasants, and venues where young Iraqis play their own electric music—sometimes Arabic, sometimes hybrid, sometimes even rock covers. But I've yet to find anyone who cares about Arab popular music who has much good, or much of anything, to say about Iraq.

By "popular" I mean commercial product, not "folk" or "people's" music, because I've also yet to find anyone who doesn't agree that Iraq has put more money into its traditional musics than any other country in the Arab world. As far as I'm concerned, anybody who thinks Saddam ain't so bad—who believes Ba'ath anti-imperialism, or gains for women, or improvements in the standard of living somehow compensates for the regime's brutal Stalinism— should take a look at Samir al-Khalil's terrifying *Republic of Fear* and think again. So you can attribute Iraq's musical activism to vainglory or cultural bribery or bread-and-circuses or repressive desublimation or virulent nationalism or megalomaniac pan-Arabism or totalitarian taste without getting an argument from me. And you can mention that Iraq's musical traditions would be in much better shape if the Jewish instrumentalists who were once their chief caretakers—and who ended up nurturing them as Israeli citizens in an urban folk club called the Cafe Nuh near Tel Aviv—hadn't been chased out in anti-Semitic crackdowns, the last shortly after Ba'athism's 1968 takeover. Neither point negates what Iraq's musical activism has achieved—respect for, and training in, the diverse traditions of a nation that may wave the glorious name of Babylon in the world's face but was in fact cobbled together by the British after World War I finished the Turks. Music doesn't negate so easy—it can thrive under the most perverse circumstances. I've heard and believe complaints that in both the folk and classical domains the reclamation job has sometimes been more vulgar, compromised, and inauthentic than one might hope. But purists and scholars always say such things, as they should. Cultural preservation is imperfect by definition. And it still beats cultural destruction a mile.

"You have to understand," one Arab told me, near tears. "For us, Baghdad is like Florence." He didn't add that Cairo was like Rome, or bring in the Medicis either. He was just an aesthete who hated bombs, and like most aesthetes these days, he was in despair watching his world explode. I wish I could spin some grand theory about the political spaces opened up by the shared pleasures and subcultural energies of this war's various popular musics. But not only don't I see any upbeat endings, I feel like a facile fool for every time I found one in the past. I can only counsel extreme cultural humility. Pop optimists who assume rock and roll is on the side of good should ponder the depressingly mixed evidence while avant-garde pessimists tempted to crow I-told-you-so consider the efficacy of their radical engagements and disengagements. And any American with the decency to mourn the Arab lives wasted in this conflict could take a tiny step toward learning how to make amends by getting to know the cultures being twisted and pulverized in his or her name. I'd start with Abed Azrié's *Aromates* on Elektra Nonesuch, darkly aggrieved artsongs by an expatriate Syrian highbrow who clearly deserves a Florence of his own. And *Yalla: Hitlist Egypt* on Mango, cheerfully defiant popsongs from two teeming Cairo subcultures whose instinct will be to hate the USA we were born in for as long as they exist.

Village Voice, 1991

Ghost Dance

Wednesday there was e-mail from Jessica Hopper of Hyper PR in Chicago, apologizing for having to tell us where her bands were headed now that CMJ had been postponed. "Nothing like profound tragedy to make our myopic punk rock world and scene squabbles seem truly meaningless," she began, struggling like everyone else for language that would grab and hold. "We're planning to donate the cost of our unused seats out to CMJ to the Red Cross and various rescue funds. It's hard to know what to do, a feeling I'm sure everyone can identify with." Perhaps it was because I'd learned from Charles Cross's *Heavier Than Heaven* that Hopper was staying in Kurt Cobain's house the morning Cobain shot himself (undetected, in a separate building) that I found her use of the exhausted, inescapable "tragedy" so much more striking than that of, say, Justin Timberlake, who seemed every bit as honorable and distraught. I mean, this woman had some expertise—Cobain's death was a profound tragedy too. But the difference in scale is qualitative. Rock and roll overcame tragedy in Cobain's music as surely as tragedy overcame rock and roll in his life. This time, it's tragedy in a clean sweep.

Talk blues till you're blue in the face, cite all the music we love that has a darkness to it, and rock and roll still remains a uniquely American reproach and alternative to what a European existentialist long ago dubbed the tragic sense of life. Invented by and for teenagers in a time of runaway plenty, it's not blues by a longshot, and from Chuck Berry to the Beatles to the Ramones to Madonna to OutKast, a fair share of its masters have made extinguishing darkness their lifework. They come in knowing that love hurts and everybody dies, but they have the inner confidence to remember there's more to life, and to prove it. The music's confidence—in addition to its deeply democratic form, its African slant on melody and rhythm, and its Cadillacs with cherries on top—was why rock and roll took over a Europe that was only a decade past World War II. We were too, of course. But our mainland hadn't been attacked by a hostile power since 1814. War had never endangered our lives, ravaged our world, happened in front of our eyes. Now, as we count our dead, adjust our expectations, replay those crumbling towers in our minds, and prepare for horrors to come, it has. Tragic-sense-of-lifers like to grant the Bomb a crucial role in rock and roll consciousness. I've always suspected that was liberal rhetoric, that at most '50s nuclear fantasies added edge and flavor. Now I'm sure of it. Our inner confidence, if it's there at all anymore, will never sound the same. If I live long enough, I'll finally have something to get nostalgic about.

Of course, what made the confidence doubly winning was its commonness—its commitment to music/language at its most vernacular. That's why the worst flatline of our president's Oval Office chat the night of the attack came when he avoided the King James version of the 23rd Psalm for one of the Business Writing 1 translations that palliate well-heeled fundamentalism all over suburbia. "The folks who did this" was mind-boggling enough. But how could even George W. have imagined that "You are with me" would get anyone's heart beating like "Thou art with me"? Just when we needed a jolt of moral certitude, the glad-handing frat boy grayed out like the policy wonk we wish he was. We vernacular fans can see the connection between "the folks who did this" and the hard-wired rootsiness that afflicts a gamut of sloppy thinkers from Pete Seeger to Lee Greenwood, just as we can connect "You are with me" to L.A./Stockholm megapop. And I hope we sense that in this time of unprecedented trouble, the long-impacted grandeur of "Thou art with me" is the kind of vernacular we need. As a Bible-believing Christian turned convinced atheist, I never miss a chance to shout that rock and roll is secular music. But that hardly means it doesn't have religious sources or express religious feelings. I know, religious feelings got us into this hell. And I can now guarantee that there are atheists in the valley of the shadow of death. I doubt there was anyone without religious feelings last week. Death is every atheist's window on the eternal.

I hadn't yet pinned this down Tuesday when I finished retrieving my daughter from school in Queens. But I already knew I wanted to begin my next show on the *Voice*'s fledgling Web radio station with the atheist's hymn: from "God is a concept by which we measure our pain" to "I don't believe in . . . ," John Lennon's "God" summed up a mood, and for Carola and me that was reality. Soon I figured out where I'd end, too: with Sufi shaikh and Istanbul medical professor Orüj Güvenç chanting "Bismillah ah-Rahman," one of the names of God. But though devising a playlist was the only way I could think of to pretend I had a use in the world without confronting my own inanity, finding the right songs was a lot harder than it was during the attack's geopolitical cause and CNN forerunner, the Gulf War. "What's Going On" seemed way corny, and "From a Distance," unfortunately, was no longer an apposite metaphor. This was a time for some of the rage music that I love as art and rarely need in life. Punk for sure, "Hate and War," but before I even got there I was on the only metal band I care for deep down, Motorhead.

"Bomber" is a classic piece of hard rock power-mongering, identifying with the thing it loves and hates: "Scream a thousand miles / Feel the black death rising moan / Firestorm coming closer / Napalm to the bone / Because you know we do it right / A mission every night / It's a bomber / It's a bomber / It's a bomber." But it doesn't vaunt itself the way metal usually does—it's too fast, too crude, too prole. And though the poorly read might get the impression Lemmy thinks napalm is cool because he too attacks every night, he doesn't—the only reason Motorhead fans don't know he's written as many antiwar songs as Bruce Cockburn is that they've never heard of Bruce Cockburn. I prefer Lemmy's because he understands the attractions and uses of violence better than Cockburn—whose greatest moment, to his undying credit, expands on the theme "If I Had a Rocket Launcher." The same goes for a lot of loud rock and roll, where what's praised as sexuality is often sublimated aggression. But that didn't make my song hunt any easier, and casual listening, to escape or find solace or get some fucking work done, was a trial—most records I could hardly bear to play. Everything lacked the proper focus and gravity. Everything seemed too sure of itself.

As the trauma recedes, my ears are coming out of their shell some. So I suspect it will take more than one unspeakable catastrophe to destroy the aesthetic I've made my calling, and wish I had faith there won't be another. But for all the solace I've derived from other people's nominations— Joy Division, Neil Young's *After the Gold Rush*, and especially the Ramones' class-proud *Too Tough to Die*, a favorite of missing firefighter Johnny Heff, known to his fans as punk rocker Johnny Bully—the record I've played like a teenager is one I ransacked for my show that first night. I wanted a victory song, which in rock and roll too often means a plodding march steeped in the European triumphalism metal takes from the symphonic tradition, and I also wanted a reconciliation song, a rebirth song. These cravings weren't rational; maybe I should have known better. But I felt compelled to locate my copy of Alpha Blondy's formerly nutty "Yitzhak Rabin." And in some crevice of my memory, prised open perhaps by the artiste's Rimbaud-worshippin' penchant for desert mysticism and other Islamic BS, I zeroed in on Patti Smith. And that's how I got to *Easter*.

Amazon bestseller Nostradamus has nothing on *Easter*. The booklet says "Till Victory" is about "the destruction of the machine gun by the electric guitar," and I hope that's a prophecy. Meanwhile, an anthemic melody, one that like all great Kaye-Kral-Daugherty reclaims European vainglory as Americanese vernacular, channeled my rage into "Take arms, take aim, be without shame" and "God do not seize me please, till victory." After the Springsteen-styled hit that seems so beside the point now, "Ghost Dance," a Plains Indian chant meant to resurrect anyone's forefathers, segues to the minute-and-a-half spoken-word "Babelogue," where I was amazed to hear Smith ranting "In heart I am Moslem; in heart I am-an-am-an American" before launching the fierce and no longer suspect "Rock N Roll Nigger." And only later in the week did I register "25th Floor," an unhinged rocker about fucking in a men's room high above Detroit: "Oh kill me baby / Like a kamikaze / Heading for a spill / Oh but it's all spilt milk to me." It spills into another rant, about shit and gold and alloys and "all must not be art," and also "the transformation of waste" repeated like a mantra. Great song. It's aggression changed back into sexuality, it's "some art we must disintegrate," it's the music I'll take away from the death of the World Trade Center and God knows what else. It's a transformation of waste. It's a dream of life. It's a small thing that will have to do.

The Moldy Peaches Slip You a Roofie

The concrete details of a vivid emotional experience have faded, and my notebook is only so much help. But this much I know. On September 10 I spent several hours with the Moldy Peaches and (was it?) twenty kids between the ages of one and twelve. We were in the house where Kimya Dawson grew up, the house where she still lives at twenty-nine, though God knows she's been around. It's a small house by the standards of Bedford Hills, a leafy hamlet an hour north of midtown—a family house, built by Kimya's great-grandfather. And from seven in the morning until six or so at night, the four rooms on the first floor are devoted to the family business: a fully licensed daycare center. Even Kimya's systems analyst dad joined on about a decade ago, thus occasioning one of the day's many remarkable sights—a man over fifty changing the diaper of a toddler not his kin.

Kimya's twenty-year-old partner Adam Green, who grew up in neighboring Mount Kisco, was at ease, and I enjoyed the kids a lot—the pictures two of them drew me are on my office door. But Kimya—dressed in unlaced platform sneakers with unmatched socks, Bermudas that showed off the tattoos on her ample calves, a T-shirt I don't remember, and her big poofy yellow Afro—was in her element. She spent a fair portion of the afternoon buried in children as she mediated disputes or praised art projects or doled out turns on the guitar. At the same time she and Adam told their story. The generationally separated distant acquaintances got close in 1994, when Kimya went to work at the Mount Kisco record shop, Exile on Main Street, after dropping out of Olympia's Evergreen State College in a dispute over sexual harassment protests. She would drive her young friend to the city for shows and they'd hang out in his basement making music. There was a "Little Bunny Foo Foo" seven-inch in 1996 and an eleven-song demo in 1998, with the rest of what turned into their eponymous debut cut in 2000, after Kimya had done another residency in the Northwest and quit drinking. Kimya and Adam have both recorded solo albums; the Moldy Peaches—occasionally still a duo, more often now a six-piece filled out with their antifolk buddies—is for the songs they write together, most often contributing alternate lines in turn, as in a party game William Burroughs might have invented for Peter Orlovsky.

It was raining, so the fluorescent plastic vehicles and swing sets and playhouses in the yard went unused as kids crowded indoors. Adam and Kimya played me the antifolk anthology they'd compiled, due out from Rough Trade early next year, discreetly skipping the occasional dirty word and the track that begins with the nipples of the female singer's girlfriend poking out of the Mediterranean. But it was hard to carry on a coherent interview, so we went for a tour of sleepy Bedford Hills and happening Mount Kisco. I took in the big secluded place where Adam used to live—his shrink and prof parents now have an apartment in Manhattan, as does he—and was deeply impressed by the greensward surrounding the public schools they'd attended. Eventually we returned to Kimya's, where her mom bid farewell, warning affably, "Today we let you work. Next time we're gonna make you *play.*"

....

Some may see the Moldy Peaches' childishness as icky affectation. But while there's no arguing with squeamishness, an affectation it clearly is not. It's deeply embedded in someone who has spent the better part of thirty years waking up in a houseful of kids, who as a twenty-one-year-old dropout from one of the most permissive colleges in civilization could establish a fruitful creative relationship with a superbright thirteen-year-old wiseass. (Adam's parents sent him to study film at another progressive bastion, Emerson in Boston. He didn't last a term. "I don't even care about film. I care about movies, not about film. And I don't even care about movies.") Thus the Moldy Peaches' penchant for performing in costume—traditionally, sailor or Peter Pan for him and bunny for her, although at the Mercury Lounge Thanksgiving Eve Kimya thanked her Aunt Patrice for her new designs, including the cape that had Adam zooming about like Captain Marvel Junior—grows out of a lifetime of dress-up; they even record in costume. Thus a seven-inch that went: "Little Bunny Foo Foo / Hopping through the forest / Scooping up the field mice / And bopping 'em on the head." Thus songwriting as party game.

And thus songs that hang growing up upside down till it shows its underpants. Some capture an innocence unknown to 'N Sync: "My name is Jorge Regula / I'm walkin' down the street / I love you / Let's go to the beach." Some unleash the id with an intimacy that could make Macy Gray blush: "Tried to buy your love but I came up short / So I fucked a little waitress in return for a snort." This is if-it-sounds-good-say-it music, played and sung with a pretty/ noisy imprecision that transcends the gap between folk and punk like nothing since *The Velvet Underground*, which had the advantage of not knowing the gap existed. Its lyricism is heartbreaking—so tenuous, so vulnerable, so palpably subject to change. But the same record is also funnier than *"Love and Theft."* First time through I merely felt privileged to reaccess the punk miracle. Fifty plays later I think I've never heard anything like it, though there's some Jonathan Richman in there and some might cite Beat Happening. To me, everything cloying and manipulative in that defunct piece of in-group politics seems effervescent and loving in this cult band a-borning. I hope they can do it again, forever and ever. But I'm not innocent enough to think anything so young can last, even till the next record.

I could be wrong. Packaged with demolike black-and-white art and hand-printed track listings, *The Moldy Peaches* has the look of a single spontaneous outburst rather than something recorded over four years, and though the older songs include the opening "Lucky Number Nine" (first words on album: "Indie boys are neurotic"), and the essential "D.2. Boyfriend" (about being yourself in junior high so you can be as cool as Kimya later), the recent material is what stands out. It's where they leave their id showing: "Who mistook the crap for genius / Who is gonna stroke my penis" (that's Adam-only, simultaneous with Kimya's "Who is dancing on the ceiling / Who is gonna hurt my feelings"), or "You're a parttime lover and a fulltime friend / The monkey on your back is the latest trend," or their cover-stickered rock and roll singalong "Who's Got the Crack": "I like it when my hair is poofy / I like it when you slip me a roofie / I like it when [pregnant pause] you've got the crack." But it also includes the guileless "Jorge Regula" and the Kimya feature "Nothing Came Out," where all she wants is to maybe spoon and she needs to get drunk before she can admit it.

Another 2000 recording is their punk apotheosis, a loud and distorted if not crack-pated generational war cry called "NYC's Like a Graveyard." It yells its resentment at rock stars double-dating, yuppies getting married, bar-hopping hippies in twelve-step programs, "suckers and fuckers and stupid retards"—all "corpses" even if they "like the way I play my guitar." "All the tombstones skyscrapin'," they observe. "If you hate me go on hating," they dare. "New York City's like a cemetery," they conclude. They used to climax their set with that unintentionally prophetic judgment.

....

I love the Moldy Peaches for how they *play*—not their instruments, nothing so sublimated, just play. They're not afraid to make a mess because they know life is a mess anyway, and although the mess can be painful, some inner confidence lets them fool around with it. You could attribute this to their privileged upbringings, I suppose. But if it were that easy Exile on Main Street would be Tower, and anyway, not only does Kimya come from service-sector people on the poorer side of town, she's black, albeit lighter-skinned than either parent. I just figure that growing up, they both maintained contact with their outer child, who was never scolded for touching his or her wee-wee and lived to tell the tale.

I met them on a Monday. On Tuesday the planes came. On Friday the band had a gig at the Merc, and I actually thought they might show, but instead Kimya invited everyone she knew to a Saturday barbecue in her backyard. My family and I stayed home. It was a month before I had the guts to play the album again—I'd loved it so, and I was afraid it would seem too small, too self-involved. It didn't. It seemed huge.

Halloween they capped a month-long tour with their friends the Strokes at the Hammerstein, adjusting nicely to the big stage. Where at the Merc they were sometimes too cute for comfort, here they were fast, loud, and tricky within a deliberately simplistic framework. They didn't "rock," they bashed. I could hear fans up front shouting "Jorge Regula" back at them.

Three weeks later they hit a packed Merc still bashing. It still suited them, too, as did the new song in which Kimya invites the world to lick her pussy. Someone requested "NYC's Like a Graveyard." "It's no fun to play anymore," Adam muttered. But I wouldn't put it past them to change their minds, if they last.

Village Voice, 2001

Attack of the Chickenshits

Steve Earle

Extry, extry: "Nashville Ex-Junkie Makes Nice to Traitor, Is Picked On by Nashville Talk Show Host!" That's what I call dog bites man. And also what I call great hype. I don't think Steve Earle wrote "John Walker's Blues" as a publicity stunt. I think he wrote it as a politically inclined guy with an idea for a song. But that doesn't mean he minds whatever attention he gets out of it. He's an artist, folks. Artists are supposed to get our attention.

There's been a fair amount of it, too. After all, as the executive editor of AlterNet learned by interviewing a shrink: "Meaningful art helps people process and digest experience and move toward catharsis." But is the song in question, how you say it, meaningful? To find out, an AP staffer in Nashville checked with a "popular-music scholar at Middle Tennessee State University," who obliged by comparing Earle's attempt to get inside American Al Qaeda combatant John Walker Lindh to Woody Guthrie's "Pretty Boy Floyd," Bob Dylan's "Hurricane," and Johnny Cash's "Delia's Gone." Somebody might have mentioned that Guthrie and Dylan, at least, seem to like their subjects a lot more than Earle likes Lindh. But at least the scholar didn't say "John Walker's Blues" was as good as those other songs. So peace be upon him.

Fact is, we're deluged with meaningful art, the tide's been rising for months, and Earle's *Jerusalem* is neither the best nor the worst of the stuff that's made it to shore. Nor should anyone pretend that this tiny brouhaha is costing Earle play he didn't relinquish voluntarily years ago. Even on 1986's *Guitar Town*, back when he could pass for a Music Row comer competing with . . . Dwight Yoakam? (John Anderson?), he was uncommonly class-conscious, and by 1988's *Copperhead Road* his albums were breaking AOR rather than country. In 1994, much mayhem later, his heroin addiction completed his radicalization by landing him in prison, which is more than you can say for most heroin addictions. He emerged a thoroughgoing leftist with a specialty in capital punishment, and though he did most of his jail time in a rehab center, nobody writes better about prison: "Over Yonder" on *Transcendental Blues*, "Ellis Unit One" on the *USidetracks* odds-and-sods, "The Truth" on *Jerusalem* itself. Earle identifies with any unlucky asshole who makes the wrong choice in the wrong place at the wrong time. Poof, he's John Walker Lindh.

Scaremongers notwithstanding, Earle doesn't glorify Lindh and also doesn't compare him to Jesus—merely illustrates the poor sap's mania by having him *compare himself* to Jesus (who is, after all, one of Islam's prophets). In fact, the song is so measured and literary I find it hard to believe the brouhaha will reach Wal-Mart when the album is released September 24. But I do wish I knew something about Lindh that suggests he was ever far enough gone to claim Jesus—much less that he was driven to jihad by "soda pop bands" on MTV. Such problems often come up with Earle. He's gifted, but he plays it fast and loose. So I also wish I was sure he meant it when he says: "I'm nervous, not for myself, but I have taken some serious liberties with Walker, speaking as him, in his voice." Because while "John Walker's Blues" is salutary just for putting flesh on Lindh's humanity, it's more limited and self-interested than the free-speech claque wants to admit.

As is occasionally noted, there's another song out there that enters the mind of the Muslim Other, and it is indeed significant that the scaremongers never mention it. Although Bruce Springsteen isn't quite as staunch a leftist as Earle, the size of his following makes him a much bigger threat to the right. Nevertheless, *The Rising* is such an unequivocal act of patriotism that for the moment the chickenshits are leaving him alone—such an unequivocal act of patriotism that the surpassing gentleness of Springsteen's impersonation of a suicide bomber arouses no suspicion. Or maybe "Paradise" is over their evil heads. It's a mysterious song, and although I'm no mysteriousness fan, a far stronger and deeper one than "John Walker's Blues." Where Earle lays out Walker's confusion, Springsteen gets inside his protagonist's spirituality, warmly and sympathetically—and then pulls the plug, with the paradise that's a holy goal in the beginning a vacant mirage by the end.

If these value judgments seem irrelevant, critical bean counting just when people are digesting experience and moving toward catharsis, please remember that good songs generally enhance understanding better than flawed ones. So I prefer not only "Paradise" but Toby Keith's "Courtesy of the Red, White, and Blue (The Angry American)," with its truthful and jovially vindictive "Soon as we could see clearly / Through our big black eye / Man, we lit up your world / Like the Fourth of July," and Alan Jackson's "Where Were You (When the World Stopped Turning)," with its truthful and chillingly complacent "I watch CNN but I'm not sure I can tell you / The difference in Iraq and Iran." They're more evocatively written and more coherently conceived. As the profiteers who run this country plot their oil grab in Iraq, even we leftists who believe the U.S. was morally obliged to invade Afghanistan had better recognize that these are dangerous works. But that doesn't make them any less engaging or revealing, and denying their power won't make it go away.

While *Jerusalem* is as clearly a response to 9/11 as *The Rising* or the two country songs—and maybe more so than my cathartics of choice, Sleater-Kinney's *One Beat* and the Mekons' *OOOH!*—it only deals directly with the Al Qaeda attacks and their military aftermath in "John Walker's Blues" and the climactic title song. Yet it's the most topical record of the bunch, front-loaded with references to assorted tyrannies of class—HMOs, maquiladoras, immigration barriers, escapist media, the assassinations of JFK and MLK if they count, and of course the prison system. With Earle slurring his drawl more pointedly than usual and Will Rigby's drums front and center on the rock tracks and breaking out of the quieter ones, the material works up a pretty good head of consciousness, and because his arrangements travel so light, they generate more musical get-up-and-go than *The Rising*'s weapons of mass reconciliation. A good thing, too, because the music helps patch over all the stitches Earle drops.

Does the man really think the daring young president of the Cuban missile crisis would have finessed Vietnam? That we're all criminals inside? That caper movies, girlie pictures, and silly love songs distract us from our higher calling? Does he know the Constitution favored the propertied classes more in the good old days than it does now? And while we understand that Emma Goldman and Abbie Hoffman partake of the usual lefty virtue-by-association, what the hell is Aaron Burr doing among the patriots in his inspirational liner notes? Burr was the prototype of the profiteering politician. Is this some meta-ironic traitor joke?

If so, I wish Earle had expended his tiny store of subtlety someplace else. I wish "John Walker's Blues" was as complex as "Paradise," that the all-things-must-pass of Earle's "Ashes to Ashes" cast as cold an eye on banality as the Mekons' "Stonehead," that the only perfect things on the whole record weren't consecutive love-in-vain songs by a guy who'd been married six times as of his last bio. But you know the drill—it's ill-advised to seek political wisdom from a pop musician unless that musician happens to be named Linton Kwesi Johnson. They're artists, folks.

But for just that reason, their misconceptions and imprecisions don't always do them in. Certainly they don't here. No doubt Earle wants to convince America to end the death penalty and hate the rich, but on this album those specifics are means to a broader end: being a musical leftist, period. As is known to anyone who reads the press kit, the seeds of *Jerusalem* were planted by the president of Earle's label—and no, Sean Hannity or is that Tom Vanderbilt, not to make a quick buck, how dumb. Danny Goldberg is just a lifelong civil libertarian who likes to stir up trouble. I haven't asked him—which I could, we talk once in a while—but I bet I know what he was thinking.

What has been the chief domestic casualty of this war on terrorism that keeps changing its spots? The Bill of Rights as exemplified by political dissent, most believe. How to fight back? Exercise the right to dissent. That's the joy of this record, which, with a crucial push from drummer Rigby, gives off a sense of freedom and defiance that's rock and roll, not protest music. This artistic effect is made possible in part by all the play Earle has relinquished—by what might be construed as his ultimate political ineffectiveness. *The Rising* is dragged down, with a few magnificent exceptions, by the overburdened emotions and conceptual commonplaces of the great audience that inspired it. *Jerusalem* travels light and gets where it's going.

Its final destination is the best, too. Where all its other political songs are embittered, "Jerusalem" doesn't have the stomach for bitterness. It watches Israelis roll their "death machines" over "the ground where Jesus stood" and asserts without the slightest justification that this too shall pass—not in the all-things-must-pass sense, but in living time. On *The Rising*, that promise would sound like a big lie. Here Steve Earle is just expressing himself. Here a hymn to hope is what free speech is for.

Facing Mecca

Youssou N'Dour

Youssou N'Dour's dignified, devotional *Egypt* is his boldest album since he formed Étoile de Dakar twenty-five years ago. Its sacral chants and Cairo strings are further from the beatwise declamations of the mbalax he invented than the rock respectability he pursued under the auspices of Amnesty International in the late '80s and early '90s. In a world where "world music" still signifies indigenous styles redecorated to entice Euro-American buyers, *Egypt* is designed to tell us that there are more ways to recontextualize a tama drum than are programmed into Jean-Philippe Rykiel's philosophy.

N'Dour is a long-standing cosmopolitan. His American star has only risen since he took his act to the tastemongers at Nonesuch. But he is also a Muslim, and, thanks to Bush-Rumsfeld-Wolfowitz Inc., determined not to let anyone forget it. So on March 7, 2003, scheduled to undertake the most extensive and expansive American tour of his life, N'Dour did a startling thing: he canceled. His explanation of why he couldn't appear to sanction Washington's impending attack on Baghdad, a remarkably nuanced statement for a musician, deserves to be quoted in full:

> It is my strong conviction that the responsibility for disarming Iraq should rest with the United Nations. As a matter of conscience I question the United States government's apparent intention to commence war in Iraq. I believe that coming to America at this time would be perceived in many parts of the world—rightly or wrongly—as support for this policy, and that, as a consequence, it is inappropriate to perform in the us at this juncture.
>
> I understand that there are many in the us who do not support the idea of their government initiating war in Iraq at this time, and I offer my greatest respect to them. I also regret the difficulties this causes those who were to present my concerts in North America and those who were

looking forward to seeing me and my band. This tour was over a year and a half in the planning and was the greatest commitment I had ever made to performing in the US.

It is my fervent wish to return to the US in better times. But I find it impossible to imagine playing concerts in America when such grave issues are confronting all the peoples of the world.

The idealism of N'Dour's gesture plus the subtlety of his analysis established him as a rock star in a grand and endangered tradition—the gravity with which he throws his weight around is more Bono or Springsteen than Dixie Chicks or Beastie Boys. Granted, his act of conscience was directed primarily at his African fanbase, which he tends prudently and loyally. He knows he's marginal here, knows most of his American audience was already convinced that attacking Iraq was a terrible idea. But the cancellation brought home our structural complicity in a war we failed to stop. And it showed us just how broad a wedge our rulers were driving between true American democracy and Islam's embattled humanists, without whom crusade-vs.-jihad will turn into a geopolitical nightmare capable of wrecking the rest of our lives.

His convictions lived up to, N'Dour visited briefly last fall and will return in a few weeks. Don't miss the chance to be transported by his latest Great African Ball marathon, set for Roseland July 9. But *Egypt* leaves no doubt that he's traveling on his own terms. Billed as an acoustic respite from the hard-driving mbalax highlights of 2000's *Joko* (*The Link*), 2002's *Nothing's in Vain* (*Coono Du Réér*) was a masterful piece of international easy listening, a savvier crossover than the likes of *Set* and *The Lion*—mellow and melodic, English moralism and French chanson balancing off tama bursts and danceable homiletics. The new record is even quieter. But its sound is Egyptian, which means a lot stranger.

Lyrics are in Wolof, the gutturals of which feel quasi-Arabic in this context, and the melodies have Senegalese contours; there's kora, Sahel percussion, Dakar backup singing male and female. But *Egypt*'s band is the Fathy Salama Orchestra, inadequately described by the booklet as "traditional musicians." In fact Salama claims intimacy with forefathers from Bartok to Barry Harris, and for these purposes simulates the semi-classical Cairo Pops sound of ugniyah's Middle Eastern hegemony with an ensemble long on folk-identified instruments like oud and oblique flute. If Um Kulthum has always sounded weird to you, so will this, and N'Dour doesn't want you if that settles the matter. But compared to Kulthum's, Salama's strings are lighter in color, touch, and pitch—suspend your disinclination and the weirdness turns into something else. From the flute solo of "Allah" to the oud break of "Cheikh Ibra Fall," from a rubato intro fit for Gordon MacRae to bellydance beats fit for a marabout, this fusion is smarter, lovelier, and more seductive than anything N'Dour conceived to impress Peter Gabriel. And the singing—from an artist whose voice, like Aretha Franklin's or George Jones's, comes to many listeners as a musical sufficiency—is captivating in its sweetness, precision, and delicacy even when you don't follow the translation-transliteration. N'Dour is perfectly capable of rocking rough. Here he's all about caring.

About what, you wonder? He's so glad you asked. Except for the finale, about Touba, the seat of N'Dour's Mouridist sect and the fastest-growing city in West Africa, all the songs extol Sufi teachers. Senegalese Islam is largely Sufi. Islam being anything but monolithic, and Sufism being highly individualistic, that doesn't mean Sufi like ecstatic Pakistani qawwali mystic Nusrat Fateh Ali Khan, or like calm Turkish musical healer Orüj Güvenc—like the fierce Chechen Muridists or the secularizing Afghan Naqshbandis either. Senegalese Sufism divides into the seminal Qadiriya, the state-building Tijani, and N'Dour's Mouridists, whose work-worshipping mercantile ethic, Calvinist in a highly un-Swiss way, dominates Senegalese politics and emigre communities like New York's. Like most sub-Saharan Islam, Sufism is very non-Arab. So for N'Dour, who for twenty years has been building bridges to Europe and America, to go to Egypt to record these pointedly pan-Sufi lyrics—in addition to praising the two Mouridist founders, he devotes songs to Qadiriya history, a Tijani anti-colonialist, a Tijani pan-Africanist, and an eccentric messianic brotherhood—is to remind his Western friends, and enemies, that in the crucial matter of faith he is not "Western," not even a little bit.

Deprived of their insistent rhymes, the translations' generalities don't always catch and hold, although the auxiliary material on the Nonesuch website shores them up. Nevertheless, *Egypt* is more than just beautiful—it's a persuasive political act. One reason the rock star whose fame matters has become a rarity is that the rock star whose music matters has too. N'Dour doesn't have this problem. Forget Bono—he has his eye on Bob Marley, and he may yet do it better.

Three Pieces
About M.I.A.

1. Burning Bright

Did I notice "I got the bombs to make you blow"? Maybe as metaphor—which it is, but not the way I thought. Had I registered Sasha Frere-Jones's trenchant comment in his *New Yorker* review of *Arular*: "What makes this genuine world music, aside from the references, is the weaving of the political into the fabric of what are still, basically, dance tunes. Any division of life into personal and political halves is absent"? Maybe as rhetoric, without understanding what was at stake. But then I learned that this twenty-eight-year-old art school grad with Elastica connections had a radical pedigree—via her father, a Tamil "revolutionary" in Sri Lanka. And then came word of an M.I.A. thread at I Love Music that morphed from rumor to exultation to, suddenly, a heart-rending roller coaster of a political debate.

Outsiders commented or raved or asked questions or noodged the discussion back toward music or imposed their own left or neocon agendas. But the chief participants were two Sri Lankans exiled by ethnic conflict: a Tamil who critically supported the Tamil Tigers, or LTTE, as the only chance of ending Sinhalese oppression, and a half-Sinhalese half-Tamil who thought the Colombo government bad and the Tigers much worse. Coming in late was an anti-LTTE Tamil who'd suffered Sinhalese bombings and interrogations and still feared the Tigers could assassinate him in exile, as they had other dissenters. As bearers of belief and experience, all three were credible even when they contradicted each other, but extracting an overview was impossible. My normally reliable panel of geopolitically informed leftist democrats knew nothing about the Indian Ocean island. So I did some reading. Because it's true: M.I.A. makes an issue of the Tamil Tigers. If we care about her, she wants us to care about them. My conclusions are brutally compressed and inexpert by definition, but let me try.

Ethnic enmity in the former Ceylon will ring a bell with fans of colonialism in Rwanda or Ireland, where divide-and-conquer also set the stage for civil war. The minority Tamil Hindus had a leg up until independence, whereupon the Sinhalese Buddhists took their revenge, though never at Tutsi-Hutu levels. The 1956 replacement of English by Sinhalese as the official language, onerous educational and other discrimination, and the gradual impoverishment of the Tamil northeast had inspired many resistance groups by the mid '70s. These were soon dominated by the LTTE, a Marxist-inflected ethnic movement committed to establishing an independent homeland called Eelam. Armed struggle, which began in 1983, has cost 65,000 lives in a nation of under twenty million.

The Tigers' signal achievement was the invention of modern suicide bombing, particularly the infamous "jacket," and as of 2001 they had seventy-five of the 188 suicide bombings worldwide since 1980 on their dossier. The Sinhalese upped the ante with the civilian bombing (of "suspected terrorists") we know so well from Palestine, plus widespread rape and occasional firing squads. Like the IRA, the Tigers have been generously funded by exiles, most from India's larger Tamil population. The U.S. declared them a terrorist organization in 1997. Feared assassins—Rajiv Gandhi is counted among their victims—they appear less given to random violence than their Palestinian counterparts, and since September 11 have all but abandoned suicide bombing. Both UNESCO and Amnesty International have recently censured them for the heinous practice of conscripting children by force, Senderostyle. But they're legitimate enough that Colombo has been pursuing detente with them for years.

As the daughter of a known rebel in a war zone, M.I.A. spent most of her young girlhood intimate with violence. She escaped Sri Lanka with her mother and two siblings at ten or eleven. British racism was no fun, but it beat war, and she excelled in school. Her father, Arul Pragasam a/k/a Arular, joined the Tigers from the more conciliatory EROS group. He has never lived with her and hasn't seen her since 1995. Extensive online and library research revealed scant reference to Arular, but he's definitely an LTTE bigshot. Circa 1976 he trained with the PLO in Lebanon, where he took advantage of his engineering degree to become an explosives expert. Wonder whether he designed any jackets.

Sinhalese depredations have been atrocious. But my reading suggests that more Sri Lankan Tamils want equality than want Eelam. So from this distance I'm not pro-LTTE, and strongly advise fellow journalists to refrain from applying "freedom fighter" and other cheap honorifics to M.I.A.'s dad. But I also advise them to avoid the cheaper tack taken in last week's *Voice* by Simon Reynolds: "Don't let M.I.A.'s brown skin throw you off: She's got no more real connection with the favela funksters than Prince Harry." Not just because brown skin is always real, but because M.I.A.'s documentable experience connects her to world poverty in a way few Western whites can grasp. Moreover, beyond a link now apparently deleted from her website to a dubious Tamil tsunami relief organization, I see no sign that she supports the Tigers. She obsesses on them; she thinks they get a raw deal. But without question she knows they do bad things and struggles with that. The decoratively arrayed, pastel-washed tigers, soldiers, guns, armored vehicles, and fleeing civilians that bedeck her album are images, not propaganda—the same stuff that got her nominated for an Alternative Turner Prize in 2001. They're now assumed to be incendiary because, unlike art buyers, rock and roll fans are assumed to be stupid.

M.I.A. has no consistent political program and it's asinine to expect one of her. Instead she feels the honorable compulsion to make art out of her contradictions. The obscure particulars of those contradictions compel anyone moved by her music to give them some thought, if only for an ignorant moment—to recognize and somehow account for them. In these perilous, escapist days, that alone would be quite a lot.

Village Voice, 2005

....

2. Quotations from Charmin M.I.A.

- They were asking me to comment on really heavy world issues, like what I thought about America, globalization, President Bush. I had to wonder, "Why me?"

- If I represent anything, it's what it's like to be a civilian caught up in a war.

- My mum brought me up going, "Ah Gandhi, he's such a nonviolent man. You turn the other cheek, huh." And then now it seems like what President Bush is teaching us is if somebody steps to you, you just kill him. Don't even ask any questions. Just take him out. He's the biggest bloody 50 Cent he is.

- I really felt like I needed to know what I wanted to tell my kids—if being good was striking twice as hard.

- Fighting terrorism is affecting the world more than terrorism. If this is being good, we better stock up on weapons.

- I use political references or words to reflect everything—whether you're poor, whether you're from the street, whether you can't pay the bills, whether you're just the underdog all the time.

- Education is so important. I think especially if you are the other, then it's always good for you to know what people think about you.

Village Voice, 2005

....

3. Right, the Record

The deepest cut on *Arular* is "Amazon," where M.I.A. the favela funk thief depicts herself as a cultivated Brit kidnapped by Brazilian criminals. She's missing from Acton, her London hood, but after she fell for that palm tree smell, "bodies started merging." The vertiginous excitement of pan-ethnic identity, so unlike the purity the Tamil Tigers kill for, imbues every pieced-together track, but only on "Hombre," a pidgin-Spanish proposition with a sitar intro, does it get quite so explicit. Violence is everywhere, dropped casually like a funk grenade or flaunted instructively as in the oft-quoted "It's a bomb yo / So run yo / Put away your stupid gun yo." But not for a moment does the violence seem vindictive, sadistic, or pleasurable. It's a fact of life to be triumphed over, with beats and tunelets stolen or remembered or willed into existence. This is the territory I've always wished Missy Elliott would risk, and let's not be coy about how M.I.A. got there. "Banana Skit" starts the album with her only message: "Get yourself an education."

Village Voice, 2005

IV From Which All Blessings Flow

Full Immersion with Suspect Tendencies

Paul Simon's Graceland

I'm here to tell you that Paul Simon's *Graceland* is a tremendously engaging and inspired piece of work. If you like him thorny it's his best record since *Paul Simon* shucked off Art Garfunkel in 1972, if you like him smooth you can go back to *There Goes Rhymin' Simon* in 1973, and either way you may end up preferring the new one. Simon-haters won't be won over—his singing has lost none of its studied wimpiness, and he still writes like an English major. But at least *Graceland* gets you past these annoyances, because it boasts (Artie will never believe this) a bottom. *Graceland* is the first album he's ever recorded rhythm tracks first, and it gives up a groove so buoyant it could float a loan to Zimbabwe.

Well, not exactly. Only in metaphor, you could say, and a metaphor of suspect tendency at that, because it implies that music transcends politics. Thus we address what *Graceland* has to be about even though it risks very few political moments—the protesty title "Homeless," a terrorist bomb metaphoring by, like that. Simon recognizes this dilemma. As he has amply publicized, *Graceland*'s groove doesn't come from nowhere—it's indigenous to black South Africa, and despite what Simon-haters may suspect, his relationship to the Soweto-centered "township jive" known generically as umbaqanga is deep and committed, and not just the way he treated his musicians, paying them triple-scale American in Johannesburg and handing out composing credits and bringing the Zulu ingom'ebusuku chorus Ladysmith Black Mambazo to New York for a *Saturday Night Live* spot and a lovely gig at S.O.B.'s. I'm talking about the music itself. This isn't the mere exoticism that flavored past Simon hits with reggae and gospel and Andean pipes. It's a full immersion. And yet there's reason to wonder whether it's enough.

At first I didn't think so. Yes, I was annoyed by the radical incongruity of the thing, the way chatty lines like "Aren't you the woman / Who was recently given a Fulbright" or a modernist trope like "staccato signals of constant information" bounced over a beat originally designed to help half-slaves forget their loneliness. But for several years I've been listening greedily to what little umbaqanga I could get my ears on, and pretty soon Simon won me over. On its own idiosyncratic terms, this is a real umbaqanga album: the rhythms and licks and colors that define the style can't go unchanged in this alien context, but I swear they remain undiluted. Yet at the same time it's a real Paul Simon album: the guy is too bright, and too fond of himself, to try and go native on us. Nor would I call it a fusion, because somehow each element retains its integrity. To use the term favored by David B. Coplan's study of "South Africa's black city music and theatre," *In Township Tonight!*, *Graceland* is genuinely syncretic: it reconciles different or opposing principles, at least for the duration of an LP.

Of course, I'm an aspiring aficionado of the township groove. Other listeners may hear *Graceland* as either utterly normal (songpoetry-with-a-good-beat) or unutterably beyond the pale (revolutionary savagery), but to me that groove sounds fresh and inevitable, with as much affinity for r&b as for the polyrhythms beloved by the tiny claque of U.S. juju and soukous and Afrobeat fans. That claque still includes me, but my allegiances have shifted. *Graceland* crystallizes a suspicion that had its inception this spring, when musicologist Charles Hamm offered me a hurried phonographic introduction to the tart, rich harmonies and far-reaching clarity of singers who had previously been names in obscure books and articles, most memorably the Soul Brothers and Steve Kekana. The three umbaqanga anthologies assembled by Earthworks—most sublimely Shanachie's *The Indestructible Beat of Soweto*—emphasize energy and drive, but the axiom that the music of Southern Africa is voice-based rather than drum-based was what jumped out at me in Hamm's living room. Over that ebulliently indigenous groove, singers reached for and attained some sort of international identification, and suddenly I realized that a rock and roll equivalent of unimaginable vitality, complexity, and high spirits was somehow thriving in apartheid's face.

Simon's romance with umbaqanga began when somebody sent him an otherwise unidentified tape called *Gumboots* a couple of years ago. As Simon played it in his car he became entranced, improvising tunes over the simple major-chord changes until he decided he had to work with these guys. Only then did he investigate and find out where the music was from, which worried him: "I first thought, 'Too bad it's not from Zimbabwe, Zaire, or Nigeria.' Life would have been more simple." But he was hooked. After consultations with the likes of Quincy Jones assured Simon that as long as he respected the music and the musicians he'd be all right, he immersed, booking several weeks of studio time in South Africa, where he cut five tracks with musicians from varying tribal traditions and assembled a trio to do more recording in the States. Eventually there were guest appearances from exiled pennywhistler Morris Goldberg, Sunny Ade steel player Demola Adepoju, Senegalese star Youssou N'Dour, the Everly Brothers, Ralph McDonald, Linda Ronstadt. Although the accordion Simon loved on *Gumboots* doesn't play a large part on *Graceland*, two American bands that feature accordion, Los Lobos and a zydeco outfit from Louisiana, back up the final two selections, which Simon hopes hit home with compatriots who find all this a touch strange.

The two American cuts are plenty lively, and would have done wonders for Simon's 1983 *Hearts and Bones*, but on *Graceland* they fall a little flat, partly because they're not lively enough and partly because they're not strange enough. Why liveliness should be an issue is obvious. *Hearts and Bones* was a finely wrought dead end, caught up in introspection, whimsy, and the kind of formal experimentation only obsessive pop sophisticates even notice— the rest of us just wondered why the thing never left the ground, and in the end so did Simon, leaving him vulnerable to umbaqanga's three happy chords. But the strange part requires more explanation. In remembrance of René and Georgette Magritte dancing to doowop's "deep forbidden music" on *Hearts and Bones*, Simon could have made like Billy Joel, who produced a vaguely "'50s" album after the heavy concepts of *The Nylon Curtain* failed to go triple platinum. But if Joel is rock's would-be Irving Berlin, Simon is some postfolkie cross between Cole Porter and Lorenz Hart, constitutionally incapable of doing things the easy way. By the late '70s he'd already applied twelve-tone theory to pop composition, so in 1985 he found himself trying to fit first melodies and then lyrics to apparently elementary structures that kept tripping him up as he went along. At some semiconscious level he understood that exoticism on this level was a hell of a roundabout way to return to the simple things, and in the end that became one of *Graceland's* subjects. It's lively, and it's also strange.

Musically, the strangeness inheres mostly in the continuing integrity of the African and American elements. The beat is still African yet a shade less driven, more buoyant if you approve and lighter if you don't, intricate like pop funk more than juju. Longer melody lines, less chantlike and circular verse-chorus structures, subtler arrangements, Roy Halee's forty-eight-track mix, guest accents, the way Ladysmith's curlicues stand in for straight response singing on some cuts—all augment the effect. Since African beats are rarely heavy, this bothered me at first. Soon, though, the buoyancy carried me away. Simon and Halee have found new resources in these musicians, and with the basic trio—guitarist Ray Phiri, bassist Baghiti Kumalo, and drummer Isaac Mtshali, all players of conspicuous responsiveness and imagination—the discovery was clearly collaborative. The record's virtuosic syncretism—juxtaposing Sotho and Shanga and Zulu, umbaqanga and ingom'ebusuku, and then moving north and west, with the African Beats' steel guitar no less striking than Talking Heads' synth guitar—is unusual, too, although it's so seamless you have to stay alert to be sure it's there. But Simon's relaxed conversational singing on top, so free of rough spots that you know it's a careful fabrication, is truly disquieting until annoyance evolves into uneasy acceptance of this abrupt musical and cultural disparity. And of course the voice comes bearing words.

Simon may still write like an English major, but he's long since stopped writing like he's still in school. His ironies can be arid and too often his ideas aren't as big as he thinks they are, but he's got the music to bail him out—to transmute cliche into reality just as it does for countless more hackneyed lyricists. What the music does for him here, however, goes well beyond the salutary effect of melody and rhythm and vocalization. *Graceland* is where Simon rediscovers the rock and roll secret, where he throws down his irony and dances. There are many ways to describe this secret—sex or youth or the primitive, spontaneity or simplicity or directness. With Simon, the terms I'd choose are "faith" and "connection," themes that keep popping up here. Although the title song describes a journey "through the cradle of the Civil War" to Elvis's mecca, which is never attained, it also hints (as Simon agreed when I asked) that somehow South Africa is a haven of grace. In "You Know Me Al," an American beerbelly ends up saying amen and hallelujah in an African marketplace. In "Under African Skies" there's the blessed assurance that "the roots of rhythm remain."

And by leading with "The Boy in the Bubble," his most acute and visionary song in years, Simon sets up every resonance. Here the African images—lasers in the jungle, a deathly desert wind, a baby with a baboon heart—are no way merely South African. Here the terrorist hides his bomb in a baby carriage and wires it to a radio in a world run by "a loose affiliation of millionaires / And billionaires"; here a boy wants to live so much he seals himself off from that world in a plastic bubble. You can hardly tell the horrors from the miracles, they're everywhere, and for a climax we have the rhetorical "and I believe" that precedes Simon's final repetition of the long refrain. Borne on the pulse of Forere Motloheloa's tireless accordion, it sounds like real faith to me, and it cements our connection to all this ironic joy-amid-pain. Simon has done the near impossible—brought off a song about the human condition. Looking for "a shot of redemption," he escapes his alienation without denying its continuing truth, and it's really like the press release says: *Graceland* "is *human* music. It celebrates the family of man." I perceive only one problem—Simon found his redemption not in all humanity but in black South Africans. The problem isn't ruinous—the man is fascinated by the subtleties of his debt and out front about its extent, and he's done plenty to pay it back. But it does deserve detailed attention.

Umbaqanga is an awe-inspiring cultural achievement. Even to call it the reggae of the '80s, as Simon has for explanation's sake, is to diminish it slightly. Those who know that in South Africa (even more than on the rest of the continent) reggae is the paradigmatic political pop, while state radio promotes a vigorously self-censored umbaqanga to divert listeners from messages of freedom beamed across the border, may consider this judgment perverse. But umbaqanga was and is created under far more duress, and anyway, Simon is talking musical influence, not politics, where reggae has its shortcomings: maybe just because its drug of choice is cannabis rather than alcohol, it's less active and less up. As Simon evidently believes, umbaqanga is the most joyful and redeeming rock and roll equivalent in memory, contravening apartheid's determination to deny blacks not just a reasonable living but a meaningful identity.

Compared to most black South African pop, which emulates American pop, soul, funk, and jazz (though by now South Africa has a jazz heritage of its own), umbaqanga honors traditional forms, which fits apartheid's fantasy of the harmless native just fine. But it's by no means tribal or rural—just like Chicago blues and rockabilly and early soul, it's a conscious urbanization. Its capacity for affirmation in the face of horror is an old story in black music, and while it doubtless serves some as an escape, it just as doubtless serves others (or the same ones at different times) as a respite, a transfusion, a promise. Pretoria may think it's harmless, and Pretoria may be wrong—so accustomed are the overseers to disdaining bush rhythms that I doubt they discern just how potent this groove is. As Neo Mnumzana of the African National Congress told me: "We have to grant the validity and legitimacy of genuine forms of expression. The regime may not see them as dangerous, but they are strengthening the people in their resistance."

Southern Africans are more interested in voices than drums, but that doesn't mean they don't regard rhythm as one of life's primaries, and umbaqanga is about the beat. By rock standards that beat is pretty elaborate, staggering ostinatos over a jumpy 8/8; the bass is usually high in the mix, leading the groove rather than stirring it up reggae-style, and as Simon discovered when he tried to write metrically identical verses, the songs' rhythmic shapes often evolve incrementally. But by juju standards, say, it's kind of square, which is just why it might appeal to Americans' crude tastes in propulsion. And though the beat is southern African first, it's also specifically South African. It must have been bent some by Afro-American models—almost all the music in Soweto is—but there's also the likelihood of direct European influence in its prehistory: because South Africa has been industrialized for so long, it's always attracted concentrations of fortune-seekers from England, Ireland, Germany, Holland, Portugal. Umbaqanga reflects the way South Africa has mixed African tribes; it reflects the forced flow of South African life from fabricated homeland to official slum; it reflects South Africa's industrialization, and its cruel prosperity too. It testifies to the resilience of apartheid's victims, but like everything else in South Africa it also grows out of apartheid. It could no more come from Nigeria, Zaire, or even Zimbabwe than Elvis could come from Johannesburg. And neither could *Graceland*.

"I'm no good at writing politics," Simon told me. "I'm a relationship writer, relationships and introspection." And of course this is true. Yet, the romantic isolation he transcends on many of *Graceland*'s songs is also social isolation, and he's pleased to acknowledge the South African subtext informing many lyrics as well as the album's gestalt. So why exactly Simon has steered away from politics proper on the album and in interviews is a question that troubles anti-apartheid activists. I spoke to about a dozen—black and white, South African and American—and not one was inclined to be judgmental. Merely by recording in Johannesburg Simon violated the letter of the U.N. cultural boycott (not deliberately, he claims). Yet except for exiled pianist Abdullah Ibrahim, who was clearly displeased but declined to comment on Simon's "personal decision," the only one who came close to insisting Simon was flat-out wrong was Amer Araim, a non–South African "international civil servant" at the U.N. Committee Against Apartheid. Elombe Brath, who's been on the picket line for a decade now, admitted "mixed emotion" because it seems Simon's "intent was honorable"; Jennifer Davis, a twenty-year exile active with the American Committee on Africa, kept using the term "gray area" and observed that "you can't have nice neat official statements in a situation of tremendous flux"; the ANC's Neo Mnumzana even suggested that "it's quite possible he might be doing a service to South African culture." Clearly, no one wanted to see black South African culture denied a chance at exposure, a chance that strictly speaking is forbidden any cultural product of a corporation cooperating with the regime (the recordings on *The Indestructible Beat of Soweto*, for example). But all were dismayed that Simon remained no good at writing politics. The most striking testimony came from grandfatherly Charles Hamm, who like Simon was in South Africa at the time of the second Sharpeville massacre, which set off the current state of emergency. The experience radicalized him, and he can't quite comprehend how Simon remained insulated. "I have trouble accepting all these lyrics about Paul Simon. It's not so much what he says as what he doesn't say."

Simon doesn't claim to be apolitical as a person—only as an artist. He has his views on South Africa, and he intends to keep them to himself. The reason, he says, is to protect the friends he's made there, especially the black friends: "I'm not gonna open my mouth. I open my mouth and they get a firebomb in their house. These people are living there. They don't like their life—but it's a life." And this makes sense. Still, I'd be curious to know just what Simon's views are, because I detect in him an ideology of anti-ideology that I simply don't trust.

This is a man who supports Amnesty International and twice honored the Sun City boycott by turning down gigs there; it's also a man who's done fundraisers for Ed Koch and refused to sing on "Sun City" because the since modified demo he was sent called out artists who'd played Pretoria's showplace of bogus integration, including his friend Linda Ronstadt. This is a man who says he "would never knowingly break the cultural boycott"; it's also a man who calls the reluctance of the world music biz to handle South African artists and product "double apartheid," which even if you find the letter of the U.N. rules misguided is very loose language. Like almost everybody who thinks about South Africa, he dreads the bloodbath: "Let's keep pushing to avoid the battle. Millions of blacks could get killed." But his sharpest political statement was on a subject closer to home: "Authoritarian governments on the right, revolutionary governments on the left—they all fuck the artist. What gives them the right to wear the cloak of morality? Their morality comes out of the barrel of a gun. Try and say bullshit on their government, write a poem or a book that's critical of them, and they come down on you. They make up the morality, they make up the rules."

No matter how true you think this is, it's truer than you want it to be for sure. But it clearly means more to an American accustomed to going off at the mouth like me or Simon than to downpressed people with their bellies and physical safety to worry about first. The idea simply isn't quite as big as is believed by all those headstrong individualists whose considered distrust of politics turns them into centrist liberals by default. The depressing saga of Linda Ronstadt in Sun City exemplifies this mentality—however sincerely she may oppose apartheid, there comes a time when humility if not solidarity must trump sincerity. Instead Ronstadt gets a personally designed cameo on *Graceland*, dueting with Simon on the verses of "Under African Skies," one of which evokes the youth of Ladysmith's Joseph Shabalala and the other Ronstadt's girlhood in Tucson. Even if I admired Ronstadt's crystal harmonies as much as Simon does, I'd object to the evasive family-of-man-ism implied by the parallel verses. The offense is compounded, of course, by who Shabalala's sister-in-song happens to be: a prominent violator of the Sun City boycott. Even if her lyric called for total U.S. divestiture, ha ha, her presence on *Graceland* would be a slap in the face to the world anti-apartheid movement—a deliberate, considered, headstrong slap in the face.

Sincere opponents of apartheid may feel I'm making too much of this, so let me add that it doesn't ruin the album or even the song for me. But *Graceland* does nevertheless circle around an evasive ideology, the universalist humanism that is the intellectual vice of centrist liberals out of their depth. It's not so much what Simon says as what he doesn't say. Apartheid's propensity to distort everything it touches comes all too close to doing this album in right now, and in a decade, when the consequences of Simon's tactic are history, it could make the beautiful music of Simon and his black friends unlistenable.

Simon wants the music to speak for itself, but the most eloquent music can only say so much; he wants to "try and bridge cultures," but he can't determine who controls the bridge once it's built. Pretoria broadcasts this music on state radio—"Homeless" and "Under African Skies," not "The Boy in the Bubble"—because Pretoria thinks it's harmless at worst and a vinyl Sun City at best, a demonstration that their hideous system doesn't preclude meaningful racial cooperation. And who knows, this time Pretoria may be right. I don't believe politics transcends music, but I don't believe music transcends politics either. They're separate realms that impinge on each other, and in times of crisis they impinge more and more inescapably. I hope Simon has succeeded in reconciling opposing principles for more than the duration of an LP, because I want to be received in *Graceland* myself. But there's reason to wonder whether he's done enough.

Village Voice, 1986

Fela and His Lessers

Insofar as it uses electric instruments or horns, all African popular music is, to use the strange Orientalist term, Westernized. Afrobeat, however, took African Westernization global. The style invented and still dominated by the late Fela Kuti is easily the most convincing Afropop fusion. Most eager-to-please African imitator-emulators barely achieve competence—the singularity of Alpha Blondy's Ivoirian reggae and Orchestra Baobab's Sahel salsa only point up how undistinguished Lucky Dube and Africando are. But Fela was no imitator, and few artists anywhere have been less inclined to kiss ass.

As an arty young Nigerian who'd gone to music college and led a highlife band on saxophone, Fela got into Black Power and then pan-Africanism via an American girlfriend in L.A., and cut some sides there that sound more like James Brown than anything he recorded when he got back to Lagos—although his first big Lagos hit, "Jeun K'oko," flaunted a tricky JB horn chart, he disavowed any direct debt to the Godfather. Figure he didn't like the way American soul was overrunning Nigeria but did hear the Africa in funk, interpreted loosely as long groove songs emphasizing forward motion more than off-beats and other rhythmic contradictions. Afrobeat as Fela developed it combined such Brownian elements as chicken-scratch guitar, full-chorus call-and-response, minor-key melodies both African and jazzlike, and a groove that owed Yoruba percussion ensembles and his longtime trap drummer Tony Allen. Topping it off—and defining it, really—were pidgin lyrics more righteously antiwhite than any others available from Africa.

So what's most Western about Afrobeat isn't musical. It's that it's not at home in the world. It's a questing music, a discontented music, a neurotic music, and this sets it apart from the other great Afropop styles. Soukous, juju, mbaqanga, mbalax, many others—with qualifications that would only distract us, all achieve a synthesis of time-honored and modern you need no grounding in the traditions they reconstitute to feel. The affirmation they fabricate initially fed off a postcolonial high, yet hasn't been brought as far down as you'd expect by post-postcolonial privation. Afrobeat was never like this. Fela was too ambitious, too defiant, too arrogant, too crazed—Afropop's most committed politico except conceivably the more cryptic Thomas Mapfumo in Zimbabwe, where ongoing civil war threatened the safety of anyone who expressed a legible opinion. Issuing pronunciamentos, taunting the feds, sporting spliffs the size of stogies, he was rock, not funk. Like Jim Morrison or Grace Slick in the throes of 1968, and unlike a sometime satirist like Luambo Franco or a homiletic progressive like Youssou N'Dour, he thought his music could change the world, even building a residential compound masquerading as a utopian community off its proceeds. It's in part because they identify with all this extra-musical stuff that Westerners form Afrobeat bands rather than mbalax bands. It also helps that Afrobeat is easier to play.

Enter MCA's giant Fela project, which in August 2001 catapulted from thirteen to twenty-eight titles. Having managed to process the first half, which generally divides a single CD between two LPs comprising one or two songs each, I grabbed a new one blind for a Sunday outing and was delighted when the title track of *Roforofo Fight/The Fela Singles* got me all the way from the Tappan Zee to Yankee Stadium. Turns out that its jumpy fifteen-minute dance numbers make that CD a prize—and that I already knew "Roforofo Fight" from the superb, gingerly edited *The Best Best of Fela Kuti*. But after September 11, any quixotic thought I'd had of devoting three days to playing each new CD twice seemed self-indulgent. In fact, I haven't played them all twice yet—certainly not *Live in Amsterdam* or the complete original "Army Arrangement" Fela hated Bill Laswell for condensing or the Roy Ayers session or the endless Ginger Baker rumble. There's enough interesting stuff on these CDs—from early highlife dates to the avant piano on the late, dark "Underground System," plus many marginally differentiated highways to an irascible infinity—that if you owned just one you'd be glad you did. And were you to play it up against *Talkatif*, the second album by Antibalas, you'd wonder why you ever thought the best of the Afrobeat revival bands had their man's funk down. Only then you might play *Talkatif* up against the bland *Fight to Win*, by Fela's scion Femi, and ask yourself where the father's musicianship would have taken him without his rage. Not far enough.

For one thing, his music had its limits, especially to the Western ear. Polyrhythm is a collective commitment in Africa, whereas the idea of the American trap set is one man reinforcing/undercutting himself. Allen's quick, light, complex pulse is the greatest trap playing the continent has produced, but over here many of us prefer things busier and/or more obvious—the eccentric cross-beats of Ziggy Modeliste, say, or the thwomp of Al Jackson Jr. Nor do any of Fela's bassists match up against Fela fan Bootsy Collins. And though Fela always claimed the marathon duration of his songs as authentic Africanism, it smacks too of authentic weedism. The extended forms of traditional cultures always get pared down as society urbanizes. Epics went on all night because people didn't have much else to do.

Yet Fela towered over the local competition like JB and P-Funk combined. This is all too apparent on a glut of Nigerian funk compilations awaiting the sales action lucky dancefloor spins might spark. From Afrodisiac's dutiful yet intermittently fun *Booniay!!* through Blow's slovenly yet sometimes catchy *Afro Beat* to Afro Strut's well-nigh scholarly *Nigeria 70: The Definitive Story of 1970's Funky Lagos*, we get music that served a social function in a time and place now part of someone else's history. At best it's created by musicians who would end up boasting about, to cite two actual instances, their big job with the Crusaders or the Capitol contract their management frittered away. There's undeniable pathos in such stories, just as there's discernible life in the music. But that doesn't mean most of us need to hear it twice.

So forgive me if after all this Nigeriana my favorite recent reissue from Anglophone West Africa was generated a few hundred miles east in Accra: Naxos World's *Electric Highlife: Sessions from the Bokoor Studios*. Highlife was the name long ago attached to Western-influenced Ghanaian dance music by people who couldn't afford the venues where it was played, and musically it's always been protean—the East Nigerian specimens on the Oriental Brothers' classic *Heavy on the Highlife!*, for instance, go on like Fela himself. But most of these tracks are in Afropop's typical six-minute range. All were recorded by John Collins, a Ghana-born white who was also one of the first to write about African music, and not one was any kind of hit I'm aware of—where the artists on *Nigeria 70* tend to show up in the reference books, these aren't even in Collins's own *Musicmakers of West Africa*. The brief trots reveal such familiar Afropop themes as "My enemies wish to disgrace me / But because of God's grace this won't ever happen" and "In olden times people trained their children well so that they became responsible people / These days such training is scarce." And yet I find all thirteen cheerful tracks inspirational, more melodically and rhythmically engaging than almost any Afro-funk you can exhume.

Pinning down their pleasures, I find myself tripping over the word "charming," a concept that always raises the red flag of exoticism. But when I examine it more closely, that charmed feeling resembles spiritual awe. As I only bothered to find out after I'd fallen for the music, Ghana had an inflation rate of a hundred percent under the second tyranny of Lieutenant Jerry Rawlings when Collins founded Bokoor Studios in 1982. So now I wonder. How did F. Kenya manage to yoke pain and ebullience describing his family problems under such circumstances? Where did the Black Beats find the perky melody that subsumes their alarm at the irresponsible young, and why did they set one to the other? Why did these artists pursue old-fashioned highlife at all, sticking guitars where the horns used to be? Something about a style that still synthesized the time-honored and the modern, I guess. Something about making the best of what small choice you have. Not designed to change the world. But custom-made to help any human being live in it.

Village Voice, 2002 · Condensed and revised

Vendant l'Afrique

The most arrogant Francophone wouldn't spend five days in Boston or Washington and tell the folks in Paris he'd experienced America—St. Louis, maybe, San Antonio, but not Boston or Washington. So I'm not going to spend five days in Abidjan, Côte d'Ivoire, and tell you I experienced Africa. Not only is Abidjan a single city on a land mass far more vast, various, and nonurban than our own, it's highly atypical even for the non–South African sub-Sahara. As shaped by Felix Houphouet-Boïgny, who for the thirty-two years before he died in 1993 was the most Francophile and bourgeois of all Africa's postcolonial leaders, Abidjan has a thing for European commerce and Northern-style modernity. Only Nairobi, almost three thousand miles east in Kenya, and Dakar, a mere thousand miles northwest in Senegal, share its reputation for amenities—highways, croissants, etc. What's more, having been flown in by MASA 95, the second biannual Marché des Arts du Spectacle Africain, I didn't spend much time in Abidjan's downtown. My base was a commodiously landscaped enclave, the five-star Hotel Ivoire, site not just of MASA but of a continent-renowned dealer in masks and (that's right) ivory and the only ice-skating rink between South Africa and the Mediterranean basin.

Yet there I was May Day evening, eighteen hours after Air Afrique had landed eighteen hours late, ten meters from a truckbed stage in the barren sandlot that was the Place Saint Jean, enjoying the Sahel-inflected harmonies of five singers and four drummers—all male elders in their forties and fifties, most dressed *à l'Africain* but one wearing a D.A.R.E. T-shirt and a porkpie hat. Although the venue was only half a mile from the hotel, there wasn't another white face or MASA badge in the makeshift crowd. This was the Programme Off, where every day from four to eight—*en principe,* as the Ivoirians say about scheduling; I never heard of an Off show that began before dusk—a dozen music acts, dance groups, and theater companies who didn't make the organizers' final cut were given a chance to peddle their wares to the attendant promoters and bigwigs. The elders made the last live music I saw at the Place Saint Jean. After that it was lip-synched hits or misses over an equally hit-or-miss PA—Gallic Afrodisco from Zaire, dance-hall with Cairo strings from Burkina Faso—capped by a stand-up comic in shades who made me chuckle even though I don't understand spoken French in France, much less West Africa. As with a lot of the Marché, I half knew what this was—imperfect free-music-in-the-park for casual pleasure seekers. But this was my first trip to Africa, and the culture shock of *différance* Côte d'Ivoire–style was severe. If Abidjan was Bordeaux, say, I wondered what an African city as huge as Lagos or as impoverished as Conakry might be like. In the end, however, I got what I wanted: to peel off a layer or two of Afropop exoticism.

Not that the business of MASA was Afropop—its business was *la langue française.* Although its professional meetings rang with North-South rhetoric and its thirty-eight official selections represented seventeen separate African nations, MASA was by design and definition a Francophone venture, funded by the Agence de Coopération Culturelle et Technique in Paris as part of its mission to prevent the uncouth gutturals of *l'anglais* from further polluting world culture. And its Francophonie had musical consequences. Since France's African empire was concentrated north of the equator, it guaranteed a strong Islamic tinge and excluded the mbaqanga, mbube, jit, benga, highlife, juju, fuji, and whatever of former British colonies. And it insured a measure of pallid Gallicism at the nightly tripleheader concerts in the Ivoire's Palais des Congrés theater, with acts from two tiny Indian Ocean nations especially egregious—Mauritius's zouk-derived Windblows, who augmented their mild fusion with a balletic ballad, and Comoro Islands folkie Maalesh, at thirty-three a member in good standing of the International Brotherhood of Sensitive Young Middle-Class Men.

I doubt in any case that even the most striking groups featured were ripe for export the way the *marché*'s marketers dreamed. Except maybe for Malagasay guitarist D'Gary, who I arrived too late to see, there was certainly no Baaba Maal, who climaxed MASA 93. There was no Youssou N'Dour, whose porkpie-hatted Senegalese manager was all over the Ivoire, or Angelique Kidjo, a sharp-witted panel participant who foisted off the dull Bénin jazz-rockers Karavan in recompense, or Papa Wemba, who sat in at several venues, among them the hotel lobby—where a tight and enthusiastic band of Zaireans called Lokito The Best played salsa, lounge jazz, and anything else a tourist might desire, including the only live soukous I heard all week. The rippling guitars that make the most beautiful sound in pop music were plentiful on radios and tape players and a PA staple at MASA's outdoor Village Gastronomique, where grillades of free-range chicken cost less than continental breakfast at the Ivoire. Maybe there were none on stage because MASA figured that portion of its sell required no bureaucratic intervention.

....

Nevertheless, I couldn't get enough of the music, which was rarely disappointing at the Palais de Congrés and continued to roll out of far-flung *maquis* and theater spaces long after the big shows ended at eleven-thirty. The experience was so intoxicating that I still regret opportunities clumsily missed—five Ivoirian musicologists playing "musique traditionelle de chambre" at the Goethe Institut, or the Bronx, a specially created ghetto rap club I didn't have the guts to seek out without a Francophone guide. At the simplest level, it was a revelation and a relief finally to encounter musical usages I knew intimately from a distance in a context where they determined the norm, and most of what I heard was ear-opening at least and tremendously enjoyable much of the time. Groups were usually large, guitar-keybs-bass-traps plus drums and perhaps horns plus singers and dancers, and since costs mount when multiplied by ten, twelve, or more, this may well present an export problem. But it also boosted musically undistinguished acts like Niger's Takeda Group, thirteen musicians and singers joined at the outset by a statuesque chorus of four male Peuls in robes and makeup Ru-Paul could take to the runway. And troupes like Guinée's Nyamakalas, who worked up a frenetic funk on kora, balafon, earthbow bass, double oboe, and such, then brought on increasingly acrobatic dancers who were upstaged by a hefty middle-aged woman singer rolling her eyes and twitching her hips, seemed committed to ritualistic scale—sixteen strong at the Palais des Congrés, in Conakry they bring it up to thirty.

Takeda Group, would-be modernists cloaking their proud tribal-national roots in a generic rock format, and Nyamakalas, practical preservationists rendering traditional culture into easily grasped entertainment, represented the aesthetic poles favored by the French and African "experts" who decided which of hundreds of aspirants would go to MASA's market. The vital, realized, reliably self-generated new Afropop styles that ought to be springing up organically in between these two poles, as soukous and mbalax once did, were not readily apparent. Yet even at the international-pop and folk-art extremes, MASA occasioned some amazing doings.

The veteran Guinéean twelve-piece Kaloum Star played the surest music of the festival, arraying confident vocals and jazzy chops over a relaxed groove Sahel in shape and Kinshasa in mood. And while Abidjan reggae heartthrob Serges Kassy, wildly received by local fans who could pay the tariff, was way too slick whatever his political message (I'm told he urged the rich to pay their taxes like the poor, always a worthy goal), the less established Tangara Speed Ghôda took the right cues from Côte d'Ivoire's only major musical export, Alpha Blondy. A professed Muslim, Tangara was Lee Perry as jive messiah in the most memorable outfit of a well-turned-out festival—shades, yellow snowhood over full dreads, purple robe over red jumpsuit, high brown combat boots, pigskin gloves, two books he never put down, and a bow and arrow. One French informant complained that his lyrics were too mystagogic, but his voice combined the gruff strength of dancehall's macho men with the embattled faith of a Bunny Wailer or Joseph Hill. Providing the other ranking international Afroprotest style, hip-hop, was Dakar's Positive Black Soul, starring Amadou Barry a/k/a Doug E. Tee, a quick-lipped prodigy who slipped effortlessly from rap to ragga, speech to song, Wolof to French to, holy shit, English. "L'anglais!" I cheered at the top of my lungs.

There were two problems with Positive Black Soul. One was the music, predictable beatbox chukka-chukka that would have sounded old in the States five years ago. My last day in Africa I thought briefly that I'd met a solution in the lobby. François Konian is a well-connected black Ivoirian who in the '80s started the first recording studio in Abidjan if not West Africa, whose current project was an African-run FM station in the city (somehow French francs always impose French control), and whose "gift" to MASA (and "the kids") was the rap club the Bronx—where, I was told, Côte d'Ivoire's minister of culture had declared that at MASA 97 this new ghetto sound would get its due as the voice of the nation's youth if not, as Konian's interpreter insisted, "the future of African music." But while the Ivoirian rap stars Konian introduced, R.A.S. (Rien à Signaler, "Nothing to Say"), wisely sought site-specific beats in indigenous percussion, the cassette they brought me was way pop even so. I hope they like the Brand Nubian tape I gave them in return.

The other problem with Positive Black Soul went a lot deeper and couldn't be blamed on them. It was that horrible hip-hop staple, death— before or during their show, a scalper had been gunned down by police. I didn't delude myself about solutions for that one, especially since I was part of the problem—the need to keep things orderly for *acheteurs* and visiting dignitaries like myself could only make the flics more trigger-happy. But the incident, *comme on dit*, did serve to point up MASA's fantasy quotient in a relatively prosperous nation where scalpers get shot and Serges Kassy's fans can't afford the Palais des Congrés. Early in the professional meetings, which would have seemed as platitudinous as the confabs at any other alternative music convention if the autonomy the Africans harped on wasn't of such historical moment, someone used the phrase "cultural resources that are a sort of wealth." This was the dream. If Africa's so musical, people wanted to know, why isn't it rich? But rich it ain't, and rich it is unlikely to become. Konian argued that African Francophonie was just the latest imperialist con game, a cover for exploitation—that MASA's 1.3-million-franc budget was three times what it would cost to train two students from every French-speaking African nation in each of five crucial music-business skills. His numbers may have been off, his motives mixed. But he obviously had good reason to conceive development differently than the Agence de Coopération Culturelle et Technique.

....

Two images, then.

While awaiting my chicken at the Village Gastronomique on the final night, I was approached by the sweet young manager of Zizimazi, a Programme Off act who'd been moved down from the Place Saint Jean and was scheduled for eight. He wondered what I'd noticed most about Africans— their warmth, perhaps? He also wondered if I'd wait to see his group, but there were no signs of movement on the tiny stage. After midnight, however, I returned, and at one-thirty Zizimazi actually went on. As promised, the singer was fairly fantastic, a lithe tenor in a sleeveless white jacket, white shirt, and gaily patched grey trousers who did splits and rolled in the grass to the delight of an adoring claque. Later I learned that in two years this was the third time the group had played out. They were all in school or had day jobs—the singer was a bookkeeper. But like most aspiring African musicians, they couldn't amass enough capital to invest in instruments.

And then there were the surprise-hit preservationists, the teenaged Merveilles de Guinée, a side project of Ballets Africains choreographer Mohamed

Kémoko. At first I took them for another of the percussion-heavy dance troupes that had long since sated my appetite for unadorned polyrhythm, but it was nice to see women drumming for once, and over forty minutes or so the solo turns and acrobatic derring-do kept getting sexier and more spirited. The audience was already deeply into it when they unveiled their showstopper—a polio survivor who walked out on his hands like a crab and proceeded to carry off a phenomenal series of steps and leaps and feats of strength with his matchstick legs folded on his chest. He was thrilling, he was corny, he was miraculous, he was hard to look at without cringing. He controlled a cultural resource that was a kind of wealth. And to convert it into crass old economic wealth he would happily dance on his hands for us.

Village Voice, 1995

Dakar in Gear

The work of fiction Mark Hudson's *The Music in My Head* most recalls is Nick Hornby's *High Fidelity*, another tale of a record collector defeating his mania on the road to mature love, la dee dah. Only it's not much like *High Fidelity*, because plot isn't the payoff. You want Motown-quality entertainment, Hornby's your man. You want music from the inside and a mad sprawl of a book that evokes it every which way, go down to Stern's and buy this award-winning travel writer's only novel, which hasn't found an American publisher. Amazon.co.uk has it too, but the Brit branch isn't selling CDs yet, and this book demands its soundtrack, a Stern's compilation also called *The Music in My Head*. As a depiction of Africa—really Dakar, except that Hudson isn't always circumspect about the distinction—Hudson's novel is tendentious, impolite, enthralled, and more convincing than most white people's depictions of Africa. As music writing it's stone brilliant, and it's generated the album to prove it.

Hudson's protagonist, the exaggerated composite Andrew "Litch" Litchfield, is a middle-level biz hustler with a Hunter Thompson swagger to his prose who on a Gambia holiday circa 1980 remakes himself as the herald of "world music," a term and phenomenon that come to perturb him greatly.

His life is changed by the voice of Sajar Jopp, who readers may recognize as Youssou N'Dour; other key pseudonyms include not just Michael Heaven (Peter Gabriel) and Cherry Jatta Samba (Salif Keita), but N'Galam, Tekrur, which is how Hudson feels constrained to designate Dakar, Senegal. Maybe his lawyers worried that a municipality could sue, and you can see why. On page five, Litch calls N'Galam "a place that, while regarding itself as the Athens of Africa, was recently described by the Economist as 'one of the least secure places in the world,'" and scarcely a chapter goes by without his fearing he'll be set upon by one of those cunning natives who lounge around affably in the heat only to spring into action at night. While it might be argued that Litch is a fictional character flirting with mental breakdown, Hudson is obviously fascinated by the cool, tough Tekrurian/Senegalese vibe that says: "I may be unemployed, I may know nothing, but I am a man—so back off!" The first chapter of his *Our Grandmothers' Drums*, set in the calmer confines of a Gambian village, relates how he was almost robbed in the Dakar airport. This overheated vision of an African city may be a grievous insult. After all, what would Hudson make of a place as scary as Lagos or Kinshasa? But it opened up West African music for me.

Regarding "probably the best band in the world," Sajar Jopp's, Litch observes: "The trouble with this kind of music, or rather the great thing about it, is that it tends not to stop in one groove for long." In this it's totally unlike the "glossy tumbling soukous hedonism" that evolved from "the beautiful, soulful old Congolese rumba," which after the juju bubble burst was "the great hope for African music. Down there in the mad military kleptocracy in the torrid belly of Africa things were so bad that the only option—for those who could afford it—was to drink, dance and try to forget it." Personally, I've always been a sucker for soukous's nonstop party. In the right mood I could relate to the solemnities of Keita and N'Dour, Baaba Maal and Ali Farka Touré, but I figured such stuff was made for a major thinker like Peter Gabriel, not little old me. Even if West Africa had stronger singers, wilder drums, and rockinger guitars, as in general it did, each element seemed to go its own way rather than serve the collective good. Yet before I'd even read *The Music in My Head*, the CD had sensitized me to what I'll call the Dakar Overgroove.

How to capture this aural gestalt in a phrase when Hudson devotes half a novel to it? Desert mystics conquering the fleshpots? Overloaded camions careening down a potholed road? Frantic macho cohering and clashing, stopping and going, crashing and cohering again? I'd encountered its prototype in two of Hudson's star exhibits, the early dance music of Keita with

Les Ambassadeurs and especially N'Dour with Étoile de Dakar Etoile. Yet the cantering guitar-and-drums riff and piercing vocal call-and-response of Étoile de Dakar's standout 1977 "Thiely" only continues a demonstration begun by Hudson's lead cut, Number One de Dakar's 1978 "Nongui, Nongui," where dramatic horns-and-drums do the hookwork and gruff Pape Seck states the theme. And what's truly gratifying is that Hudson doesn't seem stuck in the good old days: exhibit three, Thione Seck's long, elegiac "Laye M'Boup," was recorded in 1994, and the synth you can make out in the detailed modern mix belongs there like everything else.

Hudson can defy all proper principles of compilation sequencing by jumbling six pre-1980 tracks with six post-1992, ignoring the intervening world-music years, because the Overgroove prevails. He's onto something that overwhelms cogent chronological transitions: an emergent urban energy that's always in gear as it runs stop signs and screeches around corners. Admittedly, however, his greatest prizes are audiophile nightmares from 1980: tracks six and seven, Étoile 2000's literally garage-recorded anti-Youssou smash, "Boubou N'Gary," all unkempt echoplexed fuzzbox and excitable tama drum, and Gestu de Dakar's aurally crude and otherwise unknown "Djirime." Horns blare sourly, drums kibitz, two singers fall in and out, and a fast-thinking guitarist provokes Hudson to wonder whether he's Joycean or Proustian.

After that the album tones down some; tracks ten and eleven, both recent, seem comparatively slick as they protest unemployment and reprise Mandinka kora traditions, and on the finale, Coumba Gawlo says amen with a gorgeous not-quite-pop ballad that sets all this male turmoil aright with some female principle. This selection is the ultimate proof of Hudson's ears; Gawlo's album has other good songs, but "Miniyamba" is superb in a modern mode the proud discoverer of Gestu de Dakar probably doesn't have much use for. Yet as someone who resists the aesthetic of the raw and luxuriates in what Paris did to soukous, I have to admit that the older, cruder stuff—busy, contentious, fit to bust—defines the Dakar Overgroove.

Is it powered by "those whose voices testify to the most unspeakable levels of dissipation and abuse, to the closest identification with the age-old agonies of their race," as Litch puts it? Except conceivably for the wasting effects of diet, I detect no dissipation here. But "people who have nothing to live for but music"? That's what the Étoile 2000 album put together by the Dutch CNR label in 1996 sounds like. "Boubou N'Gary" was such a big hit for the disaffected Youssou bandmates the garage's owner was bankrolling—including intense tenor El Hadji Faye, rock-besotted guitar man Badou

N'Diaye, and Yamar Thiam, who couldn't stop sticking his tamas in if you paid him—that it generated a mercurial career. Springing into action at night, they were clearly one of the great crazy bands.

But soon they were gone, and Hudson's skill in proving that their spirit lives on is largely sleight-of-hand. Two of the other '90s tracks are folkloric reclamations, and two more flirt with the pop compromise the lustrous Gawlo sidesteps. So the protector of today's Dakar Overgroove turns out to be none other than Youssou N'Dour. Tell me 1994's *The Guide* (*Wommat*) is, as Litch would have it, "fucking boring," and all I'll respond is that 1990's *Set* isn't. But N'Dour continues to record for his Senegalese base, and while the rawness of Étoile de Dakar is missed, the drums are a lot noisier than world music's folkies like them. The most impressive recent N'Dour I've heard, including the just-released *Spécial Fin d'Année*, is 1996's *Lii!* The seven songs begin more decorously, more confidently, perhaps because they're sure they have tunes. But soon N'Dour and his three drummers are driving them past their own choruses and over the top. The Overgroove has changed for sure—matured, la dee dah. But it still sounds like something worth living for.

A God After Midnight

Youssou N'Dour

When Youssou N'Dour's Super Étoile band came on the Hammerstein Ballroom stage at midnight, squat, dark-suited warmup vocalist Ouzin N'Diaye's penetrating high notes had me wondering when the thirty-nine-year-old god of African music had gotten old and ugly. But Senegal is a land of singers, and I've made such gaffes before. So a few minutes later the taller, rosier N'Dour, resplendent in a floor-length white robe, was projecting over cymbals and an organlike synth wash in a voice so full-bodied and mellow that I was abashed I'd been taken in yet again. For over three hours the star and his twelve musicians showed us why his Dakar shows are religious experiences. The music went on almost nonstop, its rhythms effortless but hardly smooth or euphoric, its byplay varied and eloquent and not always predictable—twice a keyb went for a schlocky, wind-chiming art-rock cross of harp and steel drums that sounded super. There was a seven-minute, five-man tamafest and a song for the murdered Senegalese immigrant Amadou Diallo that got the three-quarters African audience going with no notable rabble-rousing. Several times a dancer in a zooty charcoal-gray suit took the stage to propel his legs and feet outward like shotputs or cannonballs, boom-boom-boom-boom-boom. On the floor, white onlookers swayed to the pulse that always sustained the synth underpinnings, guitar sallies, and tama clusters while mostly male Senegalese combatants exploded in bursts of limb and corkscrewing pelvis.

N'Dour left briefly to exchange his robe for an even handsomer rust-colored suit, and he didn't spend every minute singing. But at three-thirty, forty-five minutes after he'd solicited and received what appeared to be a show-topping twenty-minute singalong on the huge Senegal hit "Birima," he was still performing feats of volume, clarity, and emotional outreach such American marathoners as the Grateful Dead never get near. His intensity was relaxed, confident, commanding, nothing like "tight"—the kind of unassailable cultural authority that's almost disappeared from today's pop. Midway through, on the English-language hit "7 Seconds," Stevie Wonder followed the sound of his own harmonica onto the stage, where he traded vocal improvs with N'Dour until he couldn't take it any further. It was an aptly wonderful moment—one among more than anyone could be bothered to count.

Village Voice, 1999

Franco de Mi Amor

The best shorthand for the many-named hero christened François Luambo Makiadi and known as Franco is to coin a cliche and call him the James Brown of Africa. As individual artists the two had different strengths: Brown made his name as a vocalist before his genius as a dancer swept his singing before it, while Franco was a groundbreaking guitarist famed and feared for his lyrics. But both were bandleaders above all, and as such they were paradigm-shifters—so much so that their masses of admirers raised them into cynosures, demigods, animi. Despite their awkwardness negotiating the political messes that occasionally enmeshed them, they weren't shy about wielding power, and each was explicitly committed to black consciousness—as opposed to colonialism in Franco's case, the other man in Brown's. They were big men who changed their worlds in a big way.

But though Brown is a byword in Africa, Franco is scarcely known in America, a disparity that did not go unnoticed by the Sorcerer of the Guitar, the Grand Maître of Zairean Music, the 285-pound powerhouse who inspired a biography that his Boswell, Graeme Ewens, called *Congo Colossus*. After Brown first visited Kinshasa in 1969, Franco declared himself unmoved—Brown "danced like a monkey," he told colleagues in OK Jazz, and didn't show sufficient respect for his ancestral roots, especially as embodied by the Grand Maître. But some of his men got Brown's message anyhow, and with Franco that counted. Not only did his OK Jazz band breed a phenomenal number of major Congolese musicians, but—much more than Brown, let it be said—the headman recorded their songs and encouraged them to develop side projects that he'd sell on his own label. My surmise is that some sort of byplay with his musicians got him grunting the perfect English-sounding JB parody-homage at the end of "Edo Aboyi Ngai."

The eighty-four albums listed in *Congo Colossus*'s discography aren't the 150 Franco claimed, but they're plenty for a recording career that lasted thirty-six years, from 1953 until his death at fifty-one in 1989. True, overproduction is the standard African antipiracy strategy, and by the late '70s albums would commonly comprise only three or four songs that roughly approximated the standard structure of the continent-sweeping Afropop style we will call soukous although Franco—who associated the French-derived term with his romantic rival Tabu Ley Rochereau and tradition-blasting upstarts Zaiko Langa Langa—preferred the older "rumba." With props to Zairean musicologist Pierre Kazadi, Ewens outlines this structure more precisely than is altogether wise in such a volatile force-field. First a melodic section following the contours of a lyric that with Franco is almost always in Lingala—a tonal pidgin, originally the patois of the Congo docks, that serves as a working-class West African Swahili—is varied and repeated vocally and instrumentally. And then comes the sebene, soukous's signature selling point, which has been credited to both Franco and one of his mentors, long-repatriated Belgian-born guitarist-producer Bill Alexandre, but which predates both and only flowered in its countless variegations after

Zaiko launched their '70s youth movement. The sebene is an "improvisational episode" or "groove" in which three guitarists repeat short phrases off which the lead player improvises, generally remaining close enough to the source riffs to reinforce them and break them down simultaneously. Eventually younger players like Kanda Bongo Man shucked the verse to play nothing but sebene—"speed soukous." The intricate rush of the sebene is what you hear in your head when you recall what soukous sounds like.

Which is a lot easier than recalling what Franco sounds like, especially for Americans. Compared to West and South African genres, there's never been much soukous released in this country, but Franco's neglect is remarkable even so. In part this no doubt reflects his long relationship with Paris-based Sonodisc, which has never tested the U.S. market. Sonodisc has reissued much of Franco's music on CD, although only one of the four titles I recently tried at Stern's down on Warren Street corresponds exactly to any original album in Ewens's discography, and two were all but untraceable. According to Ken Braun of Stern's, who had to abandon a Franco box set when Sonodisc failed to finalize permissions, I could wait a long time.

This confusion makes two excellent recent compilations even more valuable: last year's *Franco: The Very Best of the Rumba Giant of Zaire*, with pro forma notes by Jon Lusk on Manteca, and the just-released *Rough Guide to Franco*, with informative notes by co-compiler Ewens. Commendably, Ewens repeats only one track from the earlier collection: "Attention Na Sida" ("Beware of AIDS"), by general agreement Franco's last great song as well as a way of implying that, actually, this voracious womanizer probably did die of AIDS no matter how much he and his people deny it. Because both collections begin at the beginning and end at the very end, they mutate more than is convenient. The twenty explicitly Latin-influenced early songs on RetroAfric's *Originalité* cohere better, the verse-and-sebene workouts on several Sonodiscs I've acquired flow better, and there aren't many things in the world as beautiful as *Omona Wapi*, cut with Rochereau for Rochereau's label and still in print in condensed form on Shanachie. But between them these two overviews place the colossus in history while showcasing music whose illustrative function doesn't compromise its capacity to startle and delight.

Forced to distinguish, I'd say the Manteca is more the instant hit, the *Rough Guide* more the groove carnival. The Manteca starts with the old theme song "On Entre O.K., On Sort K.O." (an exemplary piece of wordplay for a band named after its sponsor's initials, not some Yank slang), the *Rough Guide* with a "Merengue" that has no speed-merengue in it (this was 1956, after all). The Manteca is never better than when it moves from a satire on Mobutu's public executions of 1965 (in the Kikongo tongue of Franco's mother, based on Kikongo folklore about a sorcerer and featuring ninety seconds of terrified chatter in the middle, it led to a six-month exile in Brazzaville) to that James Brown takeoff to a gut-wrenching Kikongo mourning song for his younger brother to the catchily harmonized "AZDA," a totally entrancing pan-African smash that sings the praises of a Volkswagen dealership. The *Rough Guide* lays out a wide range of Afro-Latin beats and sounds (try "Likambo Ya Ngana"'s retro accordion and femme chorus) before sandwiching two lilting satires around a funereal declamation denying that Franco is a drug dealer and then breaking into the nonpareil Afro-Parisian "Chacun Pour Soi." Both collections are striking for two things above all: endless variety in a supposedly formulaic style and nonstop melody in a supposedly rhythm-bound one.

Because the soukous we know best is the slick, pealing, high-energy stuff rolled out so gorgeously in Paris in the '80s, these records may be pokier than you expect. More than half their tracks precede the soukous era proper. And the admonitory "Attention Na Sida," while staunchly danceable—its organizing riff copied, in fact, off 1978's "Jacky," which got Franco thrown in jail for describing a woman who fed her lovers what Ewens identifies as "excrement," isn't exactly an up. Rarely on any of these twenty-two tracks does the sebene rise up and carry you away, and when you listen for Franco's guitar you discover that his career-making style came late if at all to the lace-surfaced shimmer that is soukous's hallmark—the fluidity that suffuses *Omona Wapi* and buoys "Ekaba Kaba" on Celluloid's extraordinary *Zaire Choc!* soukous compilation. Gruff, sardonic, magisterial, he picked single-lined riffs and melodies at less than quicksilver speed; you can always tell the music passed through his brain before reaching his fingers. His plangent, forthright sound is his own, but if you want an analogy to his approach, say he plays like a John Lennon with more chops and a head for business—a John Lennon who could hire all the Eric Claptons he needed. And because Franco had a great head for business and music both, he knew very well he needed them.

In this his guitar is like his singing. Franco is famous for his shifting corps of vocalists, totaling thirty-seven by Ewens's count. A few of them could do it all—notably the faithful Josky and the virtuosic Sam Mangwana, whom Franco lured away from Tabu Ley for three fruitful years preceding Mangwana's solo breakthrough. But most were there to provide a sweetness Franco knew enough to value and knew he didn't have in him—more than I can pretend to tell apart, although Ntesa Dalienst's solo album *Belalo* has won Dalienst, who was with Franco from 1976 till the end, a special place in my mind's ear. Whatever Franco's technical limitations, he remained OK Jazz's primary singer as well as its primary guitarist, if only because no one else was equal to lyrics that aren't just one reason Zaireans loved him, but also speak volumes as an enacted language to attentive listeners who'll never know a word of Lingala. Liner notes and trots help—I had a flash when I learned that the entrancing, sax-hooked, sixteen-minute verse-and-sebene "Très Impoli" included imprecations against guys who raid their friends' refrigerators and show the holes in their smelly socks. But just from the way he delivers and accompanies his words you know what kind of artist this is. You know that he maintained his credibility as a man of the people by addressing them plainly. You recognize that his failure to pursue the European-American market like Rochereau and Mangwana meshes with his Africa-first anticolonial *authenticité* rhetoric. You realize that it was his stubborn Africanness that kept him from riding Afro-Parisian soukous's supersonic express all the way to glory.

After all, Franco was confident he could accelerate quicker than a heartbeat under his own steam. His live shows, celebrated throughout Africa but staples at the club he owned in Kinshasa, really were carnivals. He appeared only twice in New York, first on a frigid November night in 1983. Not really knowing much about him, my wife and I got to the Manhattan Center late. The lobby was dead, the elevator lonely, the list makeshift. Then we opened a door and wham—lights, action, music. I don't want to say it was like being teleported to Zaire, I've never been to Zaire, but that was certainly the illusion. Although the room wasn't jammed full it seemed to be teeming, perhaps because there were some forty people on the stage, all surrounding a fat man sitting on a chair and playing guitar. Beyond a vague vision of the color and motion of the female dancers and a physical memory of rippling sebenes, I can't bring back a single detail. But none of the hundreds of soukous albums to come my way since then has matched the experience. And Ewens says that wasn't even a good show! Anyone who could have made such a thing happen thousands of times inhabited a different reality than you or me.

Although Franco was always a troublemaker, not afraid to pick fights with government officials or profit-skimming businessmen, he was also a stooge for Mobutu Sese Seko, one of Africa's most rapacious tyrants. It was that or emigrate for a man of the people whose every artistic tack proves how much he loved the Congo and particularly Kinshasa: Kinshasa belonged to Mobutu, a demagogue who courted pop stars and gave disloyalty no quarter.

Nevertheless, it's undeniable that Franco made noises more regrettable than any James Brown ever uttered about Richard Nixon in far less parlous circumstances. Also like that monkey man, he never stopped believing this is a man's man's man's world. One of his early sobriquets was Franco de Mi Amor, bestowed in the '50s by the new female cooperative saving clubs that included many of his most passionate fans, presaging a cohort eventually ranging, Ewens suggests, "from innocent teenagers, widows and divorcées to adulteresses and outright prostitutes," and seventeen of his eighteen children by fourteen mothers were girls. Like many ladies' men, he could write convincingly from a woman's point of view. But he knew whose side he was on in the battle of the sexes, which was his greatest subject; the supposed breakthrough "Mario" criticized a man who was living off a rich older woman, never a socially acceptable pattern. His only song manifesting the kind of protofeminist effort apparent in Youssou N'Dour, say, was written by Ntesa Dalienst.

And still "Mario" is a great song—great if you know what it means, great if you don't. Musicians make lousy ideologues, we've figured that out by now, and what endures about the Grand Maître isn't his ideas but an attitude perfectly comprehensible to non-Lingala speakers. This was a man who knew his place but was never constrained by it. He absorbed lessons from Cuban records and a Belgian producer and a ne'er-do-well guitarist who boarded with his mother, and he got rich giving those lessons back to Kinshasa in no uncertain terms. We always think of him as the embodiment of a seismic musical tendency, and he was. But as we listen closer we get to hear him as the individual christened François Luambo Makiadi. He couldn't be one without the other.

Note: In 2008 and 2009, Sterns released two musically and annotatively magnificent Ken Braun–compiled Franco collections titled Francophonic *and* Francophonic Vol. 2. *They're now where to start—but not by any means stop.*

Forty Years of History, Thirty Seconds of Joy

Just before midnight at Manhattan's Irving Plaza last November 8, two hours after the announced showtime for the Congolese soukous ensemble JB Mpiana & Wenge Musica BCBG, I listened along with as many as eighty smartly dressed Africans while a band comprising two guitars, two synthesizers, bass, congas, and trap drums was gradually augmented by six vocalists. Four of these were singers, two animateurs charged with whipping up the crowd with shouted slogans and namechecks. All wore identical white T-shirts bearing the message "Peace Grows." Guitars purled, synths percussed, voices joined and split off—always melodic, always in pulsating motion. I was especially impressed by the sweet, piercing showpiece of a little guy sporting an overstuffed baseball cap and multiple eyebrow rings and by two singers who at around one a.m. climaxed the loosely synchronized choreography with competitive somersaults.

Helluva show, except for one thing. Where was JB Mpiana? So the band vamped on as frontmen teasingly promised "the boss" until at last a light-skinned big man progressed out to the vacant center mike. No T-shirt for the boss—he wore a jacket with a JB Mpiana billboard on the back and brought along two female dancers, the plumper of whom chewed gum through the entire concert. Less than two minutes after Mpiana added his pretty, soaring vocals, the wonderful music entered some other realm—a serial climax I felt would never end and couldn't believe would last another twenty seconds. By my watch, it went on for twenty-two minutes, but the lull was so momentary that there was no appreciable pause, just a more relaxed ecstatic number that didn't subside for twenty-five more minutes, when finally, on my feet for over two hours, I wandered to the back of the somewhat fuller house and sat against a wall, even dozing briefly, only to arise circa two-thirty, re-energized by a gently undulating sung chorus that continued for, say, seven minutes and culminated in fans affixing U.S. currency to the musicians' sweaty bodies. I was so entranced I didn't notice when Mpiana, who had stopped singing somewhere in there, left the stage. The guitarists kept rippling and the chorus kept harmonizing until the venue lowered a screen behind which the band wound down as the crowd strolled toward the exit. I assume the music ended. But I don't know when. Next day my legs ached.

I've witnessed at least two dozen soukous shows featuring most of the modern greats. Quite a few were terrific, but the only one that ranked with Wenge Musica's was Franco's equally ill-publicized 1983 affair, when my balcony ticket spilled me directly onto the otherworldly spectacle of forty singers, players, dancers, and aides-de-camp surrounding a fat guitarist sitting on a straight-backed chair and overseeing a not dissimilar sebene, as the Congolese call those sustained climaxes. In the quarter century since 1983, Franco had died, Zaire had disintegrated, and soukous had fallen into apparently irreversible disrepair. Yet there at Irving Plaza was one of four rival versions of a "fourth-generation" soukous band creating an alternative reality matched by few I've experienced in a lifetime of music-going. Hey, soukous is like that. So I floated home, took a lot of notes, and put the night in my memory book. Not everything in this world is meant to be understood.

Six months later, I pulled from my crammed to-read shelf University of Montreal anthropologist Bob W. White's *Rumba Rules*, which soon proved the third rather good book about Congolese music in English. The others are by British journalists who've lived in Africa: Graeme Ewens's Franco biography *Congo Colossus* (1994) and Gary Stewart's general history *Rumba on the River* (2000), both of which end their stories with Franco's death in 1989. Subject to academic publishing's teaching-load and peer-review stumbling blocks, White's book suffered even longer lag time, appearing twelve years after he completed his fieldwork in Kinshasa in 1996. It barely mentions Mobutu Sese Seko's soon-assassinated successor Laurent Kabila, Kabila's own successor (and son) Joseph Kabila, or the war that has killed four million Congolese and counting, mostly well east of Kinshasa in the Kivus.

Yet although Mobutu still maintained an aura of invincibility in 1996, by then Kinshasa had crossed the line from capital of kleptocracy to anarchic dysfunctionality—ransacked twice as aid dried up post–Cold War and Zaire's economy crumbled, with Mobutu ensconced in villas far north in his home village or farther north in Europe. Great soukous records still surfaced, but most of them were laid down in Paris or Brussels, many by emigres. The deep reason Ewens and especially Stewart stopped in 1989 was that they couldn't stand what had become of the music they loved. Still a believer, White explains what happened next—including that night in Irving Plaza.

Rumba Rules isn't perfectly turned. Because most of White's sources have done fieldwork and quite a few are Congolese, the obligatory academic nods have some jam, but they still drag some, and his grand thesis—that "popular music and politics acted together to reinforce a uniquely modern tradition of authoritarian rule"—feels as if a few too many disaffected African intellectuals were whispering in his ear. Nevertheless, it's good that he addresses soukous's knotty political ramifications at all, and most of the book is fascinating, even enthralling. White is diffident and relaxed about interlacing the personal and the scholarly. His description of his stint as an animateur in Général Defao's Big Stars is idea-packed and entertaining, and his analysis of four recent love lyrics as encoded cries of social uncertainty and isolation— the kind of interpretive leap that leaves many popular culture scholars flat on their ass with a twisted ankle—isn't just convincing, it's wrenching. Also illuminated are the Mobutuist complicities of Luambo Franco, the compulsory daily *animation politique* in which workers at every level were required to sing and dance Mobutu's praises, the evolution and devolution of Wenge Musica, how hard it is to play simple Congolese chords or shake an insecticide-can maraca, the cassette trade, equatorial chieftancy, and the rise of libanga, the prepurchased shout-outs now integral to bandleaders' cash flow.

But best of all is his detailed account of a Big Star's life. There's the borrowing of stage clothes; the mud river of a street that fronts the rehearsal space the band is lucky to have; the regimentation, waiting, discomfort, waiting, and fatigue; the routinized arrangements; the four- or five-hour shows; and, several times every night, the "thirty seconds of joy" as a chorus accelerates almost imperceptibly into a sebene, that "source of joy and wonder for hundreds of thousands of young people in the Congolese capital"— and also for White himself and perhaps even his barely paid bandmates. White can't let the sebene go. He says terrible things about Franco, whose sardonic populism paralleled Mobutu's and whose music was greater for it. He posits a Foucauldian reduction in which Franco's social criticisms were like Mobutu's own, serving merely and solely as a safety valve for political resistance as they helped line his capacious pockets. He even repeats the "urban myth" in which Franco had a special chair reserved for him in Mobutu's office. Yet his acknowledgments name Franco as a "profound" influence "whose music continues to haunt me." An irresistible concoction that dominated Afropop for decades, soukous is like that.

The vast, ethnically irrational territory King Leopold II of Belgium mapped out as the Congo Free State is so rich in metals, diamonds, rubber, and lumber that, as Adam Hochschild's 1998 *King Leopold's Ghost* established, it became the model for European exploitation of Africa, always a step or two more brutal and unmitigated than its French, English, German, and Portuguese counterparts. Michela Wrong's 2000 *In the Footsteps of Mr. Kurtz*, a wide-ranging journalistic account that zeroes in on protagonists large and small, describes its disastrous nationhood under the somewhat less brutal but much more inefficient Kabila. Beginning with an annotated list of 161 acronyms, more than fifty of them parties to the Congolese conflict it outlines invaluably if sometimes numbingly, Gérard Prunier's 2009 *Africa's World War* is almost as dismissive of Laurent Kabila as of Mobutu himself, although it holds out shreds of hope for Joseph and Congo's future. But from the perspective of that Wenge Musica show, it's striking how thoroughly these three very good books ignore music.

Perhaps resisting the stereotype in which, as Wrong puts it, "Congolese either make music all the time or are petty crooks," Hochschild instead emphasizes Africa's influence on cubism. Prunier makes up for attributing Wenge Musica's 1998 sinking-ship song "Titanic" to Papa Wenge by revealing that soukous siren Tshala Muana clocked dollars as Laurent Kabila's private dancer, but he's so busy tracking alliances and troop movements that he does well to mention music at all. That leaves Wrong to mention that soukous "managed to entrance a continent for more than thirty years" before moving on to La Sape, the mania for designer labels crystallized circa 1980 by the great soukous singer and convicted immigrant smuggler Papa Wemba, known among many other things as *Le Pape de la Sape*.

I propose that these excellent historians are making a mistake. While buying the Afrocentric claim that European and American wealth were built on African resources and labor, I would add that, never mind cubism, the dominant movement of twentieth-century music was built on reconstituted African usages. Economically, this is of small import. Usages are hard to monetize, especially when Europeans and Americans prefer them reconstituted. But it insults their aesthetic power and originality just to bemoan how seductive they are—to complain as do two of White's African sources, for instance, about the propensity of "the masses" to "clothe themselves in the flashy rags of power so as to reproduce its epistemology," or of musicians to avoid "workshops and conferences" discussing their nation's problems. One reason African usages took over twentieth-century music was their unparalleled ability to transform tedium, suffering, and worse into—White's word again—joy. Some would say that for the Congo oppressed—as for the highlife audience in inflation-wracked early-'80s Ghana or the beaten-down township laborers enlivened by state-sanctioned mbaqanga under apartheid—this joy is cheap distraction and escape. In some cases that may be a relevant characterization. But what exactly are these people supposed to do? Stay in school? Attend a workshop? Organize a revolution? Just keeping your spirit intact is a major achievement under the circumstances. Indirect victims of many wars, young Kinois live to fight another day—or maybe, finally, know peace.

That's not a prediction and I'm not a pollyanna. It's just an expression of respect—a respect magnified by gratitude. At this distance, soukous has gotten hard to come by. One reason I'm fortunate to have caught that Wenge Musica show is that their only available album, *Bouger Bouger*, was recorded in 1988. So to check out Général Defao's Big Stars, I tracked down their primary extant CD, which cost me a substantial chunk of the estimated Congolese per capita income and came with a DVD of videos lip-synched in a public park. These days, YouTube is a good source, and should you luck into a chance to attend a soukous show, take advantage—likely as not, it'll beat any record. Above all, be glad that a bunch of overworked Africans wearing "Peace Grows" T-shirts can still offer strong evidence that the tradition continues.

Barnes & Noble Review, 2009

Tribulations of St. Joseph

Ladysmith Black Mambazo

Think of Joseph Shabalala as Bill Monroe.

Really, how many other musicians invented a style single-handed? And note that both inventions are thought of as "traditional." Bluegrass is a radio-informed jazzification of '20s fiddle-banjo-mandolin that came to be regarded as the embodiment of mountain purity by suburbanites nationwide. Something similar happened to iscathimiya, to use the commonest of the many Zulu names for what Ladysmith Black Mambazo made of mbube, in the '50s the prevalent form of the old group-singing culture of South Africa, where ad hoc choruses can still be convened at will. Shabalala's transformation of the "bombing" style in which every man in the group sang his lungs out on the same notes was literally visionary. Iscathimiya's esoteric syllable-forming and sound-making techniques, which come easier to Zulu speakers but have to be taught and assiduously practiced, and its smooth surfaces, which required rehearsal on a scale unknown to the amateur men's choruses of the '60s, both came to him in dreams where the singers resembled angels. A devout Christian, Shabalala is big on angels.

Far from being traditionalists, Ladysmith revolutionized mbube, though if a single imitator approached their beauty, clarity, spirituality, unpredictability, or humor, evidence hasn't reached these shores. Barred from the weekly singing contests they always won, they went pro in 1972, recording many successful albums whose covers depicted them as tribal warriors or a heavenly host—images apartheid's promoters of Bantu authenticity smiled upon. In 1986, the year Ladysmith attracted international attention on Paul Simon's *Graceland*, Shabalala formed the South African Traditional Music Organization to preserve the competitions he'd helped render obsolete. Now he opposes Westernization in a nation whose hard-won freedom he warmly celebrates. All over the world, his group is a well-loved signifier of South Africa's heroic, long-suffering, exotic past.

I've reviewed fifteen Ladysmith albums since 1984 without finding a mediocre one, and the new *Raise Your Spirit Higher* is their best in years. But it has nothing on the group's sold-out performance at Poughkeepsie's 984-seat Bardavon Opera House February 21, proof for anyone put off by their aura of solemnity or lionization by world-music softies of how good they can sound and how silly they can be. More than most harmony groups they seem to sing in one impossible voice, its grain and color and layers of pitch more resonant than George Jones's or Marion Williams's, only usually the sixty-two-year-old leader's subtle, sharp, lovely, undiminished tenor darts above the bed of a chorus phrase, never compelled to extend itself because this is never a music of solo turns. Also undercutting the one-voice effect are a panoply of sounds and sound effects: clicks, ululations, whoops, whistles, kisses, yawns, yelps, gulps, gasps, glottals, gibbers, whinnies, clucks, birdcalls, r-r-rolled r's, long guttural trills, and the motorcycle noise you get when you expel breath while shaking your head from side to side. Sometimes these are interjected by somebody in back, sometimes by Joseph, given name employed because consanguinity is the rule in a group where Shabalala sons have replaced Shabalala brothers over the decades. The sounds aren't necessarily funny, just humorous, like the ancient showbiz shtick and modified Zulu dance moves that for two hours divert audiences who can scarcely understand the group even when they speak English. Ladysmith get their share of laughs, and they work for them.

Despite the tendency to perceive Ladysmith as not merely traditional but eternal, they've evolved. The durable, definitive *Classic Tracks*, compiled in 1990 from early non-U.S. catalogue, has an acerb quality in which Shabalala's nasal leads and everyone's pronounced vibrato undercut a sweetness far less dulcet than anything cooked up on, for instance, 1997's gospel crossover *Heavenly*—or the lovely *Raise Your Spirit Higher*. From the gentle opening lead (with background clicks) of "Wenyukela," its sounds are round, its timbres soft, its harmonies sweet. Three of the nine songs in Zulu praise Jesus, one a wedding. Two advise the young to get it together and show some respect. One promotes foreign investment, another safe driving; yet another quizzes a racist to an end the crib sheet fails to clarify. The English lyrics suggest that the Zulu ones are less banal than their summaries. Not only does the pan-Africa of "Black Is Beautiful" include "black and white, Indians and coloureds," it admits a strange, moving aside that begins: "We were fearful that our voices would be transferred into the machines." So figure there's play and eccentricity in the words as well as the music. But also figure Shabalala means tranquility to predominate.

This is healthy, enlarging, miraculous—as long as it's understood to be artifice. Shabalala's genius is no reason to elevate him into a feel-good saint. His history is that of a taskmaster and patriarch, and his emotional resources far exceed the antimodern, apolitical positivity he preaches, not to mention Western comprehension. Shabalala's quietism remained resolute in 1991, after his brother Headman died in a roadside shooting by a white security guard. And it sustained again when, in May 2002, as this relentlessly positive album was being recorded, his wife of thirty years, Nellie, was shot and killed, and he himself injured, outside their home. A month later, Joseph's son and Nellie's stepson Nkosinathi was accused of hiring the assassin in what police claimed was a funding dispute between Nellie's group, Women of Mambazo, and Nkosinathi's, White Mambazo, now known as Junior Mambazo. Six months later, Joseph married a woman he'd just met. Last September Nkosinathi's trial was suspended after a witness disappeared. And on February 21, Joseph beamed at a crowd of middle-aged folkies in Poughkeepsie as four of his other sons clowned around.

Bill Monroe was one tough bird. I wonder what he would have made of Joseph Shabalala.

Music from a
Desert War

Barely two months had passed since France turned back the jihadist push into Mali, so the three April-scheduled albums that arrived in March had obviously been recorded during or before the bad time: Malian ngoni king Basseké Kouyaté's breakout *Jama Ko*; the first recording in a decade from northern Mali's Tuareg-dominated Festival in the Desert; and *Nomad*, Niger guitarist Bombino's major-label debut. All had politics, and two were explicitly anti-sharia. Given the continent's hallowed tradition of governmental malfeasance, its music has a way of obscuring political dilemmas in futile pan-African entreaties, and in Mali calls for national unity are de rigueur even though Mali's boundaries were invented by Europeans. Since sharia proscribes music itself, however, this was different.

Although I've followed African music for four decades now, that long meant sub-Saharan Africa: black Africa, jungle and bush and savannah Africa, animist-Christian Yoruba and Zulu and Congo and then Muslim Wolof and—after the first Iraq war had drawn me to Islamic music, Mediterranean Africa's included—Wassoulou and Bambara Africa. It was hello Bamako, next stop Timbuktu—the world of black African and then brown African Islam, which can mean Sufi or animist or cosmopolitan but also sometimes conservative Islam, a world where "northerner" is how Bamako sophisticates refer to their unruly fellow citizens in the sand. Yet I was surprised to fall hard for 2005's *Rough Guide to the Music of the Sahara*—which, I told *Blender* readers, evoked "the intensely pleasurable illusion that before all the other musics you know, there was this." I am no kind of mystic and prefer my awe-inspiring vistas vernal. But Saharan music gets you like that.

Bigger than Europe with a population smaller than Slovakia's, the Sahara is divided among some of the world's poorest nations: Niger, Burkina Faso, Mauritania, the ex-Spanish Western Sahara, and Mali itself, among others, including the poorest stretches of wealthier Libya and Algeria. With the highly questionable exception of Algeria, all are ruled by elites at least as corrupt as most other African nations' elites. Many ethnic groups once roamed and continue to populate this desert, with the most musically significant the

Afro-Berber Sahrawi in the west and the somewhat lighter-skinned Afro-Berber ex-lords of the central Sahara, the Tuaregs.

Musically, Mali is the region's most significant nation by far, although the preponderance of its major artists are sub-Saharan—Afropop feminist Oumou Sangaré's forested Wassoulou is further south than Senegal. The big exception is the first world-renowned Saharan musician, the late Ali Farka Touré, a Songhai from Niafunke, about 350 miles north of Bamako and ninety miles southeast of Timbuktu. As with Tinariwen, the earliest of several Tuareg bands to achieve international visibility—their 2011 album is on alt-rock powerhouse Anti- and features input from most of TV on the Radio—I respect and sometimes enjoy Touré but seldom warm to him. I know you have to be a hustler to get your music out of Niafunke, but he always overdid the tendentious theory that blues was invented in Mali and, like Tinariwen, favored the kind of solemnity that impresses folkie primitivists more than it does cultural impurity fans like me.

My first Saharan breakthrough was 2003's *Festival in the Desert* CD, where only seven acts appear to be Tuareg—most arrestingly the female emigre troupe Tartit and the percussive chants of several local aggregations. Skillfully sequencing related idioms so unfamiliar they might otherwise "all sound the same," the wide-ranging *Rough Guide* selection is more representatively Saharan from bellydanceable Berber-Andalusian opener to poetic-devotional Berber-Algerian closer. Soon followed two Tuareg guitarists from Niger and a Sahrawi from Western Sahara, each with his own individual garage-Hendrix sound, Bombino's the most finished but not therefore the most inspired. With Bamako already boasting its own seductive guitar tradition, suddenly Sahara's southern fringe was the new hotbed of an archetypal instrument fast losing cachet in the U.S.

The Sahara remains sparsely documented even as we're warned that it could be the new frontier of Islamist expansionism, and Americans need to realize that its human meanings go well beyond its store of oil, gas, and uranium and the geographical barrier it provides between the Middle East and black Africa. But reliable information is hard to come by, especially in English, which had little colonial presence there. Banning Eyre's shrewd yet warm and unpresumptuous 2000 *In Griot Time*, a nuanced tale of his apprenticeship with Bamako master guitarist Djelimady Tounkara, never gets to Timbuktu. Michael Benanav's 2006 *Men of Salt*, which recounts a five-week trek to and from the Saharan salt mines of Taoudenni, is memorable on the harshness of the sand and the brilliance of the camel but begins with Benanav's discovery that he won't meet any Tuaregs on his quest, because they're above such things and because their battle camels fared even worse in the 1973–74 drought than the pack camels he learns to love. And so far we have just one book-length source on the current conflict, by British anthropologist Jeremy Keenan, who knows everything there is to know about the Tuaregs except that nobody's perfect.

I'm exaggerating, but not by enough. Never does Keenan's new *The Dying Sahara* hint at the Tuaregs' proud and extensive military history, much less the long involvement in slavery he acknowledges in his 1977 *The Tuareg*. Tuaregs were active slave traders in the nineteenth century and after, and like many other African worthies, especially Berbers, kept mostly sub-Saharan slaves well past slavery's independence-era illegalization, probably into the present—in relations Keenan reports are long on intermarriage and short on corporal punishment, which is nice, but human chattel is human chattel even so. In part because Keenan's fieldwork was done in Algeria—where only 25,000 of the 1.2 million Tuaregs reside (almost all are in Niger and Mali)—he is obsessed with the machinations of Algeria's internal security arm, the Département de Renseignement et de la Sécurité, or DRS. Keenan believes that with the full cognizance of France and the U.S. the DRS launches false-flag terrorism operations designed to justify the War on Terror, and regards AQIM—Al-Qaeda in the Islamic Maghreb, often named as the cutting edge of Saharan jihad—as a DRS front. His inferences seem credible and to some extent convincing. But when a periodical as unbeholden to capitalism as *Counterpunch* fails to mention the DRS in two of the best-informed accounts of the Malian conflict I've located (by Vijay Prashad in 2009, who calls AQIM "a small shop with a large sign," and Gary Leupp in 2013), I have to assume he's not telling the whole story.

One reason these quandaries matter to me is that I'm nosy about politics—when I get interested in a place I want to understand how it works. But with the three Malian albums now burst upon us it's deeper than that, because all three respond to the current crisis, in which, let's see now: (1) MNLA, the Mouvement National de Libération de l'Azawad, launched yet another Tuareg war to carve a desert nation called Azawad out of Mali and its neighbors; (2) Mali's outgoing president, an elected military man unprepared militarily for this rebellion and no fiduciary paragon either, was overthrown by the usual cabal of junior officers; and (3) said junta was unable to stop AQIM and its motley allies, their ranks bolstered by a portion of the well-armed Tuaregs who had formerly sought their fortunes in Gadaffi's militia as they morphed from brutal gangs of smugglers and kidnappers flying a Muslim flag into actual jihadists imposing unspeakably brutal sharia law all the way to Timbuktu itself: stoning adulterers, severing hands, forcing the veil on women who'd never worn one, and, as mentioned, banning music.

None of these records addresses Islamism's Malian advance directly. In fact, only Bombino's was recorded—in the Nashville studio of producer Dan Auerbach—after its full extent became clear. But having lost three band members in a now-suspended Tuareg rebellion in Niger, the only Tuareg guitarist to go international had other things on his mind. Just thirty-three, Bombino is fond of the word "nostalgia," and he has a right. His homeland has been ravaged, the justifiable legal claims of Niger's Tuaregs on the country's foreign-controlled uranium industry met with ruthless expropriation campaigns. But the title *Nomad* doesn't merely indicate Bombino's longing for his land and his friends. It's a call to a vanishing way of life probably insupportable under any government. So his invocations of "heritage" and calls to "unite"—amid lyrics that are also notably woman-friendly, in keeping with the matrilinear retentions that distinguish Tuareg Islam along with its animist retentions—don't necessarily make sense as policy. But as is inevitable with songs in a foreign language, the translated lyrics are subsumed by the music: declarative melodies over straightforward handclaps-and-traps in which Tuareg Hendrix worship manifests itself, as usual, more in sonics than in licks. The adaptability and ambition of that music lends emotional weight to political and cultural goals many of us would have problems with. As so often in the Sahara (and everywhere else), ideology functions as an animating myth—a means to aesthetic vitality and power.

Basseké Kouyaté's *Jama Ko* hit me with music as well, and I wasn't ready for it. The ngoni Kouyaté commands is a high-pitched lute he was the first to play standing up and then modified down to registers lower than his ngoni-playing father could foresee when Basseké was born in 1966. It seemed a folk instrument nevertheless when I first noticed him adding acoustic intricacies to Youssou N'Dour's *Rokku Mi Rakka* in 2007. His two earlier albums with his Ngoni Ba band are enjoyable but unsurprising Africana: warm, unobtrusively grooveful collections that, should you investigate, celebrate national unity, mother love, and the simple pleasures of getting down. *Jama Ko*, however, busts out of the box in a more urgent mood. The tempos are quicker, the rhythms busier, the solos trickier and more frantic; fortified by a female chorus, Kouyaté's wife and lead singer Amy Sacko has gained a soulfulness that's pained at times, and she's spelled by three male singers who teach, admonish, and in the case of visiting dignitary Taj Mahal nut out. Quickly I heard that a lot was at stake. When I read the notes, I found out what.

Without question Kouyaté, a Bambara from north of Bamako in Ségou, is committed to multicultural fellow feeling, the key democratic value in a still tribalized Africa—that's why he called another album *I Speak Fula*. He also disdains fundamentalist Islam—two forceful new songs praise opponents of the nineteenth-century Sufi jihadist Oumar Tall, who ruled Ségou until the French took over in 1893. But the proximate reason he's feeling so intense on *Jama Ko* is that as recording began the junta deposed ATT, as two-term president Amadou Toumani Touré is known, supposedly because he'd been unable to quell the rebellion, although ATT's vainglorious replacement Amadou Sanogo soon proved better at beating down his predecessor's allies than at turning back Mali's enemies. Kouyaté had counted ATT a friend since the two were introduced by ATT's press chief, who gets a praise song on the album, as do a mine owner, a big-time cotton farmer, and a wealthy patron from Ségou. Granted, some or all of these powerful men may help save Mali, and anyway, African musicians who don't flatter the rich are rarer than those who do. But I'm glad Kouyaté also includes a high-strung antiwar song on which Amy Sacko is joined by Timbuktu diva Khaira Arby, thus exploiting one gratifying Saharan musical peculiarity, which is that women play a much larger musical role in Africa's Muslim north than in the animist regions. That Arby had to flee her city as the Islamists overran it is also germane.

It was Arby's U.S. label that put out the Kickstarted *Live from Festival au Desert Timbuktu*, the first album from the annual event since the 2003 edition that got me started. Then luminaries as luminous and culturally impure as Robert Plant appeared. This time, Arby is the luminary, on the strength of her sand-blasted "La Liberté" and her guitarist Oumar Konaté's hymnlike "Bisimillah"—meaning "in the name of God" and intensified decisively by Leila Goby's soprano. All respect to Indo-Canadian world-music chanteuse Kiran Ahluwalia joining Tinariwen to add some Pakistani ecumenicism via Nusrat Fateh Ali Khan's "Mustt Mustt." But Ahluwalia excepted, outsiders were scared to come, as I sure would have been—full-scale war began just two days later. And once again the urgency is palpable, especially in a run of little-known acts that begins seven tracks in. Pointedly multi-tribal Timbuktu Songhai Samba Toure and Mauritanian diva Noura Mint Seymali share the mood, but it's Tuaregs who define it—on Igbayen's "Traditional Chant" and Tamnana's stomped and clapped "Odwa," I was reminded of how *Men of Salt*'s Benanav learned to yell back in the cool night so his guide would know his camel hadn't lost the trail. There was a power there, that compelling illusion of eternal things, only now under extreme threat.

But assuming they're anything more than thugs with a hustle, AQIM and the more Tuareg-identified fundamentalist faction Ansar Diné also believe they do battle for eternal things. Which should remind us above all how hateful it is to brag that you fight, as the poet once put it, with God on your side. Believing in cultural impurity comes at a price. It makes the world you live in, even in its aesthetic aspects, a more limited place. But in other respects that world is larger too. So it's good to learn that guitar band Imharhan and synth-inflected Amanar evoke what Benanav calls "the obvious air of permanence about this way of life" no less than Tamnana or Igbayen, both predicated musically on nothing more modern than yelling, clapping, and stomping. There's more than one way to get an eyeful, or an earful, of the eternal.

Unsurprisingly, I hope, I don't believe in Azawad, although I do hope, sure I do, that Mali finds leadership more humane than either Sanogo's or ATT's—leadership capable of providing something like justice to the Tuaregs, a consummation that would be more likely if my own nation cared to help it happen. But I'll keep listening to all this stirring music whatever its political shortcomings—shortcomings dwarfed, after all, by those of the political actors themselves. Benanav once gave his guides a laugh when he told them how beautiful he found a landscape of black mesas and red sand ridges. Their idea of beauty, they told him, was anything touched with a little green. "One does not live in the desert. One crosses it," the nomads say. This music is a way to do that—a way to access the eternal without ignoring the shortcomings of the day-to-day.

Barnes & Noble Review, 2013

V Postmodern Times

Growing by Degrees

Kanye West

Kanye West did not arrive unheralded.

Between his production credits and his Jay-Z connection, *The College Dropout* was winter 2004's presold hip-hop debut the way the Game's *The Documentary* was winter 2005's. Relative to Jayceon Taylor's bullet holes and career in sales, West was pretty anonymous—he lacked that realness thing. But when *The College Dropout* blew up, the preppy-looking double threat became *E!* material. Did he worship Christ or Mammon? RZA or Puff Daddy? Backpack or bling? Was he respectful or, oh no, arrogant? Was he put on earth to save hip-hop from whatever? West's jewelry was appraised. It was learned that his sainted mother was an English prof and his absent father a Black Panther turned Christian marriage counselor. He scandalized the scandalmongers by insisting he had more jam than Gretchen Wilson, who beat him out in the Grammys, then wrote a quasi-apology that had diamonds in it. When he tacked on a verse about Sierra Leone, he was chided for his failure to earn a degree in geopolitics first.

All this celebrity profiling preceded the August 30 release of West's heralded-to-the-nth sophomore *Late Registration*. Though a few journos obtained clandestine preliminary copies, most got the jump editors demand in the instant-information age via one-shot listening sessions. Old fart me just biked over to Virgin at ten-fifteen August 29—*Late Registration* was on the sound system, isn't that illegal?—and bought a copy with a knot of collegiate-looking African-Americans at the stroke of eleven-fifty-eight. Since then I've immersed—the realistic way, with breaks to let my mind and ears adjust. But I still couldn't tell you how it ranks against *The College Dropout*, and neither could West. He's too close to have any perspective, he wouldn't tell the truth if he did, and his judgment is so skewed he's crazy about that Common joint he produced.

Statistically, chances are it's worse. Few albums meet the measure of *The College Dropout*, a winsome thing that performed the rare feat of deepening with overexposure—the samples, the jokes, the skits, all that shallow stuff. While *Late Registration* may harbor something as brilliant as "All Falls Down," "Slow Jamz," or "We Don't Care"—the wickedest opener since Eminem's "My Name Is," flipping pop morality the bird in a laff riot of racial solidarity and sociological fact—it can't harbor anything as startling, because *The College Dropout* set the surprise bar too high. Nor can it harbor anything as funny, because if it did we'd already know—like Eminem, West has cut down on the comedy now that he's taken seriously, and let's hope he gets over it. Nevertheless, no reviewer's deadline is long enough to plumb this music. The one-dimensional "Hey Mama" tosses off an oxymoronic "I promise you I'm going back to school" before milking West's oft-dissed flow to rhyme "chocolates," "doctorate" "profit with," and "opposite." The epic grandma eulogy "Roses" lauds the extended family and interrogates the hospital system while plucking heartstrings you thought were tougher than that.

In both cases, as is the rule on this record, the rhymes are real good and the music is better—not the samples per se, from the obscure black folkie Donal Leace and a newly unearthed Bill Withers demo, but their contextualization and deployment. West's prize catch, audibly enriching at least half his new songs, is co-producer Jon Brion. It's silly to marvel over the rap–Fiona Apple hookup—we expect guts and imagination of our saviors, and modern pop's canniest orchestrator acts as West's own personal Bernard Herrmann. Unlike Herrmann, Brion doesn't have to be tweaked or seized to solve a musical problem, because he'll do the job himself, adding an unprecedented third element to West's proven meld of hitbound soul hooks and rhythm tracks made or played. There's never been hip-hop music so complex and subtle, and no matter how much you prefer simple and direct, some of these songs will sneak up over the long haul—via the folded-in orchestra of "Bring Me Down," the treated John Barry of "Diamonds from Sierra Leone," the Otis-with-strings of "Gone," the Chinese bells and berimbau that finish "Heard 'Em Say."

Each of these songs offers more exquisite details than I could earmark in twice this space, many of them literary, which the English prof's dropout son rightly claims as his calling. But secret brilliance is more likely to emerge from the sops to his hip-hop base, including several added late. The star-as-shorty reminiscence "Drive Slow" winds down into a dire fog. "Gold Diggers," marked by cognitively dissonant Jamie Foxx–as–Ray Charles backup, lays on misogynistic cliches until all of a sudden the oppressed black male West seems to be defending ditches a non–gold digger for a white girl. "Crack Music" enlists the Game himself in an unpackable gangsta tribute-critique. The seven-minute starboast "We Major" drags collaborator Nas down into

West's self-criticism. And when you think on it, the champagne-party come-on "Celebration" is the most ambivalent big-dick lie ever. I suspect the penis in question belongs to R. Kelly—the narrator is one conniving dude.

Mammon in practice, Christ in spirit—that's neat. RZA over Puffy because RZA subsumes Puffy as West subsumes them both. Arrogant for sure, only that's not why he always samples. Anyway, he's as good as he thinks he is—a backpacker at heart who, like many brilliant nerds before him, has accrued precious metal by following his dream. He wants everybody to buy this record. So do I.

Village Voice, 2005

The Slim Shady Essay

Eminem

As shtick, Eminem's somewhat petulant late-2005 decision to prepare the second act of his American life in rehab was tedious, like the Hollywood role that in late 2002 persuaded pundits to validate an artist whose three hip-hop albums had already enriched public discourse more than they ever would. For Marshall Mathers the Vicodin fan, on the other hand, rehab came right on time, just as Eminem the artistic seeker needed a film credit to broaden his options. The loser in both cases was Slim Shady, the bad-boy projection of Marshall Mathers who surfaced on Eminem's indie *Slim Shady EP* in 1997 and went public after former N.W.A. mainstay Dr. Dre oversaw 1999's *Slim Shady LP* for Interscope. Not that Slim went away. But his logorrheic schizo-slapstick was swamped by the rock anthems of 2002's *The Eminem Show* and disappeared altogether from the agonistic *8 Mile*. When Slim once again fulfilled his destiny as a pain in the ass on the only album Eminem has released since *8 Mile*, 2004's preemptively entitled *Encore*, he was taken to task for his immaturity by a music community a lot less discerning than he is—or than Eminem is.

That I have a right to expect readers to follow the shifts and feints of Marshall Bruce Mathers III's triune persona is proof of the respectability that became his lot after *8 Mile*. Though a superior vehicle in its class, the film's neorealist romance diverged from Mathers's true story in many ways. It gave fictionalization Rabbit Smith a nicer mother, a saner love life, a healthier hip-hop scene, a John Updike reference, and a job stamping auto bumpers where Mathers's employment had been strictly service-sector. By presenting Eminem as a working-class hero financing his demo on OT, it finally convinced the sociologically inclined of what he'd claimed from the very beginning: that his descriptions weren't prescriptive nor his threats literal. But this missed the bigger point—that rock and roll perennial, the triumph of smarts over school. It missed the organic intellectual and the little big man talking circles around the bully who stole his lunch money. It missed the natural-born alien who knew just from living that character and identity are mutable, with race an example rather than a defining case, and that moral responsibility in the public arts is equally mutable—a fact he accepted, explored, exploited, and expanded as the good people cringed.

In *8 Mile*'s climactic battle-rhyme scene, Rabbit is the anti-Slim: he preempts his black rival, Papa Doc, with improvised confessional poetry that lays out every embarrassing personal revelation his opponent might level at him and then outs the motherfucker as a graduate of Detroit's top private school. Thus Rabbit is "real" and Papa Doc isn't. When hip-hoppers embrace this tired trope, the tendency is to throw up one's hands—it's a philosophical survival mechanism, who can blame them? But when cultural arbiters deploy it, keep your eye on the queen. The ninth-grade dropout is acceptable when he pulls himself up by his bootstraps, faces his demons, expresses himself, and so forth. But should he become a teen idol by mastering postmodern media theory and African trickster tradition at the same time—not that they're so different—he's a menace. That stuff is for the university certified, who can be trusted to keep kids away from it.

According to official legend, Slim Shady was invented by Eminem—Marshall Mathers the artist, which means Marshall Mathers most of the time—while Mathers was taking a shit. This was in 1997, after his indie-rap debut *Infinite* tanked. Eminem was already the acknowledged talent of the otherwise African-American hip-hop crew D12, supposedly (though let's hope not) the dozen best rappers in Detroit except they could only find six qualifiers. Like rappers since the beginning, each had a handle. Sometimes a handle implies a persona, like the Fresh Prince or Ol' Dirty Bastard. Sometimes it doesn't, like MC Run or Jay-Z. And sometimes it falls in between—try to imagine Chuck D and Rakim, or Big Boi and Lil Jon, with each other's handles. D12's handles—Kuniva, Kon Artis, Bizarre—suggested characters.

But in addition, these characters had alter egos. "Everybody in my clique had an alias. They was like, 'You can't just be Eminem. You gotta be Eminem aka somebody else.'"

When hip-hop scribes try to explain Slim Shady to the condescending, they generally cite seminal gangstas N.W.A. and the Geto Boys. But though these groups were certainly provocateurs—N.W.A. greatly overstated their eagerness to break the law, and the Geto Boys trumped them by mixing in slasher-flick shock-horror—their personas, as groups and individual rappers, had one layer. The trickiest thing about them they shared with every other rapper who ever ran afoul of the thought police: a bare-faced willingness to tell a core constituency that their particular rap flava "represented" "reality," which most in their hoods would scornfully deny, while indignantly informing anyone who accused them of inciting violence and such that their songs weren't sermons, G-d damn it, but stories, no endorsement implied—as Foucault might put it, representations. These cheap and apparently contradictory claims have their truth quotient, and both work for Eminem. But a more precise precedent for Slim Shady is the Gravediggaz, who stuck their heads out in 1994, when Prince Paul of Stetsasonic/De La Soul and Wu-Tang Clanner RZA—both of whom also generated other fronts, as in the meta-ironically multicultural Handsome Boy Modeling School and the sexist excuse for a man that is Bobby Digital—joined Fruitkwan and Poetic to demonstrate that the ghetto was grislier than any horror movie: "So you wanna die, commit suicide / Dial 1-800-CYANIDE line / Far as life, yo it ain't worth it / Put a rope around your neck and jerk it." By the time Shady erupted, former Ultramagnetic MC Kool Keith had gone underground under such aliases as Dr. Dooom and Dr. Octagon, as had former KMD brother Zev Love X, a/k/a MF Doom, Viktor Vaughn, and King Geedorah.

As usual in hip-hop, this formal innovation originated with African-Americans. But unlike the Missy-slims-down, Andre-3000-goes-alt-rock persona tweaks with which pop icons pursue longevity, the illing alter ego is an underground move for black rappers, whereas the white rappers who are such embarrassingly big deals in undie-rap are into bad poetry, social protest, and woe-is-me. Slim Shady trumped both alternatives. Extreme though his tales and rhetoric were, there was nothing sci-fi or "horrorcore" about him; he was understood—by his intended audience, not the moralizers he outraged so efficiently—as a projection of Marshall Mathers's antisocial impulses. But far from self-expression, this triumph of the id was a fabrication—a cross between Cartman of *South Park* and what Eminem biographer Anthony Bozza calls an "avenging angel." And as I wish I didn't feel obliged to explain so late in the game, Eminem's audience got this. There are always nuts who'll believe what they want to believe, and Moby wasn't nuts to observe: "I'm thirty-five. I can understand the ambiguity and the irony. Nine- and ten-year-olds cannot." But Stan's little brother notwithstanding, neither was Eminem ironic to claim that his music wasn't intended for nine-year-olds. Twelve-year-olds, maybe—in these media-saturated times, hip to jokes their elders just don't get.

Eminem was unusually ambitious for an unknown rapper—contacts were handed not a tape of *Infinite* but a vinyl pressing. He had a right, because he was also unusually gifted—as an artist. Richard Kim's 2001 description of Eminem as a "brillian[t] . . . businessman" who "recognizes that pain and negativity, of the white male variety particularly, still sell" credits him with a commercial shrewdness that ranks low among his talents if it exists at all. Slim Shady was devised as a coherent frame for Eminem's intoxicated wordplay, trebly articulation, pop beats, and irrepressible sense of humor. He targeted not the latecoming adults who thrilled to *8 Mile* but, how about that, rap fans—in addition to hip-hop's core demographic, meaning adolescents young and old, the adepts, aesthetes, hustlers, small-time bizzers, and other cognoscenti who frequent the venues where hip-hop wannabes battle and entertain. When Dr. Dre gave Eminem a call, it was a bigger break than he'd had the arrogance to angle for.

Too much is made of Eminem's debt to Dre, whose weed-thugs-n-jeepbeats *The Chronic* changed hip-hop permanently and for the worse in 1993. Musically, Dre is a decisive but intermittent presence, overseeing just eleven tracks on Eminem's first three albums and eight more on his fourth and supposedly worst. These include such crucial songs as "Guilty Conscience," "Role Model," "Kill You," "The Real Slim Shady," "Mosh," "Rain Man," the transcendent "My Dad's Gone Crazy," and the unprecedented "My Name Is." But they do not include the equally impressive "97' Bonnie and Clyde," "My Fault," "Cum on Everybody," "The Way I Am," "Stan," "Kim," "Criminal," "White America," "Square Dance," or "Like Toy Soldiers." Dre's greatest gift to Eminem (for which he was soon reimbursed, then repaid with interest when Eminem reeled in 50 Cent) was credibility. For all the scare talk about the white takeover of an African-American genre—beefed up early by the rise of fellow Detroiter Kid Rock, who soon went swamp-rock, and late by his profit-taking enemies at *The Source*—Eminem's skin color was initially a negative. The white fans who dominate the hip-hop underground are all too eager to cheer their own, but the white guys who follow mainstream hip-hop are buying blackness. They see rappers as romantic outlaws who know how to handle themselves—and their women—in a hostile world. Only after he'd convinced them did his whiteness become an advantage, as *The Eminem Show*'s "White America" famously explains: "Let's do the math / If I was black I would've sold half."

But that was later, when Eminem was servicing the rock audience his rap audience evolved into after "My Name Is" made his name. With its addictive Dre loop, catchy-funny chorus, turf-claiming scratches, sotto voce backtalk, and he-fuck-da-police-in-three-different-voices, Slim Shady's greatest hit was radio-ready froth as Cartoon Network comedy routine—a joke Lynne Cheney herself could recognize if not enjoy as such. Yet like many jokes, it is antisocial. Its offensive content—"stick nine-inch nails through my eyelids," "rip Pamela Lee's tits off," "stuck my dick in the tip cup," "Put a bulletproof vest on and shoot myself in the head"—announces its evil intent in the voice of a high-pitched pitch man addressing his target demographic with a simple, damning "Hi kids! Do you like violence?" (In the video, "violence" becomes bizarro-funk nerds "Primus" and Lee's "tits" become the so much less sadistic "lips"; in an AC/DC-hooked mixtape version, "In a spaceship while they screaming at me 'Let's just be friends'" becomes the far nastier, and wittier, "Raping lesbians while they screaming at me 'Let's just be friends.'") Key line: "God sent me [in the video, 'Dre sent me'] to piss the world off." Key point: romanticize this, wiggers. Maybe you believe those tales of big gats and bigger dicks; maybe sometimes they're true. But this isn't. This is a verbal construct. And the construction worker is just like you.

Cut to "Role Model," a/k/a "Just Like Me," because the title, which cites the "Do I look like a motherfucking role model?" of Ice Cube's N.W.A days, never surfaces in a song whose unobtrusive Dre-beat stays well underneath the lyric and whose chorus goes: "I slap women and eat 'shrooms then OD / Now don't you wanna grow up and be just like me?" Sexual and drug abuse are barely the beginning, of course—in this song Slim Shady, for it is he, admits or claims uncountable unspeakable acts that, not to worry, no sane fan would imitate. Too bad you can't expect any mass of fans to prove uniformly sane, but you can't blame the white boy for that, can you? Only wait: "How the fuck can I be white, I don't even exist." So before you take him literally, ponder this credo: "I'm not a player just a ill rhyme sayer."

Part of the charm, brilliance, and power of MBM III's triune persona is the way it disintegrates. On the one hand, it's a subtly calibrated work of psychological imagination, on the other, three-card monte to sucker the thought police. Nevertheless, Eminem's album titles—*The Slim Shady LP*, *The Marshall Mathers LP*, *The Eminem Show*, *Encore*, and finally (so far) the greatest-hits *Curtain Call*—do signify an aesthetic evolution, from persona to person to artist to goodbye to now-I'm-really-going. Once I rated Marshall Mathers over Slim Shady because I thought the debut thinned out toward the end and because, as a card-carrying mature person (it gets me in cheap at the movies), I appreciated the depth of "Stan," "Kim," and "Who Knew," in all of which Marshall the person reflects on the surprising success of Slim the reconstructed id. Shifting and feinting, the debut's "My Fault" and "Rock Bottom" have a lot of Marshall in them, but not like *The Marshall Mathers* LP, where the illing title track, for instance, suggests Marshall the real-life homophobe-etc. rather than Slim wilding—Slim gets his own space only in "The Real Slim Shady," "Kill You," and "I'm Back." Some would include "Kim," but the song's moral is too powerful for Shady's purposes. Held up by philistines, ideologues, and ninnies as Exhibit A in *The Good People v. Marshall Mathers*, Eminem's second excellent wife-murdering song exposes, complexly but unmistakably, the shameful and indeed unmanly insanity of jealous rage. Go after something dumber—Neil Young's "Down by the River," say.

In retrospect the two albums don't sort out as cleanly. Much of *Slim Shady's* final third—particularly "Still Don't Give a Fuck," a Slim-as-Marshall? outing featuring the boast, "I get imaginative with a mouthful of adjectives / A brain full of adverbs and a box full of laxatives"—seems more precious as Slim becomes an endangered resource. And the four *Marshall Mathers* songs on which Eminem strokes his D12 homies and hangs with illustrious thugs are as hard to sit through as the Kan Kaniff skits, where Eminem impersonates a gay crank caller, rival, or bleached-blond pop god. Unlike Kool Keith and the Gravediggaz turning illing into significant fun, these clowns make up C-movies and play the gangsta game that guest has-been Sticky Fingaz once called "nigga in your nightmare." While one can sympathize with the perverse pleasure black Americans must take in throwing white America's racist stereotypes back in its face for big bucks and fabulous prizes, that doesn't render the stereotypes piquant or their consequences desirable.

Although Eminem was often slotted gangsta when he first launched his attack on civilization, this was ignorant or dishonest. True, Marshall Mathers was eventually arrested for waving guns at people. But Eminem had no penchant for the graphic threats, crime-scene yarns, and demeaning sexual demands of gangsta boilerplate, and he never came on thug. The only black presence on *Slim Shady* not counting Dre, Eminem's buddy Royce Da Five-Nine, understood this on the schematic Wild West gothic "Bad Meets Evil," where his light, articulate projection has no nightmare in it. Compare *Marshall Mathers*'s "Remember Me?," where Sticky Fingaz gutturalizes his rat-a-tat-tat, or "Amityville," a decent-enough Detroit-as-murder-capital rhyme ruined by a stupid caprice in which fake D12 sicko Bizarre watches ten of his pals deflower his little sister, or the well-named "Bitch Please II," where Dre's posse roll out "simplistic pimp shit" that climaxes with Xzibit's scintillating "Assume the position and get down on your knees."

Cut to the two ugliest songs on *The Eminem Show*: the Obie Trice feature "Drips," which equates vagina and contagion, and the dance-rap duet "Super-man," Eminem's only detailed exploration of the magic kingdom of abusive casual sex. "Bitches they come they go," he philosophizes to a just-fucked ho who "don't know Marshall" before slapping her off a barstool, and this time Dre will not be called upon to impersonate Slim's superego, as he was to un-packable comic effect back on "Guilty Conscience." "Superman" is gangsta posturing no less than the generic D12-Dre sequence that follows—whether or not it's also an autobiographical reminiscence by the guy duet partner Dina Rae called "Sweet. Sensitive. Shy." But it's also hard-rock posturing as practiced by Guns 'N' Roses no less than the "hip-hop-influenced" Korn.

The Eminem Show flatters the volunteer army of pale-faced not-yet-men who inspired "White America": "I never woulda dreamed in a million years I'd see so many motherfuckin people who feel like me." Eminem was twenty-nine, his initial audience had aged three years since "My Name Is," and over that time the resentfully heterosexual male chauvinism hipper gay critics exaggerate in his appeal had become musically worrisome. However roughly, approximately, and contradictorily, *The Eminem Show* is where Eminem the artist forges Slim Shady the unrepressed id and Marshall Mathers the self-doubting workaholic into one all too meaningful creation—an effort that would culminate in *8 Mile*'s Oscar-winning "Lose Yourself," a keyb-powered declaration of autonomy often cited as his greatest work by the older white guys who'd just then joined his posse.

The Eminem Show is a good album, and its closing "My Dad's Gone Crazy" could be the artist's greatest song. Not for the first time, but more multivalently than ever, Eminem simultaneously celebrates and calls into question his own devotion to fatherhood, always the moral constant in his public identity and the convincingly heartfelt theme of the only significant new song on *Curtain Call*, "When I'm Gone." His beloved daughter Hailie Jade is his conscience now, but there's a devilish glee in the innocent six-year-old's sampled vocals as she tries to figure out what's gotten into her illing dad. Recapitulating at a deeper level the teens-gone-wild sense of play that laces *The Slim Shady* LP, it makes one wonder, with real concern, how she'll like this song when her dad decides she's old enough to hear his records uncensored. But there's nothing else like it on *The Eminem Show*.

A year and a half after *8 Mile*, *Encore* catapulted to quadruple platinum—only half the sales of *Marshall Mathers* or *Eminem Show*, though up with *Slim Shady*—and small respect. Despite the antiwar "Mosh," the antibeef "Like Toy Soldiers," the absurdist "Rain Man," and the apologetic "Yellow Brick Road," as well as a full passel of well-executed lesser songs, it's admittedly sillier than the first two albums. But it's also a small miracle. Just as he'd once negotiated the ever-escalating challenge of arousing meaningful scandal, Eminem became one of the few rock artists to come out of a bout of meaningfulness by reaccessing the lyric freshness of his opening salvos. *Encore* also passes the basic avant-garde test of remaining both hard to resist and hard to listen to, and that it does so via the disreputable childishness of singsong melodies and toilet noises—recorded, one is convinced, during actual bouts of diarrhea and reverse peristalsis—is further tribute to Slim Shady.

Whether *Encore* will prove Slim's last hurrah is between Eminem and the vagaries of inspiration. For the nonce, however, he's gone: the very last credit for *Curtain Call*'s promo rap-doc reads "Slim Shady R.I.P." So with Slim relegated to history, the question becomes: how will he fare there? Since whatever his larger meanings Eminem is ultimately a musician, it is as music that Slim must and will survive. In the feverish mischief of its multisyllabic rhymes and trick enjambments, the music he makes out of the poetry he makes out of speech creates its own place in hip-hop tradition, and by subordinating bass to treble like no other major rapper, he extracts musical meaning from racial difference as well. His delivery implies not only childishness but whiteness; the hook sense Dre and Interscope encouraged in him generated a wealth of tunelets; his bass lines tend toward the bouncy rather than the soul-shaking. The sound this all adds up to, most itself when it's least rock, has its own signature, integrity, and pleasure principle. It's not as deep as competing hip-hop sounds from Eric B. & Rakim to Kanye West. But its capacity for self-replenishment is something special. It revisits childhood not unlike the early Beatles, and while I would never equate the two—in his old age, this Slim Shady fan treasures *The Beatles' Second Album* more than *Rubber Soul*—I think it could enjoy a comparable afterlife.

Meanwhile, though he's still despised by ethicists on all sides, the moral panic Eminem set off has faded away. Either you accept the irony and multiple-persona defenses or you do not; either you believe that the young suss his complexity or you do not; either you agree that he reflects more than inflects a racist, sexist, and homophobic America or you do not. Neverthe-less, a few observations are in order.

Half a lifetime ago, rejected by an African-American girlfriend, Eminem let fly some epithets on a basement tape not intended for release. After *The Source* unearthed it, he uttered three remarkable, unironic words about these epithets: "I was wrong." He has also said, accurately and often, that his white-ness impeded his early progress. And beyond that he has never suggested that hip-hop is not an *intrinsically* African-American form. He has reached out to black rappers at every level of fame and achievement, and stuck more loyally than was good for his music with the low-talents of D12. In short, no matter what *The Source* wants its demographic to believe, Eminem's racial attitudes have been admirable if not impeccable.

About women the evidence is dicier, but let me begin with something nobody ever says: Eminem is not a sexy guy. Of course girls (and some guys) think he's cute; probably he's run through lots of pussy. Nevertheless, to any-one who listens to much hip-hop his sexlessness is striking. Most hip-hop artists strive to present themselves as both sensualists and cocksmen. In the rare instances when sex occurs at all in Eminem's music, it is emotionally fraught, and his relationship with Kim is beset by the kind of jealous insecu-rity mainstream male hip-hoppers never, ever cop to. So his obsessive gibes and worse at his mother and significant other proceed explicitly from a fail-ure of confidence that in most hip-hop is masked. In "Kim" particularly, this etiology is intensely moralized—which didn't stop Eminem from stabbing a Kim doll to death on tour as his fans egged him on.

How ironic was that? I wasn't there, and wouldn't be sure if I had been, but let's guess—probably a little and definitely not enough. Which brings us to the gay question, which despite the confusing incomprehension of his adversaries is all too straightforward. Effectively, Eminem is a homophobe. But the proof isn't the endlessly cited "fag or lez" lines in "Criminal"—which go, in toto, "My words are like a dagger with a jagged edge / That'll stab you in the head whether you're a fag or lez / Or the homosex, hermaph, or a trans-a-vest / Pants or dress? Hate fags? The answer's yes." Over and over the second of these lines has been cited as a physical threat to homosexuals even though the stanza is absolutely, one-dimensionally—even for the kind of fan who wants to stab Kim dolls—about the power of his *words* to cause pain. Just before, Eminem has mocked those who believe he might actually "kill somebody" by . . . threatening to kill them—*with words*. Aesthetically, legally, and apropos all trickster and Lord of Misrule traditions, this is a crucial distinction.

Only there's a problem. Words do lacerate. They do destroy. Eminem has told us how his mother's words damaged him. So the reflexive use of the emasculating epithet "fag"—like the reflexive "nigger," which Eminem abjures, and "bitch," which he fucks with—constitutes an attack even if, as Eminem insists, it isn't meant to impute literal homosexuality. In hip-hop culture, the cliche "fag" or "faggot" has been ratcheted into a systematic slur; its generalized pervasiveness grievously insults all homosexuals and wounds many of them. For an artist who keeps his distance from other hip-hop brutalities to embrace this one is suspicious. Regarding real homosexuality, Eminem remains ignorant and fearful—the Versace jokes in "Criminal" are just one clumsy example. Yet the most physically sexual moment on any Eminem album is the *Marshall Mathers* Ken Kaniff skit. Somebody sounds like he's really enjoying that simulated blow job.

I saw Eminem perform for the first time in August 2005 at Madison Square Garden. Following the obscene-by-numbers Lil Jon and the genially uncouth 50 Cent, he entered in the suit he'd worn in a Jumbotron teaser that had him pondering suicide, and I hoped he'd keep it on. But soon he had changed into some white baggy or other. Almost every time he did a whole song, "Mosh" or "Square Dance" or, hell, "Lose Yourself," his intensity was startling even compared to that of the higher-riding 50 Cent. But often he stepped aside for D12 or some lame label signing, and while such posse-pumping is SOP in hip-hop shows, it was hard not to suspect he was feeling lazy or bored. "My Name Is," a song he is said to hate, was relegated to a medley. Also featured was a bit in which Eminem dropped his pants and mooned all those retirement rumors. Shortly afterward, the tour's European dates were cancelled for his rehab. It seems unlikely he'll disappear like Axl Rose—he's more into work, and more talented. But how many encores can he do?

What will probably ensue is a (much) less autobiographical film role or two, some unmomentous production work, and an album in 2007 or 2008. Figure the album will either be one where Eminem tries to recapitulate his shtick—which would be a miracle if he brings it off, a bummer if he doesn't, and a bummer if he comes fairly close—or something more pretentious that mixes politics and sociology, a measure of musical experiment, and a plot or concept (pray he has the sense to avoid singing lessons). But then allow me to indulge a fantasy based on Eminem's freestyles and cameos, for which I claim metaphorical but not predictive validity. The existing cameos could constitute an interim CD—from Missy Elliott's pop generosity to Shabaam Sahdeeq's underground virtuosity, one that would show how broadening full collaboration can be for an artist in the market for options. The freestyles, like most freestyles, tend to blur into each other because they're crudely recorded over crude beats. One of them, however, I've been playing for anyone I can get to listen. "We're Still #1" is the irrelevant title.

> *Peace to Thirstin Howl, A. L., and Wordsworth*
> *My mother smoked crack, I had a premature birth*
> *I'm just a nerd cursed with badly disturbed nerves*
> *You wanna be the one to step up and get served first?*
> *Ninety-nine percent of aliens prefer earth*
> *I come here to rule the planet, starting with your turf*
> *I hid a secret message inside of a word search*
> *With smeared letters runnin' together in blurred spurts*
> *I hang with male chauvinist pigs and perverts*
> *Who point water pistols at women and squirt shirts*
> *Been a bad boy since diapers and Gerber's*
> *My first words were bleep bleep and curse curse*
> *Never had it and I still don't deserve dirt*
> *My breath still stinks and I'm on my third Cert*
> *Yanking out my stitches and hollering "Nurse, nurse,*
> *You said this shot would numb it, chick it just hurts worse."*

Since seeing isn't hearing, read this piece of what some would call doggerel aloud, distorting words like "premature," "your," and "Gerber's" so that their *ure/our/er* sounds duplicate their counterparts in "prefer," "birth," and "curse." The result is an intricately articulated stammer, breathtakingly musical when you listen. Though I wish "Never had it" was "Never had shit," as it is in some transcriptions, it's a telling demonstration that as one of those aliens who prefers earth, Eminem's lacerations hurt worse.

In more recent freestyles, notably "Bully," Eminem essays some shrewd, lucid psychological analysis. My fantasy? That the artistic seeker combine the modes of "Bully," "We're Still #1" and art it up for the rap underground. It would sell like, oh, Bruce Springsteen's *Nebraska*. And the spirit of Slim Shady would live on.

The Believer, 2006

Career Opportunity

The Perceptionists

Kanye West is the first hip-hopper ever to admit he's held a job only if alt-rappers don't count. Whether it's Pipi Skid manning the kitchen in an old age home or Sole hustling "free pens and long distance calls" at the office, economic necessity is a running theme in the anti-bling subculture. Alt-rappers are only free to brag about how good they are if it hasn't made them rich. That would mean they'd gone pop. Yeucch.

Boston-born Berkeleyite Mr. Lif has put this truism behind him. He keyed 2002's *I Phantom* to two jobs—he quits one, descends into penury, then excels at the next, which destroys him by making him forget why he left the first: "Life is a gift to be enjoyed every second every minute / It's temporary not infinite." In a *Pitchfork* interview from that time, the Colgate dropout talked medical coverage versus disposable income, faithful employees cut loose, professionalism as social engineering, college kids flailing toward the wrong careers. Lif's Boston-based partner Akrobatik—who played three sports in high school, earned most of a Northeastern diploma, and in 2003 released the unspectacularly excellent *Balance*—is less cerebral than Lif, which isn't hard. But he lives Lif's theories. Akrobatik would be happy to sell half a million albums if it didn't involve turning fifteen-year-olds into "thugs and hoes." Like Vancouver beatmaster-entrepreneur Mcenroe, he's proud to have chosen the right career: alt-rap. "It's still payin' my bills, I'm still havin' fun, and my catalog is growin.'" Together with DJ Fakts One, Lif and Akrobatik form the hard-touring Perceptionists. Their new Definitive Jux album is *Black Dialogue*.

The title should clear up one question. Unlike every other alt-rapper named here thus far, Mr. Lif and Akrobatik are black. Mr. Lif, né Jeffrey Hayes, is the son of Barbadian immigrants; Akrobatik, né Jared Bridgeman, is the grandson of Barbadian immigrants. It's not unreasonable to suggest, as both Lif and Akrobatik do—with more heart and nuance than white alt-rap gatekeepers—that mainstream hip-hop sells demeaning black stereotypes to an audience it brutalizes. Nor is it crazy to say, although such charges greatly understate black fans' and artists' complicity in the sensationalizing process, that wigger race tourists are the economic motor of this exploitation. Still, six years and many dire predictions later, Eminem remains the only white hip-hopper who can top the charts; moreover, the market for bestselling hip-hop is much blacker than the market for its undie variant, where Aesop Rock, Sage Francis, and Atmosphere are headliners. Just as scoffers claim, these embarrassing facts have musical correlatives. At its best, commercial hip-hop is more compelling and original as well as pleasurable than alt-rap. Jay-Z and Timbaland and *The College Dropout* and the new 50 Cent album have more jam than any underground hip-hop ever, the Perceptionists included.

True true true, but let me tell ya—when I first saw these guys toward the end of a 2003 show at S.O.B.'s, they tore shit up. Alt-rap bills often go on for five-six-seven acts, gaining momentum at a crawl. But though Murs's monologue about "opening for every white rapper in America" would have been an up anytime, it was Mr. Lif, small and lithe and bespectacled in a hat big enough to hold his hair, and Akrobatik, a genial fullback with spiky dreads, who slammed the warmup acts' old-school party pleas into gear. I assume the Perceptionists song that got me going was *Black Dialogue*'s opener, "Let's Move": high-test rhetoric juiced by a Chem Bros homage. I didn't get many words, of course; no matter how adamantly rappers enunciate—a priority for both the staccato, argumentative Lif and the more broadly declamatory Ak—it's tough to make out songs you don't know when the DJ is bringing the noise. Maybe "Fuck a battle—we got nothin' to prove—let's move"; definitely not the references to Heaven's Gate, Miles Bennett Dyson, and "Strange Fruit." What I did grasp was that Lif and Ak were burying the sloppy democracy of preceding crews by actually trading vocals, phrase by phrase during the verse capped by Lif's faux-Caribbean "Everybody cool—hold on." This theater recalled the Holy Grail of conscious rapping, Public Enemy, except that the two frontmen were equals. Where PE's big man is a preacher, the Perceptionists' is a regular guy; where PE's little man is a clown, the Perceptionists' is a sage.

Not that *Black Dialogue* is *Nation of Millions*, which would have made history on its music alone. *Black Dialogue*'s music is merely effective—a sharp, disquieting mix heavy on drums, bass, drum'n'bass, synth blats, and orchestral riffs, tending multiplex on its three El-P tracks and loopy on its three Fakts Ones. Hedonists want their beats more luxuriant, and why not? True, the songs dip just past the album's midpoint. But they can move the crowd, and lyrically all that's missing is choruses as killer as "She watch Channel Zero" and "Don't believe the hype" (although guest chorister Humpty Hump approaches that level on "Career Finders," a wicked send-up of gangsta job skills). Among the standouts are the conscious braggadocio of "People

4 Prez," the universal soldier of "Memorial Day," the second-grade teacher of "Love Letters," and the metathematic "5 O'Clock": "Now this is dedicated to that little piece of mind / That you find every day when you leave your daily grind."

If the crowd at the Perceptionists' exultant CD-release gig March 24 was even ten percent black, the Bowery Ballroom has a balcony I don't know about. But though these white kids may have been tourists, they weren't slumming or playing bad—insofar as they romanticize African-Americans, it's about the rebel status and moral clarity of what the title song calls "the most imitated culture on this Earth." Onstage, Lif especially put flesh on these abstractions—enjoying every second, he always looked like his head was in the game, and his gesturing left hand was as graceful as a hula dancer's. But it was Ak who delivered the lines "It's black dialogue—go ahead, kid, try it on / It's much harder to master than precision with firearms / Corny niggas switch it up and rent it to Viacom / But it was taught to me early on by my mom."

Amen, brother.

Village Voice, 2005

Good Morning
Little School Girl

R. Kelly

My mind's telling me no
But my body, my body's telling me yes
Baby, I don't want to hurt nobody
But there is something that I must confess

—R. KELLY, "Bump n' Grind"

The sudden respectability of R. Kelly the artist is a confounding development in official pop taste. Child pornography charges have done for this

manifestly skillful, manifestly simplistic hitmaker what the preeminent in- **317**
spirational anthem of the '90s could not. That his fans still believe he can fly
is no surprise. But for *Chocolate Factory* to show up on dozens of critics' top
ten lists, including three in the *New York Times*, suggests less that Kelly has
responded to his legal dilemma (and fees) with the strongest music of his
life, as is commonly argued, than that an oeuvre few gatekeepers felt obliged
to take seriously is now hot news, and that credit must be given where it's
blah blah blah.

In September, seven months after *Chocolate Factory*, the oeuvre was
showcased in all its dualistic synergy on *The R. in R&B Collection: Volume
1*, which makes its move with the porn-lite triptych "Bump n' Grind," "Your
Body's Callin'," and "Sex Me" and finds spiritual fulfillment by preceding
"I Believe I Can Fly" with "I'm Your Angel," a Celine Dion duet beloved
of wedding singers, and *Ali*'s "The World's Greatest," where Kelly compares
himself to an eagle, a lion, a mountain peak, a marching band, a star ("up in
the sky"), and "the people." Those of the intervening twelve songs in which
he achieves orgasm substantially outnumber those in which he does not.
Although several of the orgasms involve affection and one commitment,
you'd never guess that *Chocolate Factory* had just bum-rushed the populace
with woman-friendly rhetoric—pledges of devotion and other idealistic fan-
cies, individualized sexual flattery, and an abject token in which Kelly not
only ranks female "backbone" above male "bullshit" but allows as how said
bullshit may be why women smoke cigarettes and snap off on their kids.
What you would guess, because it's on the compilation too, is that *Chocolate
Factory*'s lead single was the Saturday-night special "Ignition—Remix" ("stick
my key in the ignition," etc.). Nor would you gasp when *Chocolate Factory*
reversed the best-of's narrative strategy, closing with the Kelly-vs.-Isley
cuckolding contest "Showdown," the Orientalist sex fantasy "Snake," and
some pimp-and-thug—how'd he put it?—bullshit.

But the clincher is the pitiful "Heaven I Need a Hug," on a bonus disc now
available only as an import: "I gave thirteen years of my life to this industry,"
"Media, do your job / But please just don't make my job so hard," boo hoo
hoo. I know the music is one thing and the life is another, only I also know
that in pop they rarely are. "Heaven I Need a Hug" assumes the listener
knows about Kelly's tribulations—the video where some supposed fifteen-
year-old sucks Kelly's dick and he comes on her and pisses on her too, his an-
nulled marriage to the fifteen-year-old Aaliyah, and the lawsuits from other
underage girls Kelly allegedly, to use his term, sexed. It underlines a crucial
distinction, which is that whether or not Kelly is legally guilty of doing these

things, they feed into how he is perceived. Which means that when, on his hugely engaging "Step in the Name of Love—Remix," Kelly declares himself "the pied piper of r&b" ("king" was once his preferred title), his failure to think through the pedophilic implications is cavalier, stupid, or both.

Not that anyone should suspect Kelly of pedophilia per se, because teen-agers aren't children per se. His turn-on is a far commoner one—the virgin who craves your penis. This fetish has a long history in rock and roll. Its ur-text is "Good Morning Little School Girl"—attributed to Sonny Boy Williamson I and covered by, among many others, Muddy Waters, Chuck Berry, the Yardbirds, the Grateful Dead, Eric Clapton, Rod Stewart, Taj Mahal, Johnny Winter, an elderly Van Morrison, and sixteen-year-old Jonny Lang—and its permutations are endless. Most relevant here is the way modern boy groups typified by Boyz II Men developed the love-man idea traceable to Barry White, Teddy Pendergrass, and evolved doowoppers like the Moments and the Manhattans. There's a difference between teenage boys seducing teen-age girls and young studs seducing teenage girls, and Boyz II Men dare you to figure out what it is. They're polite and lubricious in equal measure, role models who'll never call that sweet young thing again.

Still, they were more teen-appropriate than 2 Live Crew, or Ice Cube's "Givin' Up the Nappy Dug Out." And in jumped Kelly, a clever beat popular-izer who encapsulated his vision with "I Like the Crotch on You." Kelly soon warmed up his voice, hooked up his tunes, and on 1995's *R. Kelly* played up the woman-friendly. But he also kissed thug booty, and no one did more to sexualize pop language and assumptions in the '90s. He made the Backstreet Boys reaction inevitable, and if he was too lightweight to loathe—I myself am partial to the dumb double entendres of "You Remind Me of Something" ("my sound, I wanna pump it," "my cars, I wanna wax it")—he was also too lightweight to feel. That's why I gave *R. Kelly* a nice review and forgot about it, why I filed 2000's *TP-2.Com*.

All love men lie. As ideals, alternatives, their lies can be healthy some-times. But no matter how much Kelly has bared his soul, expanded his palette, and seen the error of his ways, his lies smell like the foulest bullshit. Giving credit where it's due, I hope he goes broke.

Village Voice, 2004

Master and Sacrament

Buddy Guy

It was a courtesy call. Eighty-year-old B.B. King aside, Buddy Guy is the most honored bluesman standing, such a big deal he's on RCA-linked Silvertone, where he's been putting out notable albums since 1991. Yet it had been many years since I'd seen him with spit-singing harmonica maestro Junior Wells, whose 1998 death ended an off-and-on partnership of three decades. So when a death-metal guitarist I know became a blues nut working a summer job as an apprentice luthier, we made a date for a free show at Borough of Manhattan Community College's 900-seat Tribeca Performing Arts Center November 15. As a bonus I'd get a look at twenty-six-year-old Shemekia Copeland, Johnny's daughter, on profile and rep one of blues's few ranking youngbloods.

I'd hoped Copeland's set would help me hear her records. Instead it convinced me that her voice lacked the size and her songs the edge that a red hot mama needs—not to reach the specialist audience, which has been padding its waistline on marginal differentiation for so long that it can barely get to the corner anymore, but the rest of us. The major blues album is a vanishing artifact. Along with Robert Cray and Corey Harris, Guy himself is one of the few living humans with more than one. Competent work abounds—the specialist audience knows how sustaining bent notes and *aab* closure can be. But the tweak of the new is hard to come by, and not just on record. Stacy Mitchhart at B.B. King's November 27, who with his yeoman's voice and panoply of guitar options ground fatback "I'm a King Bee" and sirloin "It Hurts Me Too" into hamburger as nondescript as his originals, can stand in for a hundred others just as honorable and committed. The winner of the 2003 Albert King Award for most promising guitarist packed no more surprise than Slippery When Wet, who regaled the insatiable at B.B.'s after Bon Jovi played the Garden two nights later.

But in Tribeca, sixty-nine-year-old Buddy Guy defied all obituaries. He looked spectacular—shaved head, embroidered sky-blue overalls, pin-striped navy-blue dress shirt, black-and-white shoes midway between sneakers and spats. And when he began playing he played . . . almost nothing: quiet little pinging blue notes high up on the fretboard to which he eventually added a few crooned lines of "I'm Going Down." An audacious trick, and it worked—the full house strained to listen. Moreover, similar teases dominated the show, their pleasure intensified by blasts of sound like the raucously out solo with which newsboy-capped hipster pianist Marty Sammon finished off the opener. Guy can still big up, sure thing. He long ago decided that Hendrix kid had ideas worth stealing, and sometimes he rocked whole songs. He also freed strapping young guitarist Ric Hall to get dirty for thirty-two bars, and left space for a solo that could have been a Buddy Guy transcription by goateed hipster saxophonist Jason Moynihan. But what made the show transfixing was its dynamics—the almost sexual expertise with which Guy withheld and then slammed home the payoff. Sammon never shone so loud again, but he was attentive and imaginative throughout, as was man-mountain drummer Tim Austin. The band anticipated every shift in rhythm and volume. As Guy put it more than once, the total effect was so funky you could smell it.

The coolest touch came when—accompanied by an aide with a flashlight, his bone density ain't what it used to be—Guy walked singing and sometimes playing to the rear of the theater. Halfway back down, he guided the wrist of a female audience member—no hottie, a stout fiftysomething who looked like she worked at BMCC—until she was strumming his guitar. He provided the fancy stuff up the fretboard, and suddenly this college administrator, let's say, was playing a blues solo. Due to the miracle of cordless technology, it emanated physically from the stage even though few had their heads turned toward the three band members doing a dance routine there. It was an inspired image of formal mastery in all its generosity and artifice.

But there was more to come, and soon Guy was introducing the "friend" he claims pressured him into putting Otis Redding's "I've Got Dreams to Remember" on his songful and soulful if not altogether successful new *Bring 'Em In*: accidental teenthrob John Mayer, a VH1-favored member of the Justin Mraz school of jazzy pop-rock who caught the blues bug just when it was presumed extinct. I respect Mayer, a decent and funny guy, but I assumed he'd prove a dabbler, and I was wrong. He had his own mellow, soft-edged sound on guitar, and traded vocals with Guy even up. Modestly, he tried to duck away after the cameo, but Guy insisted he stay, so there was no blaming him for the solo he couldn't find his way out of, and if Guy good-naturedly obliterated him every time he played a little guitar, that was right and natural. Guy was the master, the last great bluesman standing. Mayer was his apprentice.

And we—we were partakers in a sacrament. Because as Guy seems to conceive it, what matters isn't Buddy Guy, but blues itself. He is its tireless exegete. Regulars say his sets change night to night, and though he was always an ace guitarist, his instrumental range and control keep growing. On the other side of his crooning, he's a brawnier singer now than thirty years ago too. If his records often fall just slightly short anyway—the best of his mature period, *Sweet Tea*, cashes in the repertoire trick of cherry-picking the underexploited Fat Possum songbook—it's because his vocal signature is more about the genre than the artist, whose personality is less distinct than King's or even Wells's. So instead he personifies the generosity of artifice.

As it turns out, however, he isn't alone, because B.B. King himself remains the greatest bluesman sitting. You don't think anyone paid 42nd Street prices for Stacy Mitchhart, do you? Talking a lot and flaunting his seniority, King never got out of his chair. But he was too old to be subtle about proving himself—his voice was powerful, and his guitar flowed into harmonic estuaries he wouldn't have dared in his crowd-pleasing, legend-building prime. I predict no revival. But great genres aren't just for specialists.

Village Voice, 2005

The Commoner Queen

Mary J. Blige

Let me preface the product report by noting that when I want to hear Mary I will play 1998's *The Tour*, just like always. Right, I call her Mary. I can't stand the male/white reflex of slipping into the familiar when referring to female/black artists, but Mary J. Blige makes it as impossible to avoid as Aretha Franklin. Not because she's so iconic or royal, "Queen of Hip-Hop Soul" though she may be, but because she feels like what used to be called a familiar—an intimate, a member of the family. While this is an illusion by definition, most of the artists who've excelled at creating it have a certain commonness in common, so that in crucial respects Mary resembles

John Mellencamp more than she does Aretha. But it's Mary the commoner who moves me. Maybe that's because she's my homie—her straight-outta-Yonkers New Yorkese gets me every time. Or maybe it's because there's no one like her.

People talk about what a great voice Mary has, but she doesn't—not like Sequence alumna Angie Stone, Bad Boy good girl Kelly Price, Biggie moll Faith Evans. Loud and forthright but hardly curvaceous, it powers a chronically off-key attack that's flat and prosey—near-spoken, as tune-carrying goes. So the ease with hip-hop that won her an instant following had a formal component. It wasn't just Grand Puba and Busta Rhymes (guesting, Busta so new the credits called him "Rhyme") meeting Shirley Brown and Dorothy Moore (influencing, and good for you if you've heard of either). It was how unselfconsciously this twenty-one-year-old from the projects brought her mama's music together with her own. The meld seemed so natural. Yet though she made Stone and Price and Evans possible commercially, they were studio pros and she wasn't. And though the new *Love & Life* is certain to become her seventh platinum album, and how many 1992 rappers can say that, the mark of the professional is not yet on her. Sure her romantic travails can be mistaken for shtick, sure she's shown poor deportment with interviewers, sure she's performed from a fake throne, sure she talks "Mary's world" like she's a star and you're not. But Mary's world isn't a star's world. She never flaunts how fine or filthy she is. She never bitches about haters or brags about her stuff. In fact, she never acts as if she's better than *anyone* except the schemer who wants her man—not even in her quest for "perfection."

For hip-hoppers, great Mary means early Mary—1992's *What's the 411?* and 1994's *My Life*, masterminded by a young Puffy Combs back when hip-hop soul was new jack swing. My position is that consistency caught up with concept only as of 1997's *Share My World* and 1999's *Mary*, after she'd dumped not just Puffy but the jerk from Jodeci she'd hooked up with and her well-known if unspecified "substance abuse." But really, who's counting? Modern r&b isn't about discrete songs. It's about texture, mood, feel—vocal and instrumental and rhythmic, articulated as they're smooshed together. In the end I treasure only three individual Mary titles: "I'm Going Down," originally fashioned by Norman Whitfield for Rose Royce; the wicked bait-and-switch "PMS," a verbatim rip of Al Green's "Simply Beautiful" on 2001's front-loaded *No More Drama*; and Babyface's *Waiting to Exhale* special "Not Gon' Cry." After that it's just the ones that are livelier or more soulful than the other ones.

Take for instance *Love & Life*'s first single, for her beau of three years, the one who really really got her to stop drinking: "Love @ 1st Sight," string-cushioned thirty-five-second apostrophe breaking into Puffyized Tribe Called Quest lope revved further by the live-and-kicking Method Man, who once shared a duet Grammy with Mary. Unfortunately, Mary has never picked up much street poetry from her love affair with rap, so Method Man's "You go mama / Nowadays I'm more calmer / And if you take a look at my life no more drama" are the best lines on a record that favors her usual "Making all my dreams a sweet reality" and "How many of us have them / I don't think we really need them / If they're not our friends." The selling point is a reborn P. Diddy overseeing a catchy set husbanded by many co-producers. It peaks in the middle, and between "It's a Wrap" kissoff and love-in-the-a.m. finale ends stronger than *No More Drama*. Up against *What's the 411?* Mary sounds older yet still girlish, rounder and smoother and pitch-improved but praise Shirley Brown not perfect yet.

And now I'll play *The Tour* again, thank you. Not for its slightly gauche show band, or even for its concentrated song selection and bonus covers. More for its hype man cheerleading like the nameless subaltern he is and the high-pitched cheers he works up; for Mary missing notes, or claiming she's getting fat and then not worrying about it. In this context, deathless nonpoetry like "I know that I was wrong for all that carrying on / But are you gonna hold it against me?" carries weight. Removed by age and race and class from these particular gender wars, I'm free to root for the good guys— strong decent females who'd "rather be loved than be judged by a buncha assholes." In Mary's world, Mary speaks for them, and to us.

Village Voice, 2003

A Hot Little Weirdo

Shakira

"She's famous for wiggling her bum," observed a British tabloid before excitedly revealing that the Colombian pop goddess Shakira "has a reported IQ of 140" and hires tutors to teach her about the cities she plays. So perhaps it's just as well I've never seen a Shakira video—maybe her bum or her "humble breasts" would have gotten in the way of my ears. Because even without the booklet photos, I find her CDs plenty sexy. Her voice, singing, songs, *music* are so throaty, spunky, eccentric, elastic, humorous, generous, excessive, embodied, and bent on benevolent world conquest. What a hot little number.

A pro since she was fourteen and a Latin American teen idol before the Backstreet Boys hit the Hot 100, twenty-eight-year-old Shakira Isabel Mebarak Ripoll was only twenty-one when she conceived a career move more ambitious than Christina Aguilera herself has ever dared: to learn English so she could dye her hair blond and take her art to the next level. But ambition comes cheap. Undeterred by the music business's diminishing returns, all too many young people still strive to achieve prominence in today's vibrant entertainment field, with *American Idol* the symbol rather than the mechanism and not as bad as it gets—many Korean hopefuls, for instance, are related to music execs. What Shakira brought to the business plan was a giant helping of the individuality Paula Abdul, who should know, is always discerning in the likes of Bo . . . Derek? Belinsky? Bice!—an individuality so much broader and more accommodating than what any indie mix-and-matcher would recognize as such. Allowing for context, Shakira's as big a weirdo as Devendra Banhart, only more talented and more focused.

Her musical idiosyncrasy announced itself with the bandoneon that kicked off her 2001 English-language debut, *Laundry Service*, and kept on coming through her surprisingly arena-rock *Live & Off the Record* and her 2005 doubleheader: June's *Fijación Oral Vol. 1* and November's *Oral Fixation Vol. 2*. Though Shakira leans on song doctors and such for melodies and arrangements, she produced all four of her U.S. albums. The South America–only late-'90s *Pies Descalzos* and *Dónde Están los Ladrones?* subject Latin-pop mush to rock-in-español mash for a blend both satiny and grainy, and the U.S. records rock it up some more. But of course, all such embellishments follow what anyone notices first about her: her voice, which a few bad people can't stand. Me, I love its size and its tenderness and the vibrato haters compare to a sheep or Alanis or a bicycle rider on a cobblestone street. I also love the personality she imprints on it—childishness versus physicality, emotional extravagance cut with sardonic self-esteem. And I love the culture with which it is imbued. Her father a Lebanese Catholic, Shakira has belly dancer genes and is ready to use them. Maybe her vibrato rubs haters the wrong way because it comes straight outta the cradle of civilization. She's a South American sexpot, but also the pre-Columbian voice of Spain's

Christian-Islamic motherlode—a happenstance she inhabits, accepts, and enjoys.

With help from the Internet I can make out the meaning of songs like 1998's mildly political "Octavo Di," which got my attention by mentioning Michael Jackson and Bill Clinton. But as both language and sentiment, her lyrics in the language she went out and learned as an adult (she already knew Italian, Portuguese, and some Arabic cursewords) are so compelling that I gravitate to *Laundry Service* and, even more, *Oral Fixation*. Awkwardly, given how much I've made of her Latin blend, the Latinest thing about her new record is her English. No native speaker would have come up with "my humble breasts," or "Don't play the adamant / Don't be so arrogant," which she pronounces as if "arrogant" rhymes with "bent." The floridity of her vocal surges is of a different order of magnitude than, for instance, Marc Anthony's, because her romanticism is rarely soothing. Sure she loves her guy, spiritually and carnally, but she's not a woman who knows her place. And though her tunes, which she always has a hand in, sometimes contour Colombian, this is a pop-rock record—one only Shakira could have made.

Shakira's stock-in-trade is love songs, their tragic side still supposedly fueled by her long-ago breakup with Puerto Rican soap star Osvaldo Ríos, their impassioned-to-feisty details presumably inspired by her life in Miami and the Bahamas with Antonio de la Rúa, the Argentine playboy to whom she got "engaged" in 2000, well before the collapse of his nation's economy cost his dad that president job. Both *Oral Fixation*s thank Antonio for "protecting" and "taking care of" her, which doesn't preclude the gloriously catty "Don't Bother," about a tall rival who cooks and speaks French, with its spoken coda: "For you I'd give up all I own and move to a Communist country—if you came with me of course—and file my nails so they don't hurt you and lose those pounds and learn about football—if it made you stay, if it made you stay, but you won't." Whoever it's about, it's great. But so are "Costume Makes the Clown," where she takes off the makeup she won't leave home without, and "Hey You," where she does the cooking herself. And though it would be silly to expect radicalism of a jeweler's daughter with UNESCO connections, concern she experiences aplenty. The opener is a nice generalized indictment of the powermongers. The closer sarcastically links Western complacency to the forgotten of—those tutors, or maybe just that UNESCO tour—East Timor.

"Life has been very benevolent to me," says Shakira the star. "Sometimes I feel like I am a rock artist trapped in the body of a pop artist," says the producer. "Sometimes I feel there's a baby inside of me that hasn't grown up," says the child. "I feel like a horse that hasn't been castrated. That's me—full of strength and very very productive," says the weirdo. "I never met a single terrorist in my whole life," says the Arab. And the former teen idol with the high IQ? "The leaders are lacking love, and love is lacking leaders." She's trying.

Village Voice, 2006

What's Not to Like?

Norah Jones

There are many things we don't know about Norah Jones. There are many things we will never know about Norah Jones. But one thing we do know—she's not a "hype." In the wake of her Grammy sweep, some who find her hopelessly anodyne may try to make her the latest symbol of all that's wrong with the record business. This would be obtuse.

Come Away with Me should be taught as a business model to anyone not prey to the alt adages that bigness is bad and consensus weakens the moral fiber. It's on Blue Note, owned by EMI-Virgin but run by Bruce Lundvall, a music man adept enough at corporate politics and the bottom line to keep the suits at bay. Lundvall glimpsed commercial potential in the jazz-schooled young singer-pianist or he wouldn't have let her make the most unjazz album the label has ever released—let her make it twice, hiring venerable popmeister Arif Mardin after Cassandra Wilson hand Craig Street turned in something too elaborate. But he certainly didn't "groom" the little lady from Williamsburg, or project her quadruple-platinum sales. As for Jones, it's credibly reported that after she went platinum she asked Lundvall if they couldn't stop selling the album—this thing was getting out of hand. She's plainly someone who just wants to play her music and sing her songs, so palpably honest and unpretentious that four million Americans and counting have bought those songs. So forget the specifics for a moment. Structurally, *Come Away with Me* is what the biz needs—executives who follow their musical instincts, artists who are in it for love. Bruce Lund-vall equals Russell Simmons. Norah Jones equals Public Enemy. Not a Clive Calder or Mandy Moore on the set. This is an exemplary biz success story in which the good guys win.

A skeptic might argue that thousands of other young women out there just want to play their music and sing their songs, and even more young men. Many of them are honest and unpretentious, a few pretty good. So how come they aren't all multiplatinum; how come most are lucky to sell twenty thou? As indicated, hype is not an acceptable answer, although megasales do start replicating themselves by means that have nothing to do with intrinsic musical value. But talent isn't an acceptable answer either. Jones's gift is clearly bigger, and more ineffable. I could hear it before the advance gathered its word-of-mouth—that mysterious gestalt bizzers on a roll adoringly and inarticulately call a "sound." Not every sound captivates every listener. But the right sound can inspire mad loyalty—definitely Al Green for me, maybe U2 or Dr. Dre or Björk for you, and in 2002, for millions of music lovers, Norah Jones.

Yet oddly or perhaps not, the attributes of that sound remain undescribed in reams of comparison-strewn coverage. The most thorough attempt I've unearthed was Jody Rosen's in the *Times*: "a lovely, pure voice that crackles now and then with a pleasing hint of grit" gets the flavors and proportions right, and "combines jazz and folk influences to make sophisticated contemporary pop" surrounds the style. Mix in her obvious restraint and famous respect for her elders and you have the basics; add that, vocally and physically, she always chooses pretty over glamorous. But with the social potency of these basics now established, we can take them further. The fact that Jones studied piano in college yet never took a singing lesson is the material basis for the belief that she imbues breathy innocence with old wisdom; she seems incorrigibly incorruptible, yet no naif. And then there's the sensual dimension, by which I do not mean sexual, although others might. Say her voice is all curves and no corners. Say there's a deep openness there. Say it makes you want to like her. Or on the other hand, get meaner with a joke no one known to Google dislikes her enough to have made: I know why she didn't come—it's the Paxil. Antidepressants help many good and vivid people be themselves. But for her own sake, I hope Norah Jones achieves her seductive serenity sans pharmacology.

Because most of Jones's material is original, it's hard to remember that she's a singer, not a singer-songwriter—the album's only self-compositions are the inviting title track and a mistake about a nightingale, plus a collaboration with Jesse Harris, the tasty guitarist who lured her from North Texas State to NYC in 1999. Harris has five copyrights, Jones's bassist boyfriend Lee Alexander four, and although Harris is edgier, one reason Jones's voice dominates the record is that her main writers are so anonymous. Harris's "Don't Know Why" towers over the album's many subsequent dispatches from the milder shores of melancholy, and Alexander's "Seven Years" feels thematic—better Jones should emulate a delicate little girl than a European bird whose natural habitat is the library. But let's hope the three covers teach all involved how complex simplicity can be: Hoagy Carmichael's Sarah Vaughan standard "The Nearness of You," John Loudermilk's Nina Simone staple "Turn Me On," and the only piece of unalloyed use value I myself have extracted from Jones's sound, a "Cold Cold Heart" that transforms Hank Williams's desolation into something playful, alluring, and negotiable—until "Why can't I free your doubtful mind / And melt your cold cold heart" drives Jones to doubts of her own. I wish we could be certain she understood how audacious this is. But the essence of her appeal is to leave the answer to that question indistinct. That's why it's not so odd that her admirers never describe her. Beyond her sound, which it would be willful to gainsay, she's become a symbol of quality for people reluctant to think too hard about what quality is.

Ladies and gentlemen, I give you the National Academy of Recording Arts and Sciences. Never take the Grammys seriously, but this year—with the biz suffering its biggest downer since disco went bust, Buddy Holly died, or Herbert Hoover was president (Lord how I miss him)—they have their meteorological attractions. Unless you believe Eminem had a snowball's chance in Harlem, or can name a bizzer other than L.A. Reid and maybe Clive Davis who knows how brilliant Pink is, Jones's five-statuette victory wasn't surprising or especially unjust. *The Rising* and *Nellyville* and *Home* (Dixie Chicks, you remember, great title gals) are overrated feel-good albums too, and *The Eminem Show* is for newbies. But although the biz needs Norah Jones structurally, it doesn't need her aesthetically, and in both respects, as hasn't been said loudly enough, *Come Away with Me* is the same record as last year's surprise winner, *O Brother, Where Art Thou?*: sincere left-field entry on music man's corporate imprint wins aging voters and consumers alike by proving that young people can too play real/honest/genuine/authentic music. This means music that cossets neither computers nor scary black guys. It also means music that pays fealty to an aesthetically respectable past authorized by public broadcasting, toney feature stories, and an educational system in which jazz is a major at North Texas State.

Some wags explain the Grammy winners' megasales another way—the they-play-their-own-instruments thing, it is said, targets an audience too old and technophobic to download. And there could be truth in the joke. But even if home burning is killing music, a convenient oversimplification at best, it's not acting alone. The NARAS posse also bears some responsibility, and in part the Grammys constitute a self-reproof and/or statement of principle—a way to compensate for the cynicism many bizzers believe they're driven to by nose-diving profits, demanding CEOs, fickle fate, and the stupidity of the young. This would be dandy if only the principle weren't so limited. It's not as if the adult alternative market many crow about is a bad idea. It's been ignored too long, and will provide succor to some lively geezers as well as many soulful bores. By definition, however, it's not much of a future. Jazzypop is more promising than neobluegrass—it's possible to imagine Jones or someone like her adding bite to the recipe without wrecking its outreach. But what we really need is more NARAS aesthetes alert enough to realize that the Neptunes deserve a prize—and that the greatest pop musicians have always wanted things to get out of hand. In this, Norah Jones is of less than no use.

Since I bear Jones no ill will, I regret to report that she has new product out. In the blurry tradition of debut divas Erykah Badu, Lauryn Hill, and Jill Scott, she has followed her first studio album with a premature live album. That this one is a DVD doesn't help a bit—showpersonship seldom sullies a presentation replete with gawky smiles, gawkier stage talk, lots of pictures of hands, five songs that aren't on the album, and ten that are—several of which become unbearable under the spotlight.

Stardom is never easy, is it? My advice is that Norah Jones study the career of Tracy Chapman, who for fifteen years has exploited the unexpected multiplatinum of her debut for all the privacy and autonomy it's worth—and who has thus remained honest and unpretentious whether you like it or not.

Village Voice, 2004

No Hope Radio

Radiohead

Can we agree that the tortured expectations surrounding *Hail to the Thief* involve more than the artistic worth of a wacky little prog band from Oxford UK? At stake isn't just whether Radiohead have returned to the songful days of yesteryear without losing their avant-nerve. At stake is nothing less than the future of rock itself. For upon these Oxonians now has fallen the dubious, dangerous mantle of Only Band That Matters.

Since I'm not known as a Radiohead fan, some may think this sarcasm, but it's not. To say Radiohead is the only youngish band standing that combines critical consensus with the ability to fill a venue larger than the Hammerstein Ballroom is a simple statement of fact. Even if you prefer Wilco or the White Stripes, you have to grant not just the Americans' lesser profitability but their lesser ambition and stature. Aptly, however, the simple statement comes trailed by two complex hedges.

Radiohead are beset not only by the usual wages-of-fame issues, which they're handling better than Nirvana, but by the reduced value of those wages in dollars and pence. When they surfaced ten years ago, the record industry was a road to riches down which sped many estimable bands, all focusing on principle with stars in their eyes. Now the same industry is in a slump worse, perceptually, than any in living memory. With sales lagging and blame flying, intelligent guitar-toting white guys, a growth sector in grunge-besotted 1993, have been marginalized commercially by hip-hop, teenpop, adultpap, and Creed. No matter how far above the cash nexus the guitar toter stands—a vantage the five Oxonians can afford—this slump exacerbates the aura of crisis and anxiety that rock bands have made a currency since the Beatles got serious. If Radiohead don't keep the artistic faith while maintaining their cultural clout, it's gonna feel like doomsday—inside what remains of the biz's idealistic wing, and also among the vaguely oppositional student types who dominate the tastemaking sector of Radiohead's audience.

Of course, the latter may not notice any difference, because doomsday is Mr. Radiohead's neighborhood. Go to their page in the All Music

Guide and find under Tones (capitalized like the Platonic forms they are): "Enigmatic, Somber, Reflective, Intense, Plaintive, Wistful, Bittersweet, Paranoid, Gloomy, Wintry, Poignant, Aggressive, Theatrical, Eerie, Earnest, Melancholy, Angst-Ridden, Brooding." Sounds pretty inviting, doncha think? No wonder they matter so much. (Right, now I'm being sarcastic.) Radiohead's eighteen Tones give them more than the Beatles (or the White Stripes, who garner a mere six) but fewer than Nirvana, with whom they share Paranoid, Angst-Ridden, Brooding, and Gloomy, as well as (whew) Intense and Aggressive—but not, for instance, Raucous, Rebellious, Fiery, Volatile, or Wry. Say hello to hedge number two, which is how partial Radiohead's consensus must remain. No more so than the White Stripes', probably. But for The Only Band That Matters to command such a wan emotional palette limits the upside of their appeal, and this bodes ill for intelligent guitar toters—while concerning their admirers hardly a whit.

Among both critics and online opinionizers, you see, the discussion of whether *Hail to the Thief* has real songs on it is invariably couched in terms of the discussants' satisfaction rather than the band's reach. So while it would be perverse for a political prog like me to scoff at Radiohead's leftish bent—expressed not just in Thom Yorke's alienated allusions but in such concrete acts as, for instance, the band's rejection of Clear Channel venues and their ideologically explicit website—its practical consequences are nugatory. Solidarity is not a big goal of Radiohead fans. Not only that, the thief they're "hailing" isn't George W. Bush. That's what Yorke says, and I believe him.

It should surprise no one that the correct answer to the puzzle of whether *Hail to the Thief* reclaims the songforms of OK *Computer* or cultivates the soundscapery of *Kid A* and *Amnesiac* is both. Once it's established that songform is on the table—that they haven't gone ahead and made the *Metal Machine Music* neocons like Nick Hornby thought *Kid A* was—what else would you expect? Radiohead's musical ideas changed when they soundscaped, so naturally those ideas now enter their songcraft. There's more melody on the new album, though it's never as elegiac and lyrical as on "Subterranean Homesick Alien," and more guitar, though it's never as articulate and demented as on "Paranoid Android." But *Hail to the Thief* flows better than OK *Computer*; it's less self-regarding. For most of the band's fans, the synthesis comes as relief enough—after all, the reason the readers of Britannia's Q absurdly voted OK *Computer* the greatest album of the twentieth century is that it integrated what was briefly called electronica into rock. But skeptics like myself—and while I enjoy mocking Radiohead's inflated reputation, I rated *Kid A* and *Amnesiac* pretty high—may demur.

Among critics and occasionally fans, there are those who much prefer their soundscaping.

First there's the obvious matter of Yorke's lyrics, which even the band's loopier admirers rarely dwell on, not because they disapprove, but because how much is there to say about, to choose something succinct: "Sit down. / Stand up. / Walk into / The jaws of hell. / Anytime. Anytime. / We can wipe you out / Anytime. Anytime. / THE RAINDROPS." That's the entirety of *Hail to the Thief*'s "Sit down. Stand up." except that "the raindrops," if you'll pardon my lower case, repeats forty-seven times, providing ample opportunity for the listener to wonder when songwriters will stop giving precipitation a bad name. Over the years, Yorke has tended to simplify and clarify his imagery. So with a few exceptions (notably "Myxomatosis," named for, if not about, a rabbit disease that swept Britain in 1953), the language on the new album is quite basic and its import fairly direct. How about that—Thom Yorke is bummed. Maybe there's more there, of course. The *Philadelphia Inquirer*'s Tom Moon argues intriguingly that Yorke casts himself here as "the last individualist in a colony of worker drones," an antihero who resists mind control by "think[ing] in junk scrambles." But in the unlikely event this theory is true, it proves mainly that Moon is cleverer than Yorke—labored concept, imaginative read.

Anyway, few Radiohead fans need or want so much specificity. All they ask is a Tone—call it Bummed, why not?—that's dramatized and rendered perceptible by the music. Music is without question foremost here, not lyrics or image or mystique. So for us skeptics, it's unfortunate that this music must begin with Yorke's singing. While stray suggestions that Yorke's vocal equipment is operatic overstate a power and range dwarfed by Jeff Buckley's as well as Pavarotti's, they certainly get at what people love about him—a pained, transported intensity, pure up top with hints of hysterical grit below, that has as little Africa in it as a voice with those qualities can. Fraught and self-involved with no time for jokes, not asexual but otherwise occupied, and never ever common, this is the idealized voice of a pretentious college boy. Its attractions for Radiohead's fanbase are self-evident. But like it or not the voice is remarkable, and many others respond as well. Opera fans? That's too simplistic, and also too kind to opera fans. But it certainly gets at who else loves him.

In the most percipient analysis of Radiohead I've found, the *New Yorker*'s Alex Ross calls a pivot tone a pivot tone: "There are times when Radiohead seem to be practicing a new kind of classical music for the masses." Ross goes into detail about why Radiohead's innovations are deeper than ELP or

King Crimson turning "orchestral crescendos and jazz freak-outs into another brand of kitsch," and he's convincing. From Eric Bachmann to Vanessa Carlton, Radiohead guitarmeister Jonny Greenwood is hardly the only classically trained young rocker out there, and from my musically illiterate fastness I always wonder, for instance, whether there isn't something else on *Pablo Honey* with a harmonic fillip as grand as "Creep"'s "regal turn from G major to B major," only nobody noticed because the song sucked. Nevertheless, it behooves the White Stripes contingent to acknowledge that for sure sonically, no doubt harmonically, and perhaps structurally, there isn't another band in the world who deliver the goods like Radiohead—including the far more elementary Coldplay, cited as inheritors because the other candidates are totally implausible, and Wilco with its famous treatments. OK *Computer*, where I've trained myself to enjoy three or four songs now, is rife with discrete pleasures and surprises. You can hear ears thinking all over their records.

Discrete is the idea. This is for the better if you believe songs should stand there hand on hips and demand you stop and listen—that in music, classical cogitation is the model of effective thought. It isn't for the better if you prefer that listeners absorb disturbing information on their feet—if you believe rhythm implies a healthier future than harmony. The reason I conceive *Kid A* as more groove than mood is that even when its details demand reflection—which usually they don't, they pass too fast and Yorke's voice is basically decorative—the music's movement implies an equally engrossing moment just up ahead. The reason most prefer OK *Computer* is that they cherish a more conventional (and perhaps accurate) conception of how minds should work. Exactly how much avant-nerve you think *Hail to the Thief* does or doesn't retain will be determined by where you stand or prance on this question. But no matter who's right, if anyone is, the future of *Hail to the Thief* is unlikely to have much bearing on the future of rock or anything else.

Village Voice, 2003

Rather Exhilarating

Sonic Youth

Forget their "edge," or whatever the edgy are calling it these days. I wish we could forget their non-youth in the bargain, but that wheeze will remain with us—they create from what they know. So let me put it this way: Sonic Youth are the best band in the universe, and if you can't get behind that, that's your problem. They haven't made a bad album since Kim Gordon, Thurston Moore, and Lee Ranaldo found perfect drummer Steve Shelley in 1985, and (forget Radiohead, forget Wilco) have released more good ones in the past decade than anyone in rock except—this is funny—Neil Young. That definitely includes the brand-new *Rather Ripped*, a light-seeming, unprecedentedly hooky thing that could prove one of their best. Ignore it to your spiritual detriment.

Sonic Nurse, the band's last record, and last of three with avant-young fifth member Jim O'Rourke, was noticeably direct and tuneful—but not, as it turned out, concise (eight of ten tracks over five minutes), nor as bracingly aggressive as *Goo* or *Dirty* or *Daydream Nation*. Excellent, but hedged. On *Rather Ripped*, seven of twelve tracks clock in under four minutes, and three more under five. But the radical departure is the new album's appearance of simplicity, especially regarding what means most with these guys: guitar sound.

Most sy guitars are thick, dirty, doubled, the better to amplify and complicate the weird scales that underlie music you can get lost in and quite often hum. On *Rather Ripped*, however, guitars are cleanly articulated, given over to tunelets and quasi-arpeggios that cycle through the songs like the good little hooks they are, so much so that when Moore and Ranaldo clash and rumble old-style—two minutes into "Sleepin' Around," on the Ranaldo horror movie "Rats" or the Gordon reverie "Turquoise Boy"—the effect is a reassuring return to normalcy. In other words, the Brechtian distance their dissonances stopped guaranteeing long ago is provided instead by super-catchy mock-pop devices—which eventually, sly devils, prove stranger harmonically than first impressions suggest. The singing, while not even mock pop—by normal standards of intonation and soulful drama, vocally this may be the least gifted great band ever—nudges their recitative tendencies toward a sweet, breathy, sincere counterpart of the guitars. Simple word choices and frequent repetitions make lyrics whose meaning never comes clear seem just out of reach.

All of which I find rather exhilarating. Of course, you may not. When *Murray Street* came out in 2002, non-old Amy Phillips notoriously asserted in this very newspaper that since Sonic Youth hadn't made a good album since (1995's) *Washing Machine*, they should break up already. Who's to say her opinion isn't worth as much as mine? Me? Well, yeah. One concept the non-old have trouble getting their minds around is the difference between taste and judgment. It's fine not to like almost anything, except maybe Al Green. That's taste, yours to do with as you please, critical deployment included. By comparison, judgment requires serious psychological calisthenics. But the fact that objectivity only comes naturally in math doesn't mean it can't be approximated in art.

One technique, which I've just illustrated, is to replace response reports ("boring" and all its self-involved pals, like my "exhilarating" or Phillips's less blatant "dull") with stimulus reports. Like for instance you could observe that, boring or not, 1998's *A Thousand Leaves* unquestionably marked a turn toward the quietude, ruminative structures, and general fuzz level always implicit in their unresolved tunings and Deadhead-manqué jams— tendencies tersely deployed on 1994's *Experimental Jet Set, Trash and No Star* and fulsomely indulged on *Washing Machine*'s twenty-minute "The Diamond Sea." On *A Thousand Leaves*, melodies were softer, lyrics kinder, instrumentals more atmospheric, and 2000's *NYC Ghosts & Flowers* ran away with the freer tendencies of that approach. But ever since then, starting with *Murray Street* and working through *Sonic Nurse* and now *Rather Ripped*, Sonic Youth have reinvested in songform. It's so much more reliable than a 401(k).

Another objectivity aid is consensus, as indicated by record guides, online compendia, and critics' polls. These establish that *Murray Street* is well-liked, *A Thousand Leaves* and *Sonic Nurse* only a little less so. The dud by acclamation (perhaps even the "bad album" whose existence I just denied) is *NYC Ghosts*, which Phillips acknowledges as the true inspiration for her kill-yr-idols hissy fit. Granted an excuse to replay every Sonic Youth album I own, I've found these judgments justifiable. *Murray Street*'s song-soundscape fusion, which at the time I didn't quite get, sounded strong, while *NYC Ghosts*, whose meanderings had captivated me in their ambiently environmental way, never fully reconnected. *A Thousand Leaves*, long my eccentric fave, proved marginally less entrancing as it sopped up its seventy-four minutes under lyric-parsing scrutiny. I'm disappointed in myself—I take pride in knowing when I've reconciled taste and judgment, and don't often get records wrong. But I still think the consensus is too extreme—and probably, given the way these things go, reactive, pumping *Murray Street* to make up for dismissing *NYC Ghosts*.

Thurston Moore claims *Rather Ripped* "isn't particularly different from any previous Sonic Youth releases," but that's just his fealty to his band's tunings talking—to a sonic signature that, having pretty much launched an alt-rock generation, is now counted boring by many non-old. Fact is, every Sonic Youth album varies within the broad boundaries of their guitaristic practices. In that capacious context, *A Thousand Leaves* did mark a turning point, which reflects not just the deterioration that afflicts human bodies as they turn forty into fifty, but also, if you'll pardon some biography, Kim and Thurston's absorption of the parenthood they undertook in 1994: the extra pressure, the lost time, the future that subsumes your own, the messy roommate you love to pieces. Concomitantly, the words of that album, insofar as they make sense, evoke a maturing marriage in a lyrical phase, with Kim's "Female Mechanic Now on Duty" adding essential sex appeal. On *Rather Ripped*, which shares its name with a legendary Berkeley record store, a similar union may be rather riven, or may not. The non-old aren't obliged to care about these things. But critics of any age ought to recognize that they're there.

Sonic Youth have certainly written lyrics that stick—for my taste, most often about music ("Dirty Boots," "New Hampshire") or politics ("Kool Thing," "Youth Against Fascism"). But where their opposite numbers Yo La Tengo put Ira and Georgia's love life on the public record, Sonic Youth don't seem to sing about Kim and Thurston. It's that Brechtian distance thing again, magnified by vocal deficiencies they play as strengths. Does Kim have a girlfriend on the side? Is her "What a waste / You're so chaste" directed at "Turquoise Boy"? How about Thurston's "Sleepin' Around"? In the end, I don't much care. What matters to me is how these unresolved intimations are allayed and disarmed by the uncharacteristic lightness of music that nevertheless gets strange when you listen hard.

Edges dull; the shock of the new gets old. But great bands keep creating from what they know, and figuring it out as they do. Try to see 'em at CB's Tuesday. They'll come up with something you don't expect, guaranteed.

Village Voice, 2006

Adult Contemporary

Grant McLennan: 1958–2006

Grant McLennan was in a grand mood May 6, with every reason to believe he had his best work ahead of him. Beloved though the Go-Betweens' six '80s albums are, 2005's *Oceans Apart*, third fruit of their 2000 reunion, had outsold them all. It also won them their first Australian Grammy, and if the category was Adult Contemporary, fine. McLennan had money in the bank. Songs were pouring out of him. That night, during a huge housewarming party that would root him in Brisbane once and for all, he planned to publicly propose to his girlfriend, Emma Pursey. At 4:30 that afternoon, he went upstairs for a nap. Early arrivals found his body in his bedroom a few hours later. The autopsy revealed a massive heart attack. He was forty-eight.

"One of the last real romantic bohemians. No watch, wallet, or drivers licence," recalled one of a thousand bereaved on the band's message board. McLennan reportedly went through a heroin phase and had trouble sustaining relationships with women; his melodic grace concealed a dark thematic undertow. His father, a doctor, died of cancer at thirty-eight, when Grant was just four: "You've lost your voice / You let it go," he literally moaned on "Dusty in Here" twenty years later. But the songwriter was famously modest, generous, polite, courtly. There seems no reason to attribute his loss to anything more esoteric than cruel fate.

McLennan is survived by his girlfriend, his mother, a stepfather he was close to, two siblings, and an adult son. But just as painfully, he is survived by Robert Forster, his Go-Betweens partner since 1977, who played and worked with him even when they lived oceans apart with band kaput. They didn't compose together, and both recorded notable solo albums—in the early '90s, McLennan's output was obsessive, unstoppable. But they were stronger in tandem; they complemented each other's tone, with McLennan's graver and sweeter. And even as naive new wavers, both conveyed a maturity—an adult contemporaneity—all the stranger for its origins in supposedly uncouth Oz. In retrospect, maybe it was too mature for its intended audience at the time.

McLennan's pick hit came early, in 1982: "Cattle and Cane," about childhood in the outback, shows up on many greatest-songs-of-all-time lists, including U2's. But now that he's lost his voice, remember 2005's "Finding You": "What would you do if you turned around / And saw me beside you / Not in a dream but in a song?" Or 2000's "The Clock": "But then the clock turns / And it's now / And its you-ou-ou-ou-ou-ou."

Village Voice, 2006

Titan. Polymath.
Naturalist.

Ray Charles: 1930–2004

Rock and roll? "A couple of guitars together with a backbeat," huffed Rock and Roll Hall of Fame charter member Ray Charles in 1959. But he dug almost everything else back then. The blues and gospel he married on "I Got a Woman," the jazz he roughed up at Newport, and the country he redefined with "I Can't Stop Loving You" were just the obvious stuff. He treasured choral accompaniment and string accompaniment, big bands and bebop, pre–World War I chestnuts and jump blues comedy and chansons translated by his French girlfriend. Born in 1930 and a pro by 1945, he spent his last four decades not as a rhythm-and-blues genius but as a pop polymath. He presaged Otis Redding less than he did Billy Joel—or really, since the main thing he liked about songwriting was royalties, Linda Ronstadt and Rod Stewart.

None of whom were in his league, because Charles was a titan. His intelligence, vitality, and will were heroic, his phenomenal musicality was intensified by his enforced intimacy with the world of sound, and his spiritual resources defied comprehension. His father a no-show, his young mother so frail she died when she was thirty-one and he was fifteen, he witnessed the playtime death of his beloved younger brother at five, just in time to be blinded by undiagnosed glaucoma.

Charles knew too much about suffering, and once he matured sub-sumed what he'd learned in vocal performances he crafted with painstaking subtlety. Sometimes joyous, sometimes blue, they made people happy even when they made people sad and epitomized an ideal of naturalness that be-came the orthodoxy toward which pop singing now strives. He also played a mean piano and some pretty fair alto sax.

Charles gave as an artist and held back as a human being. One of the few pop stars to truly control his own business affairs, he was a notorious cheap-skate, paying his band peanuts and, in a signal instance reported by biographer Michael Lydon, extracting a cameo payment "well into six figures" from the aforementioned Billy Joel. He was a serial polygamist who left a lot of bemused or bitter women behind. He kicked heroin only to avoid prison, loved nicotine and cannabis, and drank enough gin to destroy any normal person's liver long before it did his. All during the decline that finally killed him June 10, he kept going into the studio he owned in L.A., perfecting more music.

Village Voice, 2004

He Got Us

James Brown: 1933–2006

James Brown was the greatest musician of the rock era, no contest. But two of his many titles must be addressed. James Brown was the Genius. Let Ray Charles be the Godfather of Soul.

Soul was preeminently a vocalists' style, and while Brown was a magnifi-cent singer, he was no Aretha Franklin or, absolutely, Ray Charles—as an interpreter, more in Wilson Pickett's class. Also, where soul had a forgiving softness to it, Brown's byword was "hard." And so in 1965, before most white Americans even knew what soul was, he found another lifework with "Papa's Got a Brand New Bag." As he told ghostwriter Bruce Tucker: "Aretha and Otis and Wilson Pickett were out there and getting big. I was still called a soul singer—I still call myself that—but musically I had already gone off in a different direction. I had discovered that my strength was not in the horns, it was in the rhythm."

In other words, funk.

The Hardest Working Man in Show Business, sure. Just don't think, as CNN declared, that "what made Brown succeed where hundreds of others failed was his superhuman determination." There weren't hundreds of others. In fact, there weren't any—Brown was unique. Since not all geniuses get over, thank the God he believed in that he was also a workaholic and an egomaniac. Otherwise we wouldn't have P-Funk or Prince or hip-hop as we know them; otherwise we wouldn't have most of today's drummers. His work ethic was the means to the ecstasy his genius made possible.

But work was also thematic. As a lover-in-song Brown could power the romantic positivity of "Out of Sight" and "I Feel Good." But having come up in privation bleaker than even Louis Armstrong's, he was mainly a needer, and became less a lover once he mastered funk. It was a man's man's man's world because man made cars, trains, boats, electric lights; lust-in-song—"take a look at those cakes"—made man a sex machine. Thus many of his dance records celebrate discipline and self-determination, or just importune us to "Get It Together," to "Get Up, Get Into It and Get Involved," to "Get Up Offa That Thing" so we can at least "(Release the Pressure)." The greatest body of body music ever recorded, his funk is nonetheless imposingly abstract. Listen to it nonstop and its intricacy equals its energy. It's as much Bach as Ray Charles.

Listening to it nonstop can be tricky. Brown's best-known album is the self-financed 1962 *Live at the Apollo*, which established him as an r&b superstar and a businessman to be reckoned with. But though there's no music anywhere quite like the perfectly timed and articulated female fan-screeches that punctuate the ten-minute "Lost Someone," the album is barely half an hour long, living testament of a chitlin circuit now defunct as it relegates major songs to the same eight-title medley as forgotten ones. Instead the canonical work is the finest box set ever released, 1991's four-CD *Star Time*, sequenced so deftly it's as if Brown added three or four classic albums to the very few he actually managed as he toured and toured and toured some more while charting four dozen singles pop and over a hundred r&b.

As his first pop top ten, "Papa's Got a Brand New Bag" was taken by Beatles-Stones-Dylan crazies like me as a dandy novelty, which it was, turning the word "bag" into indelible hippie slang. What we wouldn't realize for many years because the action took place far from Beatles-Stones-Dylan is that it kicked off a process in which Brown would change music forever, until now, as Jonathan Lethem put it in a definitive *Rolling Stone* profile, younger listeners live "entirely in a sonic world of James Brown's creation." Lifting off from "Brand New Bag," *Star Time*'s second disc camel-walks across the four years of funk's inven-

tion—"I Got You" fare-thee-welling twelve-bar blues to "Cold Sweat" embracing modality to vamps like the incomprehensible "I Can't Stand Myself (When You Touch Me)" massaging a single chord to pieces. And at the same time his ever-changing road band bestowed upon us a cohort of crucial sidemen.

Pounding and teasing funk's topsy-turvy beats were complementary drummers: Mobile's Jabo Starks, steeped in both New Orleans second line and the stuttering float of Holiness soul-clapping, and Memphis's Clyde Stubblefield, whose straight eight maintained the pulse Starks danced over. Guitarists Jimmy Nolen and Alphonso Kellum scratched and riffed. Adding tonalities, breaks, and more riffs were future leader Fred Wesley on trombone, future arranger Pee Wee Ellis on alto, and bringing on the tenor juice Maceo Parker, whose brother Melvin had manned the drums on "Brand New Bag." Soon acid-tripping temp Bootsy Collins was transferring the funk first from the drums to the bass and then from James Brown to George Clinton. But comprehending them all was the greatest musician of the rock era, no contest. This not quite supernal vocalist, notorious for the willful nonchalance with which he sometimes manhandled drums or organ, became a bandleader as inspired as Duke Ellington himself, an unschooled master arranger who used Pee Wee Ellis and Dave Matthews the way the Beatles used George Martin. And he also became a singer whose strength was "in the rhythm" as it promised delights to come with curly intro shrieks and hooked or textured over the groove like a great horn player. Stubblefield's famous "Cold Sweat" solo needs Brown's grunts and exclamations; "I Got the Feelin'" and "Give It Up or Turnit Loose" mine his motherlode of sound effects. Everywhere his attack sharpens and embellishes the beat.

Beyond *Live at the Apollo* and perhaps *Sex Machine*, Brown's signature album-as-album is 1973's *The Payback*, the mysteriously rejected soundtrack to the forgotten blaxploitation flick *Hell Up in Harlem*. It is now honored by many hards as prefiguring gangsta, but I like how empathetic "Forever Suffering" is and note that "Mind Power"'s "starvation" talk remains perpetually apropos. Then there's the utterly unlikely "Time Is Running Out Fast," which I once found shapeless and now adore as African-cum-Holiness, with Brown uttering sounds instead of words over a conga-spiced thirteen-minute vamp, leaving the talking to Wesley's trombone. And most of all there's the deep-grooved rumination "Take Some . . . Leave Some," which includes the simple-looking lines "All my life I've dreamed of good food / Good lovin', shoes and clothes."

Very few artists would think to say such a homely thing, because very few grew up so deprived that it's true. But James Brown had a dream only a music that was physical and transcendent simultaneously could satisfy. That dream drove him forward. But the reason he got where he was going is that he was a genius.

Rolling Stone, 2006 · Substantially revised

Old Master

Bob Dylan

The third in a simultaneously startling and backward-looking series Dylan began in 1997 with *Time Out of Mind*, *Modern Times* is neither as existentially bleak as that piece of fabricated folklore nor as waggish and vivacious as 2001's *"Love and Theft."* Instead it radiates the observant calm of old masters who have seen enough life to be ready for anything—Yeats, Matisse, Sonny Rollins. This is a music-first record that leavens blues shuffles with the moderate tempos and politely jazzy beat favored by new Dylan hero Bing Crosby in the early '30s. Nice though it would be for the title to indicate "current events," the likely reference is Charlie Chaplin's 1936 movie masterpiece. In both, a legendary entertainer does what he wants because nobody can stop him, and the world is better for it.

At sixty-five, Dylan is writing modern poetry only insofar as that tradition encompasses song lyrics. Celebrating American vernacular from folk to Tin Pan Alley, he drops wonderful lines galore. Try "I got the pork chops, she got the pie." Or "I can't go back to paradise; I killed a man there." And sneaking in "The buying power of the proletariat's gone down" must have given him a kick. But what really gets Dylan off these days is jumping the beat by rushing the first line of the opening track's second stanza—which happens to be "I was thinking about Alicia Keys." Or turning Slim Harpo's "Hip Shake" into "Someday Baby." Or Hawaiianizing "Beyond the Horizon." Or the descending sixteen-note, yes, hook that runs through "Spirit on the

Water." Though it belongs on a piano, it's usually stated on acoustic guitar and then taken up by shifting combinations of standup bass and Dylan's touring band. Sometimes it fades out early, but it always comes back, and you want it to—for all eight minutes of the song.

Blender, 2006

Estudando Tom Zé

On October 5, the belatedly renowned Brazilian avant-pop genius Tom Zé released *Estudando a Bossa: Nordeste Plaza*, his fifth album since 1998. This means that between the ages of sixty-two and seventy-four Tom Zé created close to four hours of songs that I expect to be playing with pleasure when and if I reach seventy-four myself. Aware that whens get iffier in an artist's seventies, Luaka Bop, where five of Zé's seven albums have appeared—the other two are on the Brazilian labels Trama and Irara, the latter a DIY operation named after Zé's hometown in the Bahia backlands—supplied him with a second October 5 release. The box set *Studies of Tom Zé: Explaining Things So I Can Confuse You* is built around three remastered vinyl versions of Zé's "Estudando" series—"estudando" meaning "studying," the topics samba in general and the hyperromantic pop samba called pagode as well as bossa nova on the new one. Audio upgrade aside, the idea is to get you to notice Tom Zé, an artist worthy of your attention, excitement, amusement, wonder, and record-buying dollars.

Next to the U.S. and arguably Great Britain, Brazil is home to the richest popular music culture in the world—a culture of extraordinary rhythmic wealth, harmonic savoir-faire, verbal ambition, historical complexity, and intellectual ferment. If I was suitably passionate about the music it produces, I could mount an even more convincing case for Tom Zé. But I'm hardly the only Tom Zé booster who's not deeply into samba and its innumerable relatives and derivatives. Where most Brazilian pop cultivates a smoothness, Zé is rough, spiky, peculiar—blatantly avant-garde without ever sacrificing melody or ignoring groove. It's also hooky, as befits a onetime jingle writer who considers the enduring folk tune the greatest of all cultural treasures.

And it's also lotsa laughs. There's no one like him. The vaguely similar Captain Beefheart, for instance, is a big baby having a tantrum by comparison. Zé is so much kinder, wiser, saner.

For reasons I've understood better since the Zé box inspired me to finally read Caetano Veloso's memoir, *Tropical Truth*, Brazilian music doesn't mesh too good with rock and roll. In the U.S. it attracts mostly jazz fans, an affair that began with the circa-1957 invention of bossa nova by Joao Gilberto, who turned samba into a sophisticated "new thing" by complicating its chords, understating its beats, and murmuring its vocals. Veloso adores Gilberto—"popular music is the Brazilian form of expression par excellence," declares this well-read cineaste, and "Joao takes popular music upon himself as the determinant of what truth we might be permitted and could create." In contrast, the pop that Yanks were rocking around the clock in the '50s was "too simple," "unoriginal," with a "whorehouse-edge."

Tropical Truth is Veloso's eyewitness history of Bahia-generated tropicalia, which in the late '60s responded dialectically to bossa nova by reconfiguring the left orthodoxy of the broadly influential Musica Popular Brasileira movement at a higher level of radical consciousness. But ultimately Veloso's book, which praises many writers and filmmakers as well as musicians, is an argument for all of Brazil as culture and nation—and the most accomplished criticism by a pop musician I know. There's juicier writing about musicians from Robert Johnson to Ricky Nelson in Bob Dylan's *Chronicles*. But Dylan doesn't approach—nor, simple Ricky Nelson fan that he is, aspire to—Veloso's theoretical grasp. His empathy and precision had me speeding happily through descriptions of artist after artist I'd never heard of.

By 1965, the restless pop scene Veloso celebrates was a staple of both TV programming and highbrow critique; his first published essay attacked a 1966 book that inveighed against bossa nova's class bias (a whole book! in 1966!). He describes these developments so vividly that I returned with fresh ears to Gilberto, who I once considered oversubtle and now enjoy in a contemplative way, and the young rock band Os Mutantes, who I once considered overelaborate and now hear as melodically uncanny adolescent gigglefritzes who hadn't yet gone the way of all prog. Veloso is so effusive and convincing about the musicality of his tropicalia comrade Gilberto Gil, who was imprisoned with him in 1968 and served from 2003 to 2008 as Lula da Silva's minister of culture, that I also heard more on my second pass at Gil's circa-1970 breakaway albums *Gilberto Gil* and *Expresso 2222*.

Then there's the music of Veloso himself. I've been a Gil fan in principle since 1982's grooveful *Um Banda Um*, although it took Veloso to teach me that for Gil, a dark-skinned doctor's son who came late to black consciousness, harmony and melody are paramount—that like so many Brazilian musicians he's ultimately a child of Joao Gilberto. Veloso, the proudly Europhile son of a telegraph operator, has always been a trickier read, and I do mean read. His penetrating delicacy as a singer can't be denied by anyone who's caught his cameo in Pedro Almodovar's *Talk to Her*. But one reason the man is so into it is that he cares about lyrics as a songwriter, an interpreter, and a critic. Unfortunately, this leaves open the big fat question of how anyone who doesn't understand Portuguese addresses the oft-heard claim that Veloso is nothing less than the world's premier popular musician.

I began to make progress with Veloso by bearing down on 1989's *Estrangeiro*, produced by Brazilian-raised no wave graduate Arto Lindsay—its title track describes Paul Gauguin, Cole Porter, and Claude Levi-Strauss's varied responses to Rio's Guanabara Bay before exploring Veloso's homegrown tropical alienation in fact and metaphor. There's also a best-of that provides Portuguese lyrics alongside their translations so you can follow sound and meaning together. But though this is the most we can hope, it's never enough, because the best way to hear music is with your ears. That's why groove musics, usually dance musics, breach language barriers more readily than song musics. There are too many exceptions to this generalization to enumerate or explain, but sonic distinction, vocal character, vocal virtuosity, and nonverbal humor are all common mitigating factors. And where Veloso is the kind of great pop singer who makes up for what he lacks in vocal character with vocal virtuosity and vice versa, Tom Zé has significant strengths in every one except vocal virtuosity.

Although Zé was aligned with tropicalia, Charles A. Perrone's 1983 *Masters of Contemporary Brazilian Song* barely mentions him, where Christopher Dunn's 2001 tropicalia study *Brutality Garden* grants him a major chunk of its final chapter. What happened in between was that Luaka Bop headman David Byrne discovered Zé by accident in a Rio de Janeiro LP bin just when Zé was about to give up on his musical career. Zé's father was a street vendor who used a lottery jackpot to start a textile store in Irara, a settlement so premodern that Zé saw electricity and running water arrive there as a kid. He had some minor pop success in the '60s, even taking over Veloso and Gil's *Divine Marvelous* TV show briefly after they were detained. But at the University of Bahia he also studied classical music with Swiss and German emigres dedicated to dodecaphony, instrument fabrication, and avant-traditional Euro-Brazilian fusion. Usually such credentials signal the presence of interesting minds at best and misbegotten wankery the rest of the time. One reason Zé sounds like no one else is that he puts all of these avant-gardist notions into effective practice.

Veloso holds that where bossa nova made unusual chords flow, tropicalia juxtaposed standard-issue chords oddly. With Zé, it's more like juxtaposing unusual chords so they move smartly, usually in a staccato samba rhythm. He's been inventing instruments since the '70s, including a primitive sampler utilizing taped radio frequencies called the HertZé and a kazoo constructed from the leaves of Sao Paulo's ubiquitous ficus tree. And perhaps because he grew up in a culture considerably more oral and "primitive" than that of most Brazilians, he uses the avant to flavor the trad rather than the other way around.

Reimmersing in Zé's albums was both more revelatory and more pleasurable than such nice-work-if-you-can-get-it tends to be: the only ones that didn't sound even better were the first two, which had already become life favorites on a C-90 I took on vacation for years—especially the first, Byrne's cherry-picked improvement on *Estudando o Samba*, which he turned into the superb *Brazil Classics 4: The Best of Tom Zé: Massive Hits*. Recorded mostly when Zé was about forty, it mines his beginnings as a guitar-strumming chronicler of Irara with a voice that's still supple enough to sweeten his adept tunes yet never undercuts what Veloso describes as "his ill-humored observations expressed in a rural accent that revealed rather than obscured the classical elegance of his educated and correct Portuguese." Zé's minimalism is out front in such titles as "Ma," "Hein?," "Doi," "Vai," and "To" ("I'm"), with lyrics to match. The eccentric percussion—one effect involves a blender—is always beatwise. But the album sticks in the mind most vividly via its conversational melodies and the droll, sprightly guitar riffs that anchor "Ma," "Nave Maria," and "Augusta, Angelica e Consolacao," the latter two Byrne add-ons. As for how it studies samba, I can only say I know I'd love it even more if I got the references, which I bet are in the beats sometimes.

Released in 1992, *Brazil Classics 5: The Return of Tom Zé: The Hips of Tradition* elaborates this approach, although on the surface the traditions are often literary rather than musical—Faulkner, Simon Schama, Stanislaw Lem, many Brazilians. Past fifty-five by then, Zé enlisted more instrumental and vocal help in delivering his melodies, including the female choruses toward which he'd gravitate. His next Luaka Bop release came six years later: a concept album, let's call a spade a spade, entitled *Fabrication Defect*. At sixty-two, Zé changed his music considerably, and although *Massive Hits* will always be my first love, I've come to prefer this late phase. Every time I listen I discover some hooky curve or harmonic wrinkle, some sly fissure or chuckle in Zé's creaky voice, some humorous turn in the melodicism of his helpmeets, some unlikely sound, some hint of an idea.

What has become my favorite of these albums has plenty of vocals but very few words and is already unavailable every which way but digital even though it was self-released only four years ago. While devoid of Zé the cancionista, the thirty-minute, seven-track *Danc-Eh-Sa* has everything else non-Lusophones love him for: the tunes, the sounds, the beats, the irreverence. But for Zé to put himself out there in such pure form also helps me appreciate what happens when I can read along. For me, his other Brazil-only release, 2001's enjoyable *Jogos de Armar*—which comes with a forty-four-minute bonus disc of riffs, lines, and tracks lifted from the main disc to help others plagiarize him—tends to recede into the conceptual distance with no English-language documentation to pin it down.

In contrast, the three Luaka Bop albums offer English in abundance, and it adds something. *Fabrication Defect* addresses an explicit theme with Zé's typical array of warmth and irony, asperity and obscurity: that the Third World's "rapidly increasing population" of "androids" are afflicted with "inborn 'defects': they think, they dance, they dream." *Estudando o Pagode* is a scattershot samba operetta about the oppression of women with female backup all over it and many high points, from the Greek chorus of cartoon characters reciting the Hail Mary at the beginning to "Beatles by the Bushel" at the end. My favorite track, situated "Scene IV—Gay-Lesbian Parade," is called "Elaeu," a very Zéesque conflation of "she" and "I." This album has wheels within wheels. I look for excuses to play it again.

As befits its subject, the new *Estudando o Bossa* is lighter and more immediate, with nearly every fetching melody shared if not borne by yet another fetching female singer with her own register, timbre, and presence. I know there are melodic and lyrical in-jokes that Brazilians will get and I won't, and I wish someone would explicate—in English. But here there are references I do understand—two songs praising Joao Gilberto, another that has a laugh about "Ob-La-Di Ob-La-Da," namechecked singers who ring a bell. I'll take its pervasive beauty as an old man's reconciliation with a Rio lyricism whose class politics he rejected as a Bahia youth who knew something about harmony himself. Significantly, although Veloso brought Zé south and Byrne saved him from running a gas station in Irara, he's long resided not in Rio but a few hundred miles west in industrial Sao Paulo, where he can comfortably remain as spiky as he wants for as long as he likes—or not, if that's where he chooses to take his art.

The July after the Luaka Bop box, its elfin honoree visited Alice Tully Hall for his first New York concert since 1999. Wearing a Velcro-ized white jacket emblazoned with colorful designs, shiny black ovoid sneakers, white shirt, black pants, and a knee-length apron, he showed off the flexibility of his seventy-four-year-old hips, which instead of thrusting like a macho man he rotated like a coy senorita, apron skirtlike in his hands. His show all fits and starts, broken-English lectures and jokes and thoughts he never had before, he introduced his first song with eight vertical leaps, introjected others later, and scrambled on and off the lip of the stage at will. Early on his heavily accented stop-and-go patter turned to the glories of New York City—Paris is kinda small by comparison, he told us—and then to finding a limo in the yellow pages, and then to the yellow pages themselves. You know the saw about someone who can sing the telephone book? Zé sang the telephone book—first the hospital pages but then his favorite part, which goes, in his interpretation, "In case of emergency dial 9-1-1." The "9-1-1" morphed into a nifty refrain before he proceeded to a new song whose refrain went "Stand clear of the closing doors / dead souls / etc." He also performed the staccato, turf-claiming "Um Ah! E Um Oh!" and the tragicomic, English-language "Brigitte Bardot" and the lyrical, mischievous "Sincope Jaobim" in nothing like the order the program indicated.

And twice he got the audience to sing just one word. The first was "saudade," the Portuguese term for the deep, melancholy nostalgia of the language's saddest songs. The second was "Ogodo," a Portuguese name for the orisha Shango. Neither is a Lincoln Center word. But chanted over and over, both soon proved hymns to avant-trad irreverence of an irrepressible originality no other artist I know approaches.

Except in the name of its hero, no diacritical marks were exploited in the publication of this essay.

Barnes & Noble Review, 2010 · *MSN Music*, 2011

Gypsy Is His Autopilot

Gogol Bordello

I hate nostalgia so much that my favorite quatrain of the century goes: "There were never any good old days / They are today, they are tomorrow / It's a stupid thing we say / Cursing tomorrow with sorrow." Gargled out in a harsh Eastern European accent, kicked off with and topped off by a half-articulated shout and a sawing, guitar-fortified violin hook, the song is "Ultimate," which leads Gogol Bordello's fourth and greatest album, 2007's *Super Taranta!* It also led their sold-out Music Hall of Williamsburg concert July 23, the day they released their pretty damn fine sixth album, *Pura Vida Conspiracy*. My wife and I hadn't seen the band for five years, and it did our hearts good to hear Eugene Hutz give pride of place to an old credo reaffirmed. At the top of the bleachers we bopped and hugged. Nostalgic? Nous?

Not counting my beloved Wussy, the NYC-spawned Gogol Bordello are my favorite rock band of the new century, atop the Hold Steady, Vampire Weekend, even the Drive-By Truckers. Like Gogol, all three of these do something bands from Foo Fighters on the rawk side to Grizzly Bear on the prawg side do not—write songs whose lyrics and melodies please and parse. Partly as a consequence, all have enjoyed commercial success as this era defines it, and as many tomorrows will too: they make a living creating and playing music, but only because they've learned to tolerate and even enjoy touring for multiple months every year.

Yet here's the thing—few of you can even place Gogol Bordello, because they're not especially big in the U.S. Their success is a worldwide phenomenon of the "secondary markets" serviced by acts whose name recognition is based on hits long gone. (Ever hear of British Goth-poppers Placebo? In Croatia they remember.) For Gogol Bordello, the logic is different. Whether their rhythms cant Balkan or Latin or Jamaican, and by now it's all three, they always generate a crude, loud, rock-identified drive. And rock they are—Hutz plays guitar, as does Oliver Charles fulltime and utility man Pedro Erazo-Segovia when needed. Yet they're an immigrant band. The forty-year-old Hutz grew up in Ukraine until Chernobyl set his family scurrying to Vermont, and energetically explores and exploits the Gypsy roots of his Roma grand-mother. Violinist Sergey Ryabtsev is Russian, accordionist Pasha Newmer Belarusian, bassist Thomas Gobena Ethiopian, vocalist-percussionist Elizabeth Sun Scottish-born Hong Kong Chinese, multi-tasking Erazo-Segovia Ecuadoran. And their music affirms their mongrel heritage. On their excellent 2005 *Gypsy Punks: Underdog World Strike*, Hutz expostulates in his thick accent about getting "categorized" and "naturalized," "pencilled in as a goddam white," but enjoys the last laugh with his fellow "immigrant punks": "I gotta friends, we gotta band / We still make sound you can't stand."

And for more youngish Americans than you'd hope, that's true. Alt-rockers who pride themselves on their openness, critics among them, hear this sound and can't get over how Other it is. Instead of digesting the band's substance, they categorize influences they don't have it in them to naturalize. So let it be said that Gogol Bordello are not "world music" as that unfortunate term is understood by Weavers fans manque. It doesn't evince an organic culture that's in the groove and at home with itself. Instead Gogol Bordello is aggressively rootless, forcing the groove and at home with that. Although it's been a while since the band incorporated the Gypsy brass of Israeli-born Balkan Beat Box saxophonist Ori Kaplan, their rock is hectic like the dueling horns of Romania's Fanfare Ciocarlia or the fiercer Punjabi bhangra Hutz mixes into his DJ sets. They're aggressive, and that's scary for those not prepared for it.

Hutz too can be a little scary—a skinny guy with good abs and a vocabulary larger than his gutturals suggest, he's so hyperactive you're afraid he'll go into cardiac arrest next minute. Hutz stated his credo on Gogol Bordello's 2002—note highly un-guttural yet not quite fluent title—*Multi Kontra Culti Vs. Irony*. "When the Trickster Starts A-Poking (Bordello Kind of Guy)" invokes the outsider gremlins and demiurges of many cultures, Slavic included, although in recent times it's African tricksters who've gotten the ink, while many pencilled in as white believe Roma are tricksters by blood and hate them for it. Moreover, the trickster who goes a-poking is the priapic kind who led mythic rock bands in the good old days—Mick Jagger, Jimi Hendrix, even Axl Rose I s'pose. For years Gogol closed their shows with a comely-or-less maiden climbing on a huge drum held aloft by eager fans as Hutz yowled beside her or climbed on top of her. Occasionally duller versions of this kind of strut surface on the jam circuit and in the more hedonistic strains of metal. But mostly it's a lost myth. These immigrant punks are a messianic rock band in the '60s sense. They believe transcendent abandon and grotty fun are twin pathways to the divine within us that as a bonus feel really good. Nor do they forget that tricksters are also generally jokers. Their fun is funny.

Four or five years ago, Gogol Bordello seemed ready to break on through. Hutz had bonded with superbeardo Rick Rubin, and in April 2010 followed *Super Taranta!* with *Trans-Continental Hustle*, released on Rubin's Columbia-distributed American Recordings label. But for all the good Rubin or Columbia did them, they should have gone for the kind of generous revenue split that indies like their former Side One Dummy label often grant major draws. *Trans-Continental Hustle* ginned up their flattest songwriting since their 1999 debut as it leaned in toward the hard rock that's Rubin's meat and out toward the Latin beats Hutz was eating up in his new hometown, Rio de Janeiro. As happens in bands with mercurial leaders, members drifted away. But on *Pura Vida Conspiracy*, produced by Rubin engineer Dave Schepps for Dave Matthews's ATO label, Gogol Bordello regroups. More melodic than ever, Hutz even comes up with slow ones that touch the heart and hold the attention. And without slackening his messianic fervor, he shifts his goal from orgiastic rebellion toward what he has the chutzpah to call "another dimension of consciousness." As he told *Billboard*, of all places: "All the work in the studio wasn't like, 'what the fuck?' It was like 'fuck, yeah!' It's a drama either way, it's a fucking mess, but the 'fuck yeah' drama, that's our kind of drama."

To hear Hutz talk, it's all onwards and upwards. The band is proceeding apace and the Latin tinge has been on his mind for years. Indeed, *Trans-Continental Hustle* provided the Williamsburg show more songs than *Super Taranta!*, never mind that two of them constituted what suspiciously resembled a lag. *Pura Vida Conspiracy*, however, tells a more nuanced story. Its first and strongest song, "We Rise Again" (repeat: "Again"), reclaims the band's "borders are scars on the face of the planet" turf. Then follows second-strongest "Dig Deep Enough" (repeat: "Enough"), and then "Malandrino," which is Brazilian for "trickster" and insists, cornily and liltingly by Hutz's previous standards, "I was born with singing heart!" There's what sounds like a sea chantey and what sounds like a love song; there's a reincarnation hymn and a quiet tribute to the African-American trickster John the Conqueror and a reflection about navigating the sea of life that's quieter than that.

But given my special relationship with the anti-nostalgic "Ultimate," the new songs I find most striking concern Hutz revisiting his past. First he stows away to Kiev in search of his "Lost Innocent World": "Bring me place my father showed me my first guitar chord." Then "The Other Side of Rainbow" reports bleak results from his lifelong future quest: "It was black and white / It was black and white." But in "My Gypsy Auto Pilot" he runs into a "drunk girl policeman" he used to skip school with in Kiev and tells her he's spent the rest of his life skipping school some more: "I've been watching trains / Swiftly rolling by / I've been jumping them / Without long goodbyes / To uncover rules of life / And how to break them well / And the key to my gypsy auto pilot / And my story to tell." In the third repeat of that chorus, he switches to second person. He wants the policewoman to know that she also has rules to break well and a story to tell.

How priapic this encounter might turn is left unsaid, but assume nothing. Gogol Bordello has mellowed somewhat musically and Hutz has mellowed somewhat philosophically. From me, "mellow" is seldom a compliment. But a major reason the priapic rock god is a dinosaur is the evident limitations of that vision, and a major reason Gogol Bordello have always been such an up was that by linking that old style of energy and attitude to new cultural conditions they've made its defiant joy signify philosophically in our new century. That's philosophically, however—not politically. Of course Hutz has "good politics"; as you'd hope, he's supported Boycott Arizona and other immigrant causes, and *Super Taranta!*'s "Forces of Victory" is about continuing the struggle against an oppressor who transmutes from Pinochet to "any gang of four." But if you're serious about politics your future has to extend beyond tomorrow, which has never been his way. Now it's different.

The new Kiev songs are not nostalgic. Hutz's "innocent world" is definitively "lost"—too many old comrades dead, and instead of gold at the end of the rainbow there's black-and-white. So soon his Gypsy autopilot will set the pied piper of the secondary markets jumping trains again. But he'll be more thoughtful about it, and in two of the last three songs, his quest has shifted somewhat. In "Hieroglyph," Hutz calmly claims demiurge—"I'm unity I'm gravity." And both halves of what amounts to a double finale, the first upbeat and the second very much not, hew to the same hackneyed existential value: "living and loving." For a guy who believes even his old cop girlfriend needs to find herself, a guy who used to end every show yowling or humping on top of a drum, this is downright mellow.

One more thing. If all goes well—and Hutz knows better than you or I that often it doesn't—he will return to Kiev, not to settle down, but to honor the special part that secondary market has played in his story. He's sponsoring a venue called Casa Gogol there. It's due to open in the fall—as he counts time, a long way past tomorrow.

Triumph of the Id

Lil Wayne

With his first prison bid set to launch simultaneously with his first official album since *Tha Carter III*, it seemed an excellent time to ponder Lil Wayne. Only then Wayne's year on Rikers Island was delayed so the rapper could, well, go to the dentist. Some speculated that Wayne has so much bling in his mouth he was removing it for safekeeping, while jayhovawitness at the Rap Radar site snapped, "Hell, I know niggas that go to jail *just* to get their teeth fixed." Soon another Rap Radar comedian took care of the new rock-styled *Rebirth*: "Judge: Cancel the release of 'Rebirth' and we'll let you free. Wayne: OK." On February 16, however, Wayne was subjected to eight root canals along with repairs on several implants and scattered remaining original teeth, not to mention many hits of nitrous oxide or something stronger. No wonder even admirers are tempted to make light of Lil Wayne's legal problems.

The code of the streets whence hip-hop supposedly springs defines prison as part of the life, and many rappers—including Slick Rick, Shyne, Mystikal, and most recently and prominently T.I.—have been incarcerated. True, the others perpetrated crimes of violence whereas Lil Wayne finally went to jail March 8 for gun possession solely. But we Second Amendment relativists support gun laws, and seldom approve when rich guys walk even if they have undergone undue police scrutiny. And though we may not place much credence in the crime tales that once dominated Lil Wayne's repertoire, we sure don't believe he lives within the law. Prison? You could say he was asking for it.

But you also could say his disregard for the law is what we admire him for. Being a Lil Wayne fan renders you complicit not just in his musical and verbal compulsions but in the lifestyle of an unpackable, untrackable workaholic hedonist. Scarfing beats, slurping rhymes, verbalizing desires as boundless as language itself like they're a joke he's sharing with his crew as they play an ESPN videogame, Lil Wayne puts so much id into his labors he could make any cop nervous—in fact, any functioning adult. The ultimate locus of our complicity is our own infantile urges.

This complicity requires nothing like total commitment, which given Lil Wayne's uncatalogable catalogue would be a path of madness. It applies more to his high-mixtape mode, epitomized by the wild and woolly double-CD *Da Drought 3*, than to the formalizing double-platinum *Tha Carter III*, which perfected and some would say tamed that mode. And it requires no identification with the biographical Lil Wayne, M.I.A., and Kanye West I care about—their thought processes are something like mine. Lil Wayne belongs to some other species, and that is central to who he is, what he does, and how he presents himself. Maybe it's the drugs. Or maybe it's just Lil Wayne.

Biographically, Dwayne Carter is a twenty-seven-year-old from New Orleans who's been rapping professionally since he was twelve. Although thug money certainly got him started, there's no evidence he put in minute one "on the grind," to cite a title from 2000's *Lights Out*. Wayne owns luxury residences in New Orleans, Miami, and Atlanta, and has fathered four children by four different women, the last three born in 2008 or 2009. He chain-smokes blunts and has a taste for codeine-based cough syrup. He's a sports nut and an Animal Planet fan. But the really interesting stuff is his catalogue-that-isn't-a-catalogue.

In my iTunes folder subsist some 165 Lil Wayne songs, all of which went public after 2005's *Tha Carter II*, a farewell from Wayne the gangsta that launched Wayne the stoned free associater. Several times recently I've played these songs five or six hours straight without once fast-forwarding. Mostly the music percolated in the background as Wayne chuckled, chortled, croaked, cackled, heckled, jeckled, sidled, slurred, Auto-Tuned, and even enunciated over beats of varying irresistibility and originality. But every once in a while a moment previously unnoticed or fondly recalled would pop to the forefront: the mock-romantic Prince sample I'd never cared for, the triumphal Mike Jones sample I know in no other guise, the in-their-face seizure of the Beatles' "Help," some scat joke I'd missed, the endless threats to eat MCs, the murderous "Problem Solver" I first heard the day after my father died, the "Hip hop is mine now what you gonna do / I can jump on any nigga's song and make a part two." But except for *Tha Carter III* you can't buy any of this music, all of which has outlived its commercial function of seeding demand, and except for the late-2009 *No Ceilings* mixtape, you also can't download it gratis from any website I have the temerity to introduce to my hard drive. Friends less protective of their computers' immune systems report that they're easy to nab from peer-to-peer networks. Proceed at your own risk. I didn't send you.

These complications pertain because, as even casual observers are dimly aware, Lil Wayne acquired three luxury residences, three babymamas, double-platinum certification, untold blunts, and the attention of many police departments by recording every day and giving the results away. I owe my familiarity with this promotional material to the kindness of younger friends who violated their own best-practice guidelines by burning me CDs of it; the late-2009 *No Ceilings* I managed to download free with some help, after which I braved sendspace.com to obtain the earlier *The Leak 6* from yet another younger friend. As a music critic I should get over this ineptitude. But I'm betting many readers here can identify—for non-initiates, free-music-for-all is often a false rumor that's more trouble than it's worth. And nevertheless, in 2006 and 2007, Lil Wayne put out more great songs than you or I will ever hear—songs enjoyable by anyone with no principled objection to impromptu, casually connected rhymes rife with obscenities, N-words, female dogs, garden tools, and general braggadocio.

Some of these were cameos, usually in the form of sixteens he'd guest-drop for a hundred grand a pop. Others were the kind of back-patting duets that lard mixtapes like his overrated *Dedication 2* and recent *The Leak 6*. But many more were pure Wayne, free downloads that included many supposed "previews" from the oft-delayed and so-worth-waiting-for *Tha Carter III*. Having secured four or five CDs' worth all at once in early 2007, I found them hard to get my mind around. True, many jacked well-known dance and hip-hop beats, that should have helped, but as someone who only dips into that world, rarely could I ID them, and even today I can't name half the tracks on *Da Drought 3*, which is among my favorite albums of the decade. Critics aren't supposed to cop to such ignorance, and there are certainly scholars who have mastered (almost) every detail. But to me it feels like the right approach to an oeuvre in which superfluity is of the essence.

Take *Da Drought 3*'s "Walk It Out," which I'd never thought about before it came on as I completed the previous graf. Based on a stripper-ready DJ Unk track (I Googled that), it ends each of the twenty-two lines of its first half with a two-syllable short-u rhyme: stunner, stomach, rubbers, woman, dungeon, Funyun, bunion, construction, seduction, discussion, trust ya, fuck ya, fuck ya (yup, twice), busta, touch ya, Usher, Russia, flush ya, crusher, gusher, production, abduction. You may think these aren't all rhymes, but Wayne disagrees, and puts their music where his mouf is. The content is mostly sexual insults and boasts targeting unnamed rappers, some wittier than others. But the beat is beguilingly unstable—now elaborated, now deconstructed—and the verbal mood outrageous and unlikely rather than crass or obscene, though the two options do cohabit. Always there's the sense that this is word play—that Wayne has diddled the "street" "reality" of hip-hop convention until a convention is all it remains. Dope, sex, money, sucker MCs, and murder turned cannibalism—all dope themes to hang rhymes off.

"The microphone wet cuh my words like seduction," Wayne spits, summing up my argument in eight juicy words, and then later giggles us humans a future: "I am just a Martian get prepared for abduction." This matter-of-fact view of his own unfixed species identification was perfected, sort of, on *Tha Carter III*'s "Phone Home." The wordplay begins with the *E.T.*-referencing title, which reinforces the trademark childishness of Lil Wayne's nevertheless gravelly drawl and sets a storybook mood for the introductory "We are not the same I am a Martian." Second verse, the last word shifts to "alien," which is in turn sound-shifted toward famed alien Elian Gonzalez, who in early 2008 was in the news for having joined the Young Communist Union in his unphonable Cuban home. Whoever did or didn't get this, it's no accident that Wayne quickly juxtaposes the phrase "Gonzalez young college student" (actually high school, but then he wouldn't have two "oll" sounds). What it "means," of course, is itself. It's one of uncounted superfluous moments in a song about devouring MCs after the manner of the alien in that movie *Alien*, a song that concludes: "I can eat them for supper / Get in my spaceship and hover, hover."

Dwayne Carter is high a lot, and Lil Wayne hovers a lot. "I am sitting on the clouds / I got smoke coming from my seat / I can play basketball with the moon / I got the whole world at my feet," whispers the mixtape-only "I Feel Like Dying" after a chipmunk vibrato singsongs an eerie "Only once the drugs are done / That I feel like dying, I feel like dying." If I've ever been this high, which I doubt, it was forty years ago. But I consider this voice-and-percussion lament Lil Wayne's greatest track—playful, he keeps heh-hehing, yet also suicidal, as if the marijuana, cognac, codeine, wine, and Xanax he namechecks are a reason for living that will someday plunge him into a cold dark sea. You don't have to care about Dwayne Carter the person to notice this theme. Flying images recur almost as often as eating images, and often the escape they describe is from life, not into freedom. It's like his id has a flipside.

But flying is fly on *No Ceilings*, Wayne's best mixtape in years, which repeats the title in all fourteen rhymes and cites the Notorious B.I.G.: "There is no ceilings, there's only the sky, and the sky is the limit, Christopher Wallace said that." Improving beats from Dirty South one-shots and serving beats from Lady Gaga, Jay-Z, and the Black Eyed Peas, this is a gift except when some dolt like Tyga or Jae Milz gets a verse—the initiate's alternative to the Young Money crew album he furnished the big label in December. But though the boasts are mostly prime and the rhymes fun enough, it's all pretty surface—there's nothing as tricky as "Walk It Out," much less "I Feel Like Dying." And the occasional references to his forthcoming change of venue are strictly by the book. "If it costs to be the boss then I guess I gotta pay." Right.

Rebirth is much less fun, especially on two flabbergasting songs where Wayne gets back at girls who dissed him in high school. In fact, it could be the worst-reviewed album by a name artist since *Metal Machine Music*—inevitably, *Tha Carter III*'s megasales soured some initiati, and the Auto-Tuned outpourings of Wayne's inner Kurt Cobain provide a great place to vent. But riding guitar that makes DJ Unk sound like a genius, Wayne—who is in fact a longtime Cobain fan—clearly sees "rock" as a conduit for "serious" feelings disrespected on the streets: romantic self-pity, yes, but also rat-race angst, existential rage, and, strikingly, suicidal fantasies straight up. Not just "I could die now, rebirth motherfucker / Hop up in my space-ship and leave earth motherfucker," which is strong enough, but "Let's jump out of a window / Let's jump off a building baby."

Maybe Wayne's bid will be all push-ups and sit-ups, as *No Ceilings* claims. Maybe it'll even be good for him. But for someone so long on id, it might also be more than he can take—even more than he's willing to take. Suddenly I find myself caring about Lil Wayne the person.

Barnes & Noble Review, 2010

Brag Like That

Jay-Z

In August appeared two albums that qualified as blockbusters by the meager measure of our era. That both were hip-hop was unsurprising—half the blockbusters these days are—and that the rappers involved were prominent obviously wasn't a secret. But what struck me was a rarer confluence of events: a moment when commercial and critical anticipation ran parallel. Not only are Jay-Z, Kanye West, and Lil Wayne bestsellers of the first magnitude, they are also major artists-as-artists. In rock, only U2 and Radiohead enjoyed comparable status in the 'oos, and even they didn't match up—artistically in U2's case, commercially in Radiohead's.

Unfortunately, this new world order was sunk forthwith by Lil Wayne. *Tha Carter IV* eked out a sales victory over Jay-Z and Kanye West's *Watch the Throne*, and has its moments, as does the *Sorry 4 the Wait* mixtape that prepared its way, but its stunted sense of play is summed up by the T-Pain-aided "How to Hate." In contrast, *Watch the Throne* rules. Not that the raves are unanimous, or that the collaboration between the premier rapper of his generation and his most gifted protege quite matches the solo albums that led up to it. But from the first minute of "No Church in the Wild"—rolling bass over strong, simple drumbeat to stealth-thematic hook and starter rap, with organ enlarging a sound whose size is imposing from bar one—its musical command is startling. "No Church in the Wild" stitches doomy old Spooky Tooth, artier-than-Bryan-Ferry Phil Manzanera, and an expostulation from a neglected James Brown classic into an anthem that doesn't so much crush everything in its path as gather it up. Before you begin to wonder what it means, it tells you what it is. Its pop grandeur will not be denied by any better album 2011 puts before us.

That grandeur is owned by West, who had production input on twelve of sixteen tracks. It's a funkier and less ornate variant of the prog-rap of 2010's *My Beautiful Dark Twisted Fantasy*, where West rescued his faltering music from his staggering celebrity. But that doesn't make this West's record. It moves too good, and that has become Jay's way. He's always been the defter rapper rhythmically; the most prominent outside producer is his old standby Swizz Beatz; and though he made his own Euro moves on 2009's *The Blueprint 3*, which showed haters who could count—sales, years, their fingers and toes—that forty was the new thirty, they were aimed directly at the dancefloor. So what does this shared show of pop power mean?

Some might say that you know what *Watch the Throne* is before you know what it means because its essence and its significance are identical—the lyrics are shows of pop power too. *Pitchfork*'s Tom Breihan cites its "multiple name-checks of brands so expensive that you've probably never heard of half of them," and Das Racist hype man Ashok Kondabolu proposes the *Times* headline "TWO RICH OLD MEN BORE A WORLD IN FLAMES" while *New York*'s more measured Nitsuh Abebe observes, "This is an album, after all, about the relationship of black American men to wealth, power, and success." But as Abebe understands, that's only true in the long run. Right now, it's an album about two specific black American men who are closely linked but very different. Abebe explains this difference in terms of class—Jay-Z's earned street-hustler wisdom versus West's spoiled middle-class blabbermouthing. But were the middle-class kid Questlove and the street hustler DMX, class would sort out the opposite way. *Watch the Throne* is a stopping-off place for two major artists who will continue to evolve. But for now it's simplest to conclude that Jay-Z happens to be a better person than Kanye West.

Both co-kings flaunt their arrogance even by the standards of a genre where braggadocio is the main event, and neither is shy about pretending that the line of succession from Otis Redding and Martin Luther King is paved with their gold. Jay-Z's brand porn is as hardcore as West's, although he prefers luxury durables to couture, and it's Jay-Z alone who assumes Michael Jackson's mantle and then claims the Beatles' too. In most respects, however, Jay-Z is a grown man and Kanye West is not. His autobiographical tales are from the projects, not the mall. Never all that big a pimp, he leaves the group sex and coke-snorting hotties to the thirty-four-year-old who says he's outgrown strip clubs. He even boasts that he's happily married. And while both men are all too paranoid about their exalted station, Jay-Z exercises the caution of a crime boss while West emanates the self-pity of a blabbermouth.

In 2005, with Jay-Z feigning retirement and West acing his freshman-sophomore *College Dropout-Late Registration* sequence, I'd never have figured it would work out like this—that in 2011 Jay-Z would have his finger on the future while West played the fame victim. By blabbering the revolting truth about George W. Bush post-Katrina, West had even begun to manifest his civil rights upbringing. But starting with his Iraq rhymes for Panjabi MC and announced in full as of "Minority Report" on his 2006 maturity album *Kingdom Come*, Jay-Z also began to apply his intelligence to politics and express softer emotions. However dubious the dead homiez trope and the tribulations of the rich and famous, both men had a claim on those emotions beyond what Jay-Z has called "absent-father karma": Jay-Z lost his beloved nephew when the Chrysler his uncle had given the kid for graduation crashed with a friend at the wheel, and West lost his even more beloved mother in a grotesquely poetic accident in which the Chicago English professor died at the hands of an L.A. plastic surgeon.

One could venture that maybe *Watch the Throne* divvies up the way it does for rhetorical purposes—that one king plays the hero and the other the hedonist, two equally royal hip-hop archetypes. After all, *My Beautiful Dark Twisted Fantasy* lays out West's personality disorders far more subtly and satirically. More likely, however, collaborating with the undiminished master who gave him his break just set West blabbering. Jay-Z is the most irreligious of mainstream rappers, but he's been Jay-Hova since the start of his rhyming career, restoring meanings to the word "awesome" that many believed had been lost forever.

The only time I've seen Jay-Z perform, at the Garden in late 1997, I took offense at his tossed-off "Ladies grab my dick if you love hip-hop" and pegged him as Little Milton to Busta Rhymes's Howlin' Wolf—competent craftsman versus untamed genius. But the truth was pretty much the opposite. As he packs narrative, metaphor, jokes, puns, and homonyms into lines sculpted with conversational microbeats and taffy-pull vocalese and held together with internal rhymes, Jay-Z's signal musical gift is to sound like he's got nothing to prove and plenty to say—to sound like he's just talking. For an example, read along with the third verse of the new urban anthem "Empire State of Mind," right after "Big lights will inspire you." Or do without Timbaland's mocking beat and sound out the opening words of *Blueprint 3*'s lesser-known "Reminder": "All rhymers with Alzheimer's line up please / All mamis with mind-freeze please line up please / All bloggers with comments, please, I come in peace / Let's see if we can kill your amnesia by the time I leave / All mamis I whored before'll vouch for me / Tell 'em 'bout the time on your momma's couch mami." I mean, if you gotta brag, brag like that.

Not long ago Dan Charnas's excellent but hedged *The Big Payback* led me to downplay Jay-Z's criminal history, an unforced error two other excellent books could have prevented: *Forbes* staffer Zack O'Malley Greenburg's unauthorized *Empire State of Mind: How Jay-Z Went from Street Corner to Corner Office* and Jay-Z's own *Decoded*. Although some details remain murky, Jay-Z was clearly a thriving mid-level crack dealer, and that helps us understand who he has become. But he feels compelled to watch his back and dispatch his rivals not just because he came up in the crack game but because hip-hop derives its ethos from that game whatever a hip-hopper's firsthand experience. It's the ethos of Reaganomics babies who figured "no one's going to help us" and so "went for self, for family, for block, for crew"— practitioners of "the only art I know that's built on direct confrontation." Fortunately, Jay-Z was intelligent and centered enough to understand that the hip-hop training film *Scarface* was the story of a failure, not a hero—that Tony Montana's fall was inevitable. So he changed jobs.

Both books I missed amplify Jay-Z's awesomeness. Greenburg's is the easier read, full of great stories: champagne wars, the million-dollar basketball tournament he abandoned to take Beyoncé on vacation in 2003, his Rocawear profits and Def Jam presidency and Live Nation dealsmanship. Because Charnas's book loses steam around 2000, Greenburg also makes the more telling case for Jay-Z's mastery of the music business per se—what other artist of his calibre can claim signings as astute as Rihanna, Rick Ross, the Roots, and former beefer Nas for the art form, and for history Kanye West himself? But next to Dylan's *Chronicles*, *Decoded* is easily the most impressive music memoir I've read, mostly because Jay-Z is such an impressive person.

Decoded was written with the gifted and very political hip-hop chronicler dream hampton, whose only credit is a respectfully extensive acknowledgment, and it's possible a lot of the prose is hers. But given not just the complexity of Jay-Z's rhymes, many of which he is said to write in his head, but the sharpness of ideas unlikely to be entirely Hampton's, I'm inclined to credit him with the insights as well as the stories he signed off on. Given his appetite for consumer durables, I credit him with the physical object, too: $35 retail, hardbound only, on semi-gloss paper with well-designed typefaces and some 150 photos and illustrations, it's so gorgeous I wrote my notes on Post-its. Whatever you hear from gatekeepers who don't know where the front door is, I think my student Brian Parker got *The Blueprint 3* right in a final paper later published in *Perfect Sound Forever*: "the second coming." I also think Jay-Z won the *Watch the Throne* game. But it's *Decoded* that has me wondering just when popular music has seen his like.

Decoded's title refers to its annotated analyses of thirty lyrics, which while never complete and at moments underwhelming are required reading for anyone who doubts hip-hop rhyming is its own art. But it's the tales and reflections these lyrics are keyed to that leave the deepest mark. And smack dab in the center are Jay-Z's eight years as a criminal. His rationalizations for doing the work—that he sold sick people their medicine, basically—are unconvincing, probably even to him. But the character traits and psychological skills the work demanded carried over into both the art *Decoded* elucidates and the business triumphs Greenburg details: the discipline, the organizational intelligence, the card shark's eye for the tell, the unreadable, unflappable cool.

Although roughly redolent of Chuck Berry, Mick Jagger, Lou Reed, and Youssou N'Dour, these are not attributes we normally associate with our rock and roll heroes. That's why I wonder whether we've seen Jay-Z's like. Internalizing their presence enriches my feel for his music and makes me wonder where he could take it. I'd love him to explore business incident and metaphor the way he's explored his criminal history, especially if he stuck in more politics. And I'd love even more for him to take his measly half billion and figure out a way to contravene Dan Charnas's reluctant conclusion that hip-hop fortunes are still made in collusion with white corporate America rather than in competition with it. The hustler-turned-rapper who toasted "This world is full of shit" in his first video is now the rapper-turned-mogul who looks back at his hustle and sees "a culture of people so in love with life that they can't stop fighting for it." Putting those two truths together would be a worthy enterprise for any grown man.

Barnes & Noble Review, 2011

Paisley's Progress

Brad Paisley

Fifteen seconds of tune-up precede a partying rock riff that's corny even by Nashville standards. But it sure does rock, and soon it takes on virtuoso flourishes. Finally, forty seconds in, there's a rather un-Nashville lyric: "She's got Brazilian leather boots on the pedal of her German car / Listenin' to the Beatles singin' 'Back in the U.S.S.R.'" Thus begins the lead and title cut of Brad Paisley's *American Saturday Night*. So optimistic it's intrepid and shameless at the same time, *American Saturday Night* rejects the anxious escapism and dark undercurrents of actually existing country, pop, and rock convention. As it strives to touch every human being in a nation Paisley knows is less unified and forward-looking than he pretends, the farthest it deviates from message is two breakup songs of uncommon tenderness and dignity. There's not a bum track on it—unless you're one of those sophisticates who's too good for tunes more memorable than striking, lyrics that parse, pitch-corrected vocal harmonies, waveform compression, and strawberry ice cream.

Serving up an enjoyably crafted, commercially successful album in the warm months of every odd year, Brad Paisley has tasted fine to me since 1999, when I admired how confidently he opened for Loretta Lynn at Town Hall. A twenty-six-year-old newcomer riding a good little debut few in Manhattan knew existed, he seemed more at home than she did. But I never expected he'd headline Madison Square Garden a decade later. As happens in Nashville, the hits that kept on coming were soon indistinguishable from genre exercises. Beyond the funny stuff—great in "Me Neither," where he disavows a series of lame pickup lines as each is shot down, not so great in "Celebrity," where he lobs paintballs at a reality-show jerkola—what stood out most was his guitar, which got a showcase instrumental every time out. Genre exercises work fine in the country market as such, where "repository of tradition" is part of the job description. But the typical American music consumer expects forceful identities from its standard-bearers, and that goes double for dudes from the sticks.

So although Paisley was my favorite young male country artist, I pigeonholed him as a likable pro, thought of him seldom, and didn't notice when he got married in 2003. From the perspective of *American Saturday Night*, however, the marriage was a turning point. According to publicity myth, which I'm happy to believe, New York–born actress Kimberly Williams appeared to the young West Virginian as in a dream way back in 1995, when he went to see *Father of the Bride II* in the vain hope that he'd run into his high school sweetheart and was entranced by Williams's portrayal of the bride. After obsessing for a good long dry spell, during which he gathered material for songs like "Me Neither," Paisley invited Williams to co-star in the 2002 "I'm Gonna Miss Her" video, where the girl demands that Paisley choose between fishing and her and he chooses fishing. In the real America, however, he got both—far from giving up fishing after he tied the knot, he took the missis camping. The couple split their life between a farm near Nashville and a house in Malibu. They have two sons, the oldest born in 2007 and christened William Huckleberry—Huck for short.

Those nauseated by meet-cute stories should rest assured that a political angle is coming, one that culminated in Paisley entertaining an Obama soiree with bluegrass progressive Allison Krauss, his duet partner on the atypically tragic 2004 "Whiskey Lullabye," and Charley Pride, country music's only African-American star ever. (Paisley's Twitter response to the invite: "Sure we'll play? What time? Now where's your house again? 1600 Pennsylvania? Got it . . . do you have a p.a.? What about food?") Politics got me started on this album—the lead track, which only begins celebrating the ongoing mongrelization of America with the lines I quoted, and then "Welcome to the Future," inspired by Barack Obama's victory and going out on a cross-burning tale in which a high school football star tries to date the homecoming queen. But the politics that kept me going were sexual politics, which proceed from a marriage that helped him put the genre exercise behind.

That Paisley is remarkable among country stars for writing his own songs doesn't mean they're autobiographical. For one thing, he almost invariably collaborates, usually with buddies he's known since winning an ASCAP fellowship to Belmont University in Nashville. Paisley's 1999 breakthrough "He Didn't Have to Be," for instance, is based on Kelley Lovelace's experience as a stepfather, not either man's experience as a stepson. But don't think Paisley was just making nice when he promoted the artistic benefits of marriage to, well, *Good Housekeeping*: "Before, I had nothing to write about but failed relationships and life on the road. Now, I feel emotions more deeply in every sense."

There have always been country guys women swoon for—like Garth Brooks, paunch and all. And in a time when bad-ass macho powered Nashville new jacks like Montgomery Gentry and Toby Keith, Paisley's romantic come-ons had an appealing self-deprecation about them. But 2005's *Mud on the Tires* delivered something stronger: "Waitin' on a Woman," a song about how long they spend getting dressed, gender-based mortality rates, and if you stretch some the elusiveness of the female orgasm. Since then, Paisley has made the woman-friendly a mission—in a narrative voice more definitively his own.

That voice emerged on the two lookbacks at his naive youth that anchored 2007's *5th Gear*: "All I Wanted Was a Car," which does its partying with a fiddle and sets up "Letter to Me," where an older and wiser Brad assures his teenage self that the bad stuff is temporary, though he really should learn Spanish and give Aunt Rita some extra hugs. Both songs promised domestic satisfactions that included an SUV in the driveway. Deeper in came "If Love Was a Plane," about an American divorce rate Paisley reckons at sixty percent, and "It Did," about the ongoing perfection of love. Even the broad-jumping punch line of "Ticks"—"I'd like to walk you / Through a field of wild flowers / And I'd like to check you for ticks"—is more the kind of thing a husband murmurs to his wife on a fishing trip than a practical way for a singles-bar jerkola to get a butterfly tattoo into his vehicle.

5th Gear is the work of a master craftsman inspired to think about the shape of his life. Among its genre pieces are several born B sides and a soppy love duet with Carrie Underwood. But it establishes the foundation of a forceful identity. *American Saturday Night*'s politics help flesh out that identity, but an even bigger breakthrough is a maturing craftsmanship that's learned how to address familiar themes in unfamiliar ways. If the breakup tales don't suit his happily married persona, their calm, loving substratum does. The marriage proposal "I Hope That's Me" knows it's him, promising the kindness already in place; "You Do the Math" works the same for sex. There's a lookback that mourns a grandpa as it fulfills Paisley's one-Christian-track-per-album quota, and another that looks ahead to Huck's mistakes. The boys'-day-out rumpus "Catch All the Fish" is counterbalanced by the almost metaphysical "Water." And then there are the three feminist songs.

Ideologues, cynics, and disappointed office seekers may balk at this characterization, especially as regards "Then." Its narrative hooked to the endlessly evolving refrain "I thought I loved you then," the album's first single updates "It Did." My wife Carola and I, together thirty years longer than Brad and Kimberly, had had a bad day when Paisley played the Garden October 21, but not with each other, and as he topped the show off by explaining how now he loved his spouse even more, we gripped each other's arms like teenagers in love. Avers Ms. Dibbell: "He notices all the things about marriage women are always complaining men don't notice." Given how many hits Paisley has, we forgave the omission of "She's Her Own Woman," a theme only strengthened by its unbraggadocious "and she's mine." But Carola was disappointed when the concert went out on Don Henley's "The Boys of Summer" instead of brandishing "The Pants," the subject of which is who wears them: "In the top drawer of her dresser there's some panties / Go try on that purple pair with the lacy frill / With your big old thighs I bet you can't get in 'em / With that attitude of yours, hell, I bet you never will."

Complete with the rowdy male choral farewell "You wear the pants / Buddy good for you / We're so impressed / Whoop-de-doo," "The Pants" is a typically sidelong gambit from an artist who knows how to sell simple truths to a resistant audience—a master of the catchy chorus, the phrase ratcheted up a notch, the joke only a Tea Party jerkola could resent. And though that's easier with marriage songs, those soppy country staples that sometimes come as well-honed as Loretta Lynn's "One's on the Way" or Garth Brooks's "Unanswered Prayers," no country artist has ever been sharper about what connubial bliss entails. In part because it's untainted by the dread sentimentality and in part because it comes less naturally, the political stuff gets ink, as when Paisley got to tell the *Los Angeles Times*: "You can name the reasons why you feel America is the greatest country in the world, but the fact of the matter is that pretty much anything you name, aside from American Indian customs, was not indigenous—it was brought here." Note, however, that the title track of Tim McGraw's new *Southern Voice* is in-your-face biracial, that Toby Keith's new *American Ride* highlights a heartbroken tribute to his departed African-American buddy Wayman Tisdale—and that both trend-spotters, avowed Democrats unlike the "staunchly moderate" Paisley, purveyed jingoistic trash post-9/11. I say Paisley's sidelong pro-Obama songs proceed from a less opportunistic place, and that that place owes his particular marriage big-time.

It's not just that Kimberly Williams donated the max to Obama, but that this New Yorker was the woman a clear-eyed, fair-minded dude from the sticks wanted to share his life with—and even more important, helped turn that life into an American dream come true, a dream the marriage embodies and signifies. Paisley isn't pie-eyed. He tells the world that if love was a plane no one would get on; he even took marital counseling with his prospective bride. Yet by some grace of upbringing, good sense, and body chemistry, success has only intensified an optimism that preceded and enabled it. The dark and the anxious seem foreign to him, yet he's never smug—he's so self-deprecating, so funny. I've watched too many kids grow up to think all their lives turn out like "Letter to Me." But Paisley evinces so much more reach and imagination than the hard-ass thrice-removed of roots-rock convention. I love Johnny Cash. I love the Drive-By Truckers. But right now, as a decent, intellectually gifted chief executive struggles to keep hope alive, I love and need Brad Paisley even more.

The Madison Square Garden show was a two-hour knockout—even when Paisley was catching his breath and making jokes, he never stopped extracting riffs from his guitar, like Jimi Hendrix at the dinner table. But the top balconies were empty, and although "Welcome to the Future" went number ten country—doubly remarkable given its intrepidly multicultural video—its sales didn't approach those of "Then." Like Paisley's nine previous singles, "Then" went No. 1, a record. Admittedly, Paisley shares that record with the anodyne likes of Alabama and Ronnie Milsap. But if us sophisticates don't figure out that optimism isn't always anodyne, this nation will never be as unified and forward-looking as we supposedly want—and hope.

Smart and Smarter

Vampire Weekend

The nonsense about Vampire Weekend being in any definitive way "African" has dispersed somewhat with the release of their second album, *Contra*. And though they still offend the usual gaggle of indie purists, it's worth emphasizing that Vampire Weekend's indie ties are more structural than cultural— they chose the clubs-and-blogosphere route because the demo-and-a&r route was closed to art-band traffic years ago. The source of contention that remains is class—the four Columbia graduates' access to privilege and, supposedly, their celebration of privilege.

Class is America's nastiest secret, always worth raising in pop. But the concept is at its most slippery in the U-S-of-A, where economic power has long been wielded by an ever-changing alliance of the wealthy and the well-born. Although indeed Ivy Leaguers, another vexed concept, the members of Vampire Weekend come from backgrounds that are managerial if that. Bassist Chris Baio's parents are lawyers, although his dad was a child actor and he's related to '80s teenthrob Scott Baio. Drummer Chris Tomson's father is an engineer. Having escaped Iran shortly after the ayatollahs took over, keyboard maestro Rostam Batmanglij's mother Najmieh is a major Persian cooking expert, his father Mohammed a publisher of books on Iran who donated to Howard Dean in 2004. Frontman, wordsmith, cutie-pie, and scholarship boy Ezra Koenig is the son of a set designer and an academic. This is all still privilege. But it's no closer to ruling-class power than it is to the affluence of the average American geekboy who gets to insult music he resents online.

I initially ignored the ill-informed sniping at Vampire Weekend's supposed Afro-appropriations by slotting them as a fine little pop band and leaving it at that. What I didn't get at first—what you often don't get with pop bands until their light touch endures—was how fine. My epiphany came one sunny afternoon last summer, playing their debut on a whim as I drove a rented compact to a state beach east of New Haven with my wife and daughter. There was the boyish, educated Koenig delivering the album's enigmatic first verse—which cites, let me point out, not just a mansard roof but garbage and concrete. After a repeat, a non-African guitar figure strummed hard over Tomson's marchlike clatter raised the emotional ante, and then an ahistorical verse about some Argentine-with-a-long-I sea battle adduced imperialism and the insubstantiality of all things before livelying all things up with the same strum-and-clatter.

As knottier songs that were still catchy and bright followed, I got slightly lit. Hell of a summer record, I thought and soon exclaimed, and my family said amen. The overall effect recalled the Beach Boys or B-52's—not quite as tuneful, but also not nostalgic the way tuneful indie-pop can be. Celebratory, absolutely. But of what privilege? Budget Rent a Car? Hammonasset State Park? Maybe just not working on a sunny weekday. Or maybe the privilege, and thrill, of holding apparent incommensurabilities in your mind-body continuum. When education does everything it oughta, it's good for that stuff.

Like most quality follow-ups, *Contra* takes some getting used to. It's less sparkly than *Vampire Weekend*, and less frothy; the slow one that grows on you at the end is preceded by a long one that remains rather long. But when the band greeted 3,000-plus fans at a sold-out United Palace Theater January 17 with two new ones, the Afroriff-introed "White Sky" and the upful trifle "Holiday," these were cheered no less wildly than "Mansard Roof" and "Walcott" at the encore. Three consecutive tracks at the album's heart conjure a disintegrating romance with someone closer to the ruling class than Koenig while jacking Auto-Tune, Bach and/or Roy Bittan, and the Miami Sound Machine, respectively. "Cousins" is about birthrights and rocks frantic; "Giving Up the Gun" is about guitars and rocks warm calm and collected. With help from its uncontested release date and some minor marketing hanky-pank, *Contra* debuted at No. 1 in the January 30 *Billboard*, an exceedingly rare feat for an independently distributed album. At 124,000, it sold precisely a quarter of what the debut had racked up in a hundred times that long.

The next week, in a typical pattern, Lady Gaga and Susan Boyle regained their rightful places in the cosmos as Spoon's indie album entered at four and vw sank to six with raw sales dipping by two-thirds, somewhat below the statistical mean. So who knows what kind of legs *Contra* will have, what kind of audience it will crystallize. Right now, however, Vampire Weekend signify pretty big. Having declined to squeeze into the jammed club gigs of their ascent and then missed a storm-soaked festival stop last July, I'd never seen the band before the United Palace show, and they were a revelation—

not only did I have a terrific time, most of it on my feet like everyone else, but I found myself scrawling "Jonas Brothers!" in my notebook. The terrific time I'd hoped for even though I'd heard the band could be stiff. But the Jonas Brothers part had never crossed my mind. I half-knew that these were cute guys, but I wasn't ready for the squealing—not the cheers themselves, but their pitch.

Granted, this show, in a northern Manhattan neighborhood across the George Washington Bridge from Bergen County, was a made-to-order date night. In a clean-cut crowd full of the bridge-and-tunnel dabblers indie purists have bad dreams about, the preppy duds the band gets dissed for were a viable style. These were boys you could take home to mom, and they went to a good school too. Not that their talent or ambition is of superstar magnitude. But it separates them big-time from Spoon, Death Cab for Cutie, and the like.

Gossip-boy dope notwithstanding, they can all play, and stiff they're not—two years in the spotlight have generated some committed stagecraft. The warm patter, ace pacing, and energetic jumping around may not be much by Jonas Brothers standards, but it's enough to keep a crowd going, and compared to such club-and-blogosphere strategies as musicianly withdrawal, frenetic rocking, sly role-playing, and tacky extravaganza, Vampire Weekend's outgoing simplicity amounts to a conceptual breakthrough. Also, there's a counterpart in their approach to the undefinable notion of pop itself.

I've named Spoon and Death Cab for Cutie, who along with the Shins are the biggest "pop"-identified indie bands. But indie-rock, while caught up in a prog phase that looks pretty entrenched from here, continues to nurture many devotees of old-fashioned songcraft, most of whom cut retro revivalism with touches of good-natured irony. Sticking to twenty-first-century nonpunks, I'd start by listing Franz Ferdinand, the Arctic Monkeys, Rilo Kiley, Phoenix, Camera Obscura, Girls, Jens Lekman, and my beloved if elderly Wussy. But though Death Cab's mildly emo Ben Gibbard, the Arctic Monkeys' bleakly cheeky Alex Turner, Rilo Kiley's strictly gorgeous Jenny Lewis, and Phoenix's belatedly exuberant Thomas Mars all hold theoretical allure for the casual audience Franz Ferdinand briefly grabbed, Ezra Koenig reaches out far more wholeheartedly. And while several of my nominees are formally adventurous, in no case could that adventurousness be called expansive—it's ingrown, all chords and song structures. Vampire Weekend are different.

The reason is syncretism. As it happens, the kind of cross-cultural re-appropriation that's kicked up so much nonsense around Vampire Weekend is also the process by which, for example, captive Arab girls juiced the harem music of dynastic Egypt, or classically trained Creole sight readers spread jazz, or four Liverpool speed freaks beat Chuck Berry, rockabilly, Tin Pan Alley, and skiffle into a noise rude enough for the Reeperbahn. Historically, syncretism has been the main way pop musics have evolved. I began by dismissing the idea that Vampire Weekend are African, and they're not. But definitely they've grafted tiny elements from all over the place, Africa included, onto a guitar-keyboards-bass-drums pop band. Instead of looking back, they looked around. Their music feels outgoing because that's literally what it is. As Jon Pareles put it in his United Palace rave, they're "relentlessly catchy," recombining borrowed elements "with melodies that hop around wildly but still register as pop (until you try to sing along)."

Not only that, the borrowings are generally unspecific—and well beyond the ken of your average hater when they aren't. For details see Banning Eyre's expert November 2008 Koenig interview at afropop.org. Eyre isn't offended by vw's Africanisms, he's psyched by them—about time is his attitude. Koenig emphasizes that rather than hooky licks, he's drawn to the trebly, undistorted, single-line African guitar sound, a preference he explains as a reaction to grunge. When Eyre congratulates the rhythm section for almost nailing the Congolese groove of what I just labeled "marchlike clatter," Koenig responds that actually "Mansard Roof" motorvates to a speeded-up reggaeton beat. Then he reveals that its strum derives from surf hotshot Dick Dale, and Eyre tells him that the half-Lebanese Dale grew up with Arabic music. Strange are the ways of cultural imperialism.

Rereading the interview, I found myself quite taken with Ezra Koenig. Talking music with an elder who was on his side, he came across not just knowledgeable-yet-curious, eager for the lowdown on Orchestra Super Mazembe and the Washington Heights bachata scene, but exceptionally open and thoughtful in general. He's got what they used to call personality, and by indie standards he's an exceptionally arresting singer—on Rostam Batmanglij's mock-electropop project Discovery and Esau Mwamwaya's alt-syncretizing Afro-Brit fabrication the Very Best, his guest spots pop out of the mix. The Paul Simon comparisons aren't calumnies, but vocally he's much less self-involved and as a correlative more strained—he's trying, hard. He's a little shy, a little sly, sweet and changeable and impulsive, someone who's figured out he's cute without stifling his inner nerd. He's funny sometimes. He's got brains.

For the haters, I suspect that last is the nub. Although Columbia is one of the less exclusive Ivy League locations, college prep has become so insane that the envy runs hotter than it did when I lucked into a Dartmouth scholarship fifty years ago. I get that. But one result of the insanity is that these days there's privilege and intelligence aplenty at pricey places like NYU, where I teach, and Wesleyan, alma mater of the r&b-jacking MGMT, who get none of this guff. Moreover, at every school there's smart and then there's smarter. Koenig is smarter and wouldn't think of stifling it. Of course he threatens plodders and pretenders.

Holding apparent incommensurabilities in your mind-body continuum is a spiritual discipline available to anyone capable of both compassion and pleasure. Prefer T-shirts to Ralph Lauren? Well, you can still buy from sweatshops, and don't be so sure abjuring imports is the path of unalloyed righteousness—the Akron and Beatles Ts whose labels I just checked were both made in Haiti. But for most Americans it seems easier, and more natural, to turn off compassion or pleasure in turn. If there's a balancing process, for most it starts in the mind, and Vampire Weekend's rather good minds set them to sorting out ever more complex incommensurabilities. Keeping the mood playful rather than succumbing to racial embarrassment or fetishizing serotonin malfunction, both familiar indie disorders, Koenig throws up cultural contradictions and leaves it to his listeners to sort them out—or not. Many high squealers let them wash over. Many shallow thinkers take them the wrong way. How Koenig adjusts to these inevitabilities we'll have to wait and see.

And one more thing. There is no music anywhere better at this trick than Afropop, and often without apparent cogitation. One of the blithest-sounding records I know is *Electric Highlife: Sessions from the Bokoor Studios*, where a bunch of obscure Ghanaians, working in an early-'80s period of rampant inflation, sing soulfully but ebulliently about their poverty, their enemies, their faith in God. Their bravery is something to marvel at even if you worry that it's really escapism. There's no way any American pop band could equal it. But try to emulate it? Really, why the hell not?

The Many Reasons
to Love Wussy

Wussy have been the best band in America since they released the first of their five superb albums in 2005, only nobody knows it except me and my friends. I'm oversimplifying, of course. Wussy are a moderately big deal in their unhip Cincinnati hometown, and in part because so many of my friends are rock critics, their 2011 *Strawberry* finished 109th in the 2011 Pazz & Jop Critics' Poll—not bad for a band never once mentioned in *Pitchfork*. (Ever.) Nevertheless, it's a bummer how obscure they are.

When I call Wussy the best band in America, I mean I like or love—no, make that love or really like—just about every one of the forty-six songs on those five albums: *Funeral Dress*, followed by *Left for Dead*, *Wussy*, the unplugged start-to-finish remake *Funeral Dress II*, and *Strawberry*. We're talking Beatles-Stones consistency here. I love the music, always credited to "Wussy"; I love the singing, by frontcouple Chuck Cleaver and Lisa Walker; and I love the lyrics, by one frontperson or occasionally both. I've seen them live 2008, 2009, and 2012 in a 25x100 basement on the Lower East Side called the Cake Shop. All three shows were knockouts, all different; in 2009, after I took my sister along as my date, she dragged her husband to see them in Brooklyn the next night. Commenters on my Expert Witness blog traveled from as far as New Hampshire and Seattle for Wussy's NYC appearance March 3. Yet the 125-capacity venue wasn't quite sold out.

Admittedly, one oddity costs them. Fans know Wussy to be indelible melodists and wouldn't love them if they weren't. Once their songs have sunk in, you can't get enough of them, and not just the refrains—the intros, the verses, the guitar licks, the vocal interpolations, the bass and keyboard parts from attendant muso Mark Messerly. But for reasons I've never figured out, I and others have found that these recognition factors take time to register, and skeptics clearly don't put in the multiple plays. Why should they, you ask? Well, back when I was getting into Wussy's 2005 debut, *Funeral Dress*, now one of my favorite albums of the century, I had many reasons. Cleaver had led the eccentric and excellent country-rockish Ass Ponys till just a few years before. Wussy's lyrics shared with the Ass Ponys' a midwestern particularity in which garbage trucks parade and a ticket to the human-brained horse costs a dime. The guitarists—Messerly sometimes made three—immersed Flying Burrito Brothers twang in Velvet Underground drone. And Lisa Walker had one of those voices.

In an era when the most technically dazzling vocalists rap rather than sing, when *American Idol*'s fetishization of vocal calisthenics has been trumped by *The Voice* and sandbagged by Auto-Tune, when "post-rock" and dance music are preponderantly instrumental and indeed digital, when so much indie favors voices that are automated, anonymous, humongous, genteel, or classically trained, I could write a book. But instead I'll just say that one reason I adore the hard-to-find, basically acoustic *Funeral Dress II*, issued in a Record Store Day run of 500 a year ago, is that it showcases Chuck and Lisa's singing. The songwriting that was paramount in the Ass Ponys wouldn't have signified without Cleaver milking the hick factor in his pitch-challenged falsetto quaver, one of the more capable and unusual deliveries in '90s indie. But Walker's choir-primed instrument is even more remarkable—in part because Cleaver has expunged just enough choir from it.

The fifty-two-year-old Cleaver says the thirty-four-year-old Walker made him a better singer by teaching him not to drift off key—with no loss of idiosyncrasy, he gives the melodies their due. But Walker thinks Cleaver did her just as big a favor by loosening her up—"It's better to sing incorrectly." Fuller than we expect sweet, clear voices to be, sculpted by a midwestern accent that recalls Chrissie Hynde, her soprano has lost whatever angelic purity it once cultivated. There's a tartness to it—homemade lemonade with a big sprig of mint—and partly as a result Wussy's harmonies have an untamed quality. Lisa's still the smooth one and Chuck's still the rough one, but both are the strong ones, and both combine the exalted and the down-to-earth, with the spirituality of his high end exceeding that of her soft side. *Funeral Dress II* highlights such poetics as the agonizing hesitations of the co-written "Don't Leave Just Now," Wussy's one plausible shot at a country hit that could pay their bills, and such sprightly breakup rhymes as this one in "Airborne": "Something from the yours pile / Shattered on the floor tile / And you went off like Frankenstein." But it's the two voices' exceptionally subtle and responsive male-female duets that dominate.

Live over a loud, drone-drenched four-four, the structures are similar but the dynamics are different. Although Cleaver and Walker are conversational and supportive unplugged, onstage the frontcouple's wittingly yet spontaneously unsychronized shouts often make it seem like they're arguing with each other in the same words. The four band albums, whose evolution toward a bigger rock sound underwent a mutation when rumble-drumming Joe Klug replaced Moe Tucker–channeling Dawn Burman on *Strawberry*, achieve all the right syntheses—rock-meets-unplugged, urban-meets-rural, roots-meets-avant— in variants that mix plangent and distorted, plaintive and furious, lyrical and nasty, on and on. Compression is a constant. Of the forty-six songs, thirty-two run between three and four minutes, with seven below and seven above.

Most or all of what I've been describing is formal—the many different musical satisfactions Wussy's rock and roll has a bead on. Although they're aesthetes with an aural gestalt like none other—aesthetes so tolerant of exper- iment they cheerfully countenanced a stillborn remix collection by assorted Cincinnati electronicats—futurists they ain't. Cleaver is a pop polymath who's been selling used records by mail for thirty years, and Walker's onstage chatter at their Cake Club show launched an extended debate regarding Paul McCartney pre- and post-Wings—quintessential boy talk she dominated even though the music under consideration was recorded before she was born. But Wussy are uniquely progressive anyway.

The male-female partnership in American pop goes back to Nelson Eddy and Jeanette MacDonald and before. But the rock tradition is so male that for a long time its few symbolic couples were on the folky side—the Mamas and the Papas, Jefferson Airplane, Fleetwood Mac, the searing Richard & Linda Thompson. This changed materially with the L.A. punk band X, and soon unmatched pairs of husbands and wives shared the spotlight in Am- erindie's longest-running standard bearers: Sonic Youth and Yo La Tengo. Similar units of varying structure and quality followed; the best thing about indie, male-dominated though it remains, is how natural it now seems for women to find a role or call the shots there. Yet even so Wussy's gender equal- ity is pretty much unprecedented. Although Walker's guitar is relatively ves- tigial, she writes and sings half the songs and dominates onstage, rescuing Cleaver from the affectless diffidence with which he failed to put the Ass Ponys across. He's far more forthcoming as a second banana.

The couple band signifies in a social space where indie rockers age just like other humans. When Sonic Youth's Kim Gordon and Thurston Moore split last October, ripples of unease rocked quasi-bohemian bedrooms all across America, and though the band's well-established commitment to aes- thetic distance undercut the surprise factor for me, I hope I never find out how I'd feel if a similar fate befell Yo La's warmer Ira Kaplan and Georgia Hubley. With Wussy, however, identification has never been a big issue for me. It's almost as if male-female is another aspect of their principled formal balance, so far from the older bands' sprawl.

Anyway, beyond the records themselves there wasn't much information to identify with until 2009, when *Cincinnati Magazine* published a Jason Cohen profile outlining a romance so conflict-ridden that Walker disappeared with a guy from Chicago for a while. But the lyrics certainly made you wonder. As you'd figure from the titles, *Funeral Dress* and *Left for Dead* are steeped in mortality and religious disquiet. But *Funeral Dress* begins and ends with three breakup breakdowns—the co-written "Airborne" up front, "Don't Leave Just Now" plus Cleaver's bereftly obsessed "Yellow Cotton Dress" to close—and there are plenty of others; the only glimpses of possibility come in a few Walker songs with the grace to envision a future. And *Wussy* and *Strawberry*, albums three and four, are all breakup all the time—even on *Strawberry*'s catchy Cleaver dirge "Grand Champion Steer," which after capturing the underlying sadness of state fairs extends the metaphor with a flat "the affair was so god-damned obvious," or Walker's intricate "Magnolia," which intimates other dissolutions as it describes the air-crash death of Lynyrd Skynyrd's Cassie Gaines in eighteen loving lines. It is a truth universally acknowledged that unhappy love makes better song fodder than the happy kind. But this seemed a little much.

Nowhere near enough, however, to put my wife and I off the best band in America. March 3 was a Saturday. Wussy had played in Cleveland and slept in Youngstown Friday before driving all day to Manhattan so they could perform for fifty minutes and then drive six hundred miles back to their day jobs. Between 6:30 and 8:00, however, Chuck Cleaver and Lisa Walker were enjoying Sichuan takeout, drinking tap water, and finishing each other's sentences in our dining room. Hefty and tattooed, Cleaver is grizzled and hirsute enough to have once gotten rousted from his hotel lobby till he could prove he was a guest. His father was an irreligious factory worker in a small southwest Ohio town whose musical tastes somehow ran toward Manu Dibango. Supple and tattooed, Walker favors dark eye makeup and attracts her share of panting fanboys. She's a doctor's daughter from northern Indiana and graduated from a Christian college there. Both are divorced, with Cleaver awaiting his third grandchild. Cleaver works as a stonemason, although his chiropractor thinks he should quit before it's too late; Walker waits tables at a vegan-friendly hot spot in the bohemian enclave of Northside. There both reside—just a few blocks apart.

So Wussy is a couple band no more—or rather, only formally. Describing their former love life, Cleaver slotted himself as the female, sensitive one, while Walker told us she'd been diagnosed as mildly autistic, so that her "emotions are hard to read." She has a boyfriend who's helping her get her teeth fixed; Cleaver is paying that chiropractor sans health insurance and has committed to Weight Watchers in an effort to "preserve the temple." But they love how they interact musically and regard each other, both said, as "best friends." An unlikely-seeming denouement, yet as they finished each other's sentences they were making an impressive, moving go of it. At the Cake Shop they would cram a set curtailed by a late-booked private party with songs from the two breakup albums, sometimes switching sex roles as they traded miserable lyrics through a guitar roar that keeps getting bigger and is now augmented by former Ass Pony John Erhardt on steel. The music felt cleansing in addition to everything else—the roar doesn't deny what the lyrics mean, but it does affirm that the pair have found something worth living for on the other side of the misery. That something is art. A critic friend who'd caught them five times said he'd never seen them better. My brother-in-law, a lawyer who moonlights on jazz trumpet, was also there. "I loved them," he told me.

It's been said before, but it bears repeating, and Jason Cohen put it perfectly in "The Ballad of Chuck and Lisa": "Playing rock and roll is just like playing jazz or writing poetry, except with way fewer grants and teaching jobs." Wussy have yet to sell fifteen thousand albums in a career now finishing its seventh year, and its members are pretty poor: Messerly, divorced with kids, teaches special ed, and Klug, the roar's engine, tends bar and works construction. Their records are most readily available from their label—Shake It, based in the totemic Northside record shop of the same name—in part because distribution costs cut so deeply into profits when a small band takes the conventional route, and they've only truly toured once up till now. But in 2012 they're determined to hit the road and get over the hump. If you see their name on a bill within driving distance, check them out and buy some merch. Bring your friends, even. Wussy can't go on forever without you, and they deserve to.

Barnes & Noble Review, 2012

Hearing Her Pain

Fiona Apple

As the synthesizer displaced the electric guitar over the past two decades, there was a parallel development in acoustic music: the folkie ingenue strumming nylon strings gave way to the pop polymath tickling ivorine keys. All in their early thirties, the four major successes in a line traceable to Laura Nyro are Regina Spektor, Nellie McKay, Norah Jones, and Fiona Apple. The first two are obviously minor leaguers compared to Jones and her mega-platinum 2002 *Come Away with Me* or topic-at-hand Apple, who released the most acclaimed album of 2012 in June. But all are songful New York–identified originals with a fanbase, and only McKay, whose 2010 *Home Sweet Mobile Home* gestured futilely at middlebrow convention after four quirky-to-kooky keepers, is without a current release. Apple and McKay have Broadway roots, Russia-born Spektor was a classical prodigy, and Jones studied jazz piano in college. None has more than a peripheral relationship to rock and roll as it's normally conceived, and only Jones, whose fondness for country music surfaced with a spooky Hank Williams cover back when, has shown any interest in all the folkish musics on life support gathered under the rubric of Americana.

Ragtime piano did as much to transform twentieth-century pop as blues guitar, but the piano these women care about is the one in the parlor rather than the barrelhouse, its discipline harmonic rather than rhythmic. Thus they often come up short on groove even when they hire out their production, as Spektor and Apple have, to Dr. Dre graduate Mike Elizondo. The upside is their melodic facility. In an era when the indelible tune is the province of r&b hit-paraders, Nashville neo-to-pseudo-traditionalists, and old-timers who trust the mettle of blues-based forms that will never dominate pop again, all these piano players have shown a knack for writing songs that are pleasurable up front and intelligent long term.

Granted, I continue to find Jones too subtle even if or because she's the nicest person ever to go double-decaplatinum, and after half a dozen tries can neither confirm nor deny credible rumors that her quiet . . . *Little*

Broken Hearts vents the anger to which I'm sure she's entitled. Although McKay is an animal rights crank, which is to say not my type, she's also a stand-up comedian, which is to say besame mucho—a spunky, sprightly eccentric who has a history of stirring things up just because she can. Although spunky and sprightly right up to her new *What We Saw from the Cheap Seats*, Spektor is such a committed humanist that should her pop career flounder you can imagine her touring senior residences, where the ones about returning the oldie's wallet and masterpieces imprisoned in their own timelessness would win her a quick callback. Which leaves us with our topic at hand, who is certainly the most brilliant of these very talented women and almost as certainly the hardest to like.

This is not to suggest she's hard to fall in love with. Fiona Apple has had femme fatale written all over her since she debuted in 1996 at eighteen with the determinedly bathetic *Tidal*, which—in a now-vanished record-biz epoch brimming with dreams of precious metal and aesthetically complicated celebrity—went triple platinum behind a Grammy-winning single about doing a good man wrong and a video featuring a teenager in her underwear. Having beaten her three competitors to the post by five years, however, Apple has since been outdistanced by all of them: *The Idler Wheel* (we'll get to the full title later) is only her fourth album, and comes seven years after *Extraordinary Machine*. How this could be is indicated by the recording history of *Extraordinary Machine*, in which—with the aforementioned epoch on its last legs—Apple rejected the orchestrated iteration produced by the estimable Jon Brion and insisted on re-recording with the estimable Elizondo. Some prefer one version, some the other; they're different, sure, but since this is her shapeliest set of songs either way, few find the differential as stark as Apple does. She's a diva, a perfectionist, a pain in the ass. And this determines the kind of respect she gets—as a musician, and as a star in whom listeners invest their fantasies and ambitions.

The music is why we're here. Vocally Apple has more size and texture and character and drama than her fellow piano women. Her melodies and arrangements are always forceful and never predictable. The fascination she exerts, however, extends well beyond these aesthetic niceties and doesn't necessarily begin with them. Post-MTV, you'd figure all these women must work harder at their looks than Laura Nyro. But where the blonde McKay and brunette Jones are prom-queen pretty and the curly-headed Spektor retains some homegirl, Apple has always been an exotic, her enormous eyes depthless and her oval face evolving from knowing gamine to sultry analysand as the years piled on their pain. For her many female admirers, her beauty is presumably ancillary—when Jessica Hopper calls Apple "the martyr-saint, crucifying herself so that we might live drama-free," she's praising a soul sister who exposes sides of herself Hopper herself has chosen not to indulge. With men, however, the attraction has often seemed more fraught—imbued with a sexually charged preference for intensity over reliability, sparked by the kind of let-me-take-you-away-from-all-this fantasy men know in their hearts is doomed and secretly prefer that way. One achievement of *The Idler Wheel* is that it's quashed such fantasies. No longer is she seen as a tortured beauty. In 2012 she's strictly a tortured artist.

This is progress, no doubt about it. But I don't know how an emotionally engaged male heterosexual Fiona fan could have conceptualized her any way but romantically. There are thirty-three songs total on *Tidal*, the 2001 album with the ninety-word title known as *When the Pawn*, and the two versions of *Extraordinary Machine*. *Tidal*'s typically disconsolate "Sullen Girl" ponders depression per se, *Extraordinary Machine*'s startlingly cheerful "Waltz" begins "If you don't have a song to sing / You're OK," and every one of the thirty-one others obsesses on disconnects with men. For her first decade, then, Apple's "crippling doubt" and "mirror-upon-mirror confessionalism," "her pains, her insecurities," "her neuroses," her "icky little feelings," "her emotions . . . too messy for the relatively staid language of most pop music"—to cherry-pick *The Idler Wheel*'s raft of raves—all had the secret word "romantic" attached. She spent three albums elaborating her own dialect of pop music's lingua franca. In principle, love songs are OK with me, although I prefer a broader emotional palette than Apple's and have often noted that happy ones are harder to get right. But there are other things to write about, and I don't just mean partying hearty and returning people's wallets. Friendship, for instance. Mortality. Your mother. God and so forth. The pit bull you took in off the street. The little club you play occasionally. Let's face it, politics. Hell, even art as such. You can have messy emotions about any of these things.

That the three albums share a lingua franca doesn't mean they're interchangeable. The bestselling *Tidal* is sodden juvenilia, *When the Pawn* deep and dark and palpably disturbed, *Extraordinary Machine* a stab at sociable sanity—Elizondo was clearly brought in to smooth out the songs, not hype up the beats. And on *The Idler Wheel* Apple has definitely gotten on top of her disconnects—verbally, anyway. She spends less time blaming the guy or lacerating herself. The "companion" of the lead "Every Single Night" is explicitly her own "brain" even if that companion percolates heat in her belly, and "Daredevil" right after looks askance at her own risk-taking. But

"Daredevil" also addresses a presumably male other, and so it goes once again: every song after the first is about love lost, failed, or otherwise flawed. Midway through comes the oft-quoted theme statement "How can I ask anyone to love me / When all I do is beg to be left alone," and I can just imagine horny fantasists thinking, If she's going to put it that way, maybe I really should settle for Jennifer down the hall. It's a game-changing line with several parallels on *The Idler Wheel*, which is longer on the kindness and self-knowledge barely glimpsed in Apple's younger songs: "Valentine" with its "I root for you"; "Jonathan" with its "I like watching you live"; "Werewolf," where she admits flaunting the smell of blood; "Anything We Want," where she imagines a consummation. Also noteworthy is a finale called "Hot Knife." Many have observed that the entire song is a crude, eccentric sexual metaphor. No one has indicated when Apple has been so pro-sex before, because she hasn't.

My close readings constitute a scoop of sorts—the huzzahs for Apple's "self-conscious self-absorption and gritty self-loathing" rarely mention countervailing tendencies. One reason is probably that, however much Apple's tortured image is valued for enhancing her blessed artistic integrity, nobody truly believes she's much of a lyricist. That full title: *The Idler Wheel Is Wiser Than the Driver of the Screw and Whipping Cords Will Serve You More Than Ropes Will Ever Do*. To find out what an idler wheel is, read some other review, or Google it. I'll merely point out that "the driver of the screw" is otherwise known as a screwdriver and that most English speakers would just say "ropes ever will." Only then it wouldn't scan, or rhyme, that stuff. Apple does this sort of thing a lot—horrible lines like "Adagio breezes fill my skin with sudden red" or "Whose reality I knew, was a hopeless to be had" or "And last night's phrases / Sick with lack of basis." *The Idler Wheel* improves on this tendency. Because silly is good, I even kind of like the "orotund mutt" / "moribund slut" rhyme others mock, although not the "white doves' feathers"–"hot piss" metaphor others find scintillating—much less its next line: "Every time you address me." ("Address"? Really? Who talks like that?) But remember—lyrics aren't why we're here. Music is.

This is not a hooky album. Even compared to the earlier work it's not a hooky album. If like me you're skeptical about Fiona Apple in particular and pop avant-gardism in general, you could play it four or five times without hearing a single song whole. If you're like me, however, by then you'd admire how decisively producer-drummer Charley Drayton's junkyard percussion colors this music while deploying Apple's piano, sonically and rhythmically, including several boogie-woogie figures. And soon thereafter, if you're like me, the whole thing will come together in a whoosh—the kind of formally risky pop that, when it happens to work, provides pleasures almost as bracing and enduring as "Over the Rainbow," "She Loves You," or "I Want It That Way."

Because it's jagged on top and melodically facile deep underneath, the music too discourages vicarious romanticism. It impels any interested bystander to hear Fiona Apple as a tortured artist rather than somebody to love. Yet as a pop polymath whose artistic integrity works hidden variations on teen ballad and Broadway heartsong, maybe she's finally become so accomplished that she's less tortured than she and everyone else thinks—on her way to more lovable, even. No matter how much she begs to be left alone, maybe the respect she's clearly earned means she deserves what she can't stop begging for, else she'd be writing songs about God and her pit bull. I mean somebody to love. Just not anyone I know, please. Because speculate as we might, one thing is certain: Fiona Apple is always going to be a pain in the ass.

Barnes & Noble Review, 2012

Firestarter

Miranda Lambert

On September 30, Texas-raised, Oklahoma-based, Nashville-conquering Miranda Lambert launched her second headlining road trip of 2010. Dubbed the Revolution Tour to distinguish it from the Roadside Bars & Pink Guitars Tour, it kicked off in, of all places, Manhattan, at, of all places, Terminal 5, a 3,000-capacity stand-up rock venue that two nights before presented Ratatat and two nights later presented Soulive. Eric Church got the night rolling with a guitar-driven half hour he climaxed by revving his minor country hit "Smoke a Little Smoke" into a rocking showstopper that ended "Then I'll maybe break out that old rock and roll / Drink a little drink, smoke a little smoke." "Old rock and roll." Not country. Get it?

Although she was leading her own bar band before she left high school, the twenty-six-year-old Lambert got her break finishing third behind Buddy

Jewell (???) in 2003's inaugural "Nashville Star" competition. All three of her albums—2005's *Kerosene*, 2007's *Crazy Ex-Girlfriend* and 2009's *Revolution*—debuted No. 1 on the country charts. Her nine 2010 CMA nominations are the most ever awarded a female artist. Yet it took her forever to convince country radio. Not till 2008 did she score a top ten country single, and she didn't go No. 1 until *Revolution*'s "White Liar" and "The House That Built Me." She's just never been very Nashville. Early on she regularly praised the kind of tough-minded semi-folkies her songwriting cop-turned-P.I. dad always played her—Guy Clark and John Prine, Allison Moorer and Emmylou Harris—while distancing herself from "pop country" artists she diplomatically failed to name. She wrote her own songs and played her own guitar. Like the Dixie Chicks' Natalie Maines, another role model, she wasn't ready to make nice.

Lambert's CMA coup establishes that she's moved on. To an extent it rewards sheer talent—country radio seems less make-or-break when your albums debut No. 1 without it. But it also rewards both her maturation and her willingness to compromise. Are you a big Blake Shelton fan? Actually, no—but he's destined to become your fiance anyway. Is Carrie Underwood "pop country"? Maybe, but she's also a nice gal you've bonded with at backstage get-togethers. Is "The House That Built Me" a Music Row heart-tugger that doesn't represent the life experience of a hard-riding pro who's written heartfelt songs about the upside of leaving home? Doesn't matter, not with every word and note so well-chosen that half the women at Terminal 5 will sing it a cappella if you give them the chance.

With most artists coming off their third and biggest album, these would be ominous signs. But with Lambert they're more like course corrections. Due to its pyromaniac title song, which with its fierce beat and snarly vocal was taken more literally than its "Light 'em up and watch them burn" lyric warranted, *Kerosene* created more stir in New York than Nashville, and far from letting up, *Crazy Ex-Girlfriend* was fiercer: as angry as one of those stupid anti-A-Rab albums that preceded our unfortunate Iraq adventure. In the lead track Lambert shoots up a boyfriend who'd beaten her down; the crazy ex of the title song sanely leaves her pistol in the car. But the likes of "Desperation," "More Like Her," and the conflicted "Guilty in Here" offset hot-bloodedness with self-doubt. It's as consistent as it is feisty.

Still, *Crazy Ex-Girlfriend* was too feisty for Nashville—I've read three reviews of *Revolution* that congratulate Lambert for putting what they all call "bluster" behind her. This is their way of praising God that, like any self-respecting country album, *Revolution* has soft spots. I don't mean the pitch-perfect "House That Built Me"—I'm talking fuzzballs like "Virginia Bluebell," "Makin' Plans" and, worst of all, "Love Song," a strained attempt by Lambert, Shelton, and the yeomen of Lady Antebellum to snatch some of the marital wisdom Brad Paisley keeps in his back pocket. But those gestures give Lambert room for the two twistiest songs she's yet recorded: the multivalent extended metaphor "Me and Your Cigarettes" followed by the barely two-minute "Maintain the Pain," which puts a bullet in Lambert's car radio only after establishing an arrangement that, from big strings to bigger drums to arpeggiated guitar hook, is country only because the CMA says so.

It took a major songwriter to come up with those. But Lambert loves songs so much she'd as soon interpret somebody else's. Her sharp twang isn't as nuanced as it will be. But she sure does sniff out great material—her daddy taught her well—and make it her own, from Nashville quality brands like Patty Griffin and Julie Miller to folkies-and-proud like Fred Eaglesmith and John Prine. The covers kept on coming at Terminal 5. "Time to Get a Gun" was there—Lambert is very Second Amendment—and Prine's hard-rollicking "That's the Way That the World Goes Round" came 'round as a forcebeat barnburner getting the crowd in the mood for the climactic "Gunpowder & Lead." But mostly Lambert revived new stuff: Steve Earle's "The Revolution Starts Now" as a lead-in, the Blasters' Hank Williams tribute "Long White Cadillac," and the pre-climactic "Rock & Roll Hoochie Koo," once a flag-waver for her Texas homeboy Johnny Winter. And in a concert that skipped past "Me and Your Cigarettes" and "Guilty in Here," she devoted her encore to two turf claims: Merle Haggard's "Misery and Gin" for authentic country, and one called "Call Me the Breeze," ID'd as a Johnny Cash song though it was written by Lambert's Oklahoma homeboy J. J. Cale and made famous by a Jacksonville band called Lynyrd Skynyrd. That's the "old rock and roll" Miranda Lambert is targeting as she tours America with the CMA shindig approaching. She's country all right.

And that ain't all. Although Lambert's a good-looking blonde with killer dimples, she's not skinny or even lissome. She's a little chunky; she's got some thighs on her and puts them out there. Sometimes she dresses country. At Terminal 5, she wore a short black dress and high black heels that somewhere in there got kicked off so she could better prance around to John Prine or Johnny Winter or maybe even the loud two-step her "ass-kickin' group" made of "Airstream Song." Rock 'n' roll hoochie koo. She's got the CMA no matter how many firsts she wins. Now she's thinking about conquering the world.

MSN Music, 2010

Monster Anthems

Lady Gaga

Even if you've never seen Lady Gaga on the small screen or listened consciously to a minute of her music, you've probably gathered that she isn't just, well, Britney Spears. Nor is she Katy Perry, Miley Cyrus, Rihanna, Beyoncé, or Christina Aguilera. All these artists differ markedly in content, persona, attitude, and musical worth. But they all have more in common with each other than they do with Lady Gaga. And that's because they're all celebrities.

Obviously I'm playin' with ya here. Lady Gaga, whose *Born This Way* recently sold more copies in its first week than any album since 2005, is also a celebrity—by many accounts the biggest in the world. In *Forbes*'s 2011 "Celebrity 100," in fact, she and her supposed $90 million income surpassed Oprah and her supposed $290 million income "because of her social media power." But of course the *Forbes* list is no less arbitrary and mind-numbing than any of the other Best/Worst/Hottest/Scuzziest/Greediest/Intriguingest countdowns with which massive media compete for stunted brain-space. As a baseball fan who has dabbled in the list business himself and a pop critic who had his life changed when Ellen Willis wrote the gorgeous and prophetic sentence "In the same sense that pop art is about commodities, Dylan's art is about celebrity," I am both appalled and abashed by these developments. The list was boyish fun, celebrity's complexity aesthetic insight. Over the decades, however, the culture industry has had its trivializing way with both.

Defying these odds, Lady Gaga is complex. She's compared to Madonna not because both emerged from dance music but because nobody since Madonna has wielded celebrity so audaciously, a failure of collective nerve for which the pop singer who looked like a movie star is partly to blame. The visualization of music that began with MTV gave us other beauty queens—the still-fine Tina Turner, the then-exquisite Whitney Houston. But as history played out, all the pop dollies named above inhabit the world Madonna made—a world in which female vocalists are obliged to be far more glamorous than the "girl singers" who rose up after the big band bubble popped. However "attractive" they were, Doris Day, Patti Page, Jo Stafford, et al. didn't have to play the sex bomb.

Since you may not have noticed "the girl who never wears pants" declining the sex bomb role, let me quote what a friend-turned-source told one of Gaga's dozen-plus biographers: "Interscope is a long, long road which actually involves a lot of people thinking she's great to have around, but"—here's the money shot—"not pretty enough to be a pop star." Universal Music flagship Interscope is Gaga's label, three tentacles of which have their logos on her first album, and "around" means as a songwriter, in particular for the Pussycat Dolls, Universal's attempt to create a slut group in the sense that Ponzi schemer Lou Pearlman once created boy groups. Her Italian nose too big for her narrow face, Gaga really isn't pretty enough to be a pop star in the world Madonna made. Rarely does a paparazzo catch her sipping Kristal at some restaurant where the doorman has to pass on your shoes. She calls her fans "little monsters" because unlike those other pop stars, she's Other. The most gay-identified major star since Madonna only more so, she doesn't pretend her fans are all normal. Instead, she pretends they're all abnormal.

One reason Willis's idea proved so fungible is that celebrity is such a slippery concept. Take as texts the sixth and seventh tracks on Gaga's debut album. Number six is "Beautiful, Dirty, Rich": "Bang bang / We're beautiful n' dirty rich." Number seven is the title number, "The Fame": "Doin' it for the / Fame / Cuz we wanna live the life of the rich and famous." Both are dance-derived pop songs anchored by synth riffs that lead the ear to the choruses I've quoted (although Gaga's choruses often morph slightly), so that listeners home in on those phrases, which share one word: rich. But both are explicitly fantasy rather than autobiography. Clinching "Beautiful, Dirty, Rich," which Gaga has said was inspired by the posers she hung with in her cocaine period on the Lower East Side, is the insistent tag "But we got no money"; "Fame" is nailed in a final verse that ends, "My teenage dream tonight / Yeah I'm gonna make it this time."

So while Gaga is ready—and as a come-on, eager—to be taken for a Ke$ha-style party animal, she's quick to reverse that impression for anyone who's paying attention. Nor does she conceive celebrity itself conventionally. She's said many times that "fame" is an inner quality anyone can have, particularly her monsters—a quality she had back when she was a big-nosed nobody getting noticed. A year ago she told *Rolling Stone*'s Neil Strauss that she didn't "want to be a celebrity" and argued that she wasn't one cos her monsters cared about her music, clothes, and videos rather than who she was sleeping with. For her, apparently, a celebrity isn't a person whose inner fame has made itself felt in the great outside. It's a person whose fame has escaped her control, so that her inside is no longer her own. Bob Dylan knows what she's talking about.

Were a skeptic to object that Gaga, who plays up her bisexual impulses and rather enjoyed the absurd Internet rumor that she's a hermaphrodite, is an ex-stripper turned sexual provocateur who wants everyone to care about who she's sleeping with, Gaga could reply that the drama she conducts in the public eye is part of her art. Certainly the eye part looms large—few if any pop stars have put so much thought and effort into their visuals. Under her active direction, the Haus of Gaga brain trust devises more new fashion statements than I have the intellectual capacity or gut interest to catalogue. She uses makeup to glorify the unnatural, uglifying or prettifying herself as the occasion demands. The easiest and cheapest way to access her music is via her galaxy of increasingly extravagant videos, easily available on You-Tube though for some reason they've never been collected on DVD.

One even hears it said, in fact, that Gaga's songs are mere occasions for the overdetermined videos and nonstop costumery that are the true loci of her originality. Having first taken her for a dance diva whose album I was obliged to make sense of, I believe this undervalues a lifelong musician whose hook sense and vocal muscle were manifest well before her fame went public. In fact, I'm not a fan of her visuals. Shoulder pads and weaponized brassieres just don't turn me on, sexually or semiotically, and music video's genre-surfing junk surrealism is seldom improved by the kind of money Gaga throws at it, though when I knuckled down and watched some clips I often found them wittier and less grotesque than the stills suggested. Start with "Telephone." Avoid "Judas."

For Gaga and her monsters, of course, grotesque is good. That became all too clear at Madison Square Garden February 22, where my conversion experience was undercut by overkill. The gargantuan sets and painful-looking vinyl/plastic/foil/elastic/rubber/crinoline/lace ensembles, the corny searching-for-the-monster-ball "plot" and cornier "Someday you'll be standing here and I'll be in the bleachers cheering you" lies—in practice these were momentum killers. Barnstorming the arenas, Gaga has poured workaholic effort and profligate capital into the spectacle she believes her monsters crave and deserve. But that's a major reason her music is undervalued.

It's worth remembering that twenty years ago the same guff was talked about Madonna herself, and not just by rockist dinosaurs. Cultural studies wonks out to get tenure for watching television creamed over her videos and declared her music unparsable, irrelevant, or both. Little did they suspect that a decade later Madonna's 1990 best-of, *The Immaculate Collection*, would be remembered as a masterpiece—named by the poptastic *Blender*, in fact, as the greatest American album of all time. Since I consider it pretty nifty myself, I thought it would make a convenient benchmark.

Reaching back to pre-CD times, *The Immaculate Collection* culled fifteen songs from the forty-three relevant ones on six albums that included two soundtracks and spanned seven years, adding two bonus tracks. Madonna had some sort of composer credit on eleven of its selections and was thirty-two when it appeared. Gaga turned twenty-five in March. *Born This Way* is considered her second album because 2009's *The Fame Monster*, although eight songs long like Madonna's debut, counts as an EP. Since *The Fame* appeared in the fall of 2008, she has released thirty-nine relevant songs, with composer credit on every one. That is, Gaga generated about as much music in well under half the time, completing this phase of her recording career at the age Madonna began hers. Quantity isn't quality. But that's certainly worth noting.

For two gay-friendly Italian-American bottle blondes specializing in dance-derived pop, Gaga and Madonna are rather dissimilar musically, even if "Born This Way" does cop its tune from "Express Yourself." Madonna's pop is more pop—it's smoother, calmer. While both women's Eurobeats are remarkably d'void of funk, Gaga's are bigger and broader, because hip-hop and techno have bum-rushed dance music since 1990 and also because she's at root a rock chick—the new album favors an old-fashioned disco thump so unrelenting it shades toward Springsteen and Meat Loaf. Also, her voice is bigger than Madonna's—bigger than that of any rival except Xtina and Beyoncé. Where Madonna has always favored cool, allusive, cannily ambiguous lyrics, Gaga's themes are like her voice—hot and emphatically all over the place.

Lady Gaga is an upper-middle-class NYU dropout who's better educated than Madonna or her rival normals and has been known to brag about how smart she is. But you have to be pretty dumb to expect intellectual coherence from a pop star. Instead you get the spiritual coherence of a relatable celebrity persona. So who is the Lady Gaga you needn't be a monster to enjoy? Impulsive and willing to make mistakes, she uses her big ego and bigger emotions for good—to work herself hard and make waves. She campaigned outspokenly against don't-ask-don't-tell and shovels money to homeless LGBT youth. She never appears in public out of character and she never acts the diva offstage. She spends more on her shows and videos than a shrewd capitalist would. She's funnier than her putative peers, with an absurdist streak that reflects her downtown history. And none of this would mean a thing if she hadn't learned how to deploy her hook sense and vocal muscle in mammoth anthems that began with one called "Just Dance" and never stopped coming.

It would be nice to pretend that all these anthems and the keeper tracks in between firm up our connection to the artist's persona, her "vision." But within certain parameters we don't care. I do hope she doesn't really crave her ex's leather-studded, metal-drumming revenge. But that's "Bad Romance," on a brute level my favorite Gaga song, and rather than going along with it psychologically or ideologically, as a pop fan I'm free to be blown away by her skill, her energy, her extravagance, and her luck. Even back when, the Madonna experience was mellower—an almost Apollonian satisfaction in how she controlled the pleasure spigots.

I've wondered whether it might be possible to compile some sort of *Gaga Bloody Gaga* from Gaga's thirty-nine relevant songs—nothing immaculate, mess is her metier, just equally unfailing and representative. There might be enough songs there—her first two records are stronger than Madonna's were. But that kind of consistent use value can only prove itself over more time than we've had with her. We just don't know yet. If on the one hand *Born This Way* suggests the possibility that workaholism has blurred her distance vision or compromised her quality controls, on the other it could signal that she's more a rock chick than anyone so gay-identified is supposed to be. Which might be cool and even liberating in a way. If anybody can lead a rock and roll revival, it's somebody wielding her celebrity like a scimitar or like a bludgeon, or for that matter like a disco stick.

Barnes & Noble Review, 2011

Dancing on Her Own

Robyn

The Swedish dance thrush Robyn filled the 6,000-capacity Radio City Music Hall February 5 even though her widely praised *Body Talk* album—unlike its shorter and cheaper *Body Talk, Pt. 1* and *Body Talk, Pt. 2* predecessors—

had never cracked the *Billboard* 200. Robyn's Stateside audience ought to be bigger, but in New York she's doing all right, and she gave this sizable crowd an even better show than they gave her. The house was about half gay, which leaves some three thousand celebrants divided into many male-female couples, enough girls-night-out couples and groups, and me proudly surrounded by my sixty-five-year-old wife Carola and my twenty-five-year-old daughter Nina. Nina and I agreed we'd slightly preferred the sweaty August gig she'd put away at the 1,400-capacity Webster Hall. But Carola was happy with exactly what she got—not only a commodious venue but a commodious crowd.

"Somehow she creates such a feeling of acceptance," she told me at breakfast, wearing a hotpack although she'd announced the night before that dancing at her seat for ninety minutes had finally loosened up her back. "Did you notice the large couple just up to our right?" This wasn't the large black couple dancing directly across from us, but the large white couple further forward who turned and sang lyrics to each other at every opportunity (both couples, as it happens, were male-female). "I loved how everybody knew the words. Thousands of people singing 'Now I'll be dancing on my own.' Wow—what does that even mean?"

"Dancing on My Own" is the nearest thing Robyn has had to a "hit" in her current manifestation: No. 3 on *Billboard*'s Hot Dance Club Play chart. This great honor situates her where she currently belongs, in Clubworld—not the alt-rock circuit, but a less arty and somewhat pricier realm descended from disco. Since Nina came along, my knowledge of Clubworld has been based almost entirely on hearsay, reading, and of course listening. Carola and I dance more than most people our age, but at parties, and seldom to what I will designate techno—which equals dance music almost everywhere but America, where it gets major competition from the popper and crunker strains of hip-hop. As I've said many times, dance music is very site-specific. Even disco proper, which produced loads of music I loved, was dependent on sound systems, DJs, and biochemical enhancements inconvenient to duplicate at home. For those partial to lyrics, voices, and melodies, techno is much worse, its uncounted subgenres unparsable despite the occasional killer compilation and the more occasional self-sustaining longform like the Knife's *Silent Shout*.

Robyn has worked with the art-damaged Knife, who are also Swedish and whose subsequent work suggests that the eerie comedy of *Silent Shout* is as pop as they intend to get. But she's also a hip-hop fan, and her commitment to the more pop-friendly techno strain called electro comes from an unarty place—her history as a teenpop queen and, later, a club kid. The daughter of actors whose divorce inspired her first venture into songwriting at eleven, Robyn became a star in Sweden in 1995, when she was sixteen, and had two major American hits in 1997: "Do You Know (What It Takes)" and "Show Me Love." Though Robyn has always been a songwriter—in English, as ABBA taught all Swedes—her breakthroughs were doctored by Stockholm legend Max Martin, who's also had his hand in the Backstreet Boys' "I Want It That Way," Britney Spears's "Oops! . . . I Did It Again," and Katy Perry's "I Kissed a Girl," among many others. There are good songs galore on her teenpop debut *Robyn Is Here*, including plenty she wrote with her usual team, but "Show Me Love" clinches the deal with its sturdy chorus hook: "Show me love, show me life / Baby show me what it's all about." Seriously yet discreetly sexual, not naughty or oopsy, it hints at the sobriety of another Martin contractor, Celine Dion. Be grateful Robyn had other ideas.

First, however, she had to go through the awkward stage that hits teen-pop stars like clockwork. Her 1999 *My Truth* is as strained as you might fear despite the title track's convinced relativism and "Giving You Back"'s reflections on her own abortion, and the minor hits on 2002's likable enough *Don't Stop the Music* pleased no one enough in the end. This is where the burned-out skyrocket either turns into Justin Timberlake or enters rehab. Robyn turned into Justin Timberlake—in her own way, which is the only way, and on a smaller scale, but impressively nonetheless. Beyond JT, in fact, no one has done it better, including my old fave Pink, now proudly pregnant by her squeeze-turned-husband, motocross racer Carey Hart. Robyn has one of those too—Olof Inger, a fiancé she's dated since 2002 who is both a visual artist and a mixed martial artist. (Quality girlpop and extreme sports—separated at birth?).

Timberlake's march on the American entertainment industry brandished his burgeoning musicality, surprising slapstick, and adequate acting ability. Robyn's approach was less ambitious artistically, but also less conventional structurally: to record the music she wanted to record on a label she owned and ran called Konichiwa. Although this took guts for a twenty-five-year-old has-been, how much autonomy Robyn has achieved remains murky because, sanely, she works with a business manager and in America secured distribution—a full ten years after *Robyn Is Here*, her only previous Stateside release—via Cherrytree, a Universal-affiliated semi-independent best known for Lady Gaga, although Robyn got there first.

All these acts specialize in club music whose focus tracks are designed to pulse and warble from radios and shopping-mall in-stores. But for Robyn pop runs deeper than that: "I'm raised in the Swedish tradition of songwriting. If you don't have the songs, you're going to be fucked basically." Her singing, too, reaches for the kind of down-to-earth empathy that signifies for many young listeners well after their adolescence is over—which, as the club-inclined find, by no means brings an end to romantic drama. More than Britney Spears's trashy coo or Christina Aguilera's trained projection, the sincere affect of *Robyn Is Here* presaged straightforward Brits Adele and Duffy, only with quieter soul flourishes and a more boisterous sense of fun. In 2005, the Konichiwa-launching Robyn turned up the fun—pugnaciously so. But irresistible as the chirpy boasts and skanky beats of "Konichiwa Bitches," "Cobrastyle," and "Bum Like You" seem to wise guys like me, it was the addition of the breathy, emotional "With Every Heartbeat" that put Robyn's reincarnation across internationally. And it's the heartsong element that gives *Body Talk*'s faux trilogy its heft and staying power.

In the trilogy, all of which materialized within a six-month span, eighteen songs total repeat (or not) in remixed (or merely re-released) versions over two budget albums and a regular one that offer thirty-one tracks total. Robyn says she chose that route because she wanted the freedom to recharge on tour before finalizing all her new material in the studio; Cherrytree's Martin Kierszynbaum says he hoped to service Clubworld's hotbed of instaneity with the speed website comments demanded. Figure they're both telling the truth and that, as Robyn has said, she won't do it again. But it definitely didn't produce the best of all possible albums. So at Christmas, to amuse my younger friends and educate their parents, I rejiggered the three mini-albums into a mixtape yclept *Robyrt's Robyn* that would have finished top three with me for sure.

My tracklist highlights only her strongest heartsongs and pursues a narrative logic in which the hurting Robyn of "With Every Heartbeat" proceeds from the pugnacious Robyn of "Konichiwa Bitches," in which the compassionate Robyn of "Cry When You Get Older" proceeds from the defiant Robyn of the asterisks-in-original "Don't F***ing Tell Me What to Do." It moves from three Clubworld-specific manifestos to the broken-up, chin-up solitude-as-solidarity anthem "Dancing on My Own" to the story of a love affair that you can glean from the titles: "Get Myself Together," "Hang with Me," "Call Your Girlfriend," "Stars 4-Ever," "Indestructible." Of these the prize is "Call Your Girlfriend," where the pain Robyn is feeling belongs to the ex she's replacing. If "Tell her that the only way her heart will mend / Is when she learns to love again" is kind advice, "Don't you tell her how I give you something that you never even knew you missed" is even kinder. But it's also vain. The woman can write.

After "Cry When You Get Older," in which Robyn counsels the bereft young of both sexes like the big sister she's grown up to be, come five songs in which the pugnacity of the three openers takes on a social dimension, which for a second-generation artist in a putative welfare state seems to come naturally. These climax with "We Dance to the Beat," where the title repeats some sixty times with ever-changing tags: the beat of "silent mutation," "raw talent wasted," "bad kissers clicking teeth," "consolidating assets," "suburbia burning," "an eviction next door," "a billion charges of endorphin," "a love lost and then won back," "source code and conjuring," "gravity giving us a break." As a coda there's a folk song sung sweetly in Swedish, just to remind us where Robin Carlsson comes from and who she's been.

Electro means not just electric but electronic—keyboard beats and tunelets, no guitars, horns, or violins. Konichiwa Robyn's grooves are choppier, her songs full of lists. And except on the folk song, the voice is more babyish than when she was teenpop, often filtered or treated—more Betty Boop than Heidi. So among other things, she's a cartoon, which is fine with her. This is a proud habitue of the same Clubworld outsiders consider inauthentic, amoral, and even post-human—and that she knows to be "a grown-up playground where people just let everything hang out and get stupid drunk." She shares a gleeful duet with a doggish Snoop Dogg and esteems her gay audience because "feeling like an outsider is something that gay culture naturally always had to consider"; she goes out of her way to speak to, as Robyn's "Dream On" specifies, "Thugs and bad men / Punks and lifers / Locked up interns / Pigs and snitches." No one this pugnacious can be much of a pushover or sentimentalist. But for sure she's not inauthentic, amoral, or post-human.

Robyn is a muscular, thick-waisted pixie who couldn't have stood more than five-four in the platform workboots she sported at Radio City. On a scene that adores glamour, she was conspicuously pragmatic, with a band comprising two drummers and two keyboard players and costume changes limited to taking her jacket off; her only accessory was white denim cutoffs split into a skirt that from a distance resembled a T-shirt tied around her blue-and-gray camo bodysuit. Initially I regretted the slight sexualization of the calisthenic dance moves she'd pumped out at Webster Hall. But having giggled at how she first bent from the waist in the classic chorus-girl receiving position and later humped the floor like she had her own penis, I eventually decided I was being a prude about her playful grinds—not so much about sexual display as about what it takes to please an audience she called "the biggest crowd I've ever pulled by myself." We were all together and we were all dancing by ourselves. It was only New York City, the nearest

America gets to Sweden unless Vermont counts. But she had the U.S. audience share she's earned, and every one of us was different.

Barnes & Noble Review, 2011

Three More Pieces
About M.I.A.

1. Spread Out, Reach High: *Kala*

Careerwise, the recent album M.I.A.'s *Kala* recalls is Kanye West's *Late Registration*—an unexpectedly sure-footed follow-up to a brainy beat adept's can-you-top-this debut. And though West is the more universal musician, especially as Americans conceive the universe, both albums challenge sophomore slump by risking pretension. But where West hired classically trained Jon Brion, the Sri Lankan–British rapper spread out and bent down low. Originally she'd hoped to trade the grimy beats of 2005's *Arular* for the more radio-friendly dirt of Timbaland. That plan fizzled, for two reasons— not just the feds' refusal to let M.I.A. re-enter the U.S., but her reluctance to turn into Nelly Furtado once the chance was in her lap.

Plus, though she's polite about it, a sneaking suspicion that maybe Timbo wasn't all that—that there were edgier beatmakers all over the place. With visa madness blockading her new Brooklyn apartment, she turned world traveler, pulling in multiple Indian musics and encompassing Jamaican dancehall moves, Indian-Trinidadian multicontinental mash-up, Liberian vibes, a British-Nigerian rapper, Australian aboriginal hip-hop, Baltimore hip-hop, Jonathan Richman, the Clash, and a bonus afterthought from Timbaland's solo album. Though she claims this record is more personal and less political than *Arular*, that's misleading. The political was all too personal on an album obsessed with her long-lost father, a player in Sri Lanka's terrorist-revolutionary Tamil Tigers. Here, that conflict-ridden relationship is behind her. Star access enables a woman who grew up an impoverished refugee to observe the outcomes of similar histories in immigrant and minority communities worldwide. If you don't think that's political, ask your mama—or hers, who's named Kala.

Arular was about M.I.A.—her ambition, her education, her contradictions, her history of violence. *Kala* is about the brown-skinned Other now obsessing Euro-America—described from the outside by a brown-skinned sympathizer who's an insider for as long as her visa holds up. It opens with the uninvitingly spare "Bamboo Banga," which samples Indian Tamil filmi composer Ilayaraja and bends the lyric of Richman's "Roadrunner" so it celebrates a kid running alongside a Third World tourist's Hummer and banging on its door. "BirdFlu" disses dogging males everywhere—"selfish little roamers"—over another filmi sample and a barely synchronized four-four on some thirty deep-toned urmi drums. Also on "BirdFlu," high kiddie/girlie interjections add a cuteness that's sustained pitchwise on "Boyz," with its video of synchronized Kingston rudies shaking their moneymakers for the Interscope dollar. Only with "Jimmy," a Bollywood disco number a kiddie M.I.A. used to dance to for money at Sri Lankan parties, does a conventional song surface.

You've probably gathered that unlike *Late Registration*, *Kala* is less pop-friendly than its predecessor. It's heavier, noisier, more jagged. Timbaland might conceivably have found a hit for M.I.A.; London-based "dirty house" producer Switch, credited on eight of twelve tracks, will not. The eclectic world-underclass dance amalgam M.I.A. has constructed is an art music whose concept recalls the Clash as much as anything else—the aggression of the early Clash and the reach of the late (who she samples). But soon enough, the music does soften and, occasionally, give up a tune. There's melancholy melodica, Sri Lankan temple horn, the eighteen-year-old rapper Afrikanboy describing his hustles, and several child choruses, notably on "Mango Pickle Down River," where preteens rap about bridges and fridges to rhyme with the didge—didgeridoo—that provides their groaning bass.

But none of these pleasures comes as easy as the high spirits of M.I.A.'s debut album seemed to promise. And in the end, that's why *Kala* strikes deep. There's a resolute sarcasm, a weariness and defiant determination, a sense of pleasure carved out of work—articulated by the lyrics, embodied by the music. A riot of human, musical, and mechanical sounds bubbles underneath these tracks. Not a white riot, that's for sure, and not a dangerous one either—unless you believe every Other wants what you got and has nothing to offer in return. *Kala* proves what bullshit that is. The danger is all the evil fools who aren't convinced.

Rolling Stone, 2007

2. Illygirl Steppin Up

Maya Arulpragasam is a musician who performs as M.I.A. Let's just start there, shall we? Of course she's also a woman, a mother, and a soon-to-be wife. Of course she's also a Sri Lankan, a Londoner, and now an American. She can also claim success in an array of visual callings—painting and video, fashion and design. But these identities wouldn't add up to much were it not for three albums' worth of M.I.A.'s music. The first came out in 2005 and is named for her father, whose cognomen is Arular. The second came out in 2007 and is named for her mother, known simply as Kala. The third is just out and is named for Maya herself.

These name games signify, and in complex ways—even Arulpragasam's idiot detractors rarely deny that she's led a rather eventful life. Not only did she spend a big chunk of her childhood as a Tamil in Sinhalese-ruled Sri Lanka, where twenty-two years of sporadic civil war had taken 65,000 lives by the time *Arular* was released, but she survived a divorce more life-or-death than any suburban malcontent could readily imagine. Her description may read like standard hyperdrama: "My mum is a saint, and my dad is insane. That's exactly what I am—I'm a split personality between my mum and dad. I look at them both, and they hate each other." The difference is that by "insane" Arulpragasam means that her father was in some sense or other a Tamil Tiger revolutionary, while her mother, well: "My mum brought me up going, 'Ah Gandhi, he's such a nonviolent man. You turn the other cheek, huh.'"

The biographical facts remain murky and disputed. But they flared up anew on May 24, when the *New York Times Magazine* adjudged Arulpragrasam such a shallow person that it granted her twenty of its fifty-six pages, adding a fashion spread to an interminable, skillfully "balanced" hatchet job by a Hollywood journalist whose last musical subject was Rick Rubin in 2006. Replete with multiple references to Arulpragasam's impulsive politics, nonexistent musical training, and snippy ex-boyfriend, it spent less time on her beats than her clothes, gloated over new contradictions in re the father she stopped IDing as a Tamil Tiger in 2007, and misrepresented her psychological identification with the Tiger cause as ideological commitment. Thus it inspired megabyte upon megabyte of commentary—some insightful, some supercilious, and quite a lot the asinine resentment that greets any musician who dares suggest listeners introduce their overtaxed brain cells to world issues that are such a bummer. But the aesthetic ramifications of those facts are as straightforward as aesthetic ramifications can be: *Arular* is her father's album, *Kala* is her mother's album, *Maya* is Maya's album, and all three are M.I.A.'s albums. Let's just stay there, shall we?

Spiky and childish, playful and sensationalistic, *Arular* addresses her father's politics from the perspective of an exile thrust into the panethnic slums and bohemias of a Western metropolis. The misapprehension that it celebrates those politics reflects both M.I.A.'s conflicted feelings and her joyful triumph over them. Verbally, the giveaway among lyrics that do sometimes seem cavalier about violence is the armed struggle advisory "It's a bomb yo / So run yo / Put away your stupid gun yo." But the clincher is M.I.A.'s immersion in U.K. dance styles, in which the beats are generally as minimal as the cultural embrace is far-reaching. As tweaked by then-boyfriend Diplo, a Philadelphia electro wiz with a passion for the favela funk of Brazil's jammed shantytowns, the mongrel inclusivity of M.I.A.'s melange flips off the ethnic purity that so consumes the Tamil Tigers.

Arular was major, but sonically and philosophically it had a thinness about it that was blown away by *Kala*. Initially M.I.A. planned to collaborate with Timbaland, but when the INS wouldn't let her return to the Bed-Stuy apartment she'd rented, she had her usual second thoughts and elected instead to record her mother's album all over the world—in Kingston, Port of Spain, Liberia, New South Wales, and Tamil-heavy southern India, with samples or cameos from Jonathan Richman and Indian filmi and a Nigerian-born rapper and Baltimore hip-hop and the Clash. Because the dance substratum was maintained this time by British house producer Switch, the sonics were somewhat thicker, but he was just technical help. The genius was in the textures M.I.A. laid on top, in between, and underneath—indigenous sounds and the tunes that go with them, which together tendered a generosity rarely glimpsed on the flintier *Arular*. There she was intoxicated by a world that had come to her; here it was M.I.A. who made the move, rendering her politics more affectionate and informed—and if anything more radical for that. It wasn't Gandhian, not hardly, but its embrace felt maternal nevertheless. Two songs made special room for kids—the subteen Aboriginal rappers of the irresistible "Mango Pickle Down River" and, by extension, Maya herself, reconceiving the Bollywood trifle "Jimmy," which she'd sung at grownup parties as a little girl.

Having pressed to award *Kala* four-and-a-half stars for *Rolling Stone*, I wish I'd had the foresight to fight for five. *Kala* kept growing on me till I even dug the Timbaland remnant; it kept growing on me till it was my album of the decade. Soon, to my surprise and delight, the Clash-sampling "Paper Planes" was itself sampled on such hip-hop highlights as T.I.'s "Swagga

Like Us" and loomed larger yet from the soundtracks of *Pineapple Express* and *Slumdog Millionaire*. Grammy and Oscar nominations behind it, Kala finally went gold this year. All of which makes *Maya*'s music harder to hear for what it is. Tasked in 2007 with swallowing *Kala* over a long weekend, in 2010 I listened to *Maya* for weeks before I wrote, and once again it grew on me. It's spunky and dreamy, raw and sweet, a half-articulated lo-fi finger to the Grammy pomposity she exploded by shaking her babymaker nine months pregnant at the 2009 ceremony. But I still doubt it will ever resonate like *Kala* or *Arular*.

If *Arular* is about obsession and *Kala* is about respect, *Maya* is about self-involvement. Not that you can blame her, exactly. Whatever the added distractions of her union with Seagram/Warner heir and failed alt-rocker Ben Bronfman and the birth of their son, Ikhyd Edgar Arular Bronfman, Maya Arulpragasam finds herself in a dilemma few if any of her thousands of predecessors have escaped unscathed: she wanted to be famous, and now she is. So at the very least she finds herself surrounded by flatterers and unable to interact with the hoi polloi, with both problems compounded by the wealth she's marrying into. Historically these factors have made it hard to write songs about anything but yourself, and it's to M.I.A.'s credit that she tries and sometimes succeeds. But her successes are often ambiguous in ways they probably shouldn't be.

Don't begrudge her the two love songs, lyrical on the surface and unquiet underneath—"xxxo" proves a friendly earworm, and "It Takes a Muscle" is the most fetching thing on the record as well as a cover affording quick YouTube proof of her innate musicality. Don't begrudge her the lust song "Teqkilla"—one of its many liquor-name jokes justifies that gratuitous-looking "killa." Don't even begrudge her the star plaints—"Story to Be Told" and "Lovealot" exemplify the familiar trope in which the besieged celebrity merges with the besieged citizen, and the way "I really love a lot" morphs-or-does-it into "I really love Allah" is a nice provocation, especially given its "I fight the ones that fight me" tag. But there are too many of these plaints, and several stumble badly. "Meds and Feds" fails to bulldoze its own paranoia, "It Iz What It Iz" iz full of shizzit, and "Tell Me Why" hangs by the neck from M.I.A.'s emptiest couplet to date: "If life is such a game / How come people all act the same," oh dear. Climaxing the twelve-track standard-issue album is "Space," about being so high "the stars are banging next to me." Lil Wayne, step aside.

But to stumble isn't to fall, and not only does every one of these tracks have its attractions, the deluxe edition's four extras include three excellent new songs. Since all were produced by Baltimore's Blaqstarr, they were presumably moved to the back of the bus for musical reasons, but I don't know what those are. I'm not supposed to, because the lyrics aren't all that's self-involved here. From the start M.I.A. has been down with fringe dance-or-die scenes and site-specific club sound systems, an acolyte of beatmaking strategies so subcultural that my strategy is to wait till they rise to sellout level so I can skim off the cream. This M.I.A. twice provided. But now she's betting that celebrity affords her commercial leeway. So though Maya's def beat beds and sparse melodic content assert themselves eventually, all the outsider hears at first is a junkyard strewn with sub-bass and electronic squiggles, virtual drums and real motorcycles, chipmunks and dybbuks, the occasional hooky chorus and one borrowed pop tune. Then at track nine the funk recedes and rock takes over: Suicide sample to Sleigh Bells guitar-crunch to electro-march to electro-psychedelica. Maybe M.I.A. was afraid all the Blaqstarr music, which favors a slightly pop-friendly take on the rigorously primitivist Bmore ethos, would mess up this structure. But at least she could have replaced Blaqstarr's flimzy "It Iz What It Iz," with "Internet Connection" and its hoo-hoo beat, or the eerie "Believer," or, most thematically, the trance-punk "Illygirl."

"Illygirl" is narrated by an abused sixteen-year-old tough in tight jeans who claims knowledge of Bruce Springsteen, "Billie Jean," plastine (??), and mujahadeen, and brags that she has a "dream" albeit not a "scheme." On her feet but still a little lost, she's the kid-sister-in-metaphor of the queen of club, sub, and dub who fronts the more accomplished "Steppin Up," royalty who could be M.I.A. but probably isn't quite: "blowing songs up" sure, "humping on my leg" not so much. What I like about this theoretical diptych is the way it frames the hip-hop legend of the self-made thug in musical terms that make historical sense—the toughness it situates halfway between gangsta lies and "Paper Planes"'s gleeful, spiteful, sad, relentless, and altogether brilliant "all I wanna do is take your money."

The notion that M.I.A. isn't politically meaningful because her motives are mixed and her ideas are screwed up is clueless about how pop music works—namely, all kinds of screwy ways. Five years ago, before *Arular* was out here, I thought I'd look into this Tamil Tiger thing, and was shocked to find that no one I knew knew anything—anything!—about Sri Lanka. So I did some research and concluded that the Tamil Tigers were murderous ideologues and their Sinhalese overlords brutal beasts, with most Sri Lankans caught in the middle as usual. But what stands out in retrospect is that the Sri Lankan conflict was so obscure. It's not obscure anymore. And while that's due in part to the appalling slaughter that accompanied the 2009 Sinhalese "victory," it's also due in part to M.I.A.

It's the music of *Maya* that will make or break it in the end—make is my guess. But one couplet from the bonus "Believer" defines it: "I could be a genius. I could be a cheat. / It's a thin line and I'm fuckin with it."

Like she says, it is what it is.

Barnes & Noble Review, 2010

....

3. Spelled Backwards It's "Aim"

Nothing has made me happier in this horrendous moment than AIM Maya Arulpragasam's loopy, simplistic fifth album. Fuck you if you think it's "lightweight" or "confusing" or "aimless" or "ho-hum," as various reviewers have charged—it's the hard-earned proof of the happiness she's achieved after years of fretting about the asinine shaming of 2010's excellent *Maya* for the crime of following *Kala*, which was only the greatest album of the century. As no one notices, her sonorities, scales, and tune banks have never been more Asian—mostly East Asian, especially up top, although I'm partial to the uncredited oud-I-think on "Ali r u ok." That's one more signal of the self-acceptance enjoyed by this refugee on an album she says is about refugees, as is her damn right as someone who migrated/fled from London to Sri Lanka to India back to Sri Lanka back to London to—after absurd bureaucratic hoohah—the USA. Never a convincing intellectual, she makes a point of keeping these lyrics beyond basic—declaring "we" a trope, jumping on the byword "jump," riffing on every stupid bird rhyme she can think of. The recommended non-"deluxe" twelve-track version ends with one called "Survivor," which like it or not she is. "Men are good, men are bad / And the war is never over," she notes. "Survivor, survivor / Who said it was easy? / Survivor, survivor / They can never stop we." Takeaway: bad shit being her heritage, she intends to enjoy herself however bad the shit gets, and so should we.

Noisey, 2016

The Unassumingest

Lori McKenna

Ultimately, it was due to the country smash "Girl Crush" that I drove up to Boston on October 26 to interview Lori McKenna in her natural habitat, the big unluxurious cul-de-sac house in her native Stoughton that the forty-seven-year-old artist shares with her plumber husband Gene and four of their five children. A McKenna idea she tailored with her Nashville song-writing posse the Love Junkies, "Girl Crush" is all about Little Big Town's Karen Fairchild obsessing on the gal who landed the guy it's written to. But predictably, its "I wanna taste her lips 'cause they taste like you" kicked up lesbianism charges—which not so predictably backfired, so that in the end "Girl Crush" was voted the Country Music Association's 2015 Song of the Year. Thus it powered McKenna's *The Bird & the Rifle*, her first album to be anything like promoted since Warner sprung for 2007's *Unglamorous*, and in its wake I caught up with and fell for 2013's *Massachusetts*, 2011's *Lorraine*, and 2004's *Bittertown*. This was a major artist so unpretentious she could be missed entirely, an artist whose plainness of language served her elo-quence of spirit with a grace that said such nice things about democracy's upside. I wanted to sing her praises and write her story.

So on the way up, I did some due diligence on her early catalogue, and thus it transpired that my first question concerned a song on her first album, 1998's *Paper Wings and Halo*. Sung over an acoustic power strum in the loud, glottal half-drawl of an insecure folkie drowning out bar chatter, "Don't Tell Her" begins: "Don't tell her that I drink tea and not coffee / I'd prefer if you didn't talk at all about me / Even in a brief casual chat / Don't tell her how I loved your smile or things like that." Easily the most unassuming genius I've ever met, McKenna was abashed to inform me that she hadn't listened to it in years, and pleased when I told her it was a triumph even if she hadn't figured out the singing part when she cut it. Way back when, she was already encapsulating a credible situation new to popular song: shy, proud young woman safeguards her privacy while forlornly sneaking in the occasional "If you can forgive me for my faults / Maybe it can work out after all." Way back when, her command of the commonplace had a deftness worthy of the artist who would later nail the line "I wish I was a better person"—"things like that," exactly.

But because I'd come to care deeply about Lori McKenna, the biographical fallacy intruded, and I wondered where the song came from. So over coffee-not-tea at her windowside dining room table, impressed by the suburban calm of a town I suspect has come up in the world since she and Gene were newlyweds, I asked whether she and Gene had suffered some early breach. Basically the answer was nope. "He was a big kid, and nice," she once told interviewer Holly Gleason, and this was when they were in third grade. "He was one of the nicest, the protector kid"—a typically apt turn of phrase that has her stamp on it. They married at nineteen, three kids and nearly a decade before *Paper Wings and Halo*. Not that the marriage was altogether happily-ever-after—Gene worked major hours at his union job with Consolidated Gas as well as spending six months making the fixer-upper they'd bought habitable, and the biographical fallacy suggests that maybe sometimes he withdrew and/or drank. But these days, "Our biggest problem is my job."

So with her two youngest still in school, McKenna doesn't "tour smart"—that is, minimize overhead on a run of closely spaced venues over several weeks. Instead she flies out of Boston, does two gigs, and gets back Monday morning, or spends a few days with Love Junkies Liz Rose and Hillary Lindsey in Nashville, who as it happens are two of the biggest female songwriters in country music (Taylor Swift, Carrie Underwood, Lady Antebellum, you name it). This discipline runs deep. Little Lori was the six-year-old youngest of six in the Giroux family when her own mother died at forty, and she never forgets it. In addition to several Beatles posters—two "All you need is love"s, one "The love you take is equal to the love you make"—her household decor features a mirror bearing the telling legend "Mirror mirror on the wall / I am my mother after all." So she urges her kids to stick around: "I tell them, 'Stay here as long as you can handle it and save money.'" Four still live at home, with the oldest around a lot too; someone's girlfriend was driving off as I arrived at ten a.m. and the twelve-year-old was sharing the TV room with the twenty-four-year-old when I left. "I cook if I'm home," McKenna went on. "I cook my things that are easy to make, like this soup that I make all the time." Some songwriters she knows light a cigarette when they're stuck. Lori McKenna vacuums. At concerts she introduces the title song of *The Bird & the Rifle* by describing how it came to her while she was folding laundry.

The Girouxs were musical—a grandfather was a lounge singer, several siblings wrote songs, the one who's a guitar whiz still does. So at fourteen

Lori began writing songs herself, her rough models the James-and-Joni folk-ies her family was into. Gene always knew that songwriting mattered to her. And being Gene, he was nicer about it than the husband in "The Bird & the Rifle," who "loves the bird when she's singing" but is "afraid if she flies / She'll never come home again." So when in early '96 Lori drove an hour with various Girouxs to an open mike in Westborough, he minded the kids. Soon his wife stopped oversinging, coloring her declarative intensity with a conversational vibrato as songs as well-turned as "Don't Tell Her" kept on coming. Pushing thirty, she'd secured a job she could pay some bills with on the far-flung Massachusetts folk circuit.

After all, who there was better? Veteran Chris Smither, back then. And arguably the darker, bluesier Mary Gauthier, who soon emigrated like so many folkies to Nashville, the sole remaining market for the straightforward songs folkies favor. As it happened, a 2003 Nashville gig had alerted Mc-Kenna to country radio's appetite for domestic themes, and when Gauthier offered to hook her up with publisher Melanie Howard, Lori was grateful albeit soon busy being pregnant again. Only then, around Thanksgiving, she learned that Faith Hill had recorded four McKenna songs for her next album. She had to sign a one-sided four-year contract with Howard, but so what? "It didn't even matter what it said. They owned all the publishing, but everybody does that at the beginning. I probably would have given her a car if I had one."

In fact, Hill's *Fireflies* went double platinum and Lori and Gene got the non-fixer-upper we were sitting in out of the deal. It was 2005, the tail end of the record biz's sales bonanza, and fat paydays were disappearing fast. But although the bigged-up Warner album Hill's husband Tim McGraw produced for her got lost, McKenna was in a different place—as her stock rose on her home circuit, she also joined a Nashville songwriting community where her common touch and interpersonal details were gold. In addition to song placements, her break generated *Lorraine, Massachusetts,* and *Numbered Doors,* albums that target only her ardent fanbase and artists in search of mate-rial. All mix cowrites with songs solely by McKenna, which I prefer with many exceptions—prolific pro Barry Dean, for instance, helped finish *Lorraine's* glo-rious "Still Down Here," which describes heaven in terms of "strawberry cake," a Jesus who's "taller than you thought," and we earthlings in "the shadow land": "Here where we must learn to live / With what we live without."

These recordings document the fruition of McKenna's imperfect vocal style. More physically gifted singers—Sara Evans, Alison Krauss, Keith Urban, Brandy Clark, Tim McGraw himself—have recorded McKenna's songs, and that's the idea. But her plainer vocal approach is better suited to the lyrical plainstyle she's made her own, and in her modest way she knows it. "My deficiencies formed my style more than anything I was good at. If I could sing like Carrie Underwood I'd totally write different. I was lucky in that regard."

I've caught two McKenna shows, at Manhattan's City Winery and a month later and a bunch better at Northampton's folk-circuit Iron Horse. McKenna is a compact woman with long brown hair who doesn't look nearly forty-seven. Although she's never been one for funny songs, onstage she told housewife jokes that mocked her own shopping habits (Nordstrom Rack) and ignorance of football ("just clap when all the other parents clap"). In Northampton, where the crowd knew her when she only had three kids, a story about replacing miniskirts with rompers got detailed enough to require the word "vagina," and the place cracked up. There was more catalogue material in Northampton too, and a shoutout to Gene's gas company brothers. But both places she was promoting *The Bird & the Rifle* and topping it off with "Girl Crush," which she's never recorded.

Savvily produced by alt-country sachem Dave Cobb, who McKenna reports prefers feel to perfection just like her, *The Bird & the Rifle* has been positively but sparingly reviewed, gaining little traction with the Chris Stapleton and Sturgill Simpson bros who've stoked Cobb's rep. With Miranda Lambert, Kacey Musgraves, and for that matter Karen Fairchild, straight country's quality brands, my theory is that the problem is McKenna's specialty in marriage songs, which reviewer bros find icky when positive and scary when they hit bone. On this album they run five-to-three scary, and although not one of the five is nearly as bitter as "You ain't worth the spit in my mouth when I scream out your name," the killer line she unleashed on *Massachusetts*'s "Salt," some might well flinch at the killer refrain of "Old Men Young Women": "You want the lights off / He wants the lights on / So you can pretend / And he can hold on, hold on." The three positives are modest, credible, and different. The only one that whispers Gene is the fond remembrance "We Were Cool," which has them (well, maybe them) listening to Nirvana on the car cassette player.

And then there's one that fits neither category, although it's to her kids and positive as can be. An instant earworm that in its McGraw version was plastered all over country radio by February, "Humble and Kind" could prove McKenna's "Hallelujah" should we somehow end up with the nominally just society we now crave so acutely—a humanist anthem that counsels not just the suddenly endangered humility and kindness, but saying please and thank you and cooling off with a root beer popsicle. Just after I interviewed McKenna and just before electoral Kristallnacht, it was named the CMA Song of the Year, making McKenna the first woman ever to win that plaudit two years running. I'm not so pie-eyed as to read literal political consequence into this coincidence. But not only has the institutional embodiment of our most politically conservative art form twice validated a damn Yankee from the most liberal state in the union, but that Yankee lives the life the art form has fantasized about and agonized over since Lefty Frizzell crooned "Mom and Dad's Waltz," Hank Williams moaned "My Son Calls Another Man Daddy," and Kitty Wells pointed out that "It Wasn't God Who Made Honky Tonk Angels."

Given the tetchiness of country radio, I never broached the election with McKenna. I just didn't want to get her in trouble. But because her very early "Ruby's Shoes" was written for a son's school project on six-year-old integration pioneer Ruby Bridges, I did venture one question about political meanings. She answered, sensibly enough, that they were impossible to do right. But as I told her, the one with the self-explanatory title "Three Kids No Husband" does the trick pretty well. So does "Ruby's Shoes." And so does "Humble and Kind," unexceptionable on the surface and yet inimical to the cruel braggart the Electoral College but not the electorate will soon sign off on.

So ultimately, it was due to "Humble and Kind" that I could write about my visit to Boston with something vaguely resembling hope. Because ultimately, it epitomizes how much Lori McKenna cares about human connection. At the end our talk landed on the streaming economy, which dilutes her remuneration every year. But though McKenna acknowledged that her friends in Nashville couldn't stop worrying about it, she insisted that for her the money was secondary. Here's some of what she told me.

"Let's say Donald Trump becomes president and the first thing he decides is that songwriters are overpaid and we go to minimum wage, we just get paid by the hour. I still think I'd be a songwriter. I just don't know what else I could do that would be so fulfilling. I'd work at Target, I'd work at Dunkin Donuts, I'm still gonna write songs. So do I want people to hear the songs? For some reason or other that's part of it. And if I want people to hear the songs then I'll have to give them the songs. If it all somehow implodes and everything's backwards and everything's free I'm gonna have to pay people to listen to my songs. I mean as songwriters that's the only way we can do it."

Things like that.

VI Got to Be Driftin' Along

Who Knows It Feels It

Bob Marley

As Chris Salewicz's *Bob Marley: The Untold Story* isn't the first to report, many human beings worldwide—he cites Hopis, Maoris, Indonesians, and of course Africans—regard Bob Marley as a "Redeemer figure coming to lead this planet out of confusion," and some consider him nothing less than the literal second coming of Jesus Christ. Say what you will about the adoration accorded John Coltrane, John Lennon, Elvis Presley, Michael Jackson, Um Kulthum—this is another order of iconicity. Say what you will about the religious dimensions of pop fandom—Marley's Rastafarianism renders the metaphor literal. These mystifications bode ill for Marley's biographers, who number fifteen or twenty by now. Take for instance Stephen Davis, who closes with two triple-indented lines: "Bob Marley lives. He's a *god*. / 'History proves.'" And Davis's bio is one of the good ones.

Maybe it's the ganja—well, definitely it's the ganja, with its built-in third eye, its aura of secret significance. More fundamentally, though, it's the transport, the release—the suprarational rewards music lovers love music for, which Marley claims are owed solely to the divinity of the Ethiopian autocrat Haile Selassie. Who are we to gainsay him, especially we white Babylonians? He has bestowed upon us this feeling of transcendence, and not only that, articulated a political consciousness that needs articulating. "I remember on the slave ship / How they brutalized our very souls / Today they say that we are free / Only to be chained in poverty" might not turn many heads at a socialist scholars conference, but by pop standards it's a smart, blunt, hard-headed augury of militance. As a result, many all too readily suspend their disbelief when the politics turn out to herald twistier "reasonings," as Rastas call their stoned biblical bull sessions.

So when I noticed Salewicz embellishing his first-chapter account of Marley's fatal cancer with matriarch Cedella Booker's conspiracy theories and backup singer Judy Mowatt's lightning-bolt premonition, I said uh-oh. But these were feints. Davis's *Bob Marley* is wrenching on Marley's final months, Timothy White's *Catch a Fire* provides unmatched blow-by-blow on the Marley estate, and both bring their own details to the life story proper.

But Salewicz's book is faster, fuller, and fairer than either. It's faster because through plenty of incident it sticks to the story, a welcome improvement on Salewicz's bloated 2007 Joe Strummer bio. It's fuller due not to Salewicz's relatively late and limited personal contact with his subject, but to the spadework of the eleven other biographers he cites, the low-lying fruit he picked up during two years of living in Jamaica, and what looks from here like some plain old digging. As for fairer, well, Salewicz admires Bob Marley deeply without deifying him. That's what I call reasoning.

Marley was born in 1945 to the eighteen-year-old daughter of a locally prominent black family in the Jamaican high country and a much older white bureaucrat who married the mother but barely knew the son. He moved to Kingston's Trench Town ghetto at twelve and cut his first record at seventeen. For the next decade, he and fellow Wailers Peter Tosh and Bunny Livingston grew in skill and Jah love as they negotiated the rough and tough Jamaican music business. Advised by a motley crew of thuggish Kingston minimoguls, devious Rastafarian elders, and small-time American bizzers, twice joining his mother in Delaware to replenish his capital in working-class jobs, he and the Wailers were the biggest thing in Jamaica by 1970. They performed in the States, undertook an abortive Swedish film project, and ended up in London. And in early 1972 they connected with Island Records' Chris Blackwell, the great white record man who staked them to the breakthrough album *Catch a Fire*.

For most of his fans, Marley equals his Island output, and understandably so. Not only does it remain music of the highest quality, it was the engine of the cultural, spiritual, and political quest that led to his deification—his "legend," to cite the title of the Island compilation that has poured from the dorm rooms of millions of stoners since 1984. Nevertheless, this output reflects only a quarter of his tragically foreshortened thirty-six-year life, for the previous quarter of which Marley was just as prolific. More than White and much more than Davis, though in less musical detail than the scrupulous academic Jason Toynbee, Salewicz respects this truth without tackling the monumental job of codifying it. Near as I can count, the 1970 Jamaican hit "Duppy Conqueror," later re-recorded for *Catch a Fire*'s ruder, stronger follow-up *Burnin'*, has appeared on some three hundred Marley and reggae comps.

The first disc-plus of Tuff Gong's *Songs of Freedom* box is a good introduction to Marley's strictly Jamaican period, overlapping only slightly with Sanctuary's highly recommended *The Essential Bob Marley & the Wailers* and barely at all with Heartbeat's earlier, weaker *One Love at Studio One, 1964–66*. But none of these include "Nice Time," "Treat Her Right," "The World Is Changing," or "Black Progress," all of which Salewicz tipped me to, or the Toynbee faves "I'm

Still Waiting" and "Jailhouse," or "Milk Shake and Potato Chips," a touching trifle I streamed because I liked the title. There's not all that much sense to be made of a discography that embraces half a dozen producers, a hazily documented myriad of backup musicians, and material ranging from "Black Progress" to "Milk Shake and Potato Chips." But dip in and many things become clear.

As a teen, Bob would do anything for a hit, including covers of "And I Love Her" and "What's New Pussycat?" He loved American soul music but wasn't always so great at it. He was militant early, as on 1968's "Bus Dem Shut (Pyaka)," "bus" meaning "bust" and "pyaka" meaning "liar." He was on top or ahead of every rhythmic shift in Jamaican pop and several elsewhere. He shared with certain country songwriters the ability to express deep content in simple language, both personal (think Hank Williams) and social (Merle Haggard). And most important in the long run, he had the gift of tune, devising songs so compelling that many from his 1969–71 flowering were inevitably reprised on Island: "Concrete Jungle," "Slave Driver," "Small Axe," "Trench Town Rock," "Lively Up Yourself," "Kaya."

There are purists who claim Marley's music went north once he signed with Island, or broke with Tosh and Livingston, or enlisted American guitarist Al Anderson. But Salewicz isn't among them. Like most observers, he sees Blackwell as an essentially benign force who helped Marley achieve "the international sound we were expecting to have"—a quote not from Marley but from Livingston, who felt so ill at ease in Babylon that he rejected the touring life for a sporadically inspired solo career as Bunny Wailer. Marley's internationalism was better assimilated in Britain, where Jamaicans dominated the small black population, than in the U.S., where, as Marley knew too well, a much larger black population preferred competing musics of its own. A cordial but rather private man, Marley drove himself hard, perfecting his stagecraft and writing a song a day as he studied scripture, pondered politricks, acted the don, played soccer barefoot, bedded innumerable women, and fathered what Salewicz reckons as thirteen children by eight of them including his wife Rita, although estimates do vary.

Unsurprisingly, Marley's choices and circumstances embroiled him in contradictions. I hesitate to say his insatiable womanizing is the least of them, especially since some of his kids had it so much better than others—his son Ky-Mani's *Dear Dad* is a much better book about growing up in a drug-dealing culture than about music or his dear dad. But at least it's a familiar pattern. Less so is the man of peace who delivered the occasional beatdown and hired ropey-haired toughs who promoted his records by delivering many more. And what are we to make of the Marley who

Salewicz reports watched the private executions of three men who'd tried to assassinate him shortly before his 1976 Smile Jamaica concert—a comeuppance that came down a week or so after his 1978 One Love Peace Concert, which Salewicz unconvincingly judges "one of the key civilising moments of the twentieth century" because Marley got two warring politicians to grasp hands onstage for an awkward spell? But I was in fact more shocked by the famously generous philanthropist dropping thirty-five grand on a Miami dinner with a daughter of the Libyan oil minister, 1953 Chateau Lafite Rothschild included—and more saddened by Salewicz's account of Marley's embattled 1980 visit to a newly independent Zimbabwe, where Robert Mugabe's cohort was already proving more autocratic than Ras Tafari's.

To repeat, it was righteous of Salewicz to tell these tales. But that's only because they don't turn his book into a debunk. If it's foolish to deify Bob Marley, it's far more foolish to dismiss him, in effect blaming him for not living up to the magnitude of his achievement. Praise Peter and Bunny all you want—they deserve it. But credit Marley's reservations: "Is like them don't want understand mi can't just play music fe Jamaica alone. Can't learn that way. Mi get the most of mi learning when mi travel and talk to other people." And recognize in that one-world bromide the seriousness of his cultural-spiritual-political ambitions. Salewicz reports that the assassins just mentioned were armed by the CIA, while others blame the right-wing Jamaican Labour Party. Probably not much difference, and either way you can trust his enemies to know his power. Most of the fourteen million Americans who've bought the calculatedly anodyne *Legend* are in it for the herb. But Marley is very different for such people of color as the Tanzanian street vendors of Dar es Salaam's Maskani district, one of many Third World subcultures to integrate his songs and image into a counterculture of resistance.

Peter and Bunny wouldn't have brought Marley near such a consummation. Nor would the rhythmic muscle and dubwise byways of Lee "Scratch" Perry, who purists reasonably account Marley's best and toughest producer. In fact, it worked pretty much the opposite. The gunmen who invaded Marley's Kingston compound in 1976 managed to crease Bob's arm and Rita's skull. After playing the concert in bandages two days later, the two fled to England, where Marley took musical vengeance not by screaming bloody murder but by fulfilling his crossover dreams with heightened understanding, focus, and subtlety. In six months he recorded all of *Exodus*, which *Time* hyperbolically declared the greatest album of the century in 1999, and the equally blessed *Kaya*, which leads with the languorous "Easy Skanking" and climaxes with "Runnin' Away" and "Time Will Tell"—this normally unalienated visionary's haunted meditation on the confusions of fame followed by a promise of justice no tougher than anything else on his gentlest albums sonically and his most acute aesthetically. *Exodus* and *Kaya* opened the door on a three-year period during which he cemented his international fame while fighting the cancer he might have beaten if Rastafarianism looked more kindly on Babylonian medicine, amputation in particular—the disease began in a long-troublesome big toe he reinjured playing soccer barefoot.

Marley's big Kingston concerts didn't prevent Jamaica from turning into the most gun-ridden state in the western hemisphere. Lee "Scratch" Perry relocated to Switzerland. The Maskani district has been plowed under to make room for a bank. And reggae has evolved into a beat-dominated music of crotch-first sexism and toxic homophobia that's far livelier than the Bob-worshipping hippie and Afrocentric crap that surfaces wherever spliffs are smoked or tourists go dancing. In short, Bob Marley has yet to remake the world—a failing he shares with just about everyone else who's tried. But that doesn't mean he hasn't changed it. Gandhi and King and Mandela didn't leave utopias behind either, and unlike them, Marley was merely a musician no matter how much praise he proffered Jah. His music is as firmly ensconced in the pop pantheon as the Beatles' or James Brown's, and it signifies a remade world even if that doesn't make it so.

A Redeemer? We don't play that. "Redemption Song"? That we play. "Won't you help to sing, these songs of freedom / Cause all I ever had / Redemption songs, redemption songs / Redemption songs."

Barnes & Noble Review, 2010

Shape Shifter

David Bowie: 1947–2016

David Bowie accomplished several things I wish he hadn't in the '70s, from briefly reinstating mime as a legitimate art form to permanently convincing Britons that their elitist nation was the chief locus of artistic sophistication in popular music. But you have to hand it to the guy—the main reason he accomplished these things is a conceptual fecundity so bottomless that his accomplishments verged on endless.

The '60s get the ink, but the '70s were pop's golden years—economically in that they were when sound recordings became, as the trades trumpeted in 1969, a "billion-dollar business," and artistically because the '60s had opened things up so much that for all of the '70s possibilities seemed infinite whether they built on or rebelled against '60s models. And Bowie was in the middle of so much of it: a punk prophet and an arena-rock pioneer, a free spirit and a proud poser, an adept of black musical vanguards as well as white, a dynamo and an amalgamator and a shrewd hanger-on. In associative rather than chronological order, here are a few innovations I'm remembering as we adjust to a world without him. There are so many I'm sure I'll forget some.

1. Most important even though it was a publicity ploy: he broke the gay barrier. In biographical fact, he bedded what some estimate as thousands of women. But as a public cross-dresser and private omnisexual who in January 1972 told *Melody Maker*'s Mick Watts "I'm gay and always have been, even when I was David Jones," he made sexual identity a public issue in a music business where in Britain gay management had long been a way of life. Even Elton John, who came up alongside Bowie and was always gay, waited till 1976 to declare himself "bisexual" and didn't come out officially until 1988.

2. Not unconnectedly, Bowie also broke the authenticity barrier. The '60s myth was that rock and rollers were "real" men expressing their "real" selves (or, God help us, souls). Starting with Ziggy Stardust in 1971, Bowie always ch-ch-ch-ch-changed, sometimes playing new characters with sobriquets like "the thin white duke" and always adjusting if not reversing his musical tack. The idea that pop artists project "personas"? It was true pre-Bowie. But Bowie turned it into a commonplace.

3. Most of Bowie's pretensions were arty, some would say avant-garde. But because Bowie's concept of art was decidedly theatrical, he pioneered the fully staged arena-rock show. When he toured behind *Diamond Dogs* in 1974, his set was equipped with platforms and winches that enabled him to float suspended in the air as guest dancers acted out the songs.

4. His sponging was a species of genius, and he gave back. The artists he latched onto early, and whose ideas he freely and sometimes candidly purloined, included Lou Reed, whose calculatedly androgynous, Bowie-produced *Transformer* generated Reed's only hit single, 1972's "Walk on the

Wild Side." He mixed Iggy and the Stooges' seminal 1973 *Raw Power* ("weed-
ily," James Osterberg later justly complained) and produced Iggy Pop's 1977
solo debut *The Idiot*, also filling the keyboard chair in the touring band that
promoted it. More obscurely but arguably best of all, he wrote and produced
the title song of Mott the Hoople's classic 1972 *All the Young Dudes*. Check
it out.

5. In his own class among Bowie's collaborators is Brian Eno, a near-equal
partner on Bowie's Berlin albums *Low* and *"Heroes."* Eno had quit Bryan
Ferry's Roxy Music to release a string of four iconic solo LPs that at that time
were strictly cult items, and eventually would go balls-out ambient on '80s
albums like *Music for Airports* as well as producing Talking Heads and U2.
But listen to what we used to call the second sides of Bowie's Berlin albums
for the true beginnings of illbient and chillout techno.

6. Well before militantly white Berlin, Bowie also discovered weirdly
black funk, which in 1975 was still terra incognita to most rock fans. I can't
resist recalling Roy Bittan's irresistible New Orleans piano on "TVC-15,"
which tops 1976's well nigh danceable *Station to Station*. But the real coup
was his first No. 1 single, 1975's "Fame," which sounds like a James Brown rip
but is based on a riff devised by Bowie guitarist Carlos Alomar. Brown liked
it so much that he quickly recorded "Hot (I Need to Be Loved)" over the
same riff. JB stole DB's funk move. Word.

As I've said, there must be more. And there were many other innovative
musicians moving in all kinds of directions in those golden years. But few
and probably none (George Clinton?) roamed the rock universe with as
much acumen as chameleonic personamonger David Bowie. It's enough to
make you wonder whether he's capable of resting in peace even now.

Noisey, 2016

The Most Gifted Artist
of the Rock Era

Prince: 1958–2016

The only way to begin any tribute to Prince is by belaboring the obvious, which is an implausible hyperbole. Strictly in terms of his skill set, Prince Rogers Nelson was the most gifted artist of the rock era. Not the greatest genius—just the most musical in the broadest sense. Singing, playing, songwriting, dancing, putting on a show—he was fabulous at all these things and fabulous at stardom itself, a provocateur with few equals who after major reversals proved himself a profiteer with few equals as well. His shifting transgenre amalgam of funk and rock and pop and r&b was so original that he long pretended he was biracial even though both his hard-working failed-singer mother and his scuffling pianist father were African-American. His fanatical fanbase was and remains as ecumenical as his great rival Michael Jackson's, and more discerning.

With all that on the record, however, let me mention how much he owed both bizzers and rock critics. In 1977 Warner gave a black nineteen-year-old Minneapolis unknown an unprecedented complete-control contract only partly justified by 1979's "I Wanna Be Your Lover": three hooky minutes of shy-boy synth-guitar disco-funk that went No. 11 pop and No. 1 r&b. So it helped that soon *Rolling Stone*'s Stephen Holden was creaming over the accompanying album's "blatant sexuality" as Georgia Christgau's *Village Voice* review ventured prophetically: "He may not know how he feels, only that his feelings are strong enough to sing about." And while sales dipped with 1980's *Dirty Mind*, half an hour of audaciously radio-unfriendly rock demos including the three-in-a-bed "When You Were Mine," the incestuous "Sister," and the truly dirty-minded "Head," Prince's critical star kept rising.

Like 1981's *Controversy* and 1982's *1999*, *Dirty Mind* earned a *Rolling Stone* rave and finished top ten in the *Voice*'s Pazz & Jop Critics' Poll, and by *1999* there were finally more hits. But the historic breakthrough wasn't "1999" itself. It was "Little Red Corvette." It's hard to grasp now, but in 1982 the "death of disco" was still fueling hit radio's racist fear of offending its core demo with "urban" programming—not even a damn rock song about a woman too damn hot for the blatantly sexual Prince. When NYCV's WPLJ finally put it in rotation, Warner's Karin Berg phoned me just to crow about it. Beat steady and imposing, noisy guitar nailing synthed-up lyric, "Little Red Corvette" was Prince's trans-genre genius in action—without it, MJ's "Beat It" might never have cracked MTV. This kind of stage-tested, studio-documented proof that "rock" and "r&b" weren't mutually exclusive—funk patterns blunted by arena scale, soulful singing intensified by virtuosic shredding—will remain his greatest achievement.

All this action predated the summer 1984 launch of the Prince legend as we know it: the two-pronged release of the seriously gorgeous *Purple Rain* LP and the surprisingly enjoyable *Purple Rain* flick. For the next decade Prince would be the pop demigod the world mourns today, a prolific, hard-touring, reclusive cash machine who spent every spare minute laying down tracks in his Paisley Park compound—when he wasn't dreaming up movie concepts or bringing the gift of orgasm to bevies of darling Nikkis in his erotic city. The eros is my but also our fantasy—his private life was exceptionally well-guarded. But something not just soulful in his lithe falsetto, gruff baritone, and warm midrange made the fantasy irresistible. Lubricious, solicitous, insinuating, polymorphous, sometimes ungendered, his singing was confident without cock-rock aggression—friendly, good-humored, there for you.

But although the 1987 double-LP *Sign 'O' the Times* was his greatest album by acclamation, his obsessive overproduction led to musical dilution, his cinematic dreams were barely pretensions, and his sales never again approached *Purple Rain* levels. He was still creating exceptional music. But with Paisley Park badly overextended by his rock-star extravagance, Prince blamed Warner for his commercial shortfall. Thus ensued his Artist Masquerading as a Rune phase and his insistence that his contract rendered him a "slave." Exploited? Always arguable. Slave? Show some respect.

As I once put it whilst praising Prince's exceptional 1992 rune album, I am neither smart nor stupid enough to parse this African-American's racial politics. But I am arrogant enough to insist that chattel slavery is too huge a blot on humanity to exploit as a metaphor, and to observe that the political smarts my critical clan sensed in the most gifted artist of the rock era were also a fantasy. Sure he dubbed his band the Revolution and wrote one called "Ronnie Talk to Russia," but that was about the bomb just like "1999" was about the bomb—our most exhilarating bomb song ever. By temperament, Prince always believed the end times were coming. It was this innate belief that inspired his scattershot God-mongering and made his sexual extremism feel so urgent. And it's why the horror of his only child's infant death in 1996 ultimately drove him from the Seventh Day Adventism of his raising to the Jehovah's Witness millenarianism he espoused throughout this millennium. That didn't wreck his music either—because his feelings were always strong enough to sing about, nothing could. But it did put a crimp in his sexual extremism.

Yet it's a tribute to his musicality, his intelligence, his will power, and his capacity for change that in the wake of his '90s traumas he proved he'd been right about Warner all along. Marketing directly to his fanatical fanbase via an internet he saw early was made for the job, he earned a far bigger return packaging some of the many unreleased masters he owned than he would have with the most generous label deal. Yet as the decade wore on he further refurbished his legend by wangling one-offs from Columbia, Universal, and even eventually Warner. And he rebuilt his touring career as well—in 2004, he sold a million concert tickets.

Prince had always told us he just wanted to get through this thing called life. But now that his own physical life has ended, his artistic life will continue. Find the viral video where he destroys the Eric Clapton solo on "While My Guitar Gently Weeps." Reflect that he's never released a full-fledged live album. Pray his last will and testament makes that possible now.

Noisey, 2016

Forever Old

Leonard Cohen: 1933–2016

Before we contemplate Leonard Cohen's mortal soul, which left us Election Eve although the death was only announced with Donald Trump's electoral coup a social fact three days later, let's run some numbers.

Born September 21, 1934, Leonard Cohen was the oldest major musician to emerge in the high '60s. A modestly renowned Canadian poet and novelist

when *Songs of Leonard Cohen* materialized at the end of 1967, he began productive if not quite prolific—four studio albums in seven years. But over the
next thirty-four years, up till 2008, he added just seven more. And then in
2009 he exploded. In the final eight years of his life, Cohen generated three
studio albums and four live ones without slackening his lifelong perfectionism. The studio work measures up, not quite *Songs of Leonard Cohen* or *I'm
Your Man* but far sharper than *Death of a Ladies' Man* or *Dear Heather*. And
where most artists' concert albums are filler, these are summations.

True, on 2010's *Songs from the Road* many titles are a touch less than prime,
and on 2014's *Live in Dublin* performances fine-tuned in hundreds of venues
seem rather redundant even so. But what renders them so is the album that
proved how alive Cohen was at seventy-six: 2009's *Live in London*, which
blows away not just his three earlier live placeholders but his various best-
ofs, culminating his lifework as it portends the new songs that would amplify it. And having shrewdly reclaimed shiny shards of catalogue, 2013's
overlooked *Can't Forget: A Souvenir of the Grand Tour* ends by topping off
a monologue about the six stages of male sex appeal—irresistible, resistible,
transparent, invisible, repulsive, and cute—with his single greatest quatrain:
"I said to Hank Williams how lonely does it get / Hank Williams he hasn't
answered me yet / But I hear him coughing all night long / A hundred floors
above me in the Tower of Song."

Inflected by multiple religious fascinations and quests, song and sex are
the bulwarks of Cohen's legend and achievement. Emerging in 1967 as an ancient thirty-three-year-old sporting a sober haircut and dark suit, he played
the worldly-wise yet spiritual ladies man to a poetry-curious audience of
hirsute hippies whose idea of free love was let's-spend-the-night-together—
where Stephen Stills was a blond demigod who fucked lots of chicks, Cohen
was a jaded roue who bedded lots of women. And indeed, many women felt
his magnetism—many. But with males the attraction was trickier—his sophistication was a fantasy so far beyond these guys that it narrowed the appeal of his dry wit, drier melodic gift, and calm verbal command.

Me, I admired Cohen's sacramentally sexed-up novel *Beautiful Losers* before he announced as a singer-songwriter, dug his supposedly overproduced
debut album, and raved early about Robert Altman's Cohen-suffused *Mc-
Cabe and Mrs. Miller*. Clearly, only some kind of genius could have burst
upon us intoning "Suzanne," "So Long, Marianne," and "Bird on a Wire." But
that genius was inconsistent—his underproduced second album, *Songs from
a Room*, is one of several decided subclassics. Nor did his fallback pessimism
or the women and faiths he engaged so readily and discarded so inevitably

betoken true enlightenment. He was always a bigger star in Europe than the USA, and due to some amalgam of perfectionism and chronic depression never felt fully comfortable on the road, which along with copyrights provided the bulk of his income. So having toured successfully enough behind 1988's confident *I'm Your Man* and 1992's ominous *The Future*, he climbed Mount Baldy to initiate the oft-told tale: five years as a Zen monk, publishing rights sold with the huge windfall hidden in a tax shelter, long sojourns in Mumbai studying Advaita Hinduism, fine post-9/11 album, and the 2004 discovery that his windfall had been embezzled away, leaving the author of "Hallelujah" broke at seventy-two.

The dream had been to quit music, write what he pleased when he pleased, and, as Yeats advised forty-year-olds around the time Cohen was born, begin the preparation for his death. But he wanted to leave his two children something, and although abstemious by roue standards had no appetite for poetic penury. So he did the only thing he could do, and by combatting economic duress became a better man—ironically for someone who had always been old, a more mature man. After meticulous rehearsals with a road band so intelligently curated it could hit every note every night while evoking the responsive flexibility of a crack jazz combo, he embarked upon his grand tour.

There Cohen accepted himself for what he was: a superb songwriter and canny, gracious performer who after four decades was loved worldwide by an audience that would never match his sophistication but had achieved enough wisdom to enjoy *la différence*. Where before his doomed retirement he had downed multiple bottles of Château Latour to warm up for shows, now it was half a stout or nothing at all. Where before he was a compulsive perfectionist, now he was a working man who always hit the nail on the head. Where before he sometimes felt discomfited by his fans' adoration, now he was enlarged by it. I was seventy myself when I saw him at Madison Square Garden in 2012, so I have the authority to quote myself verbatim: "This was not a nostalgia trip, a comforting or at best invigorating lookback at pleasures and potencies past. It posited a clear-eyed future in which the fruits of a well-spent life remain at your disposal. Leonard Cohen is the seventy-eight-year-old sixty-eight-year-olds hope to become."

Yet simultaneously he prepared for his death by finishing twenty-eight of many available song fragments. These he spread over three albums that taken together posited a future in which his soul would leave this coil. For a while the exact date remained obscure—when a recent *New Yorker* profile surmised that it was imminent, Cohen riposted that he intended to live forever. But where 2010's *Old Ideas* packed a sardonic punch worthy of a seventy-eight-year-old road dog, on 2016's still estimable *You Want It Darker* his voice was a husk. It wasn't the first time. But in retrospect it seems a clear-eyed signal that Leonard Cohen knew exactly what he was doing, and where he was going.

Noisey, 2016

Don't Worry About Nothing

Ornette Coleman

The climax of Celebrate Brooklyn!'s Celebrate Ornette tribute in Prospect Park June 12 was supposed to come when two 1930-born saxophone legends, Ornette Coleman and Sonny Rollins, would stroll if not strut in to join the "Lonely Woman" encore and prove their unvanquished puissance. But instead the climax came early.

Before a note was played, engineer turned emcee Gregg Mann and Ornette's son Denardo Coleman, his drummer at ten and his manager for thirty years, called Rollins out. Rollins didn't strut—he had a helper. His voice was shaky. But he knew what he wanted to say: "Ornette has changed so much in music, in politics, and in human relations between people," and also: "I'm going to say something that Ornette already said to me. It's all good. Don't worry about nothing." Enter Ornette with the same helper: "All I want to do is cry. It's so beautiful to see so many people who know what life is. I want to be alive when I'm alive." The two men kissed each other's hands and were led off. The crowd cheered wildly because it didn't want to cry.

The climax came half an hour later, after saxmen Henry Threadgill and David Murray, young turks turned old lions at seventy and fifty-nine, proved for the millionth time that Ornette's "free" jazz was a cornucopia rather than a cacophony. Like Louis Armstrong in his way and Charlie Parker in his,

Coleman has the precious gift of melody, which he arrays in spiky, thoughtful, impulsive variations over rhythms that mirror, elaborate, and support it. With Denardo's version of his father's Prime Time band bonding as strong as his father's bottomless songbook, Threadgill and Murray transmuted "Blues Connotation," "Broadway Blues," and "Law Years" before Ornette was led smiling to an onstage chair, where Denardo and others quietly urged the horn to his lips. Ornette blew so frailly it was heartrending until the wandering beauty of the melody brushed the frailty away. For six or seven minutes he was unaccompanied in awed silence. Then the ensemble slowly joined in until saxman Antoine Roney steered them toward Ornette's beloved diddleybeat blues "Ramblin.'"

Standing O, forty minutes in. The music never got better. But for more than two hours a panoply of avant-gardists reminded Ornette's well-wishers of what he had wrought—species of "free" music he couldn't have imagined, which was how he wanted it. The jazz was the best-realized: saxman Joe Lovano and pianist Geri Allen pondering "Sleep Talk," James Blood Ulmer shredding "Peace," a subdued Ravi Coltrane reimagining his own father's freedom. But plenty else signified: Flea's bass funking Threadgill up; Lou Reed metal machine drones rendered by Laurie Anderson, John Zorn, and Bill Laswell; two Master Musicians of Jajouka braying and skirling "Song X"; Patti Smith praising Ornette's "alphabet based on the ancient phrases of angels." On tape, the departed Reed had told us that "Lonely Woman" ran through his head every day. Lovano, Roney, Ulmer, Allen, Coltrane, and Murray took it home.

Like the man said, it was all good—because it wanted to be alive.

Billboard, 2014

Sticking It in Their Ear

Bob Dylan

Bob Dylan changed songwriting single-handed in the mid-'60s. Before him, clarity and surface coherence were a requirement. Afterward, they weren't. Not every songwriter who followed a model he himself sometimes puts aside was better for it. And he credited this innovation to Robert Johnson, which makes sense (as might other bluesmen too). But without question Dylan freed things up for the better. Single-handed, he revolutionized a major means of verbal expression. Of course he deserves his Nobel. Though admittedly he could have been nicer about it.

Spiked, 2017

Sensualistic, Polytheistic

New York Dolls

"So everybody gets makeup, OK? You look dead on TV without it." Back in the *Conan* green room from a Camel-stoked walk to the Hilton with his girlfriend Leah, David Johansen was taking charge of the reconstituted New York Dolls, who didn't really need the help. The sextet showed a lot of denim in rehearsal, but all manner of magpie finery came out at the witching hour, with red-on-black a theme—Jersey guitarist Steve Conte's red-lined frock coat, keyb pro Brian Koonin's red derby, the red rose in nice-guy bassist Sami

Yaffa's hair. The multiple accessories to Syl Sylvain's colorful costume include a snarly-wolf wristband and Max's Kansas City kidney belt painted by his wife Wanda in Atlanta, who he called before he went on. And Johansen—whew. Jean Harlow (?) T-shirt. Stovepipe flares. Belts and rhinestones and silvery chains. They were a great band dressed to kill again.

Many reunions never get past the tour that's never as hot as true believers claim. And the creditable albums some bands manage never live up to old glories. The Dolls' new album doesn't either, but that's compared to my desert island discs—with this band, I'm the true believer. Their second shot took thirty years, a decade-plus more than Blondie or Mission of Burma or Gang of Four. With junko partners Johnny Thunders and Jerry Nolan gone in 1991 and 1992, three of the original Dolls survived till Morrissey engineered a London one-shot two years ago. His dream fulfilled, bassist Arthur Kane died of previously undiagnosed leukemia a month later, leaving David and Syl to ride the one-shot's reverberations. But although the pace has slowed and the execution filled out, although Thunders's squalling sound and drop-dead time are irreplaceable, they're still the New York Dolls.

The Dolls came together at one of Queens's less distinguished educational institutions—Sylvain, Thunders, and classic drummer Billy Murcia, who died in a 1972 drug bollocks, all attended Newtown High School, and Kane grew up nearby. Staten Islander David Johansen they met downtown, and he was different. Bluntly put, what Sylvain calls the Dolls' "skyscraper soup" wouldn't have been all that tasty without Johansen's genius as songwriter and frontman. The forced rhythms and slapdash musicianship of this fast, noisy mix-up—comprising, Sylvain reckoned, girl group, blues, Eddie Cochran, Young Rascals, and Little Rascals—read radically anti-hippie and now just seems quintessentially rock and roll. But it presaged punk, and it influenced thousands of bands—none of whom sounded remotely like the Dolls because none of them had Johansen's eye for a joke, nose for a hook, clothes sense, appetite, or humanity. Nobody does.

Since the Dolls fell apart without having approached the megasales dancing in their heads, Johansen has enjoyed a solo career that included a long stint as cruise-ship popmeister Buster Poindexter and a briefer one yodeling in the canon with the ad hoc Harry Smiths. But give the new album half a chance and it stands as a miraculous demonstration of how much this modestly cultured middle-class New Yorker—dad an opera-singing insurance salesman, mom a librarian—benefits from the proximity of dead-end kids. He's written hundreds of songs with collaborator Koonin. But when sound-check riffs evolved into songs and then a deal with the metal heavyweights at Roadrunner Records for the first Dolls album since 1974, Johansen knew he had to generate fresh material. "It's like being the speechwriter for a party," he told me, coyly leaving out the "political." The unenlightened will grouse about a fifty-six-year-old pretending he's twenty-two again, just as *Mojo*'s Kris Needs recently groused that *New York Dolls* and *In Too Much Too Soon* were "neutered," "limp" renderings of the band's pansexuality. The Dolls always were over some people's heads.

I've held off on the album's strange title because it says so much: *One Day It Will Please Us to Remember Even This*. The "even" is preemptive; those who level the self-evident charge that the Dolls don't jam like they used to should check their own jam level and say something new. But what's more mind-boggling is that after thirty years Johansen isn't looking back from his earned maturity—he's looking ahead. He has internalized his mortality so thoroughly that he realizes he won't be fifty-six forever. This is a true Dolls album—as in the *Conan*-featured "Dance Like a Monkey," which bids a "pretty little creationist" to shake her "monkey hips" now that "evolution is obsolete," or the opening "We're All in Love," with its "Jumping around like teenage girls" and its "We all sleep in one big bed." But it also expresses the worldview of a lean, strong-piped guy who understands what makeup is for and knows he may not be pretty in pink forever.

Johansen scoffed at my suggestion that his new album harbored religious feelings, and I didn't push it. Instead I'll just mention the booklet's Kali Yoga shout-out and quote a few lyrics. "Feel exiled from the divine," for instance. Or "Nature with its true voice cries out undissembled, 'Be as I am!'" in the one that ends "Sensualistic / Ritualistic / Alchemistic / Polytheistic." Or the loose talk about infinity in the two songs that lead into the perorating "Take a Good Look at My Good Looks," which begins, "Spirit slumbers in nature / And awakens in mind / And finally recognizes / Itself in time." The ghost track "Seventeen" is tacked on as a corrective. Begins: "I was down on the corner one night." Continues: "I was made all of light."

Fools may wonder why Johansen needs dead-end kids to write like this. Where's the party? But the Dolls were dead-end kids in transcendence mode. Their goal was and is the unbound, humorous humanism apparent in Bob Gruen and Nadia Beck's *All Dolled Up* DVD, a far more vivid memento than any concert bootleg. Their summum was *In Too Much Too Soon*'s future Guns N' Roses text "Human Being"; their big drug slogan was "I need a kiss not a fix." They were anti-hippie only insofar as hippies were passive (the Dolls rocked nonstop) and pretentious (David and Syl rail at twenty-minute guitar solos as if they just tuned one out on WPLJ). Heterosexuals all, they believed in universal love the way disco utopian David Mancuso believed in universal love—with a sloppy touch of the Cockettes. "I've been trying to convince Syl that what we had in the '70s wasn't sex," Johansen explained at Randalls Island in 2004, and again at Irving Plaza in 2005. A Monica Lewinsky joke, he couldn't resist. But think of it this way—maybe what they had in the '70s was love.

One attraction of Johansen's newfound Buddhist rhetoric is that it doesn't shy away from the carnal. The knowledgeable lust of "Fishnets & Cigarettes" and the pussy-worshipping "Running Around" counter the lived despair of "Punishing World," "Maimed Happiness," and the hope-deprived "I Ain't Got Nothin." And that draft for a suicide note leads into a redemptive earthly-love triptych that dovetails plausibly, if not definitively, with what is known of Johansen's personal life, in which a long marriage to photographer Kate Simon was followed by his relationship with Leah Hennessey, whose teenage daughter designed the ten-page comic that comprises the notes. He remains a votary of l-u-v.

That is, he remains a New York Doll. "This is the most fun way I can think of right now to not work," Johansen told me, but he has big plans for his lark. No "bar band" or "preaching to the choir" for this mature professional entertainer who began his career believing he was about to take over the world. "This is going to be a big record. It's like there's no rock and roll records out there. It's a fait accompli."

It isn't, but don't tell the folks at Roadrunner. Tell them they've underwritten another desert island disc. Because it's quite possible they have.

Village Voice, 2006

Index